Story & Art by Shouko Akira

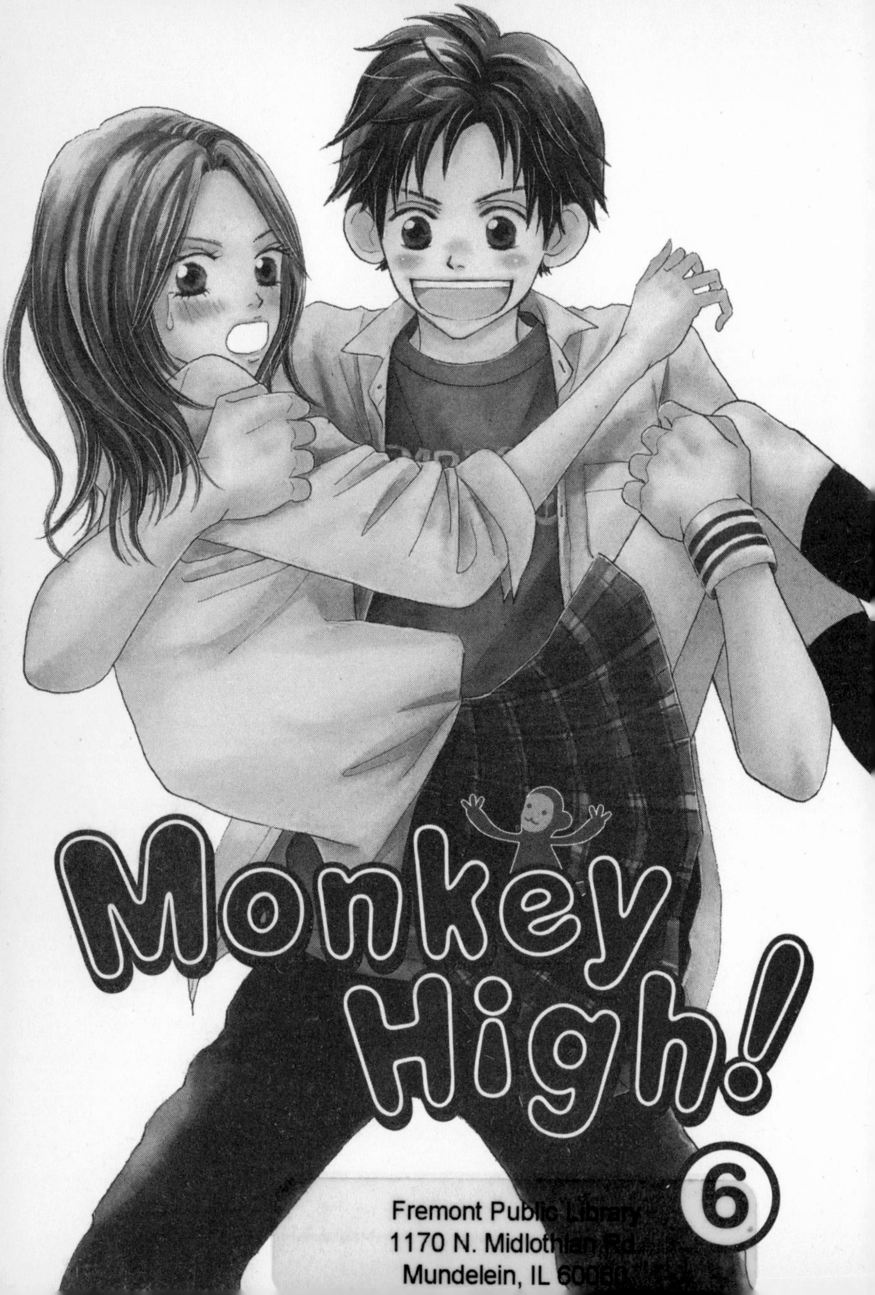

Monkey High!

6

Monkey High!

⑥

CONTENTS

Story Thus Far

Masaru Yamashita
(Nickname: Macharu)

Haruna starts going out with Macharu (often teased and called a baby monkey) at the school she transfers into. Every day is like a carnival with her rowdy classmates. So many events and happenings... And lately, it seems that Macharu's best friend Atsu really has feelings for Haruna...!

Haruna Aizawa

MONKEY HIGH
IN KYOTO - PART I

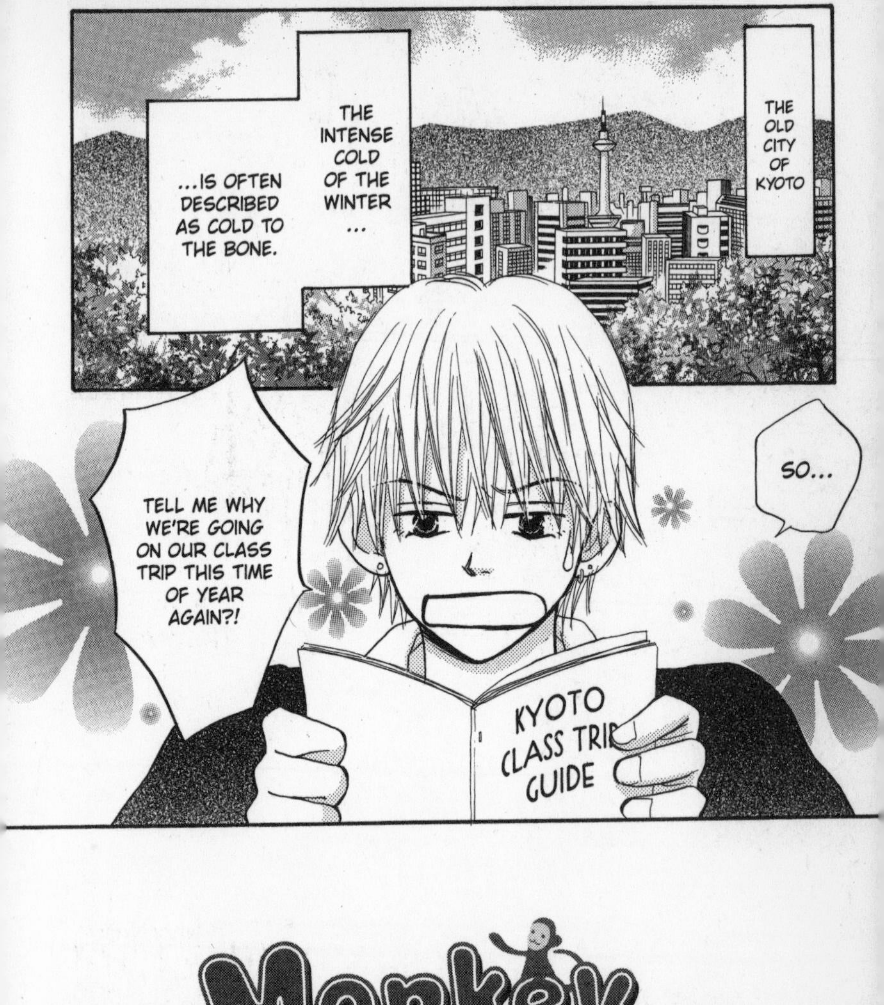
THE OLD CITY OF KYOTO
THE INTENSE COLD OF THE WINTER...
...IS OFTEN DESCRIBED AS COLD TO THE BONE.
SO...
TELL ME WHY WE'RE GOING ON OUR CLASS TRIP THIS TIME OF YEAR AGAIN?!
KYOTO CLASS TRIP GUIDE

Monkey High!

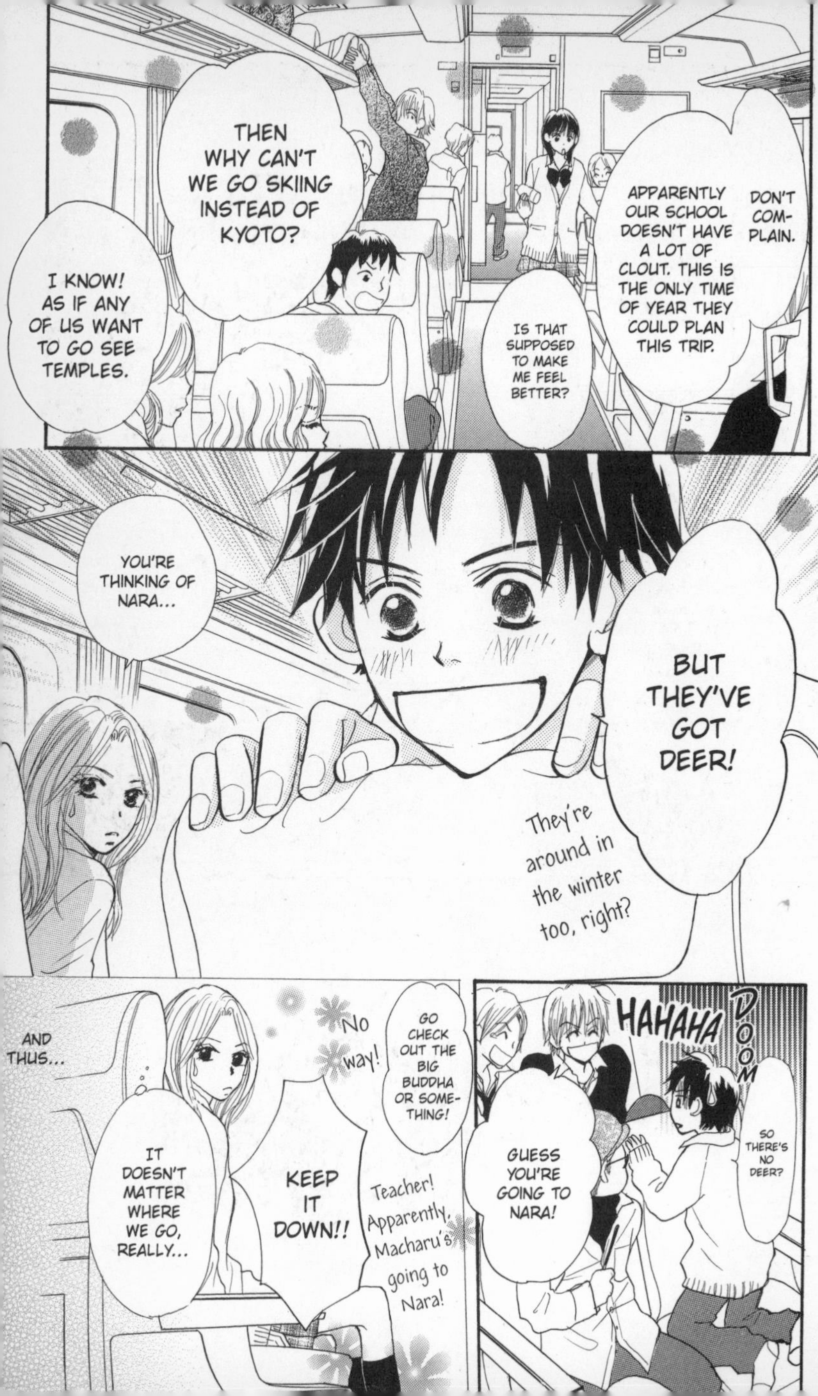
DON'T COMPLAIN.
APPARENTLY OUR SCHOOL DOESN'T HAVE A LOT OF CLOUT. THIS IS THE ONLY TIME OF YEAR THEY COULD PLAN THIS TRIP.
THEN WHY CAN'T WE GO SKIING INSTEAD OF KYOTO?
IS THAT SUPPOSED TO MAKE ME FEEL BETTER?
I KNOW! AS IF ANY OF US WANT TO GO SEE TEMPLES.
BUT THEY'VE GOT DEER!
They're around in the winter too, right?
YOU'RE THINKING OF NARA...
HAHAHA
DOOM
SO THERE'S NO DEER?
GUESS YOU'RE GOING TO NARA!
GO CHECK OUT THE BIG BUDDHA OR SOMETHING!
No way!
Teacher! Apparently, Macharu's going to Nara!
KEEP IT DOWN!!
IT DOESN'T MATTER WHERE WE GO, REALLY...
AND THUS...

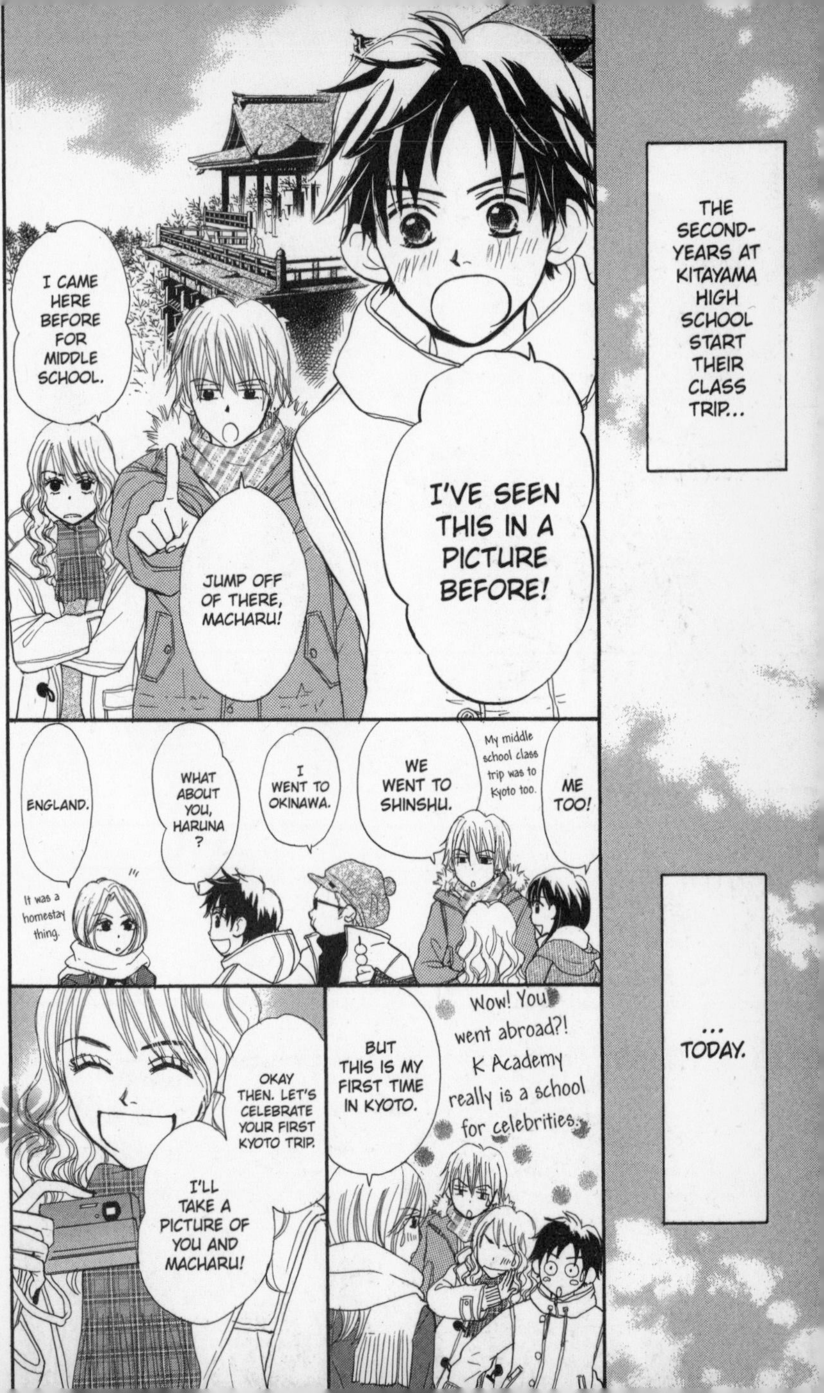
THE SECOND-YEARS AT KITAYAMA HIGH SCHOOL START THEIR CLASS TRIP...
... TODAY.
I'VE SEEN THIS IN A PICTURE BEFORE!
JUMP OFF OF THERE, MACHARU!
I CAME HERE BEFORE FOR MIDDLE SCHOOL.
ME TOO!
My middle school class trip was to Kyoto too.
WE WENT TO SHINSHU.
I WENT TO OKINAWA.
WHAT ABOUT YOU, HARUNA?
ENGLAND.
It was a homestay thing.
Wow! You went abroad?! K Academy really is a school for celebrities.
BUT THIS IS MY FIRST TIME IN KYOTO.
OKAY THEN. LET'S CELEBRATE YOUR FIRST KYOTO TRIP.
I'LL TAKE A PICTURE OF YOU AND MACHARU!

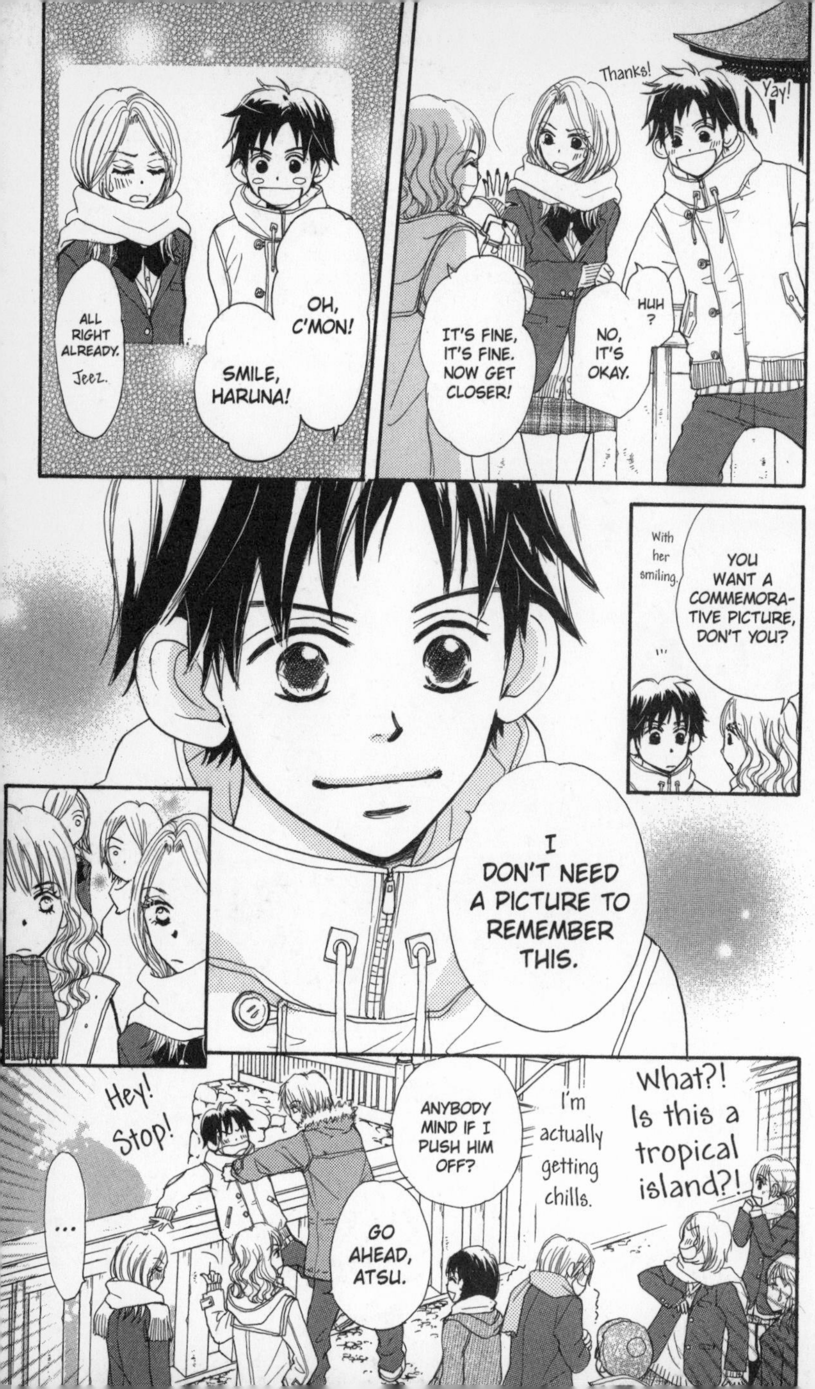
Thanks!
Yay!
HUH ?
NO, IT'S OKAY.
IT'S FINE, IT'S FINE. NOW GET CLOSER!
OH, C'MON!
SMILE, HARUNA!
ALL RIGHT ALREADY.
Jeez.
YOU WANT A COMMEMORATIVE PICTURE, DON'T YOU?
With her smiling.
I DON'T NEED A PICTURE TO REMEMBER THIS.
What?! Is this a tropical island?!
I'm actually getting chills.
ANYBODY MIND IF I PUSH HIM OFF?
GO AHEAD, ATSU.
Hey! Stop!
...

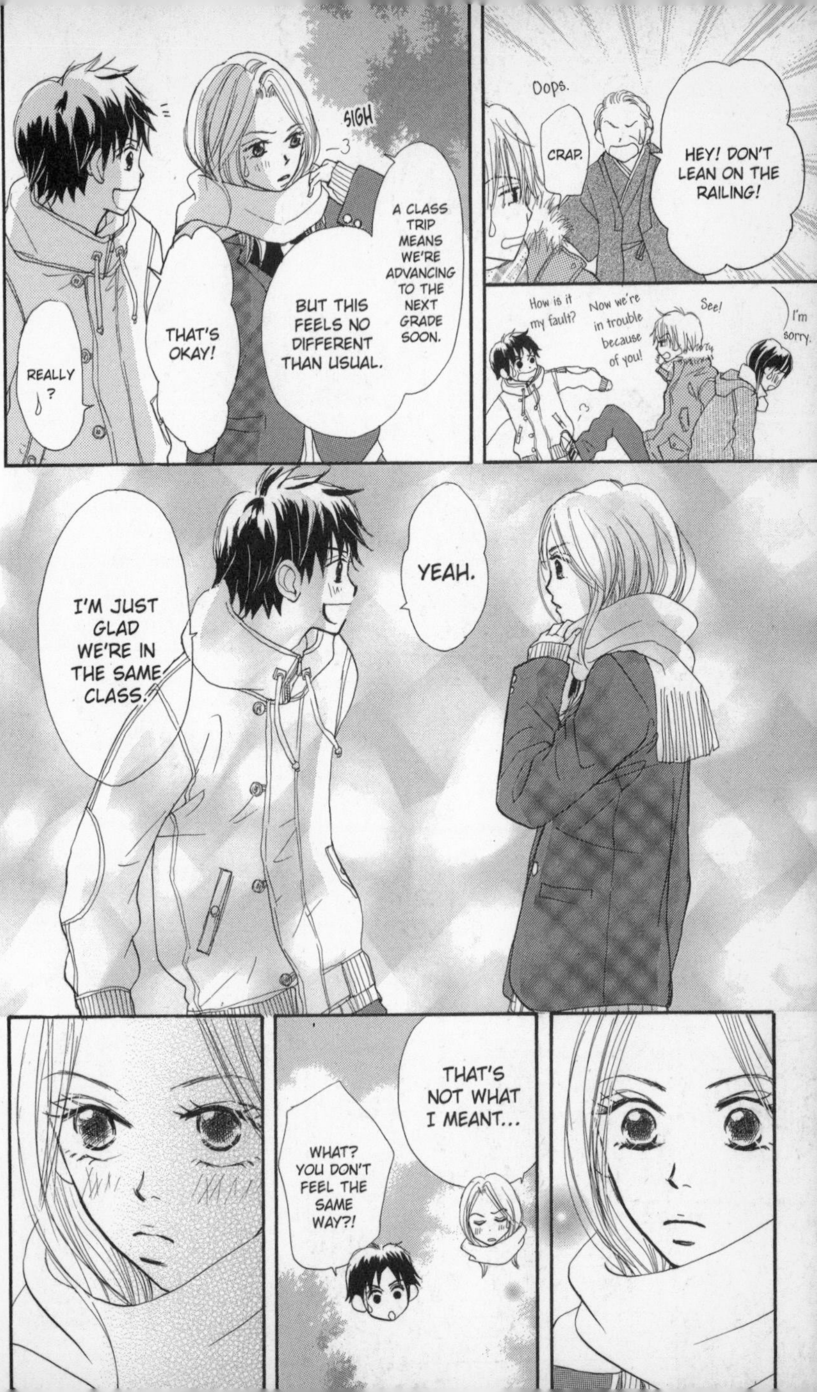
HEY! DON'T LEAN ON THE RAILING!
Oops.
CRAP.
I'm sorry.
See!
Now we're in trouble because of you!
How is it my fault?
SIGH
A CLASS TRIP MEANS WE'RE ADVANCING TO THE NEXT GRADE SOON.
BUT THIS FEELS NO DIFFERENT THAN USUAL.
THAT'S OKAY!
REALLY?
YEAH.
I'M JUST GLAD WE'RE IN THE SAME CLASS.
THAT'S NOT WHAT I MEANT...
WHAT? YOU DON'T FEEL THE SAME WAY?!

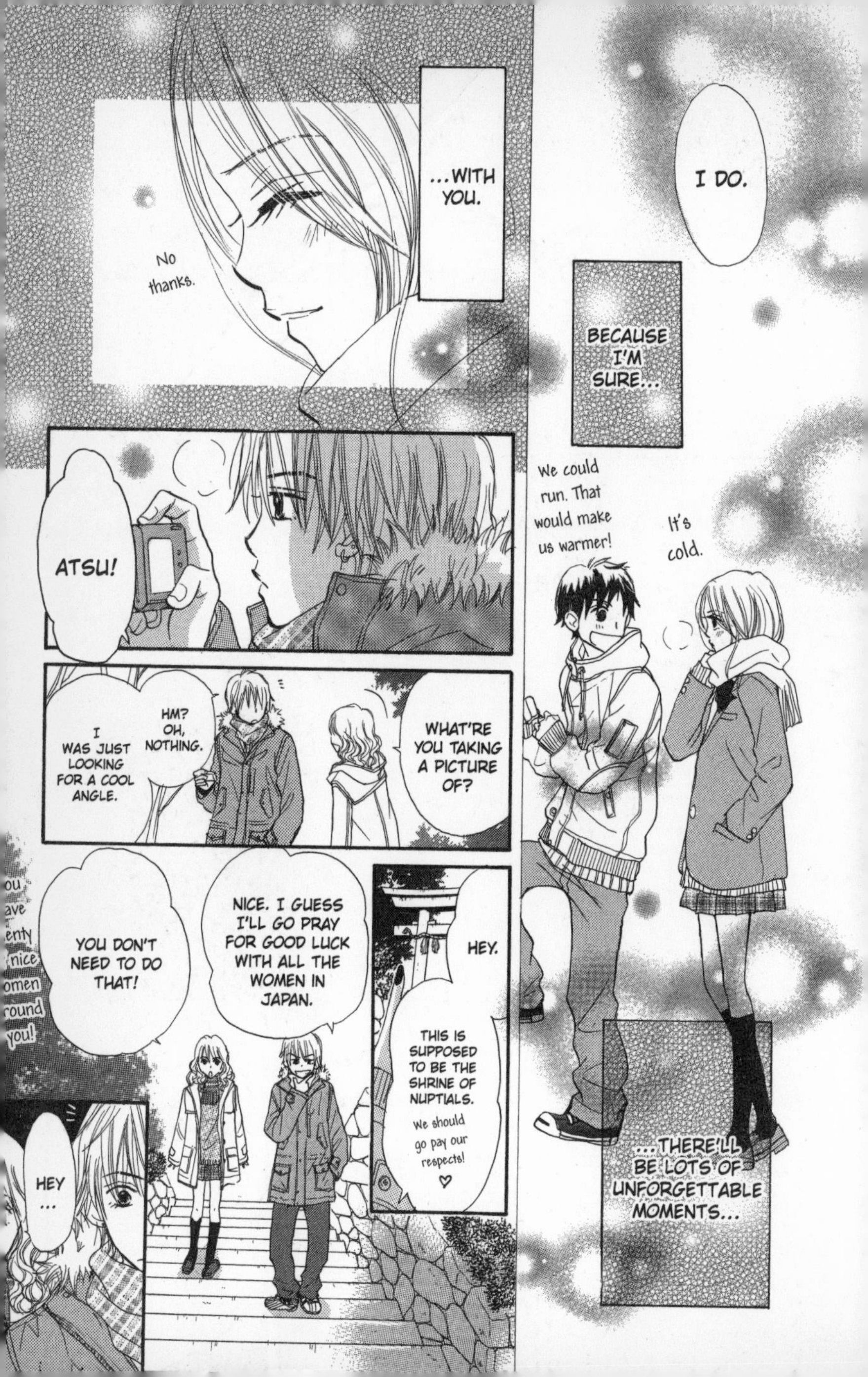
I DO.
BECAUSE I'M SURE...
We could run. That would make us warmer!
It's cold.
...THERE'LL BE LOTS OF UNFORGETTABLE MOMENTS...
...WITH YOU.
No thanks.
ATSU!
WHAT'RE YOU TAKING A PICTURE OF?
HM? OH, NOTHING.
I WAS JUST LOOKING FOR A COOL ANGLE.
HEY.
THIS IS SUPPOSED TO BE THE SHRINE OF NUPTIALS.
We should go pay our respects! ♡
NICE. I GUESS I'LL GO PRAY FOR GOOD LUCK WITH ALL THE WOMEN IN JAPAN.
YOU DON'T NEED TO DO THAT!
HEY ...

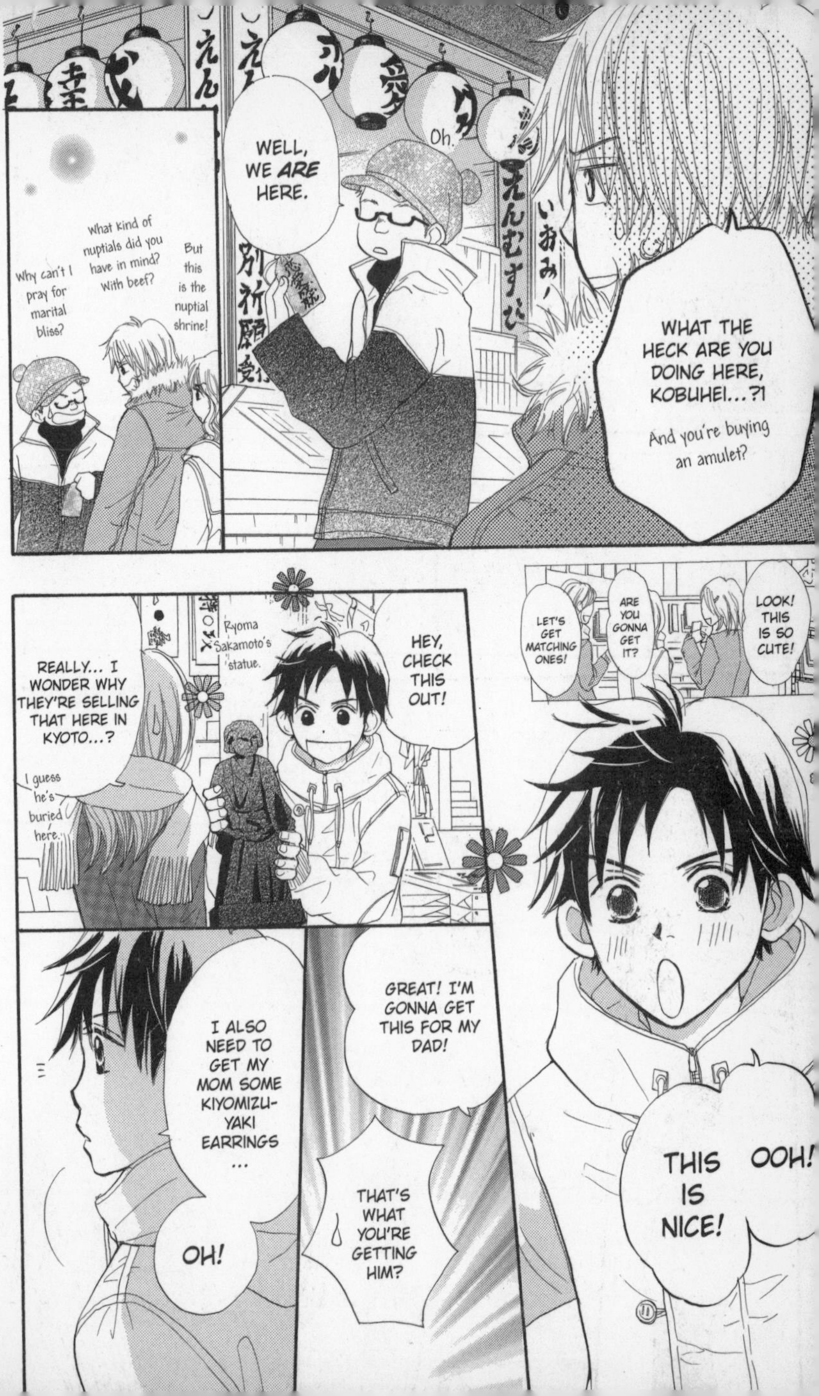
WHAT THE HECK ARE YOU DOING HERE, KOBUHEI...?!
And you're buying an amulet?
Oh.
WELL, WE ARE HERE.
But this is the nuptial shrine!
What kind of nuptials did you have in mind? With beef?
Why can't I pray for marital bliss?
LOOK! THIS IS SO CUTE!
ARE YOU GONNA GET IT?
LET'S GET MATCHING ONES!
HEY, CHECK THIS OUT!
Ryoma Sakamoto's statue.
REALLY... I WONDER WHY THEY'RE SELLING THAT HERE IN KYOTO...?
I guess he's buried here.
OOH!
THIS IS NICE!
GREAT! I'M GONNA GET THIS FOR MY DAD!
THAT'S WHAT YOU'RE GETTING HIM?
I ALSO NEED TO GET MY MOM SOME KIYOMIZU-YAKI EARRINGS...
OH!

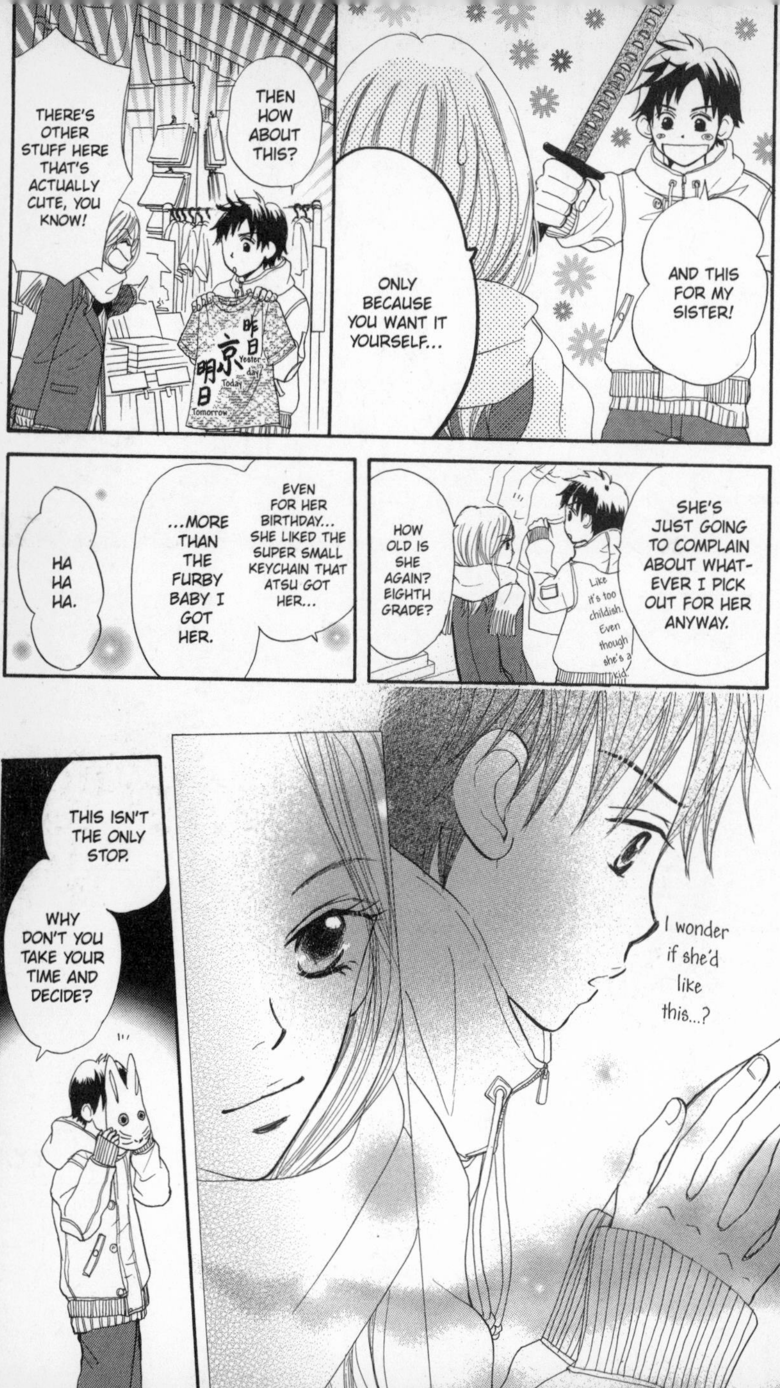
AND THIS FOR MY SISTER!
ONLY BECAUSE YOU WANT IT YOURSELF...
THEN HOW ABOUT THIS?
昨日 Yesterday 京 Today 明日 Tomorrow
THERE'S OTHER STUFF HERE THAT'S ACTUALLY CUTE, YOU KNOW!
SHE'S JUST GOING TO COMPLAIN ABOUT WHATEVER I PICK OUT FOR HER ANYWAY.
Like it's too childish. Even though she's a kid.
HOW OLD IS SHE AGAIN? EIGHTH GRADE?
EVEN FOR HER BIRTHDAY... SHE LIKED THE SUPER SMALL KEYCHAIN THAT ATSU GOT HER...
...MORE THAN THE FURBY BABY I GOT HER.
HA HA HA.
I wonder if she'd like this...?
THIS ISN'T THE ONLY STOP.
WHY DON'T YOU TAKE YOUR TIME AND DECIDE?

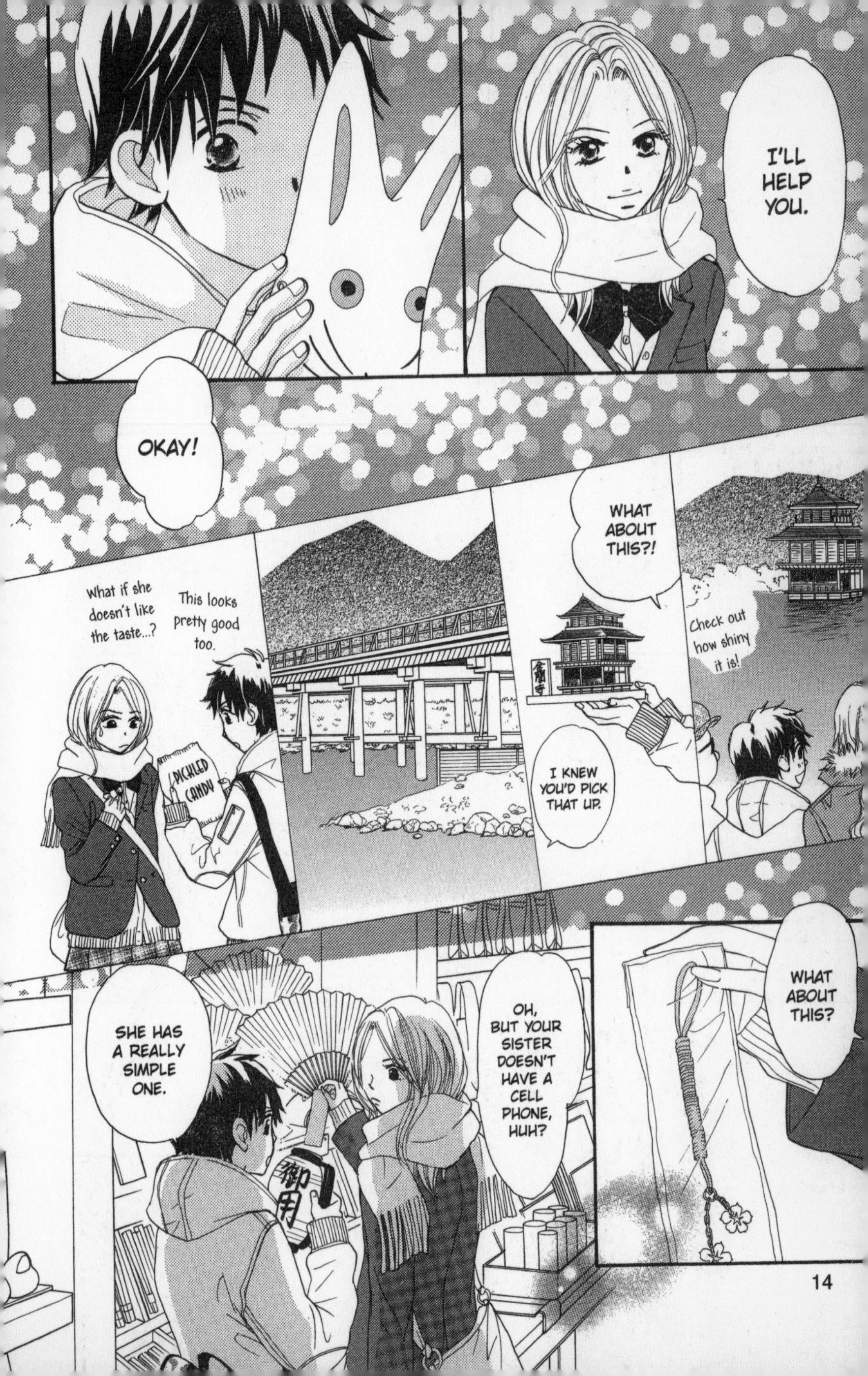

I'LL HELP YOU.
OKAY!
Check out how shiny it is!
WHAT ABOUT THIS?!
I KNEW YOU'D PICK THAT UP.
This looks pretty good too.
What if she doesn't like the taste...?
PICKLED CANDY
WHAT ABOUT THIS?
OH, BUT YOUR SISTER DOESN'T HAVE A CELL PHONE, HUH?
SHE HAS A REALLY SIMPLE ONE.

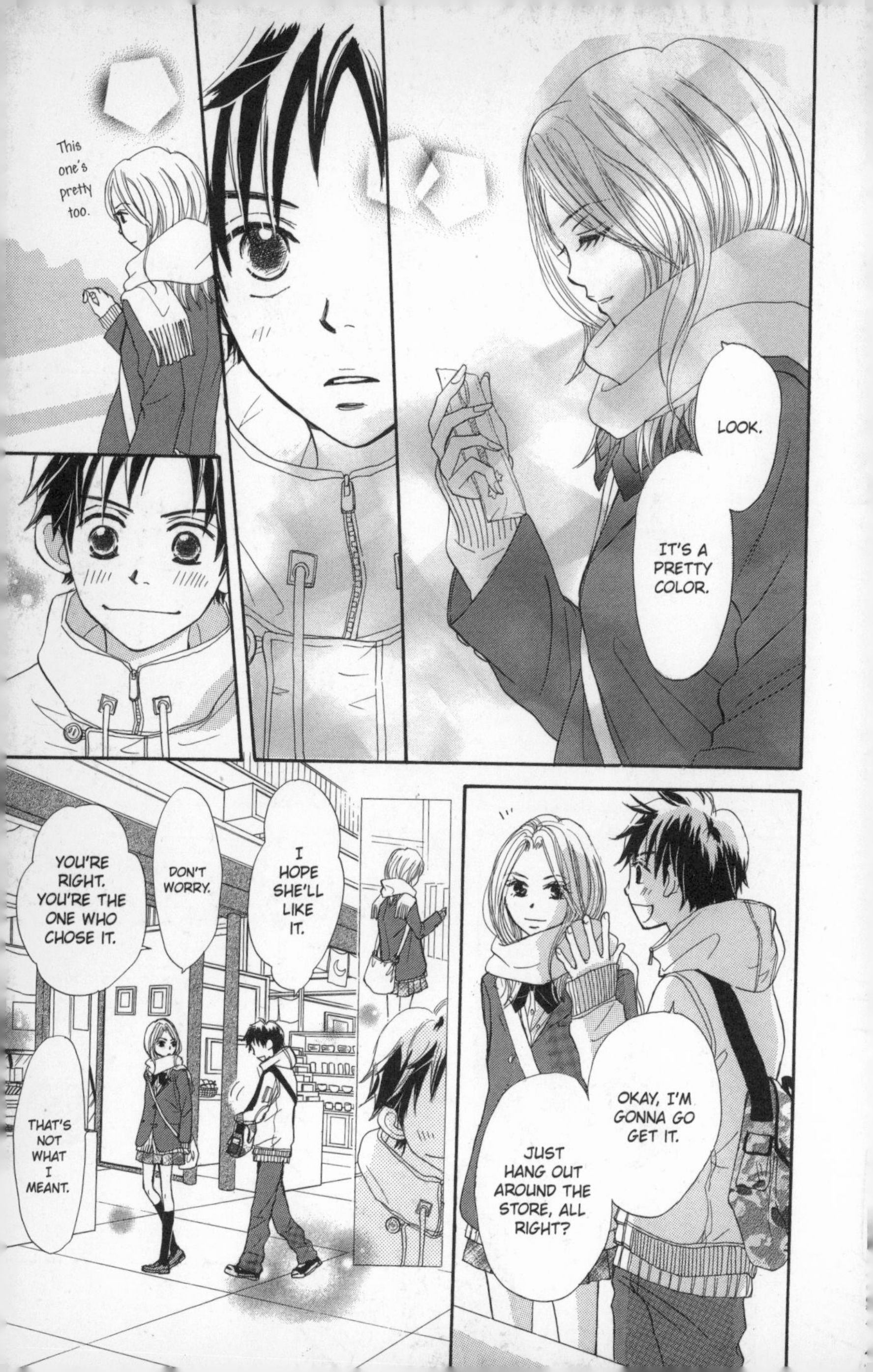
LOOK.
IT'S A PRETTY COLOR.
This one's pretty too.
OKAY, I'M GONNA GO GET IT.
JUST HANG OUT AROUND THE STORE, ALL RIGHT?
I HOPE SHE'LL LIKE IT.
DON'T WORRY.
YOU'RE RIGHT. YOU'RE THE ONE WHO CHOSE IT.
THAT'S NOT WHAT I MEANT.

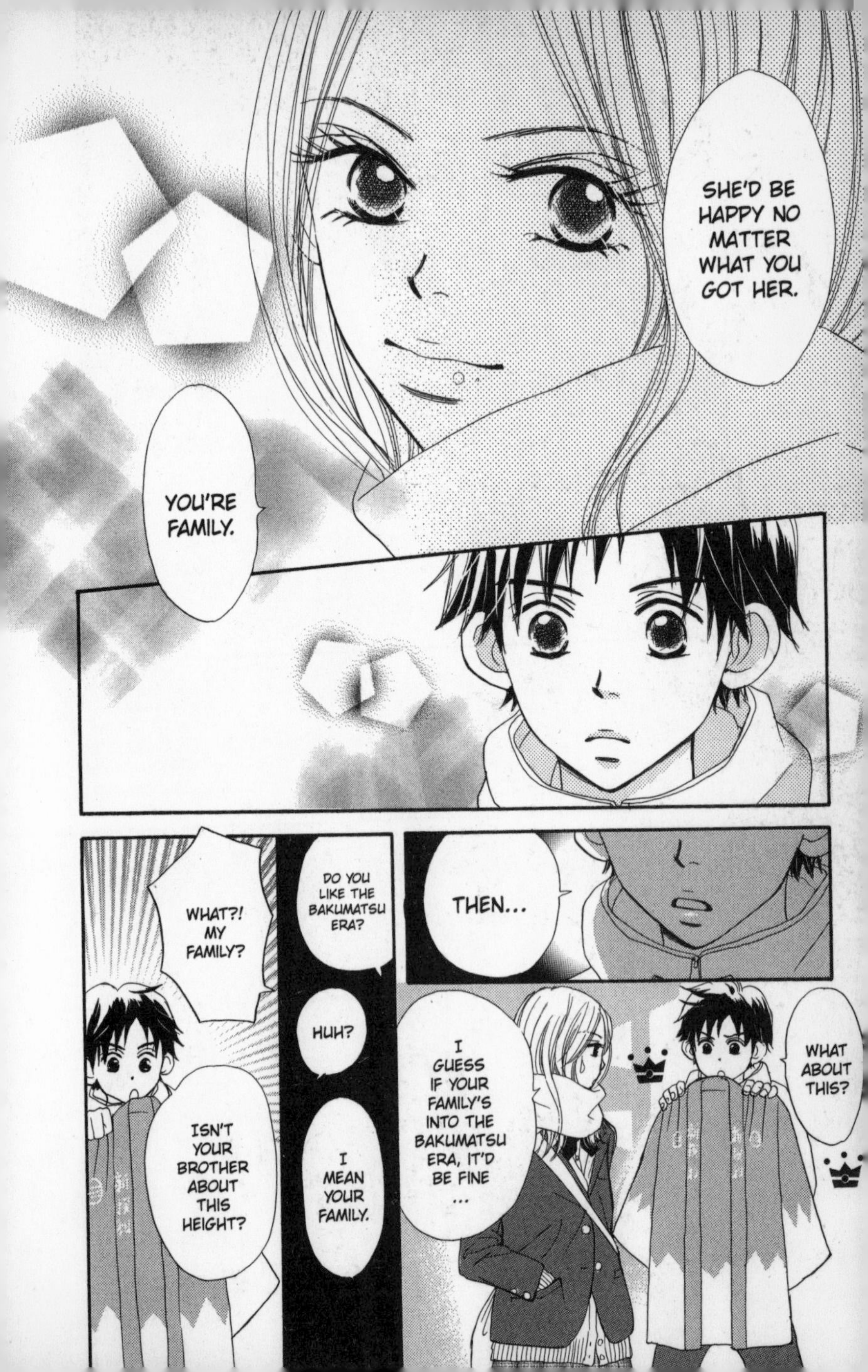
SHE'D BE HAPPY NO MATTER WHAT YOU GOT HER.
YOU'RE FAMILY.
THEN...
WHAT ABOUT THIS?
I GUESS IF YOUR FAMILY'S INTO THE BAKUMATSU ERA, IT'D BE FINE ...
DO YOU LIKE THE BAKUMATSU ERA?
HUH?
I MEAN YOUR FAMILY.
WHAT?! MY FAMILY?
ISN'T YOUR BROTHER ABOUT THIS HEIGHT?

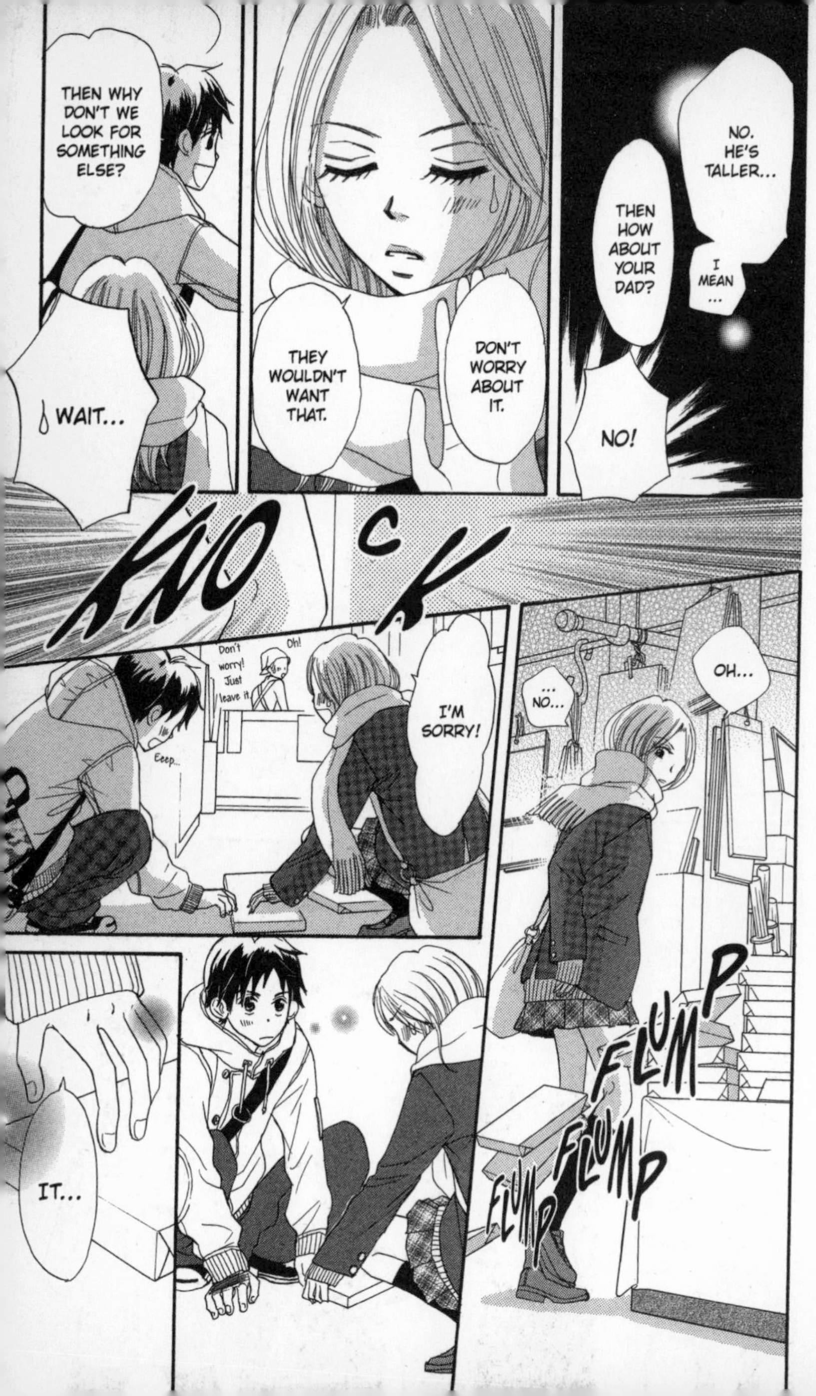
NO. HE'S TALLER...
I MEAN...
THEN HOW ABOUT YOUR DAD?
NO!
DON'T WORRY ABOUT IT.
THEY WOULDN'T WANT THAT.
THEN WHY DON'T WE LOOK FOR SOMETHING ELSE?
WAIT...
KNOCK
OH...
...NO...
FLUMP
FLUMP
FLUMP
I'M SORRY!
Oh!
Don't worry! Just leave it.
Eeep...
IT...

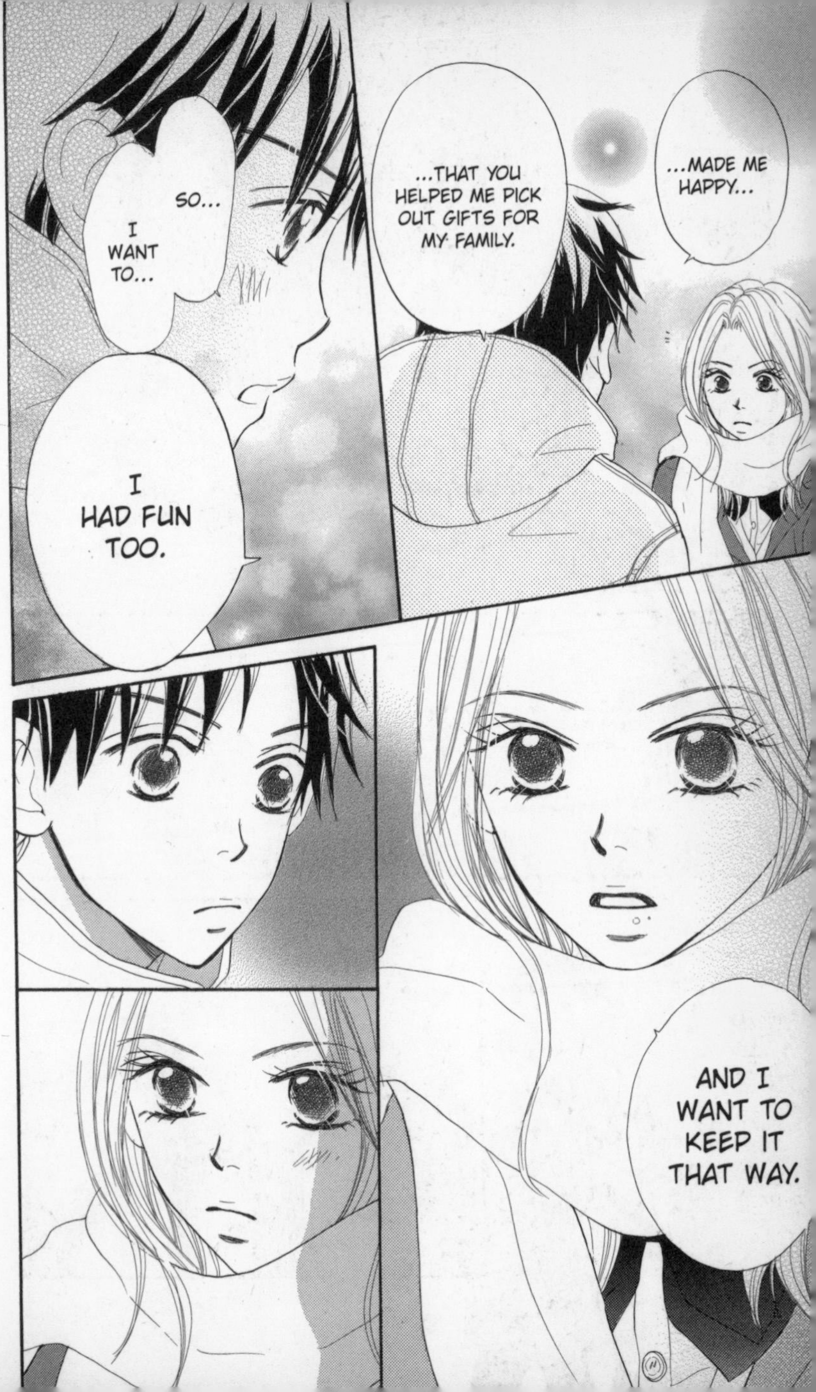
...THAT YOU HELPED ME PICK OUT GIFTS FOR MY FAMILY.
...MADE ME HAPPY...
SO... I WANT TO...
I HAD FUN TOO.
AND I WANT TO KEEP IT THAT WAY.

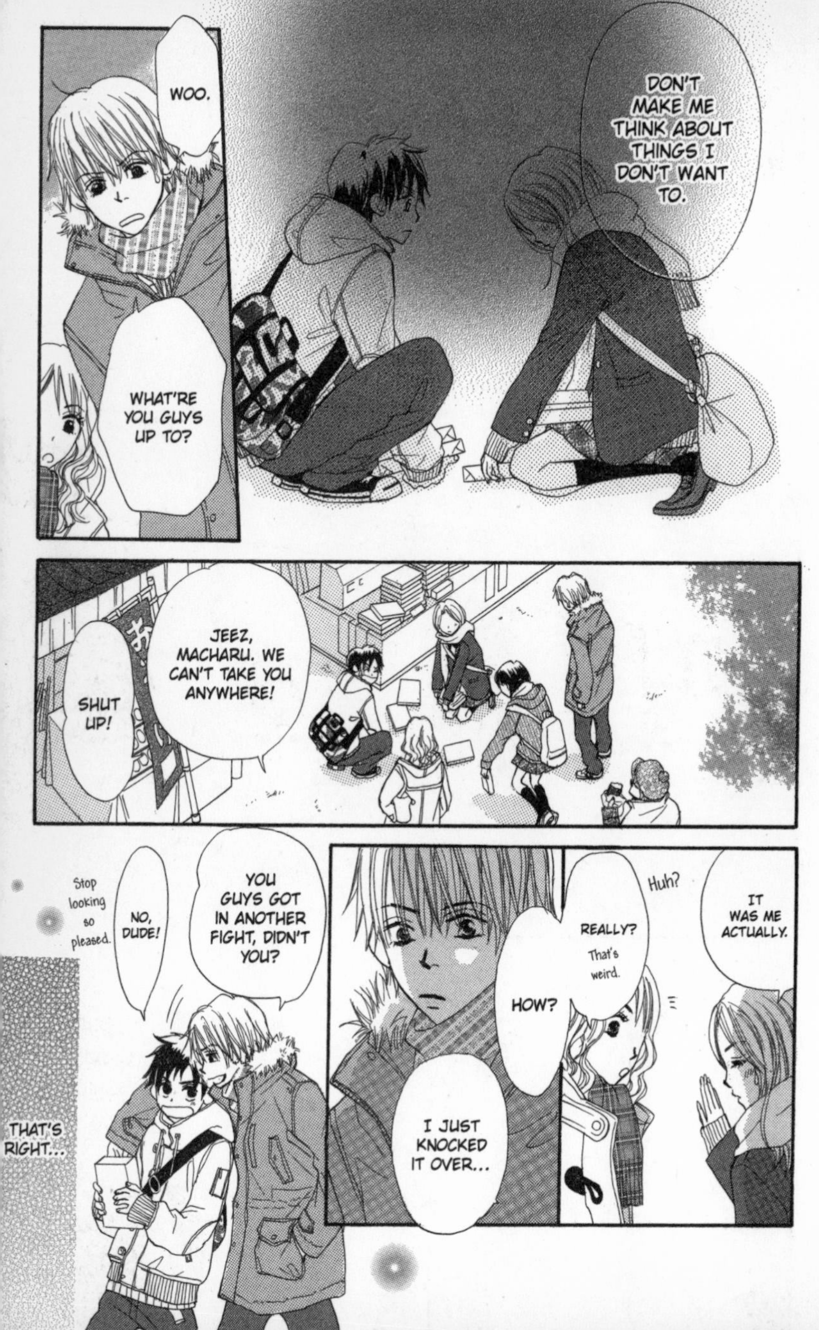
DON'T MAKE ME THINK ABOUT THINGS I DON'T WANT TO.
WOO.
WHAT'RE YOU GUYS UP TO?
JEEZ, MACHARU. WE CAN'T TAKE YOU ANYWHERE!
SHUT UP!
IT WAS ME ACTUALLY.
Huh?
REALLY? That's weird.
HOW?
I JUST KNOCKED IT OVER...
YOU GUYS GOT IN ANOTHER FIGHT, DIDN'T YOU?
NO, DUDE!
Stop looking so pleased.
THAT'S RIGHT...

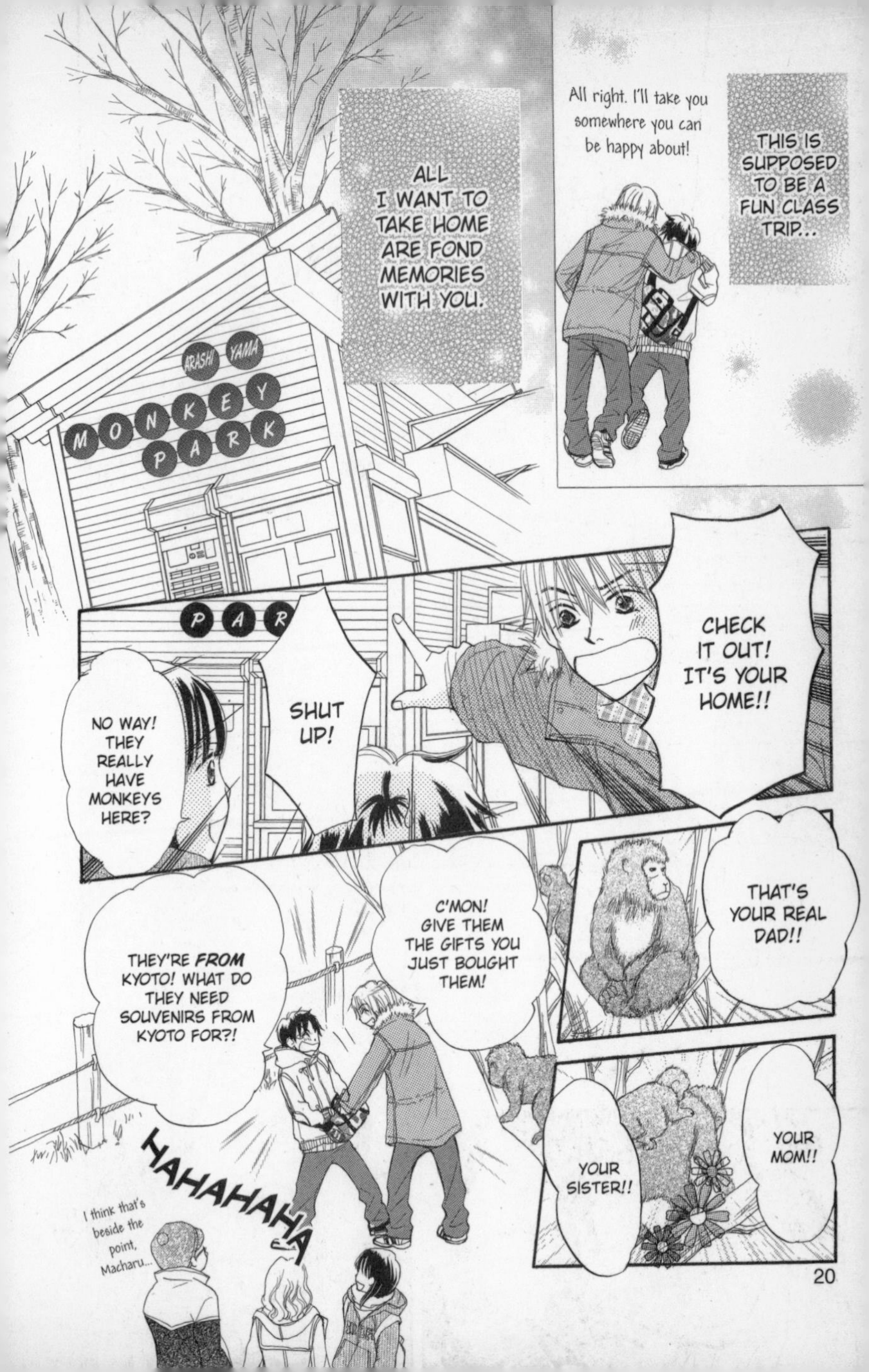
THIS IS SUPPOSED TO BE A FUN CLASS TRIP...
All right. I'll take you somewhere you can be happy about!
ALL I WANT TO TAKE HOME ARE FOND MEMORIES WITH YOU.
ARASHI YAMA
MONKEY PARK
CHECK IT OUT! IT'S YOUR HOME!!
SHUT UP!
NO WAY! THEY REALLY HAVE MONKEYS HERE?
THAT'S YOUR REAL DAD!!
YOUR MOM!!
YOUR SISTER!!
C'MON! GIVE THEM THE GIFTS YOU JUST BOUGHT THEM!
THEY'RE *FROM* KYOTO! WHAT DO THEY NEED SOUVENIRS FROM KYOTO FOR?!
HAHAHAHAHA
I think that's beside the point, Macharu...

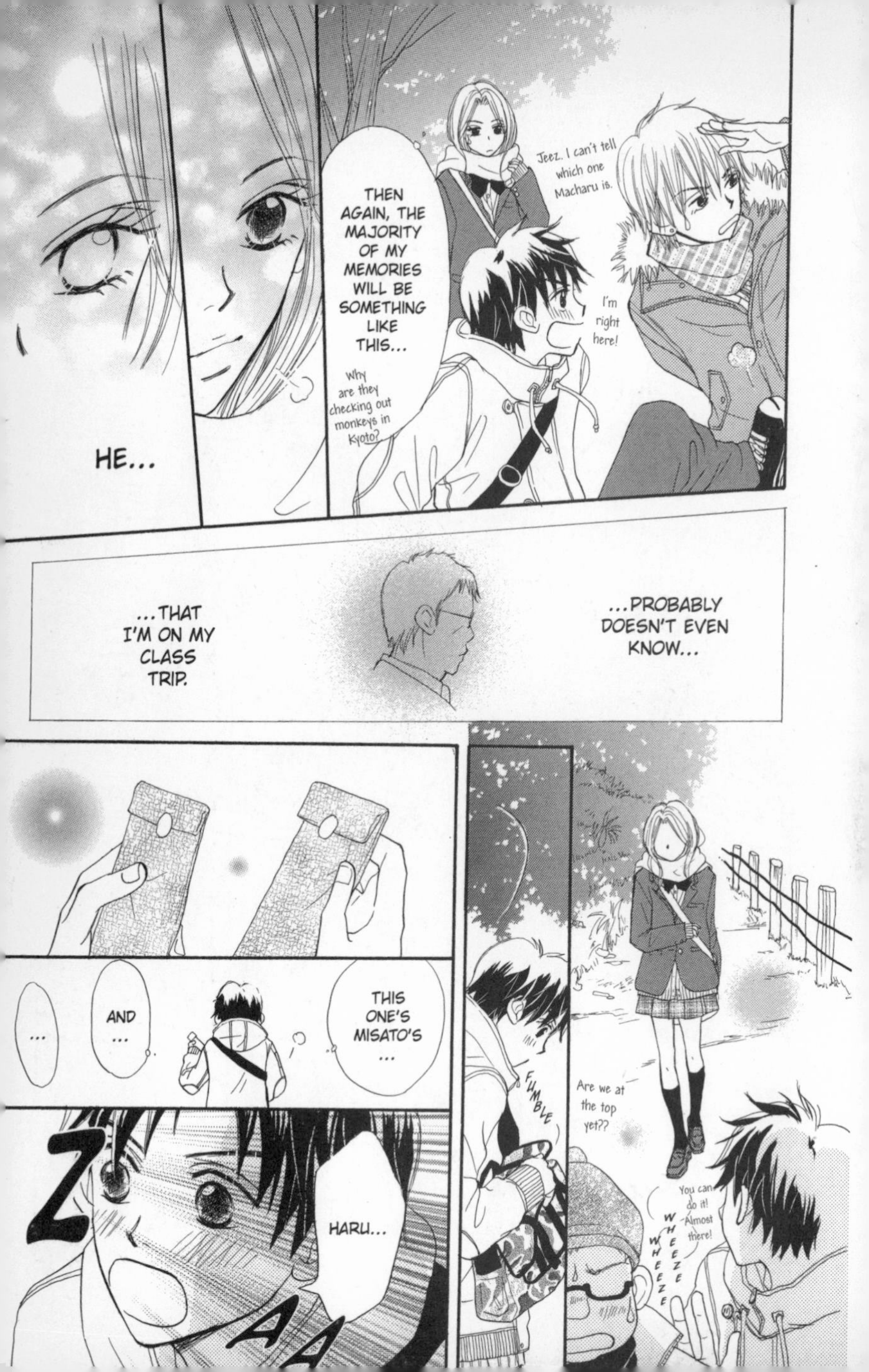
Jeez. I can't tell which one Macharu is.
I'm right here!
THEN AGAIN, THE MAJORITY OF MY MEMORIES WILL BE SOMETHING LIKE THIS...
Why are they checking out monkeys in Kyoto?
HE...
...PROBABLY DOESN'T EVEN KNOW...
...THAT I'M ON MY CLASS TRIP.
FUMBLE
Are we at the top yet??
You can do it! Almost there!
WHEEZE WHEEZE WHEEZE
THIS ONE'S MISATO'S ...
AND ...
...
HARU...
ZAA

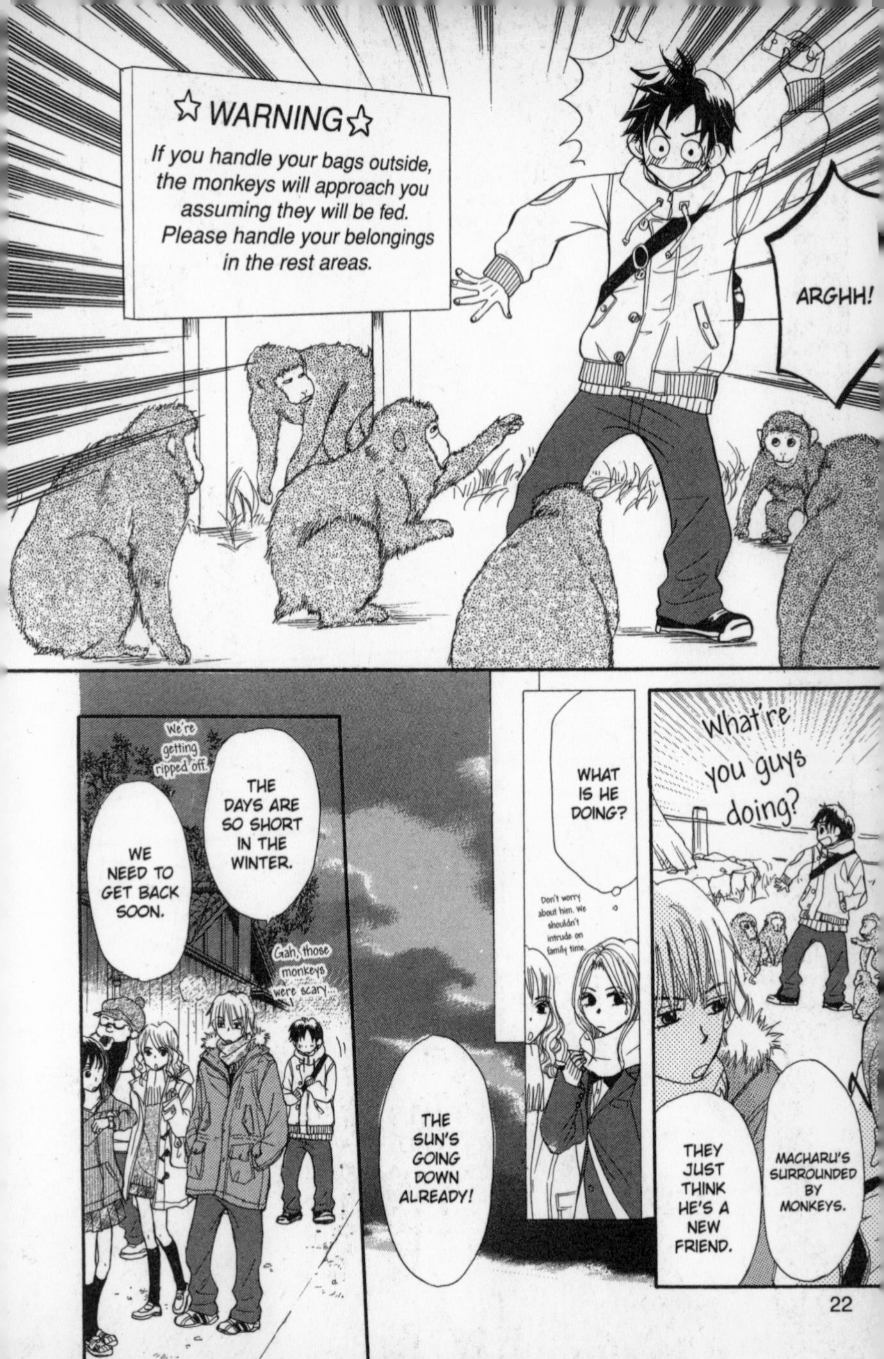
☆WARNING☆
If you handle your bags outside, the monkeys will approach you assuming they will be fed. Please handle your belongings in the rest areas.
ARGHH!
What're you guys doing?
MACHARU'S SURROUNDED BY MONKEYS.
THEY JUST THINK HE'S A NEW FRIEND.
WHAT IS HE DOING?
Don't worry about him. We shouldn't intrude on family time.
THE SUN'S GOING DOWN ALREADY!
THE DAYS ARE SO SHORT IN THE WINTER.
WE NEED TO GET BACK SOON.
We're getting ripped off.
Gah, those monkeys were scary...

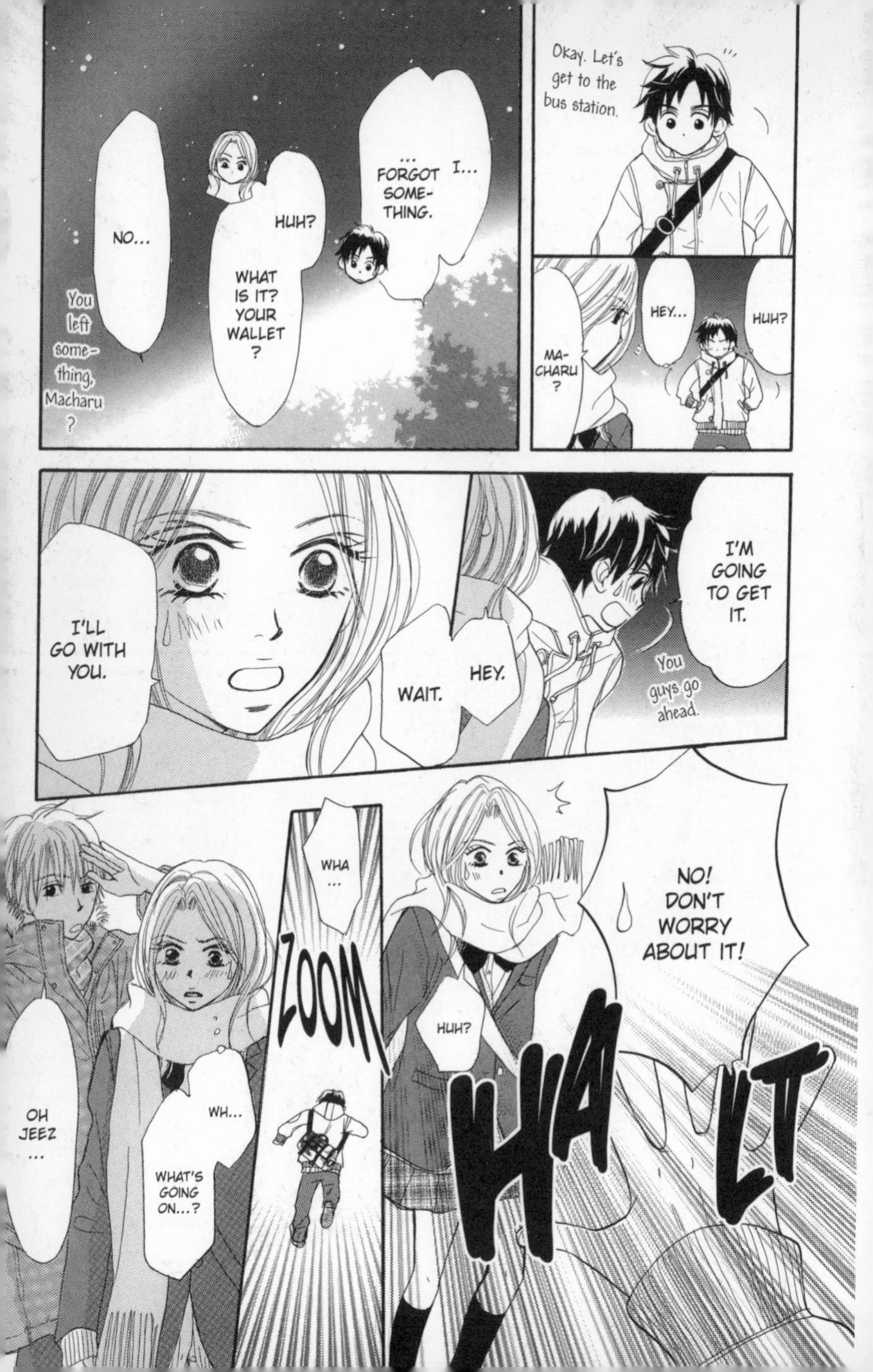
Okay. Let's get to the bus station.
HUH?
HEY...
MA-CHARU?
I...
...FORGOT SOMETHING.
HUH?
WHAT IS IT? YOUR WALLET?
NO...
You left something, Macharu?
I'M GOING TO GET IT.
You guys go ahead.
HEY.
WAIT.
I'LL GO WITH YOU.
NO! DON'T WORRY ABOUT IT!
HALT
HUH?
WHA...
ZOOM
WH...
WHAT'S GOING ON...?
OH JEEZ...

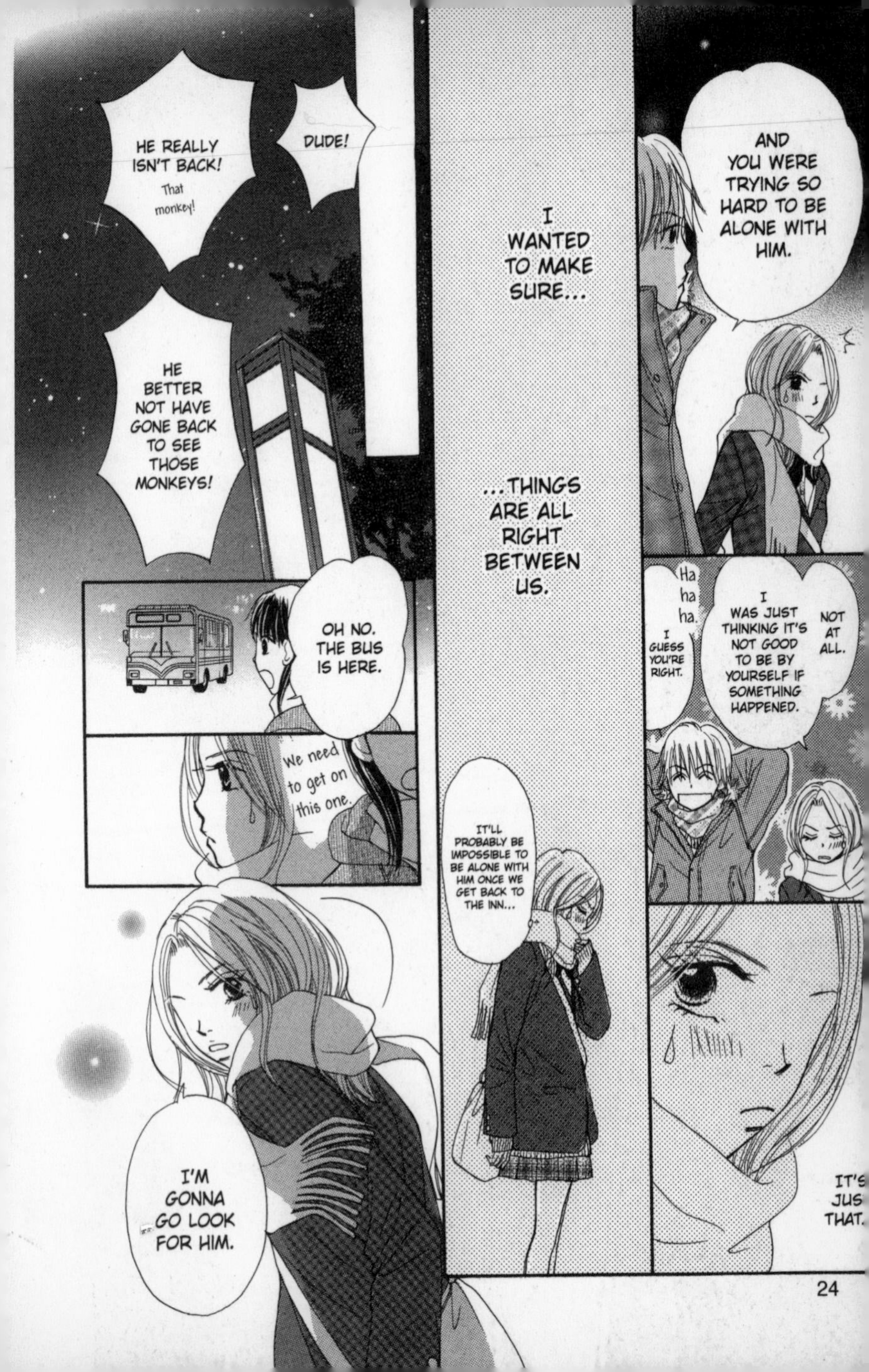
AND YOU WERE TRYING SO HARD TO BE ALONE WITH HIM.
NOT AT ALL.
I WAS JUST THINKING IT'S NOT GOOD TO BE BY YOURSELF IF SOMETHING HAPPENED.
Ha ha ha.
I GUESS YOU'RE RIGHT.
IT'S JUST THAT.
I WANTED TO MAKE SURE...
...THINGS ARE ALL RIGHT BETWEEN US.
IT'LL PROBABLY BE IMPOSSIBLE TO BE ALONE WITH HIM ONCE WE GET BACK TO THE INN...
DUDE!
HE REALLY ISN'T BACK!
That monkey!
HE BETTER NOT HAVE GONE BACK TO SEE THOSE MONKEYS!
OH NO. THE BUS IS HERE.
We need to get on this one.
I'M GONNA GO LOOK FOR HIM.

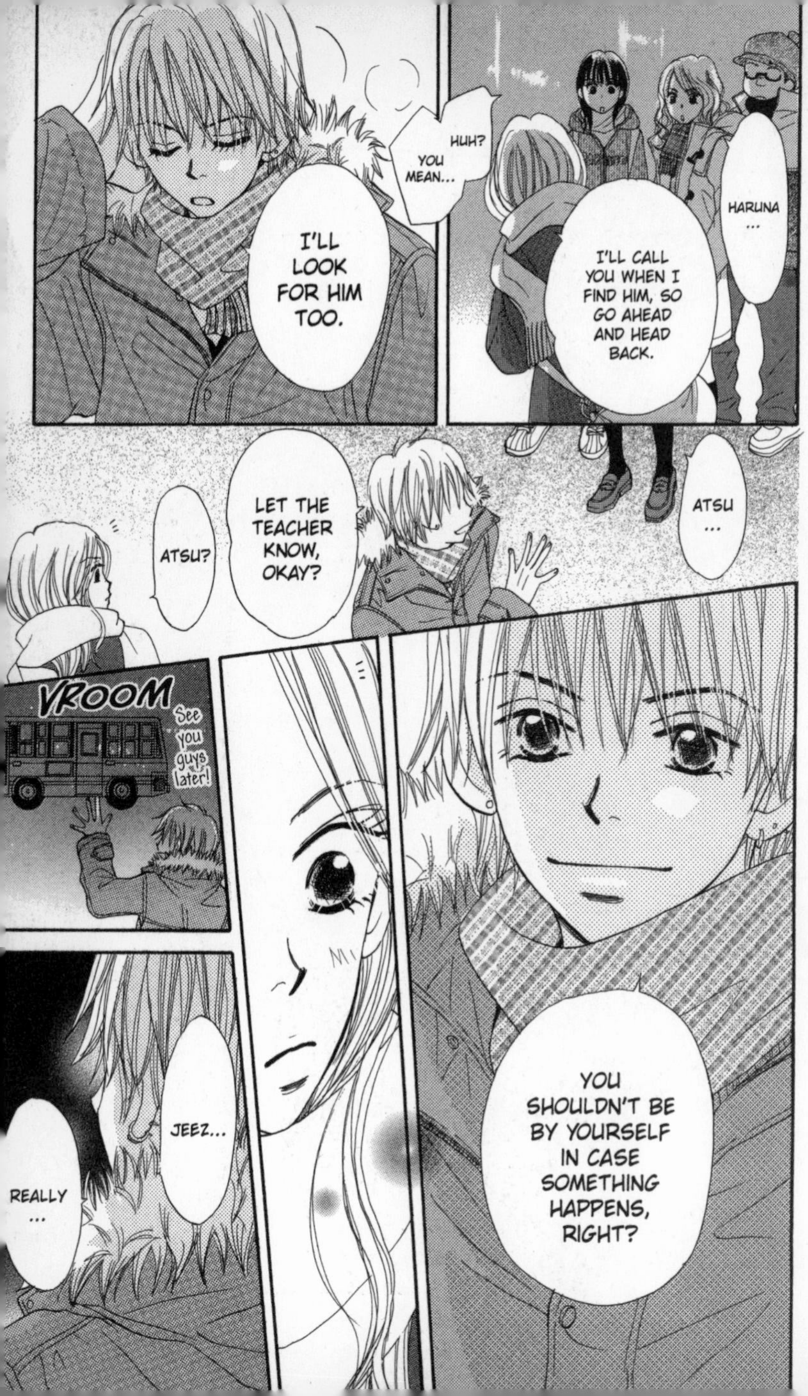
HARUNA...
I'LL CALL YOU WHEN I FIND HIM, SO GO AHEAD AND HEAD BACK.
HUH? YOU MEAN...
I'LL LOOK FOR HIM TOO.
ATSU...
LET THE TEACHER KNOW, OKAY?
ATSU?
YOU SHOULDN'T BE BY YOURSELF IN CASE SOMETHING HAPPENS, RIGHT?
VROOM
See you guys later!
JEEZ...
REALLY...

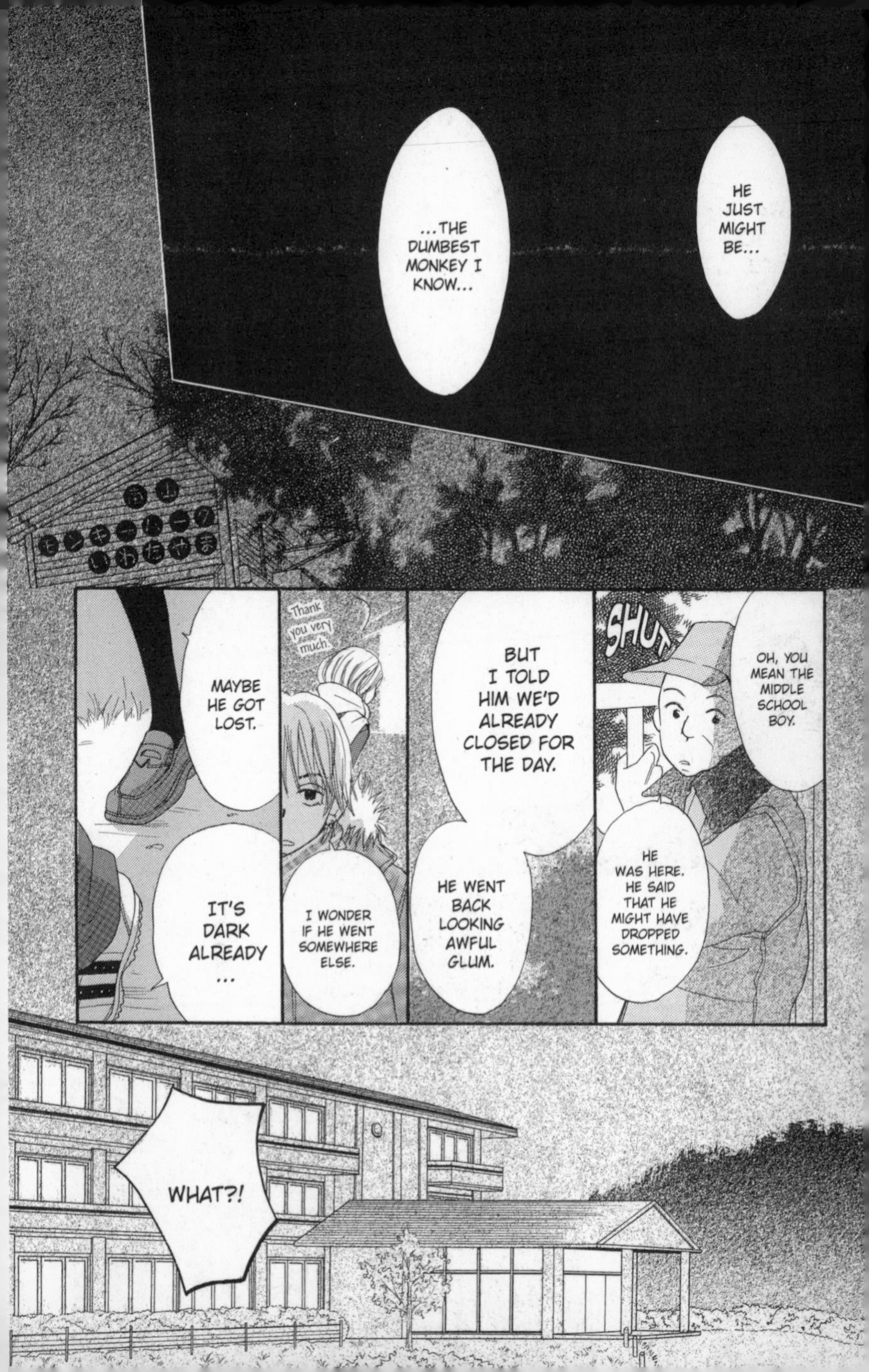
HE JUST MIGHT BE...
...THE DUMBEST MONKEY I KNOW...
SHUT
OH, YOU MEAN THE MIDDLE SCHOOL BOY.
HE WAS HERE. HE SAID THAT HE MIGHT HAVE DROPPED SOMETHING.
BUT I TOLD HIM WE'D ALREADY CLOSED FOR THE DAY.
HE WENT BACK LOOKING AWFUL GLUM.
Thank you very much.
I WONDER IF HE WENT SOMEWHERE ELSE.
MAYBE HE GOT LOST.
IT'S DARK ALREADY...
WHAT?!

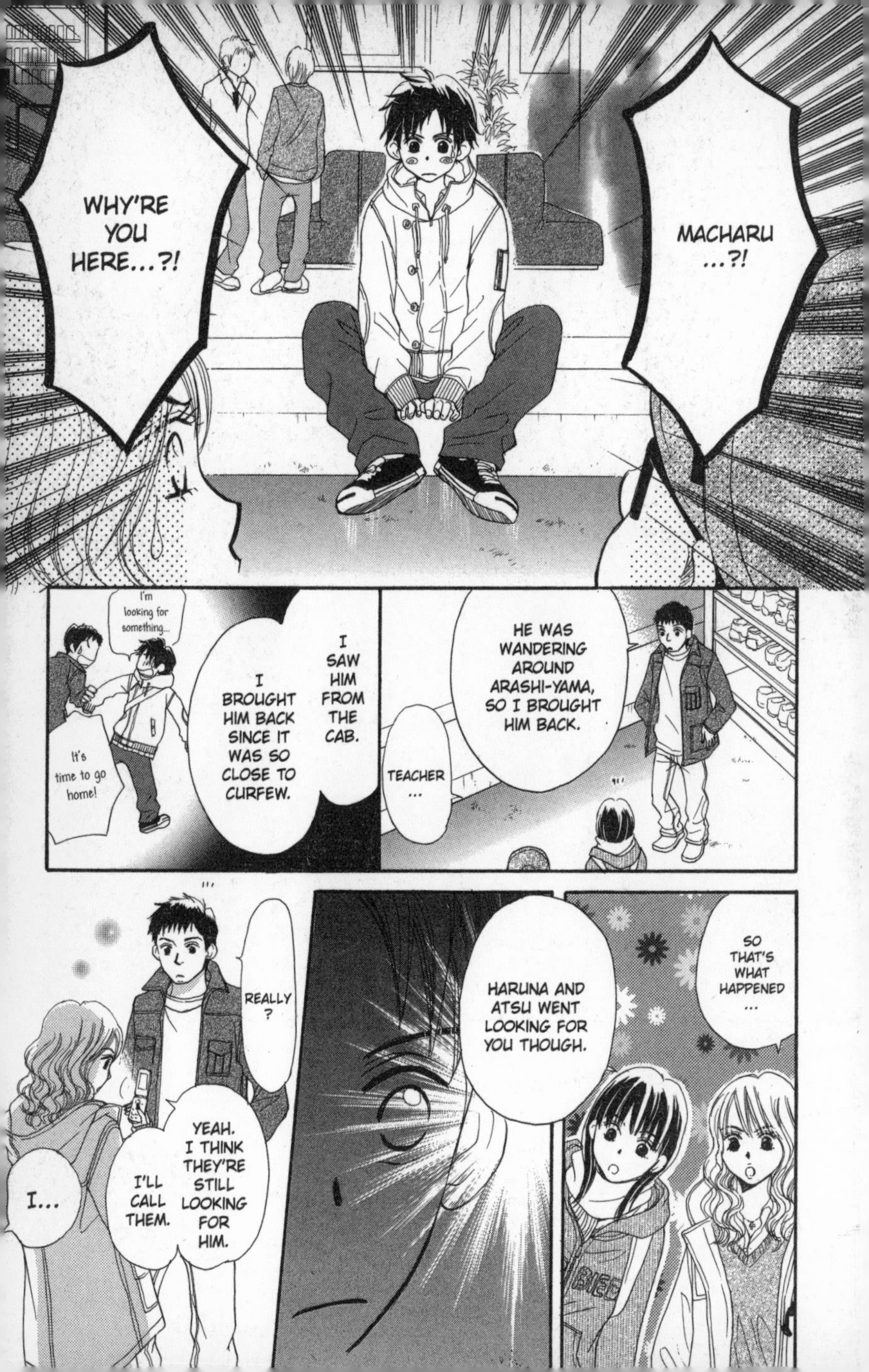
MACHARU ...?!
WHY'RE YOU HERE...?!
HE WAS WANDERING AROUND ARASHI-YAMA, SO I BROUGHT HIM BACK.
TEACHER ...
I SAW HIM FROM THE CAB.
I BROUGHT HIM BACK SINCE IT WAS SO CLOSE TO CURFEW.
I'm looking for something...
It's time to go home!
SO THAT'S WHAT HAPPENED ...
HARUNA AND ATSU WENT LOOKING FOR YOU THOUGH.
REALLY ?
YEAH. I THINK THEY'RE STILL LOOKING FOR HIM.
I'LL CALL THEM.
I...

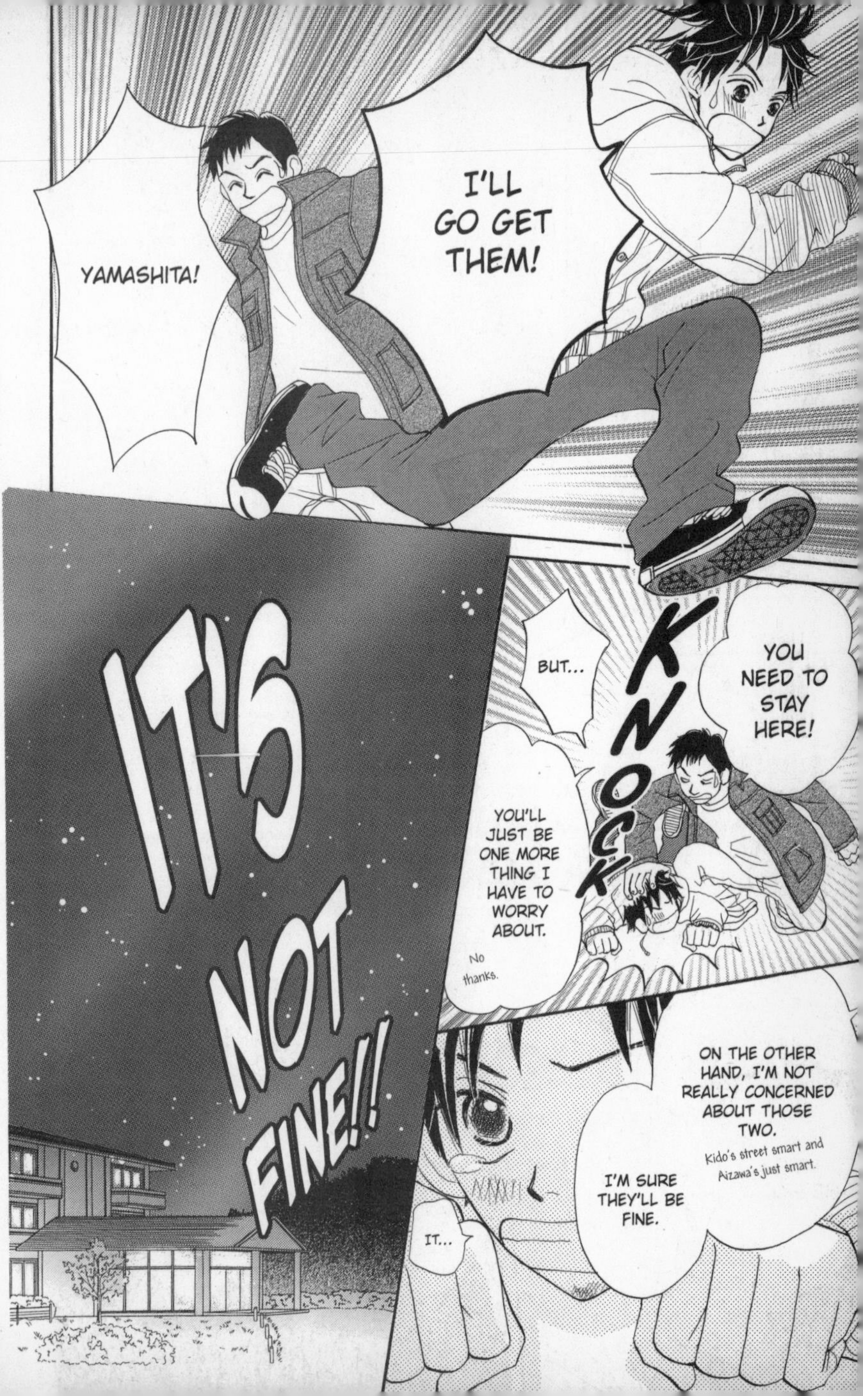
I'LL GO GET THEM!
YAMASHITA!
YOU NEED TO STAY HERE!
BUT...
KNOCK
YOU'LL JUST BE ONE MORE THING I HAVE TO WORRY ABOUT.
No thanks.
ON THE OTHER HAND, I'M NOT REALLY CONCERNED ABOUT THOSE TWO.
Kido's street smart and Aizawa's just smart.
I'M SURE THEY'LL BE FINE.
IT...
IT'S NOT FINE!!

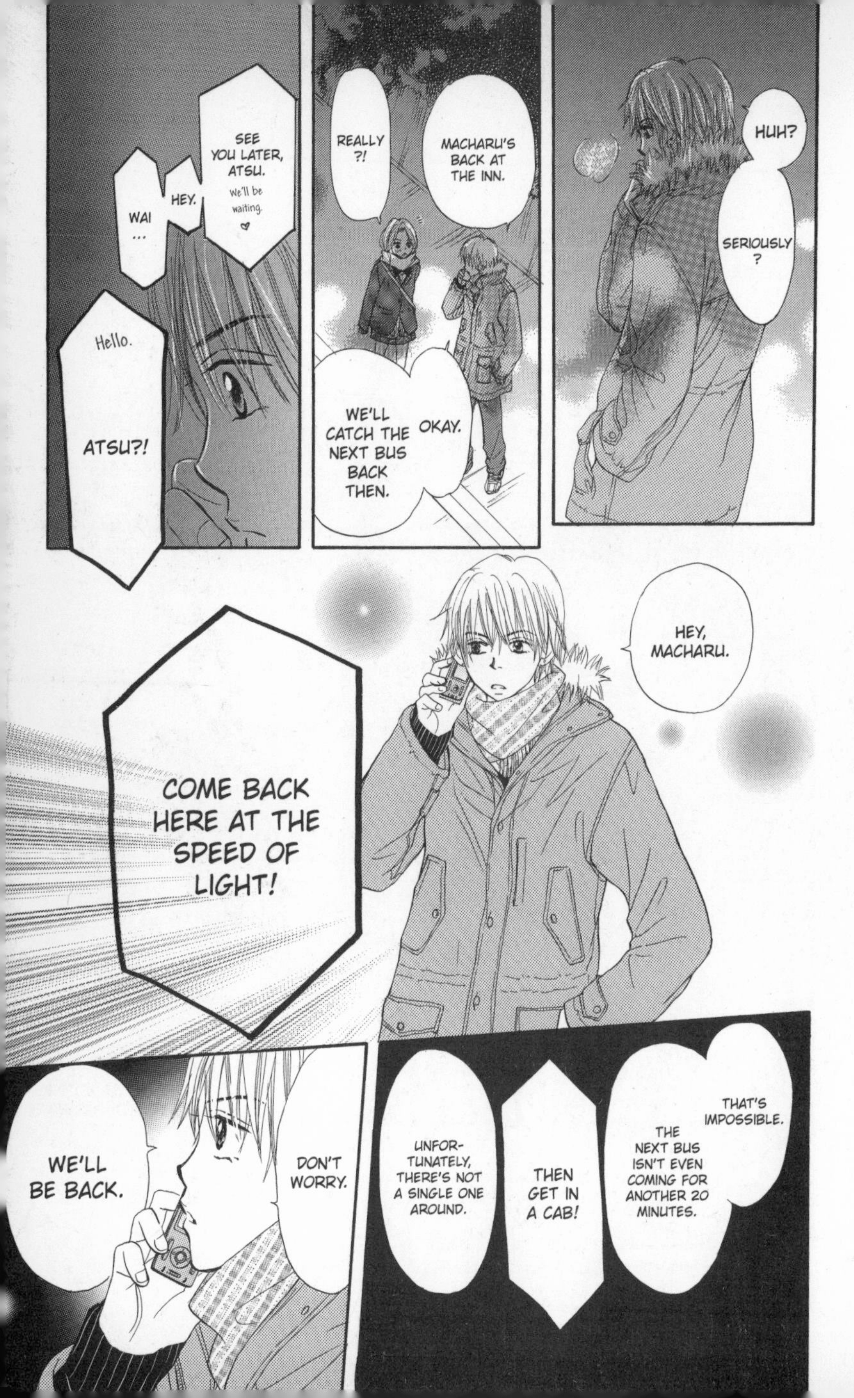
HUH?
SERIOUSLY?
MACHARU'S BACK AT THE INN.
REALLY?!
OKAY.
WE'LL CATCH THE NEXT BUS BACK THEN.
SEE YOU LATER, ATSU.
We'll be waiting. ♥
HEY.
WAI...
Hello.
ATSU?!
HEY, MACHARU.
COME BACK HERE AT THE SPEED OF LIGHT!
THAT'S IMPOSSIBLE.
THE NEXT BUS ISN'T EVEN COMING FOR ANOTHER 20 MINUTES.
THEN GET IN A CAB!
UNFORTUNATELY, THERE'S NOT A SINGLE ONE AROUND.
DON'T WORRY.
WE'LL BE BACK.

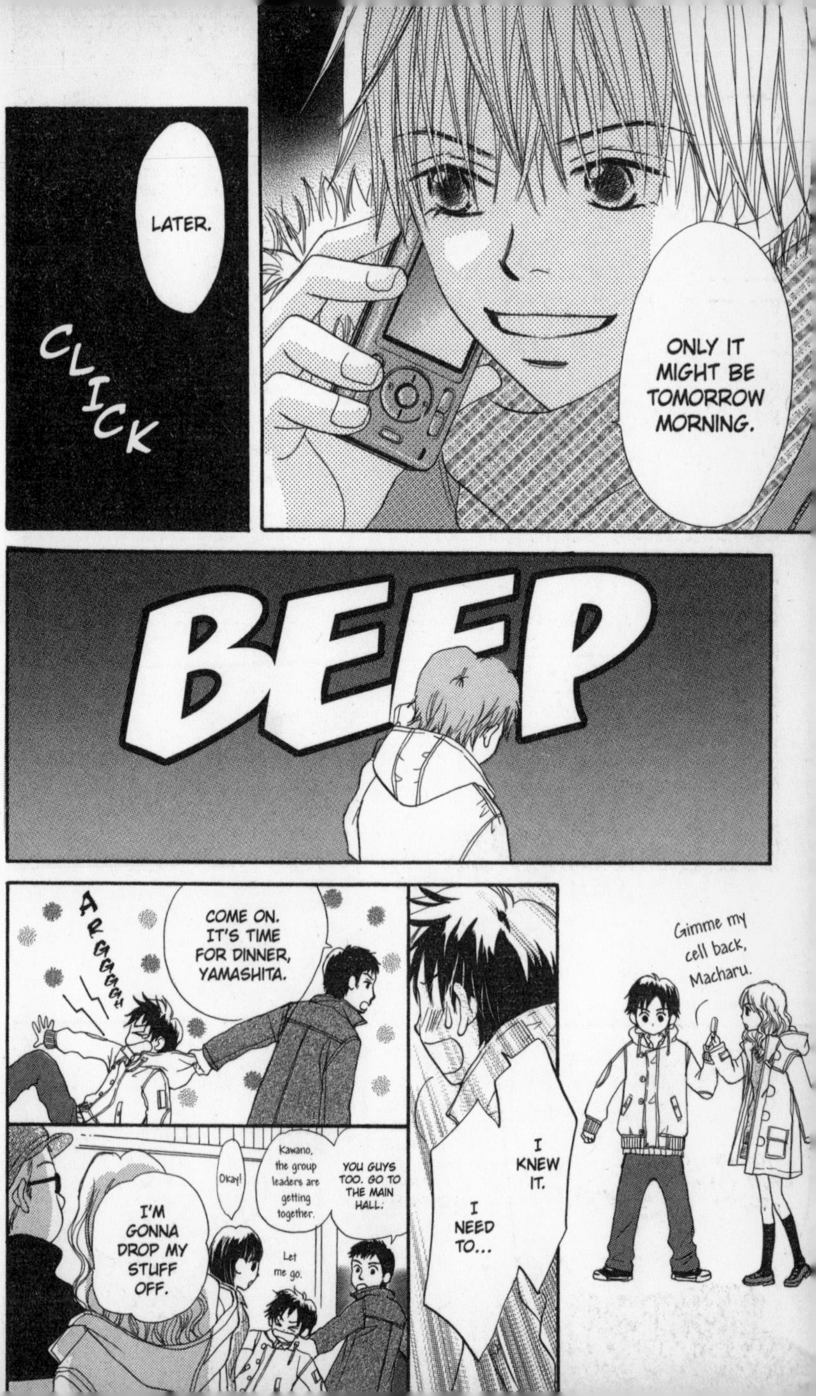
ONLY IT MIGHT BE TOMORROW MORNING.
LATER.
CLICK
BEEP
Gimme my cell back, Macharu.
I KNEW IT.
I NEED TO...
COME ON. IT'S TIME FOR DINNER, YAMASHITA.
ARGGGGH
YOU GUYS TOO. GO TO THE MAIN HALL.
Kawano, the group leaders are getting together.
Okay!
I'M GONNA DROP MY STUFF OFF.
Let me go.

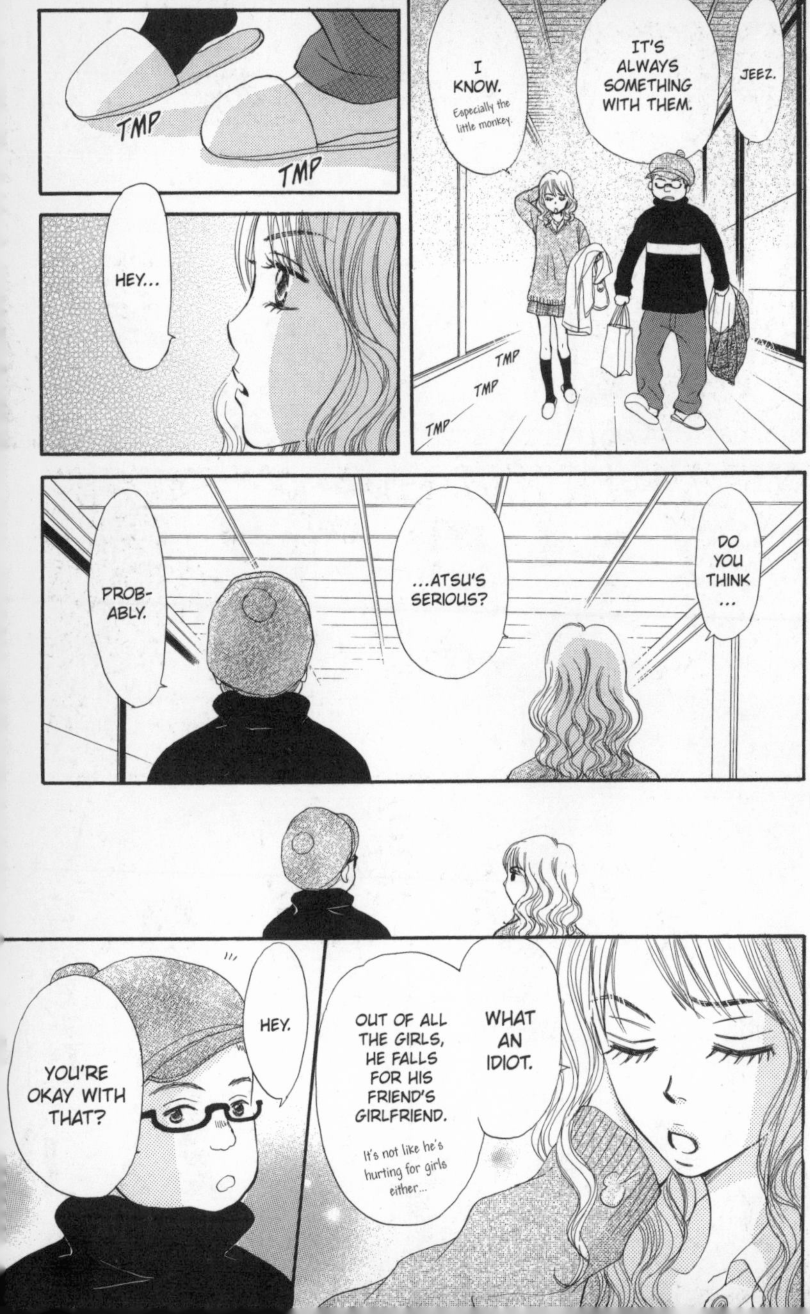
JEEZ.
IT'S ALWAYS SOMETHING WITH THEM.
I KNOW.
Especially the little monkey.
TMP
TMP
TMP
TMP
TMP
HEY...
DO YOU THINK ...
...ATSU'S SERIOUS?
PROB-ABLY.
WHAT AN IDIOT.
OUT OF ALL THE GIRLS, HE FALLS FOR HIS FRIEND'S GIRLFRIEND.
It's not like he's hurting for girls either...
HEY.
YOU'RE OKAY WITH THAT?

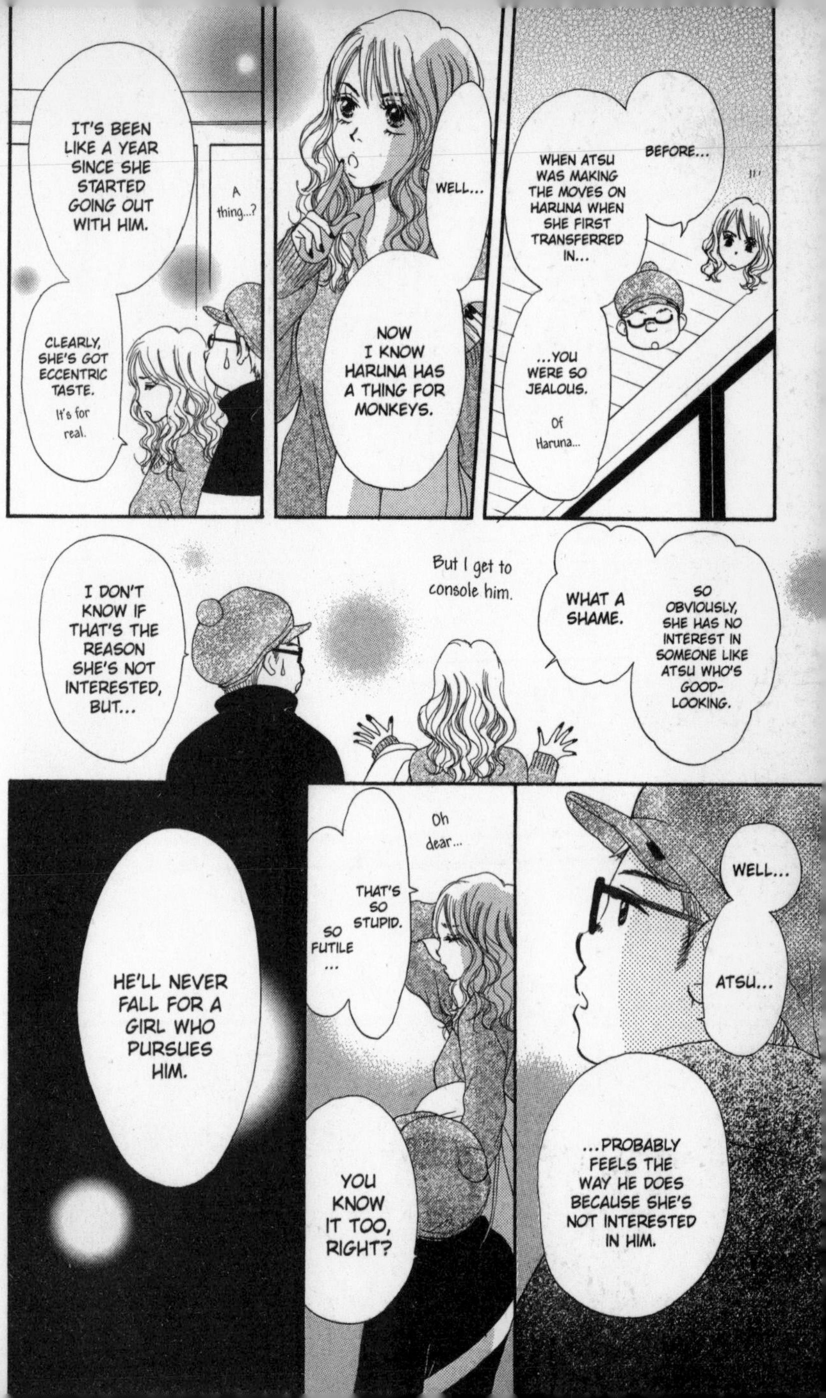
BEFORE... WHEN ATSU WAS MAKING THE MOVES ON HARUNA WHEN SHE FIRST TRANSFERRED IN...
...YOU WERE SO JEALOUS.
Of Haruna...
WELL...
NOW I KNOW HARUNA HAS A THING FOR MONKEYS.
A thing...?
IT'S BEEN LIKE A YEAR SINCE SHE STARTED GOING OUT WITH HIM.
CLEARLY, SHE'S GOT ECCENTRIC TASTE.
It's for real.
SO OBVIOUSLY, SHE HAS NO INTEREST IN SOMEONE LIKE ATSU WHO'S GOOD-LOOKING.
WHAT A SHAME.
But I get to console him.
I DON'T KNOW IF THAT'S THE REASON SHE'S NOT INTERESTED, BUT...
WELL...
ATSU...
...PROBABLY FEELS THE WAY HE DOES BECAUSE SHE'S NOT INTERESTED IN HIM.
Oh dear...
THAT'S SO STUPID.
SO FUTILE...
YOU KNOW IT TOO, RIGHT?
HE'LL NEVER FALL FOR A GIRL WHO PURSUES HIM.

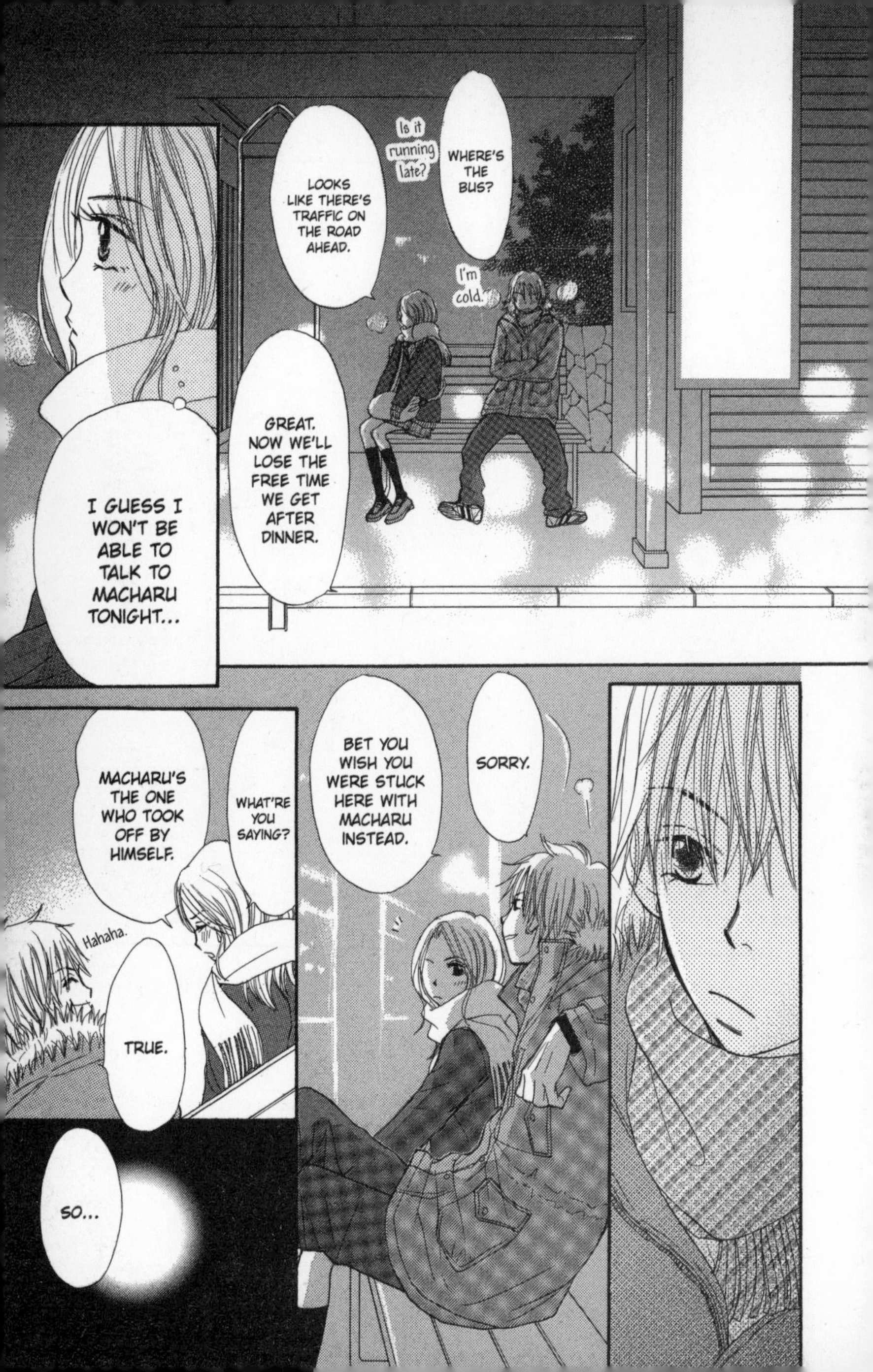
WHERE'S THE BUS?
Is it running late?
LOOKS LIKE THERE'S TRAFFIC ON THE ROAD AHEAD.
I'm cold.
GREAT. NOW WE'LL LOSE THE FREE TIME WE GET AFTER DINNER.
I GUESS I WON'T BE ABLE TO TALK TO MACHARU TONIGHT...
SORRY.
BET YOU WISH YOU WERE STUCK HERE WITH MACHARU INSTEAD.
WHAT'RE YOU SAYING?
MACHARU'S THE ONE WHO TOOK OFF BY HIMSELF.
Hahaha.
TRUE.
SO...

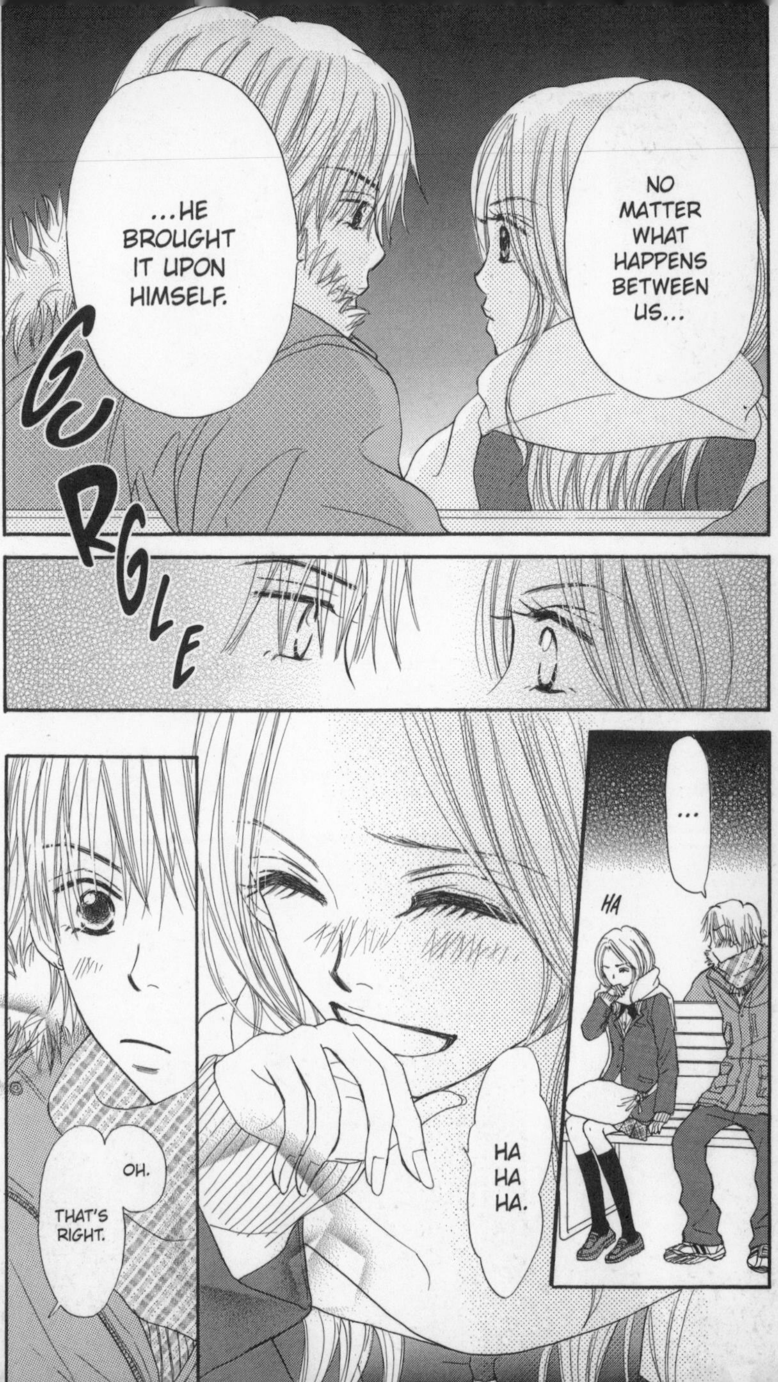
NO MATTER WHAT HAPPENS BETWEEN US...
...HE BROUGHT IT UPON HIMSELF.
GURGLE
...
HA
HA HA HA.
OH.
THAT'S RIGHT.

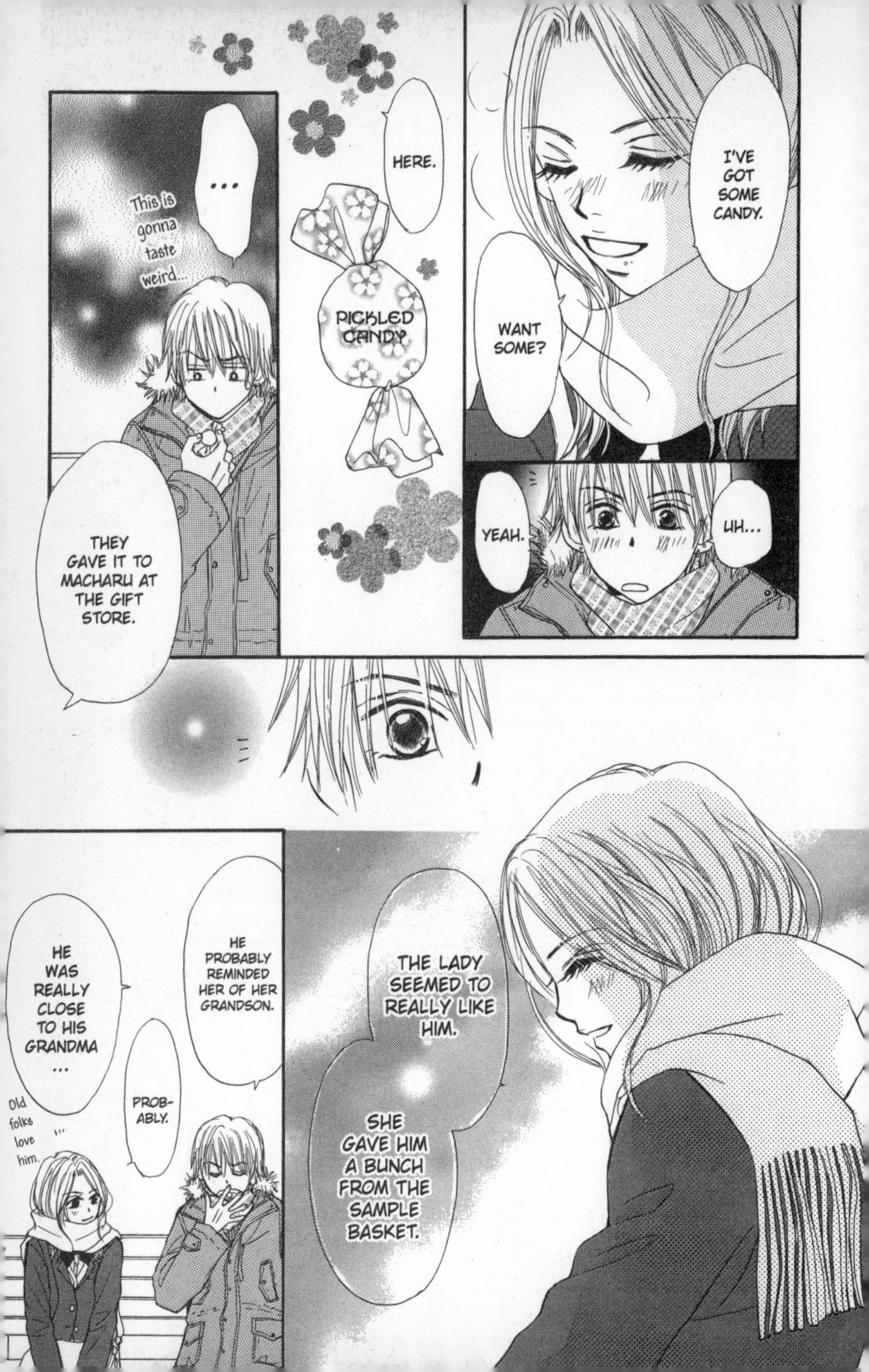
I'VE GOT SOME CANDY.
WANT SOME?
UH...
YEAH.
HERE.
PICKLED CANDY
...
This is gonna taste weird...
THEY GAVE IT TO MACHARU AT THE GIFT STORE.
THE LADY SEEMED TO REALLY LIKE HIM.
SHE GAVE HIM A BUNCH FROM THE SAMPLE BASKET.
HE PROBABLY REMINDED HER OF HER GRANDSON.
HE WAS REALLY CLOSE TO HIS GRANDMA...
PROBABLY.
Old folks love him.

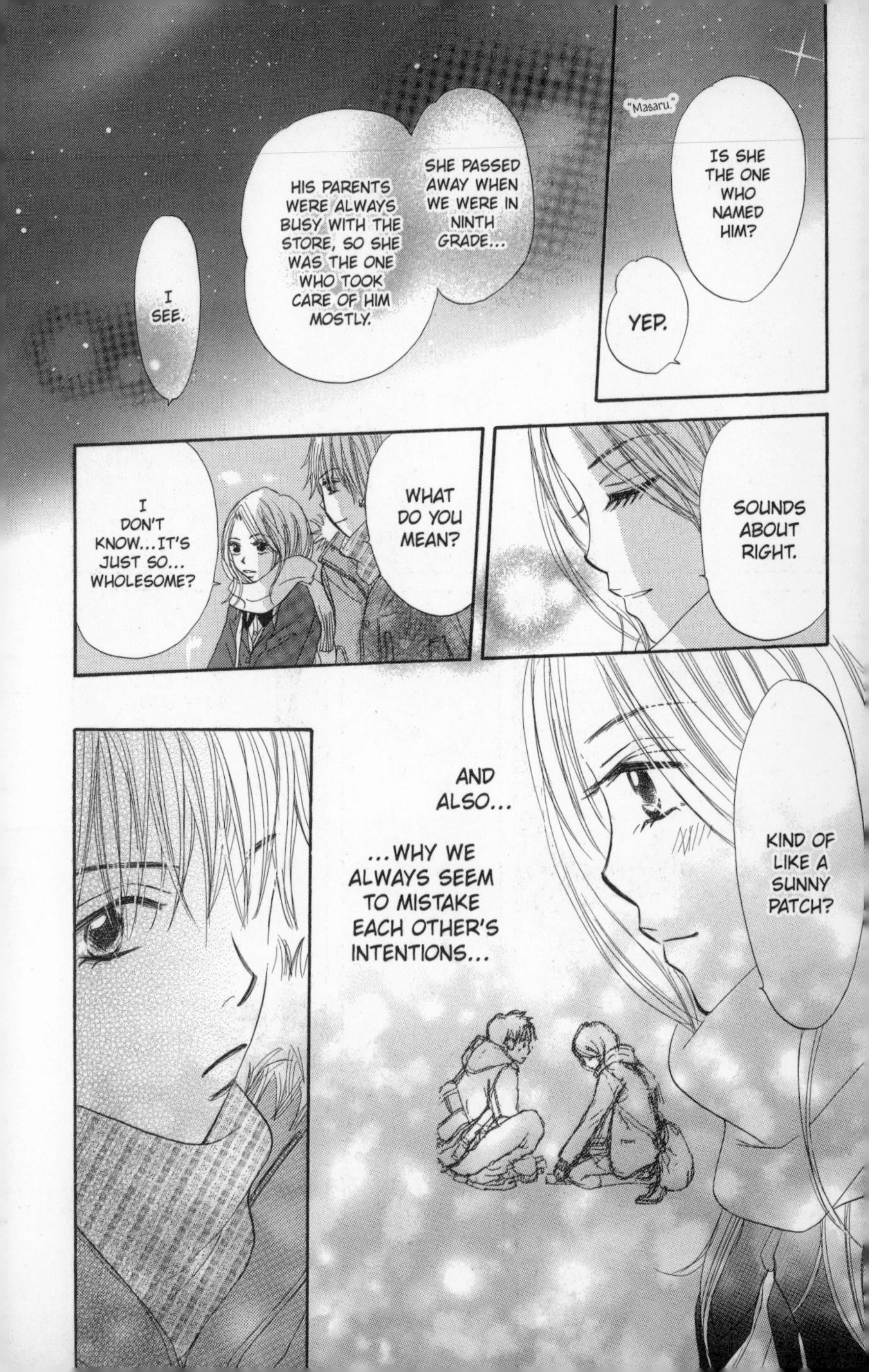
"Masaru."
IS SHE THE ONE WHO NAMED HIM?
YEP.
SHE PASSED AWAY WHEN WE WERE IN NINTH GRADE...
HIS PARENTS WERE ALWAYS BUSY WITH THE STORE, SO SHE WAS THE ONE WHO TOOK CARE OF HIM MOSTLY.
I SEE.
SOUNDS ABOUT RIGHT.
WHAT DO YOU MEAN?
I DON'T KNOW...IT'S JUST SO... WHOLESOME?
KIND OF LIKE A SUNNY PATCH?
AND ALSO...
...WHY WE ALWAYS SEEM TO MISTAKE EACH OTHER'S INTENTIONS...

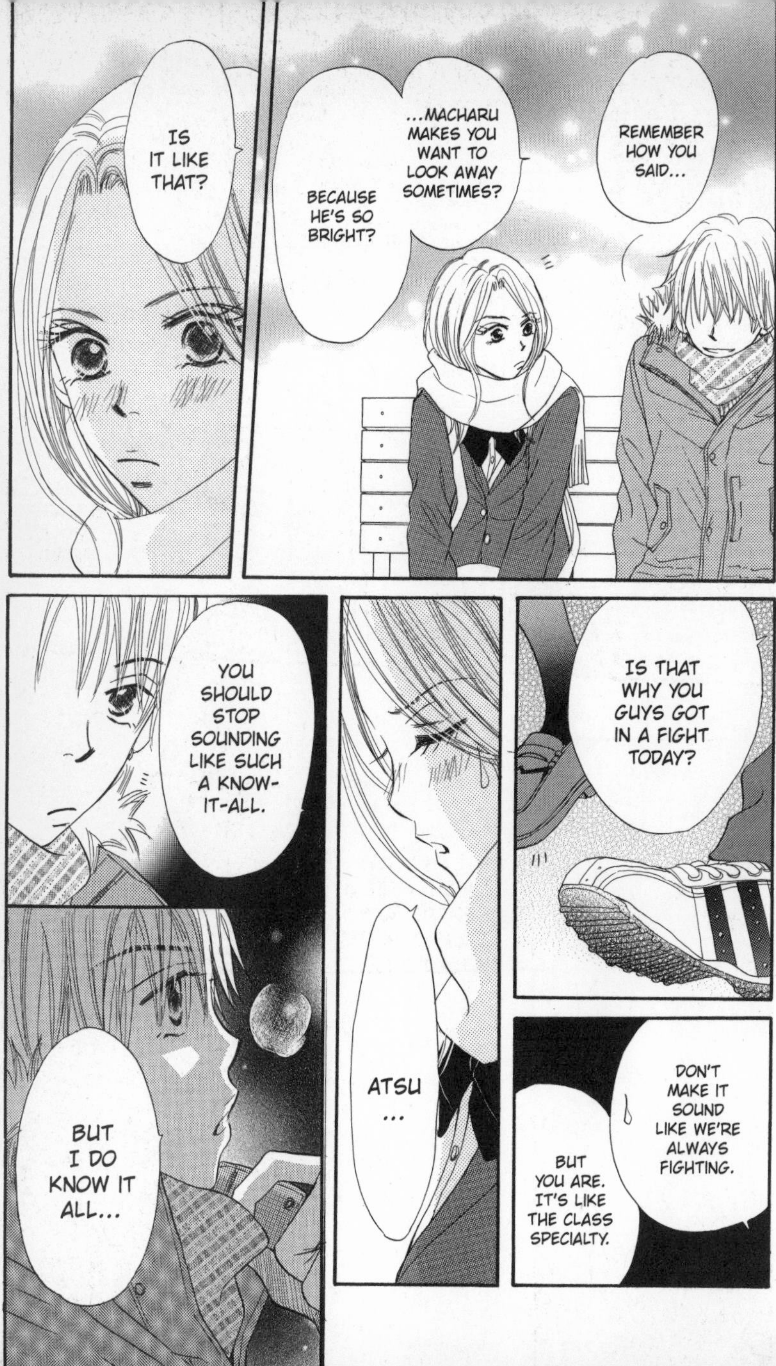
REMEMBER HOW YOU SAID...
...MACHARU MAKES YOU WANT TO LOOK AWAY SOMETIMES?
BECAUSE HE'S SO BRIGHT?
IS IT LIKE THAT?
IS THAT WHY YOU GUYS GOT IN A FIGHT TODAY?
DON'T MAKE IT SOUND LIKE WE'RE ALWAYS FIGHTING.
BUT YOU ARE. IT'S LIKE THE CLASS SPECIALTY.
ATSU ...
YOU SHOULD STOP SOUNDING LIKE SUCH A KNOW-IT-ALL.
BUT I DO KNOW IT ALL...

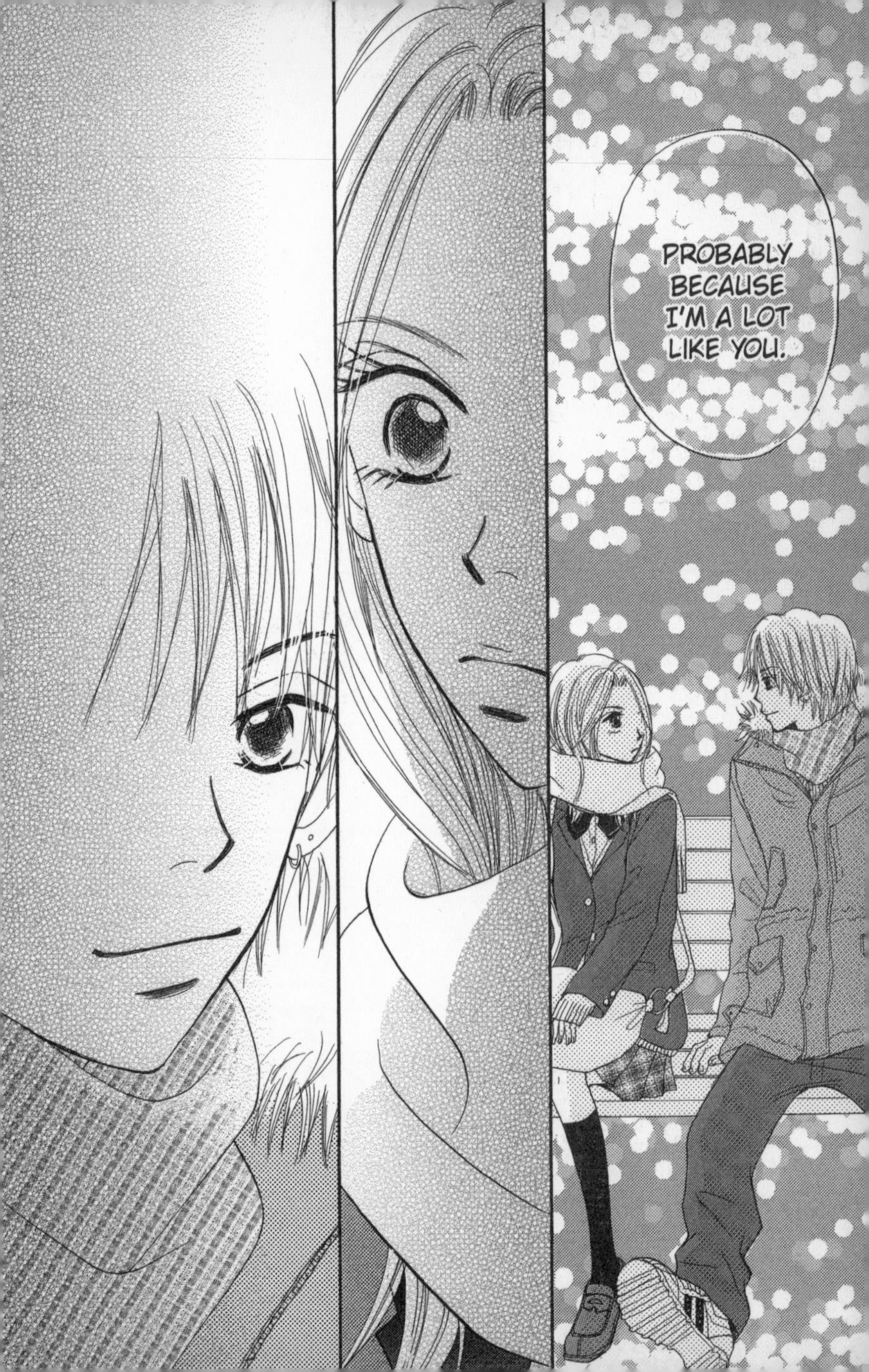
PROBABLY BECAUSE I'M A LOT LIKE YOU.

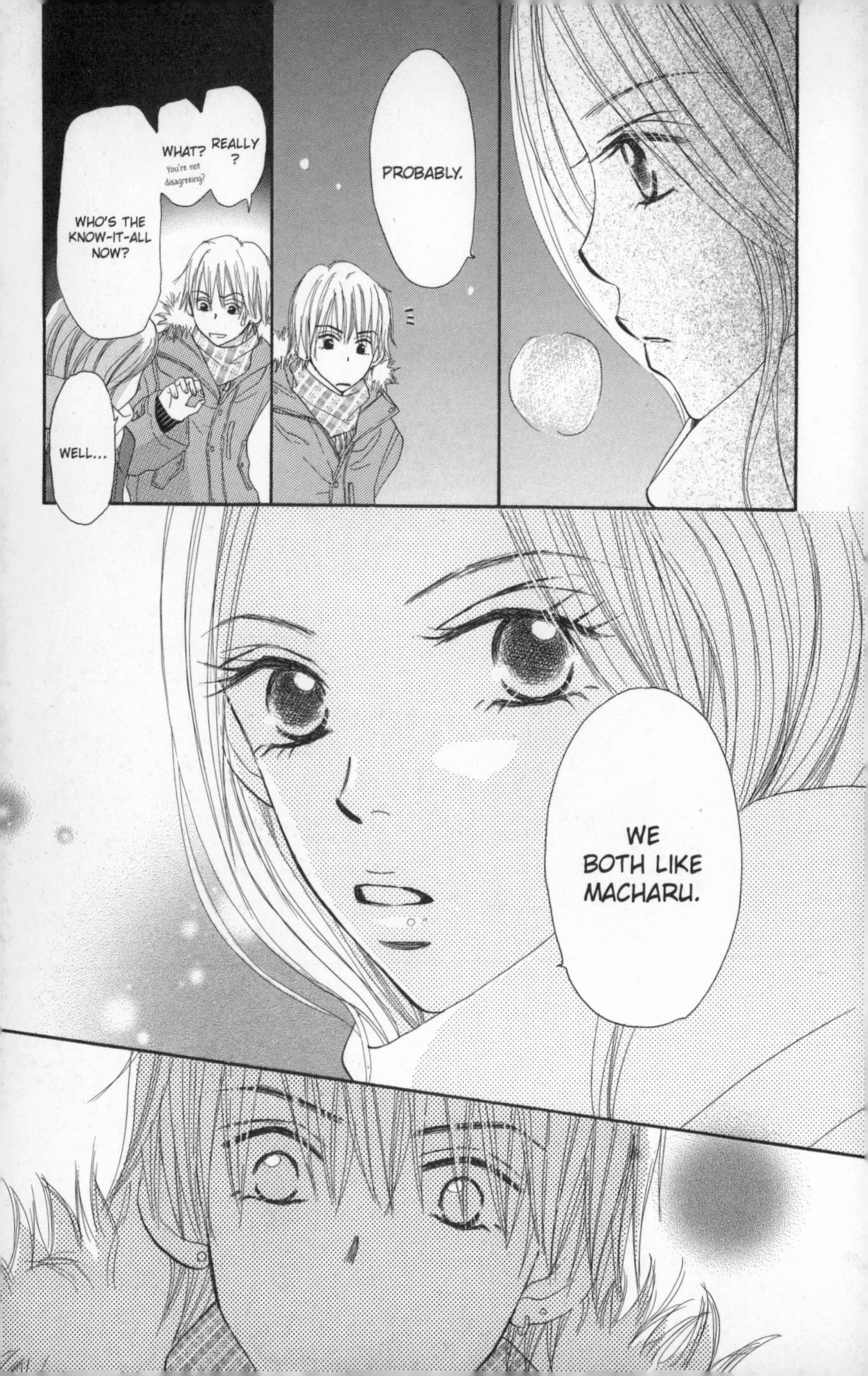
PROBABLY.
WHAT? REALLY? You're not disagreeing?
WHO'S THE KNOW-IT-ALL NOW?
WELL...
WE BOTH LIKE MACHARU.

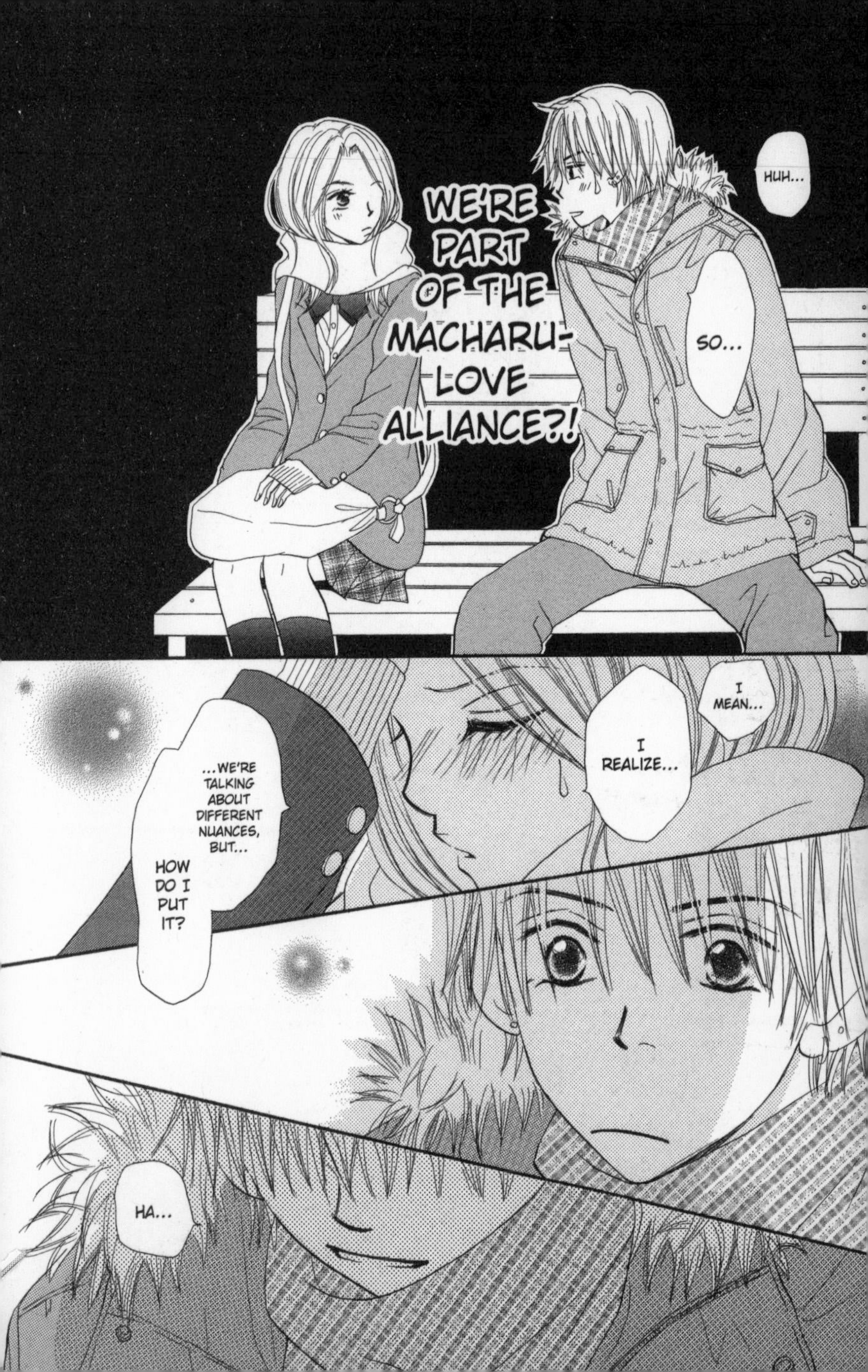
HUH...
SO...
WE'RE PART OF THE MACHARU-LOVE ALLIANCE?!
I MEAN...
I REALIZE...
...WE'RE TALKING ABOUT DIFFERENT NUANCES, BUT...
HOW DO I PUT IT?
HA...

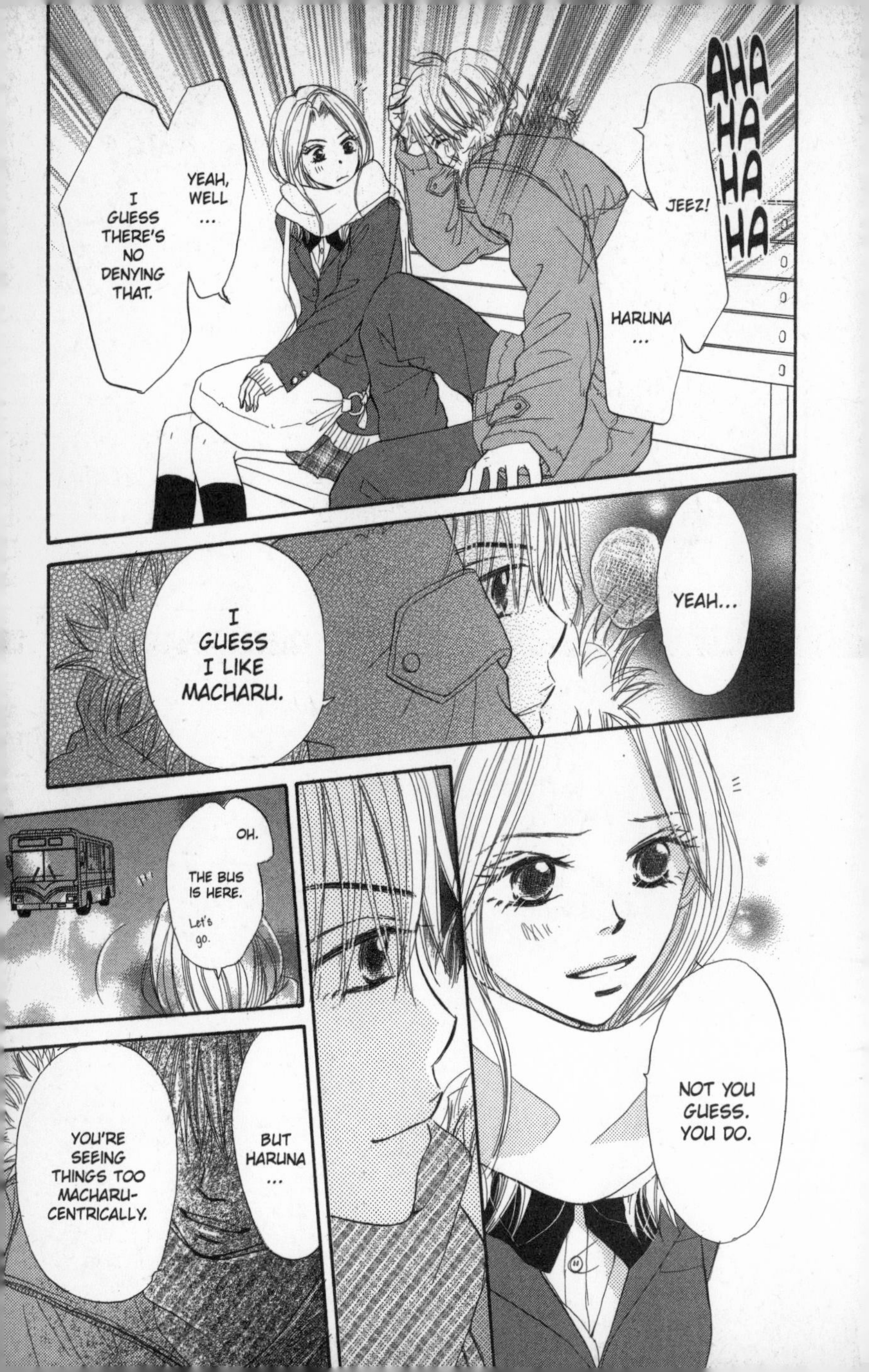
AHA HA HA HA
JEEZ!
HARUNA ...
YEAH, WELL ... I GUESS THERE'S NO DENYING THAT.
YEAH...
I GUESS I LIKE MACHARU.
NOT YOU GUESS. YOU DO.
OH. THE BUS IS HERE.
Let's go.
BUT HARUNA ...
YOU'RE SEEING THINGS TOO MACHARU-CENTRICALLY.

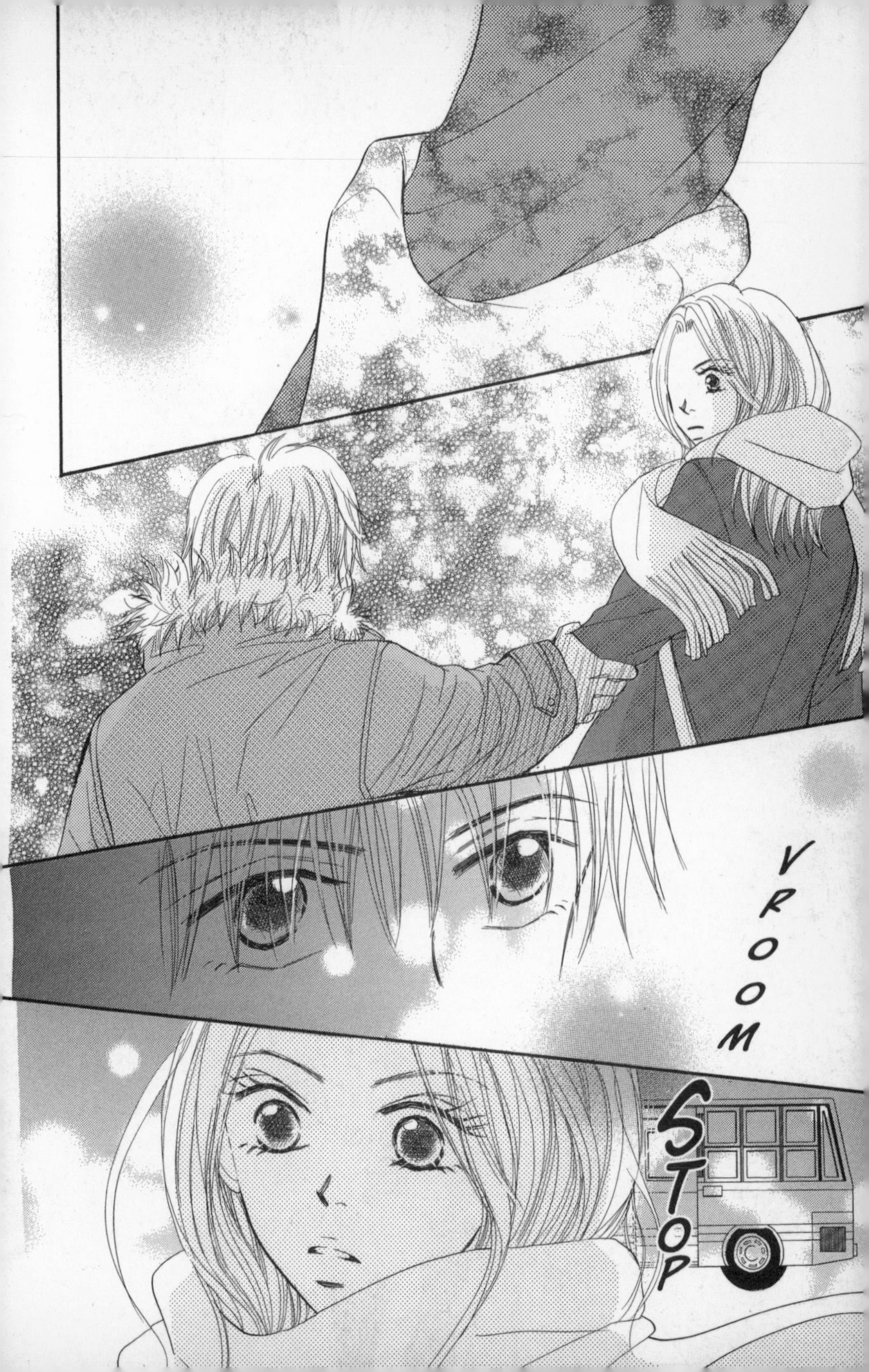
VROOM
STOP

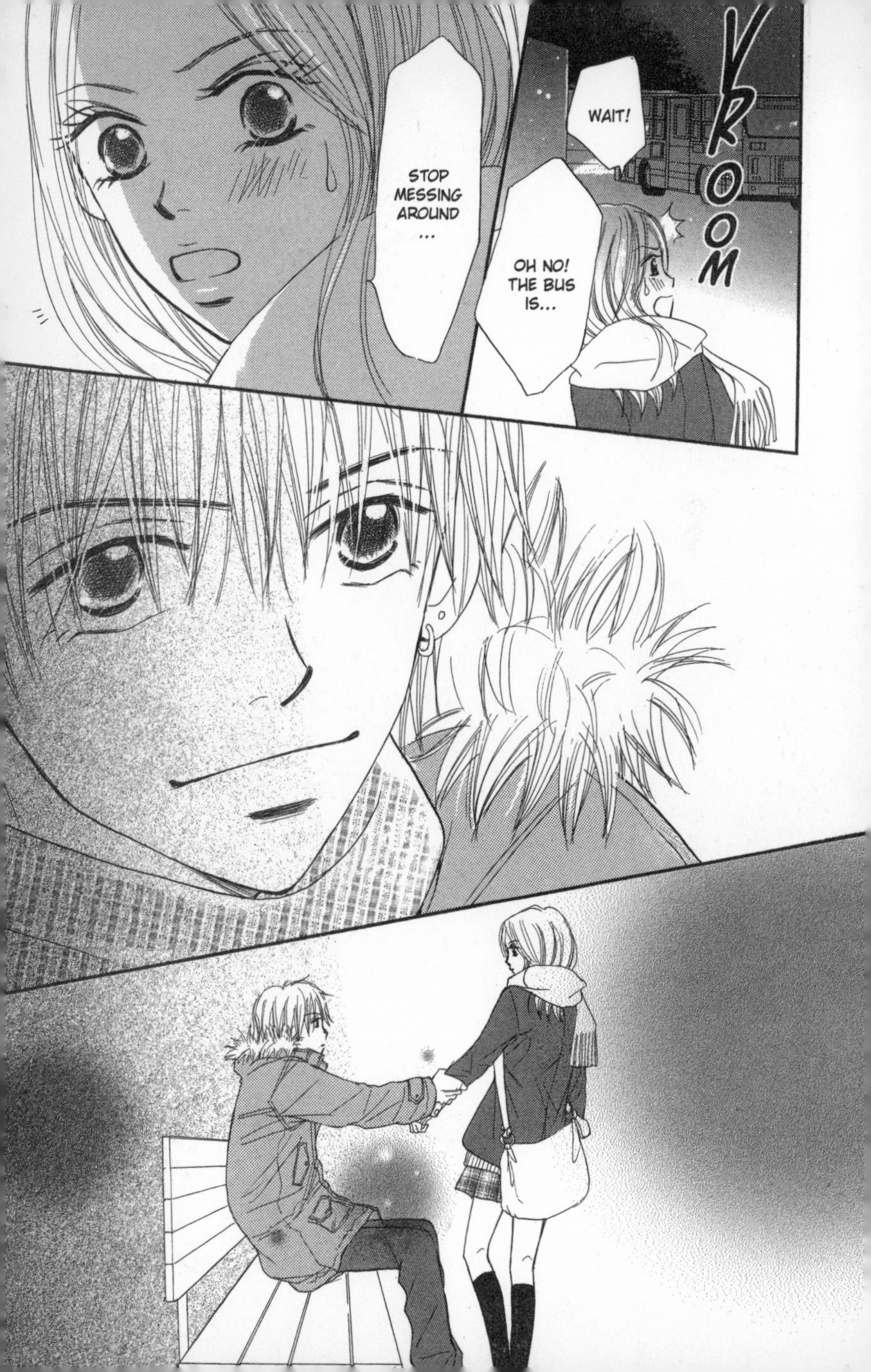
VROOM
WAIT!
OH NO! THE BUS IS...
STOP MESSING AROUND ...

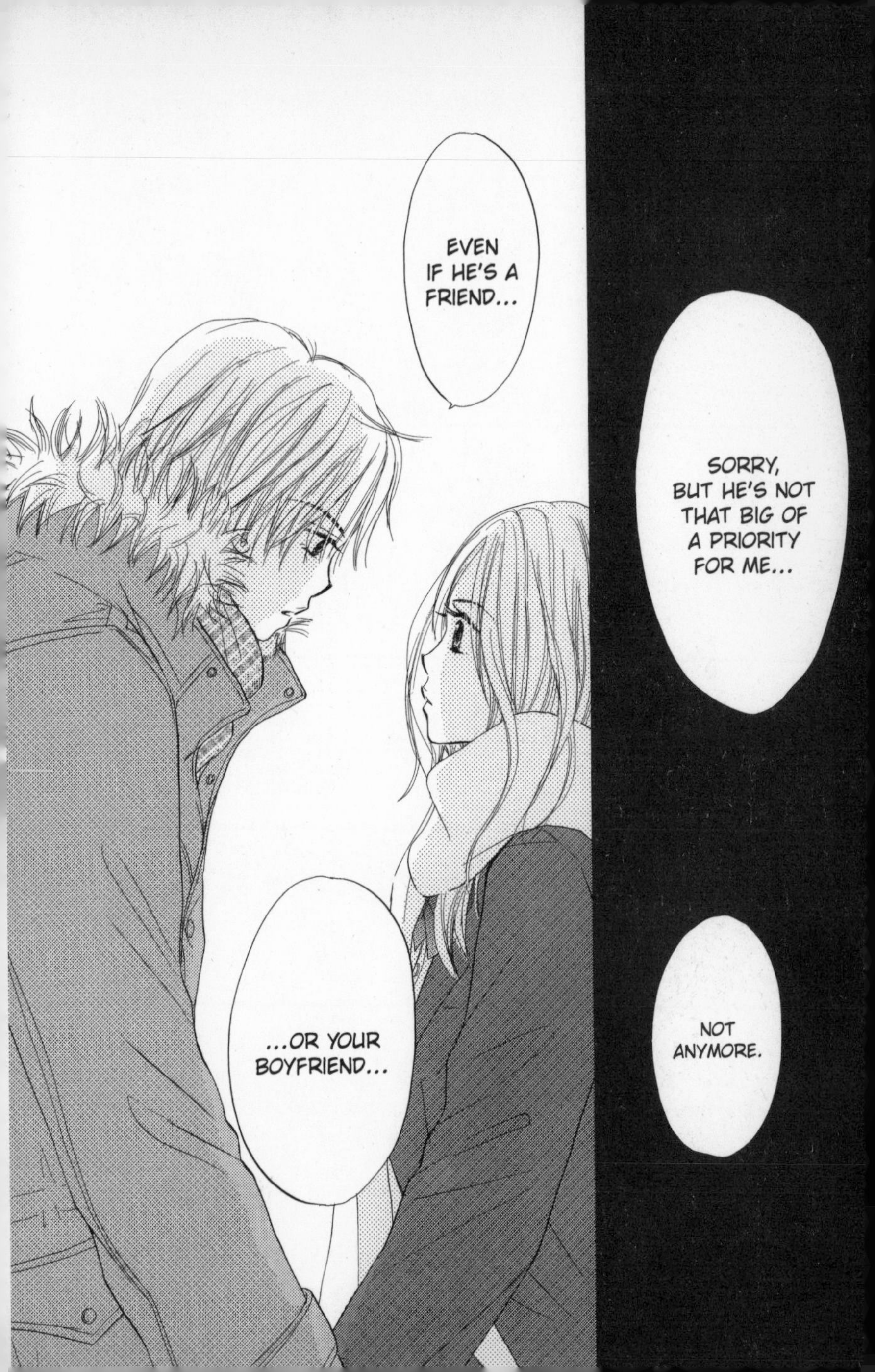
SORRY, BUT HE'S NOT THAT BIG OF A PRIORITY FOR ME...
NOT ANYMORE.
EVEN IF HE'S A FRIEND...
...OR YOUR BOYFRIEND...

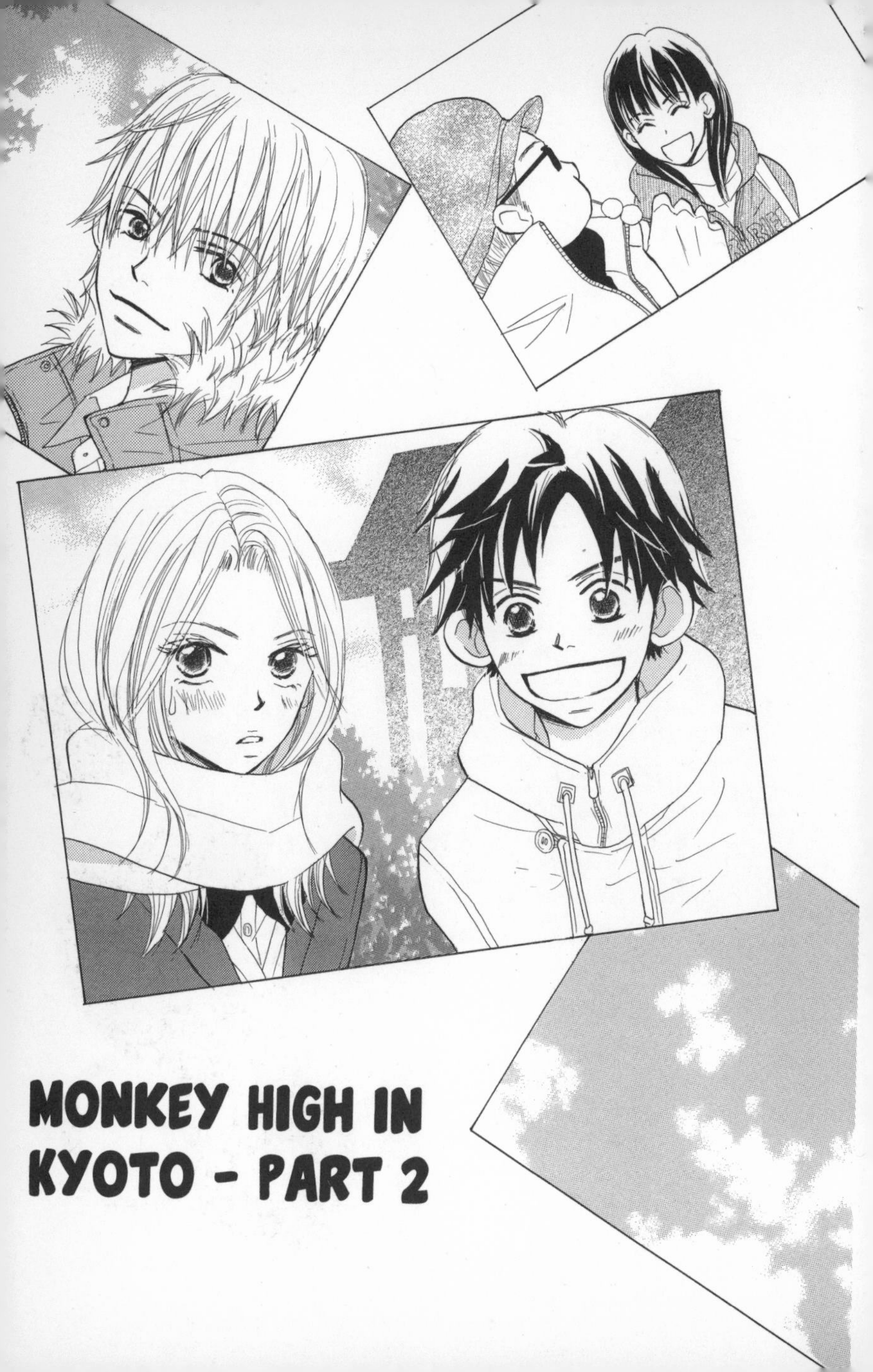

MONKEY HIGH IN KYOTO - PART 2

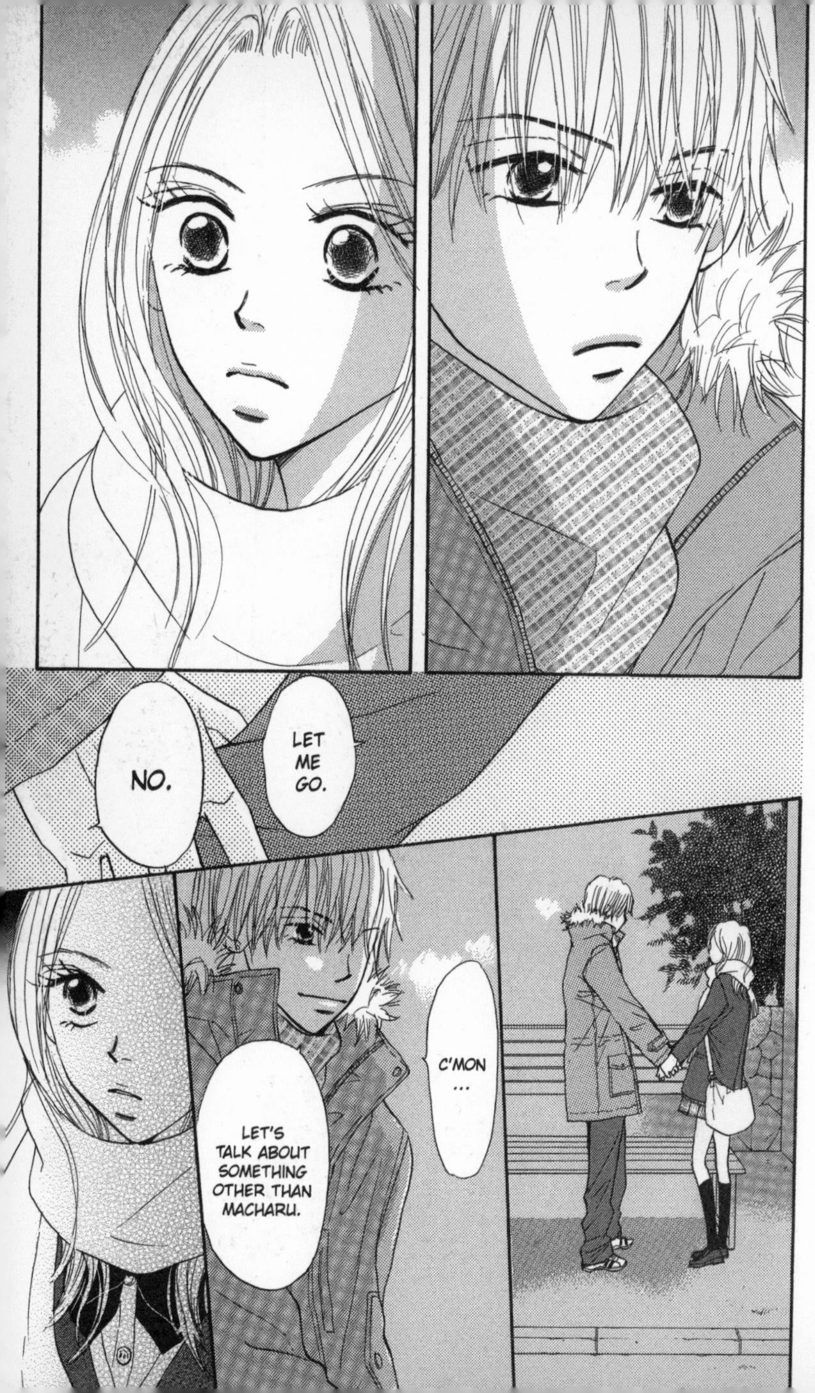
LET ME GO.
NO.
C'MON ...
LET'S TALK ABOUT SOMETHING OTHER THAN MACHARU.

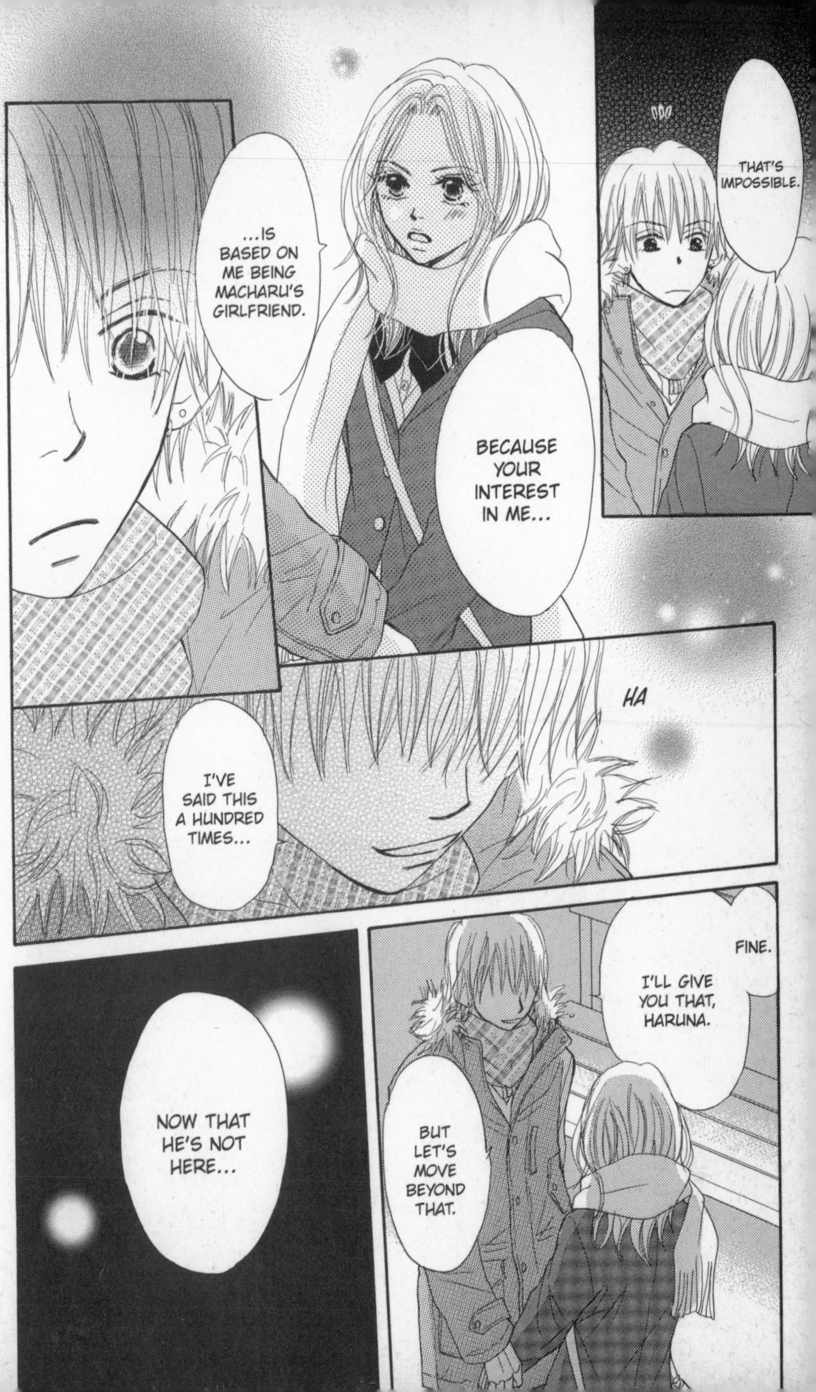
THAT'S IMPOSSIBLE.
BECAUSE YOUR INTEREST IN ME...
...IS BASED ON ME BEING MACHARU'S GIRLFRIEND.
HA
I'VE SAID THIS A HUNDRED TIMES...
FINE.
I'LL GIVE YOU THAT, HARUNA.
BUT LET'S MOVE BEYOND THAT.
NOW THAT HE'S NOT HERE...

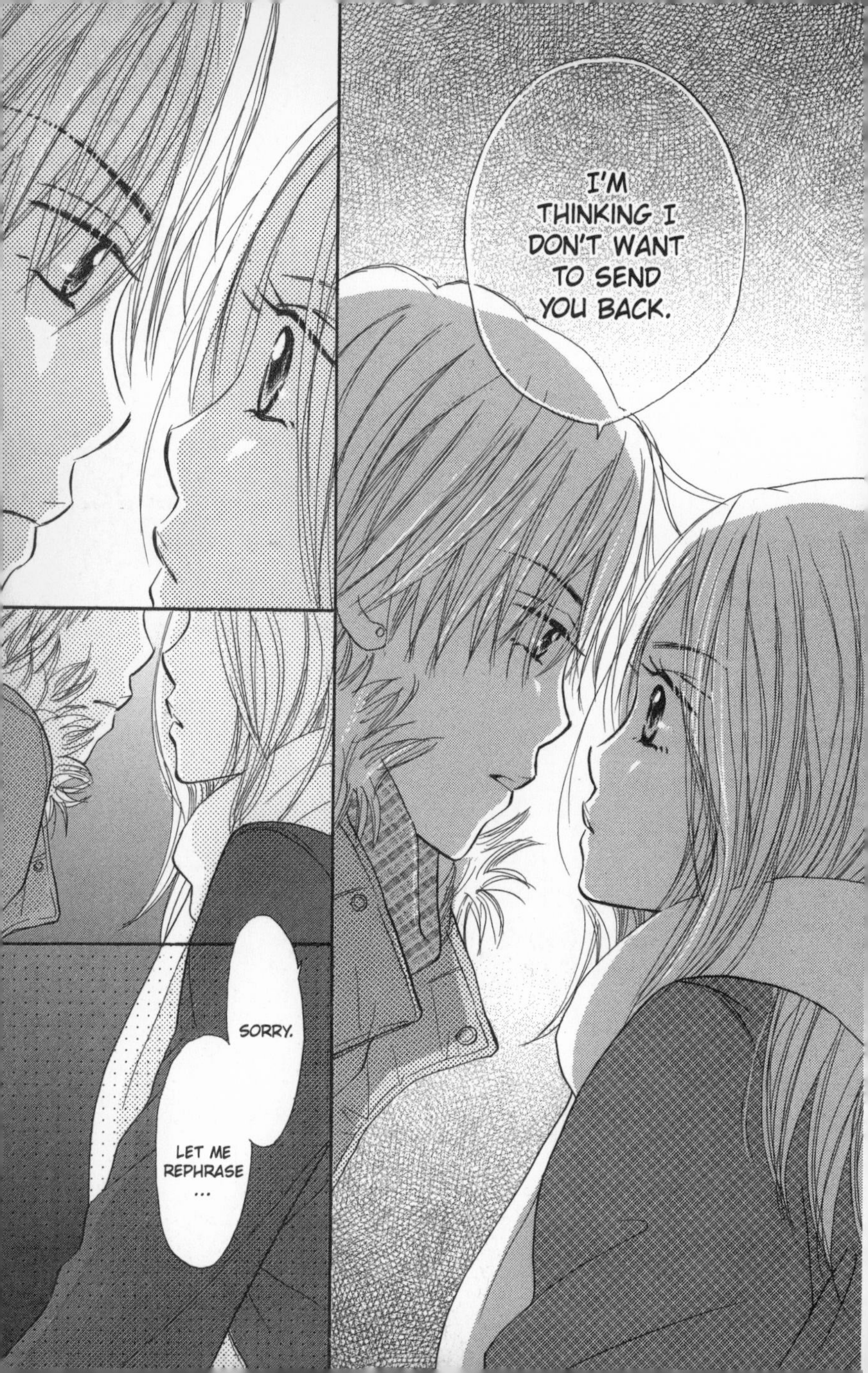
I'M THINKING I DON'T WANT TO SEND YOU BACK.
SORRY.
LET ME REPHRASE ...

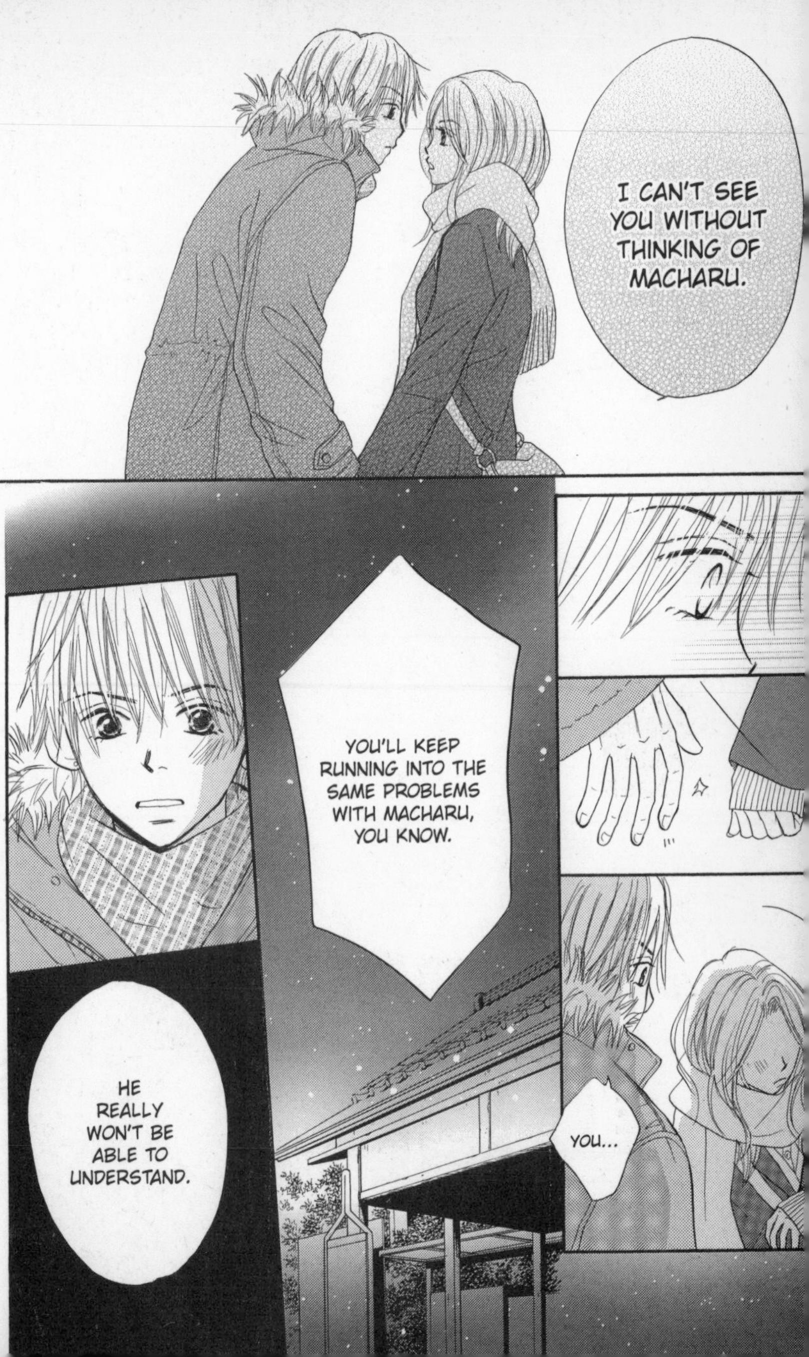
I CAN'T SEE YOU WITHOUT THINKING OF MACHARU.
YOU...
YOU'LL KEEP RUNNING INTO THE SAME PROBLEMS WITH MACHARU, YOU KNOW.
HE REALLY WON'T BE ABLE TO UNDERSTAND.

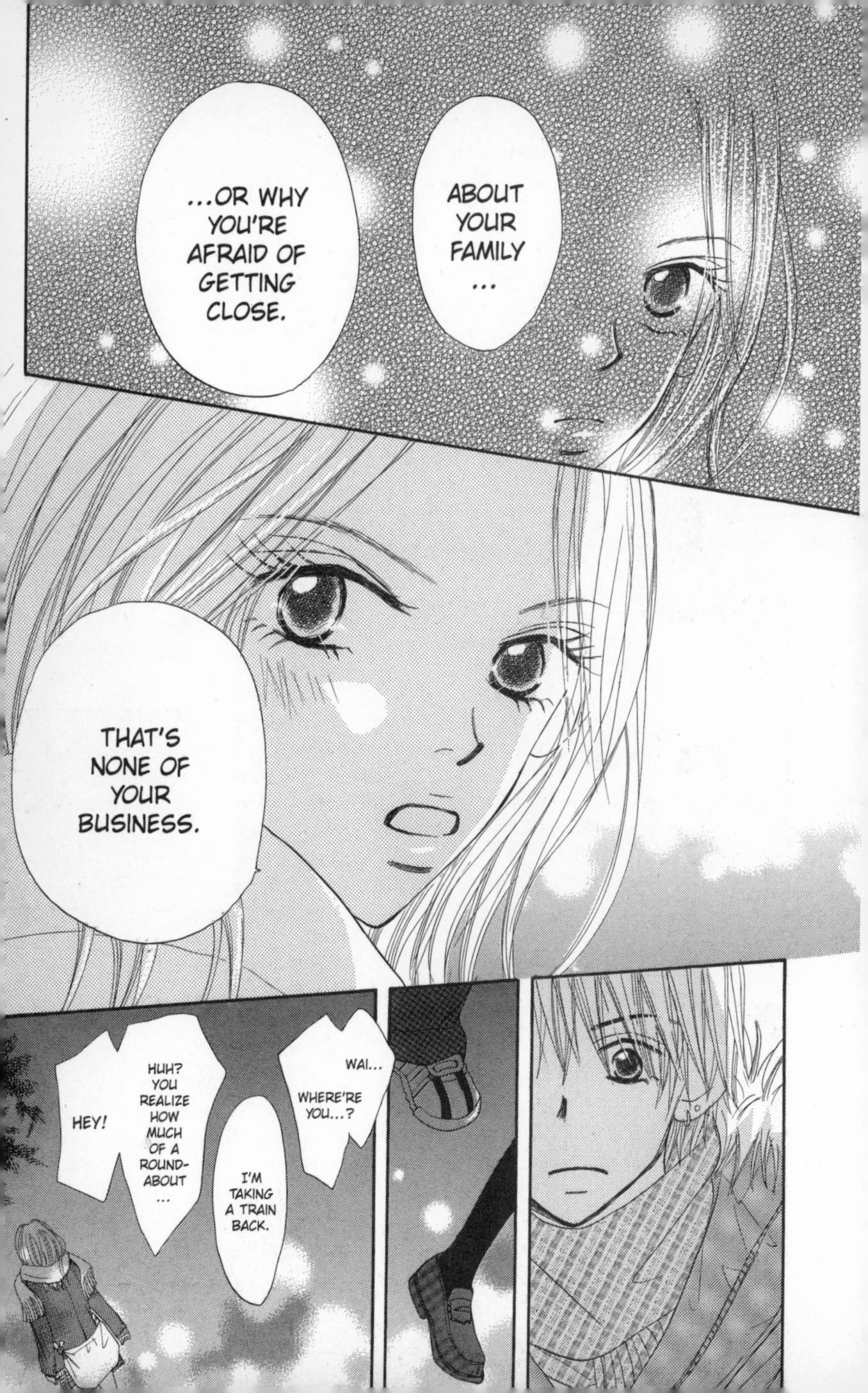
ABOUT YOUR FAMILY...
...OR WHY YOU'RE AFRAID OF GETTING CLOSE.
THAT'S NONE OF YOUR BUSINESS.
WAI... WHERE'RE YOU...?
I'M TAKING A TRAIN BACK.
HUH? YOU REALIZE HOW MUCH OF A ROUND-ABOUT...
HEY!

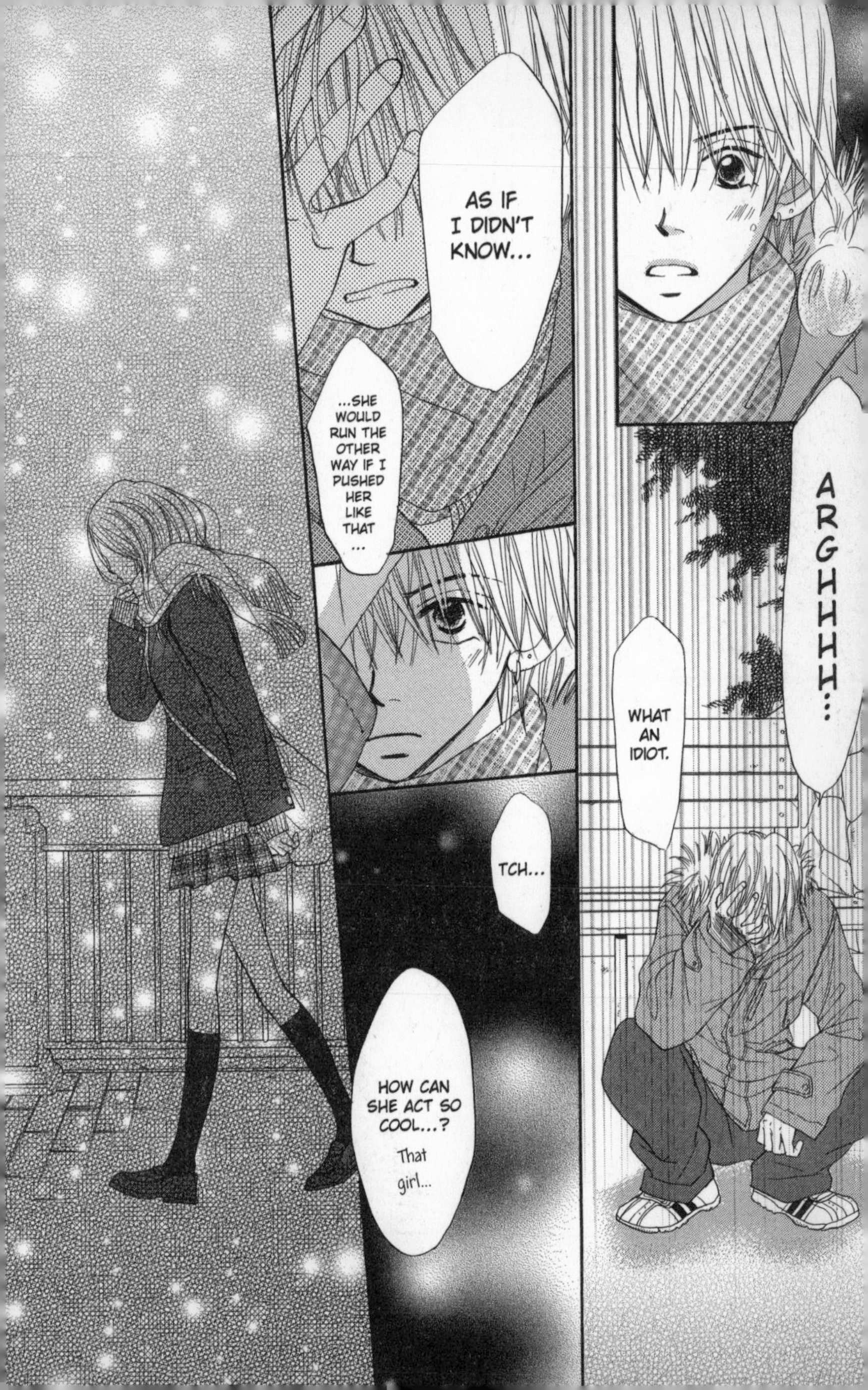
ARGHHHH...
WHAT AN IDIOT.
AS IF I DIDN'T KNOW...
...SHE WOULD RUN THE OTHER WAY IF I PUSHED HER LIKE THAT...
TCH...
HOW CAN SHE ACT SO COOL...? That girl...

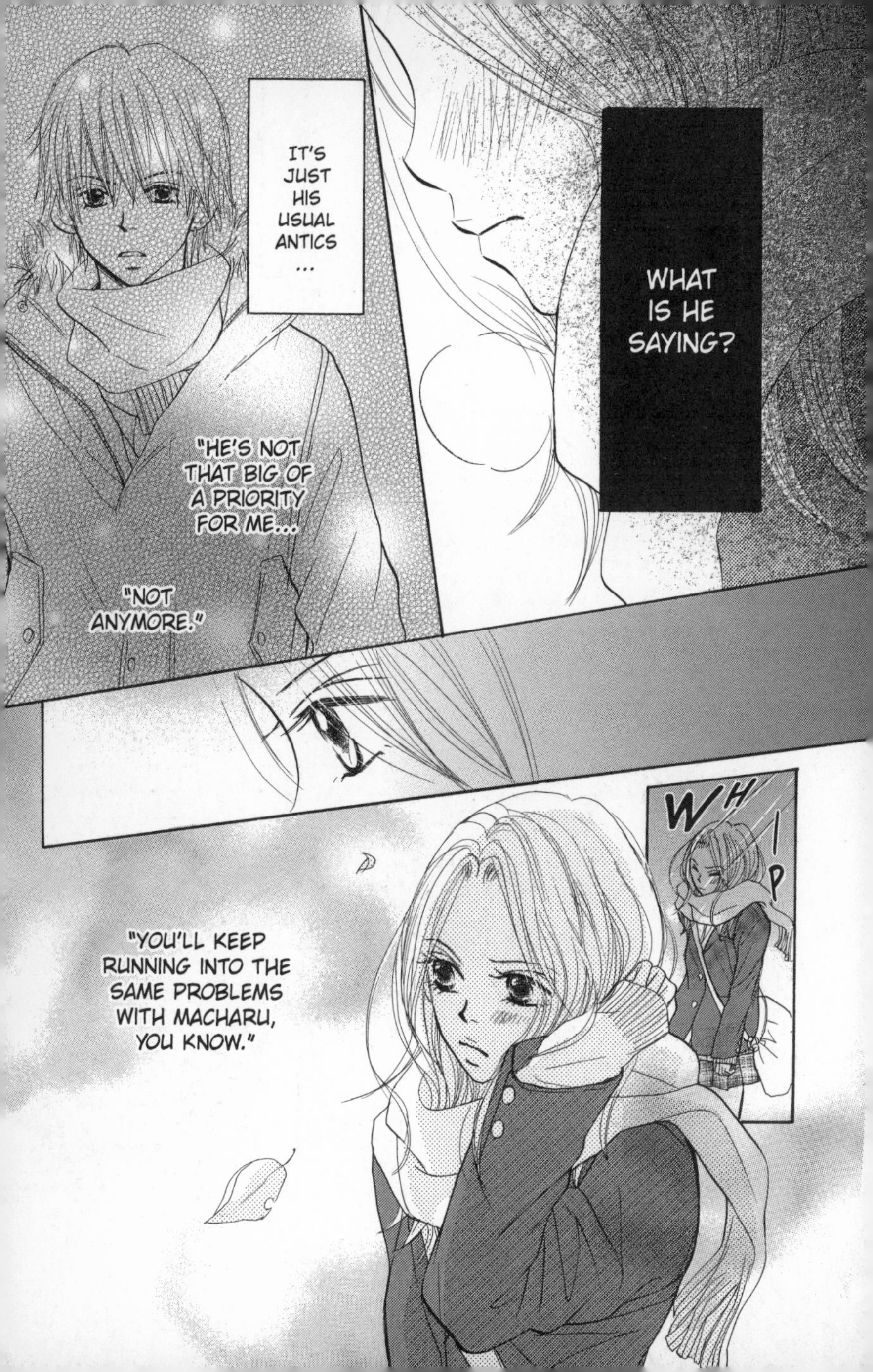
WHAT IS HE SAYING?
IT'S JUST HIS USUAL ANTICS...
"HE'S NOT THAT BIG OF A PRIORITY FOR ME...
"NOT ANYMORE."
WHIP
"YOU'LL KEEP RUNNING INTO THE SAME PROBLEMS WITH MACHARU, YOU KNOW."

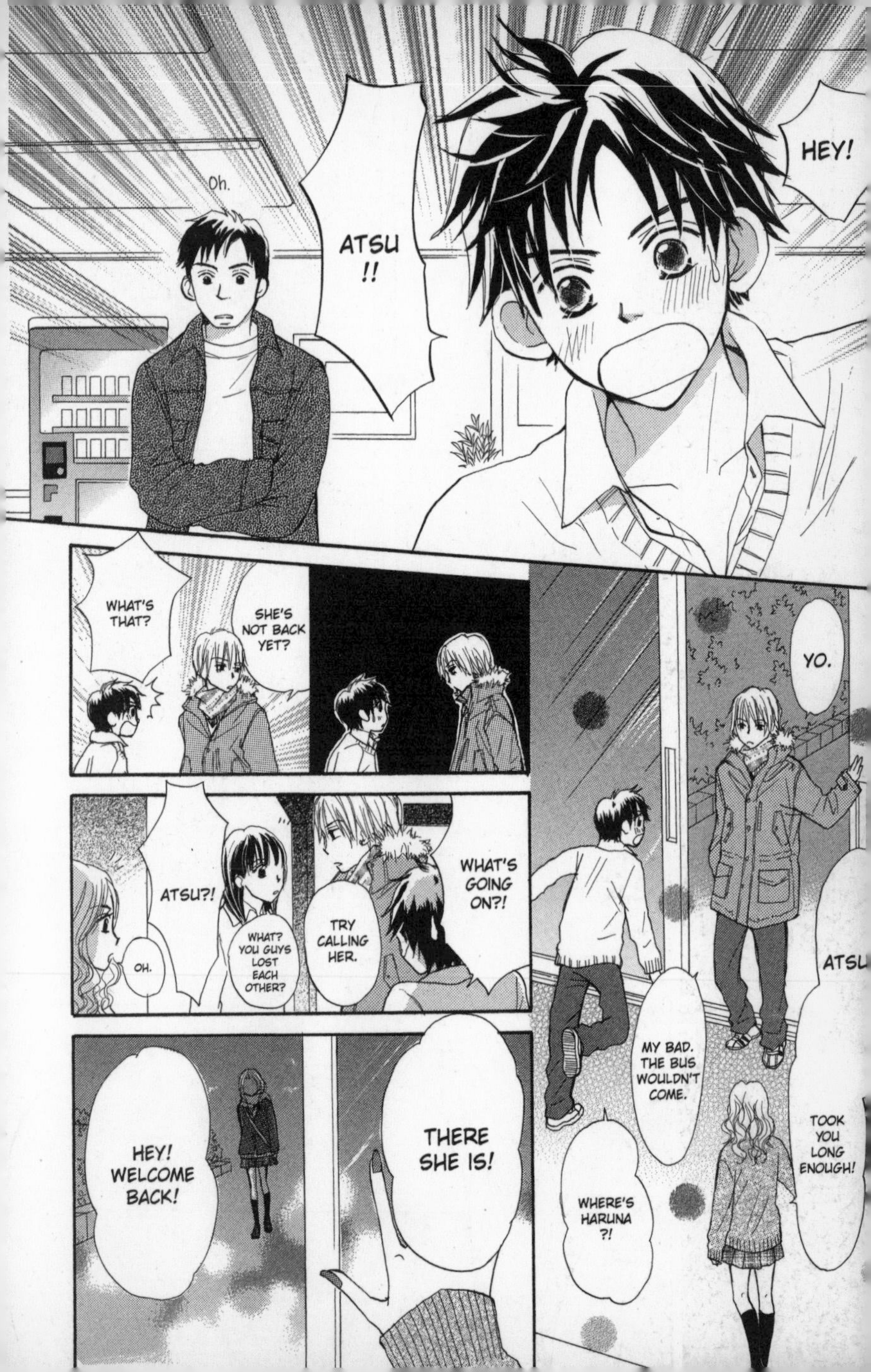
HEY!
ATSU !!
Oh.
YO.
ATSU
TOOK YOU LONG ENOUGH!
MY BAD. THE BUS WOULDN'T COME.
WHERE'S HARUNA ?!
SHE'S NOT BACK YET?
WHAT'S THAT?
WHAT'S GOING ON?!
TRY CALLING HER.
ATSU?!
WHAT? YOU GUYS LOST EACH OTHER?
OH.
THERE SHE IS!
HEY! WELCOME BACK!

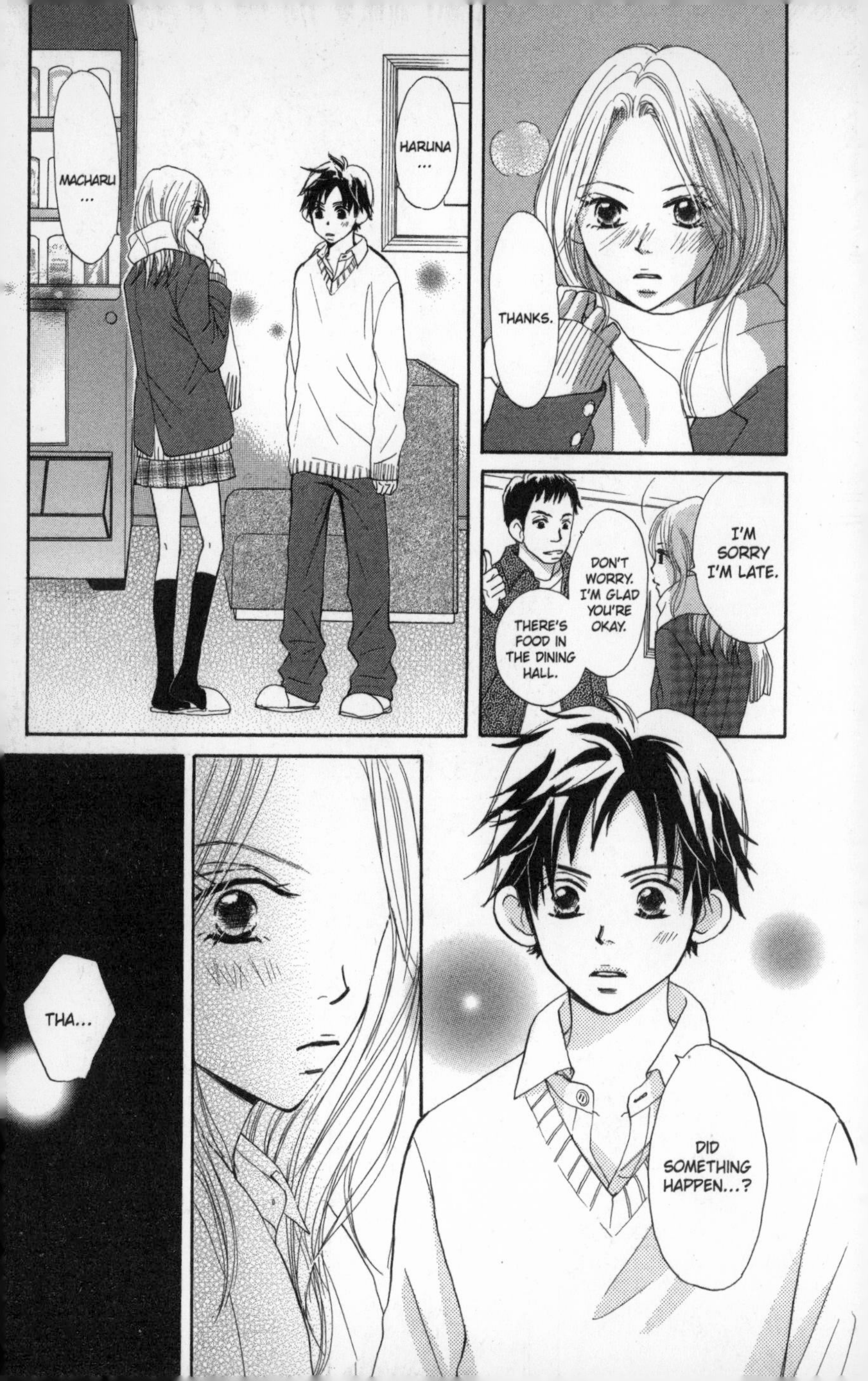
THANKS.
I'M SORRY I'M LATE.
DON'T WORRY. I'M GLAD YOU'RE OKAY.
THERE'S FOOD IN THE DINING HALL.
HARUNA ...
MACHARU ...
DID SOMETHING HAPPEN...?
THA...

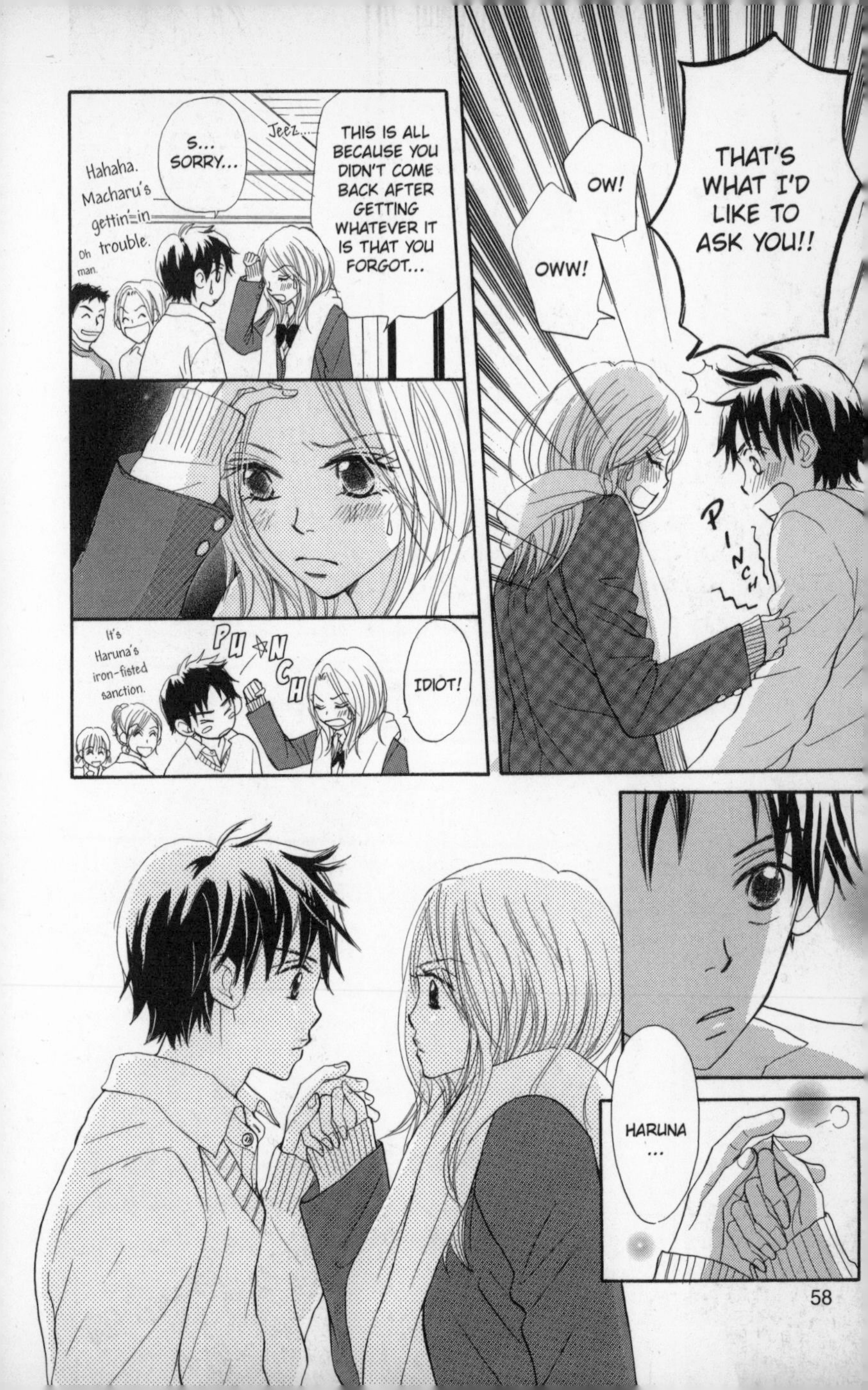
THAT'S WHAT I'D LIKE TO ASK YOU!!
OW!
OWW!
PINCH
THIS IS ALL BECAUSE YOU DIDN'T COME BACK AFTER GETTING WHATEVER IT IS THAT YOU FORGOT...
S... SORRY...
Jeez...
Hahaha. Macharu's gettin' in trouble.
Oh man.
IDIOT!
PUNCH
It's Haruna's iron-fisted sanction.
HARUNA ...

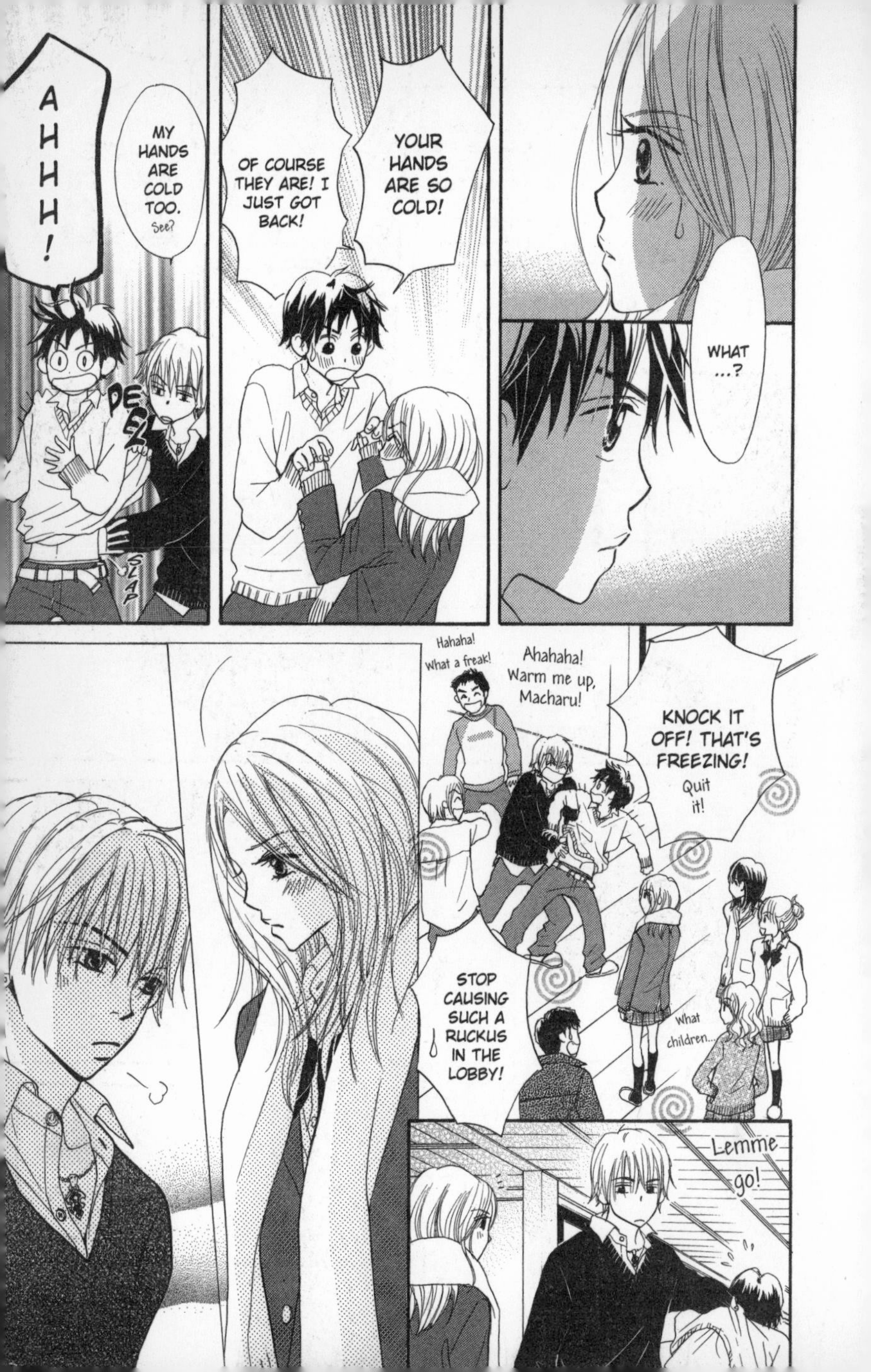
WHAT ...?
YOUR HANDS ARE SO COLD!
OF COURSE THEY ARE! I JUST GOT BACK!
MY HANDS ARE COLD TOO. See?
AHHHH!
PEEL
SLAP
KNOCK IT OFF! THAT'S FREEZING! Quit it!
Ahahaha! Warm me up, Macharu!
Hahaha! What a freak!
STOP CAUSING SUCH A RUCKUS IN THE LOBBY!
What children...
Lemme go!

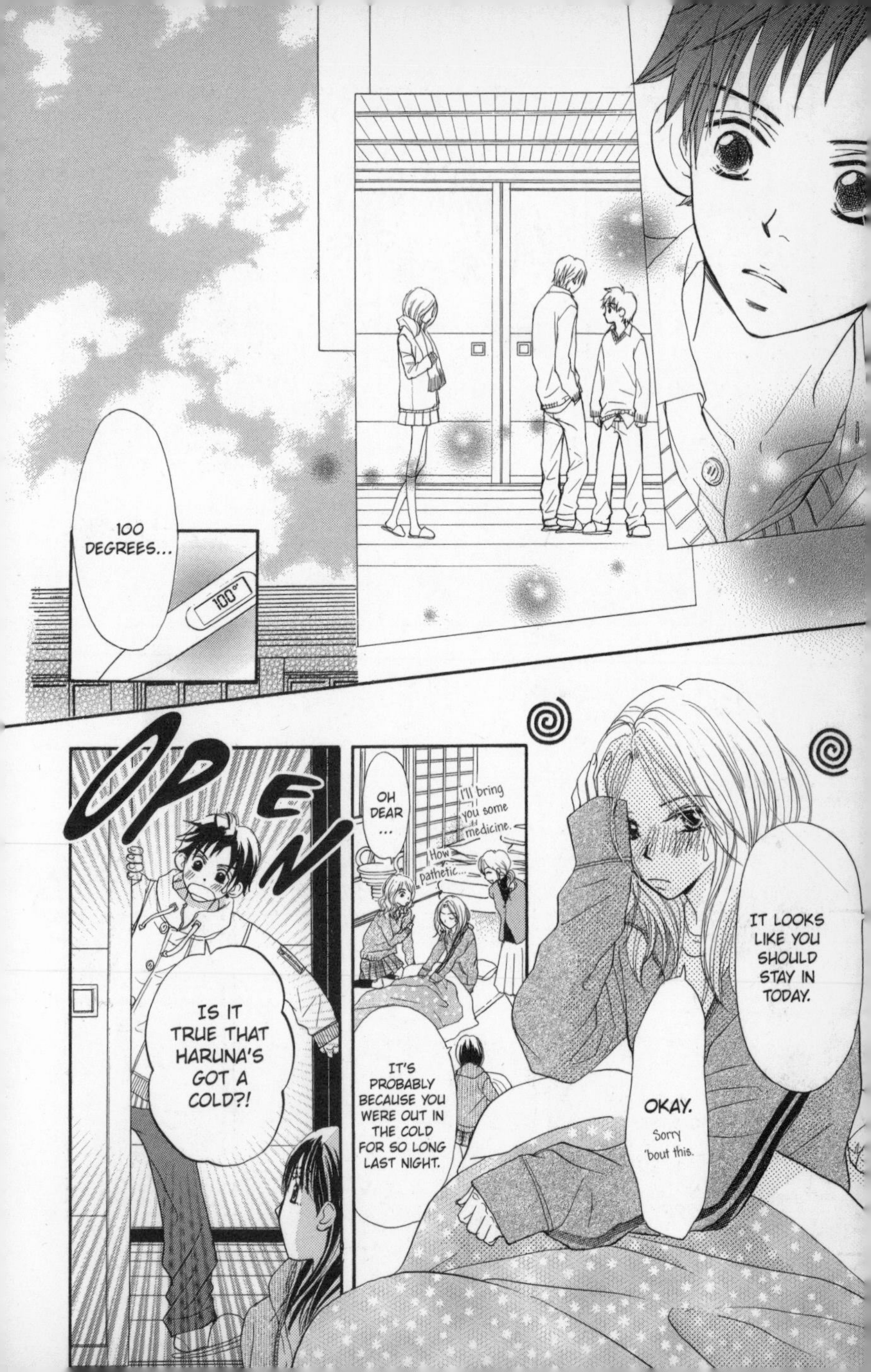
100 DEGREES...
100°
IT LOOKS LIKE YOU SHOULD STAY IN TODAY.
OKAY.
Sorry 'bout this.
OH DEAR ...
I'll bring you some medicine.
How pathetic...
IT'S PROBABLY BECAUSE YOU WERE OUT IN THE COLD FOR SO LONG LAST NIGHT.
OPEN
IS IT TRUE THAT HARUNA'S GOT A COLD?!

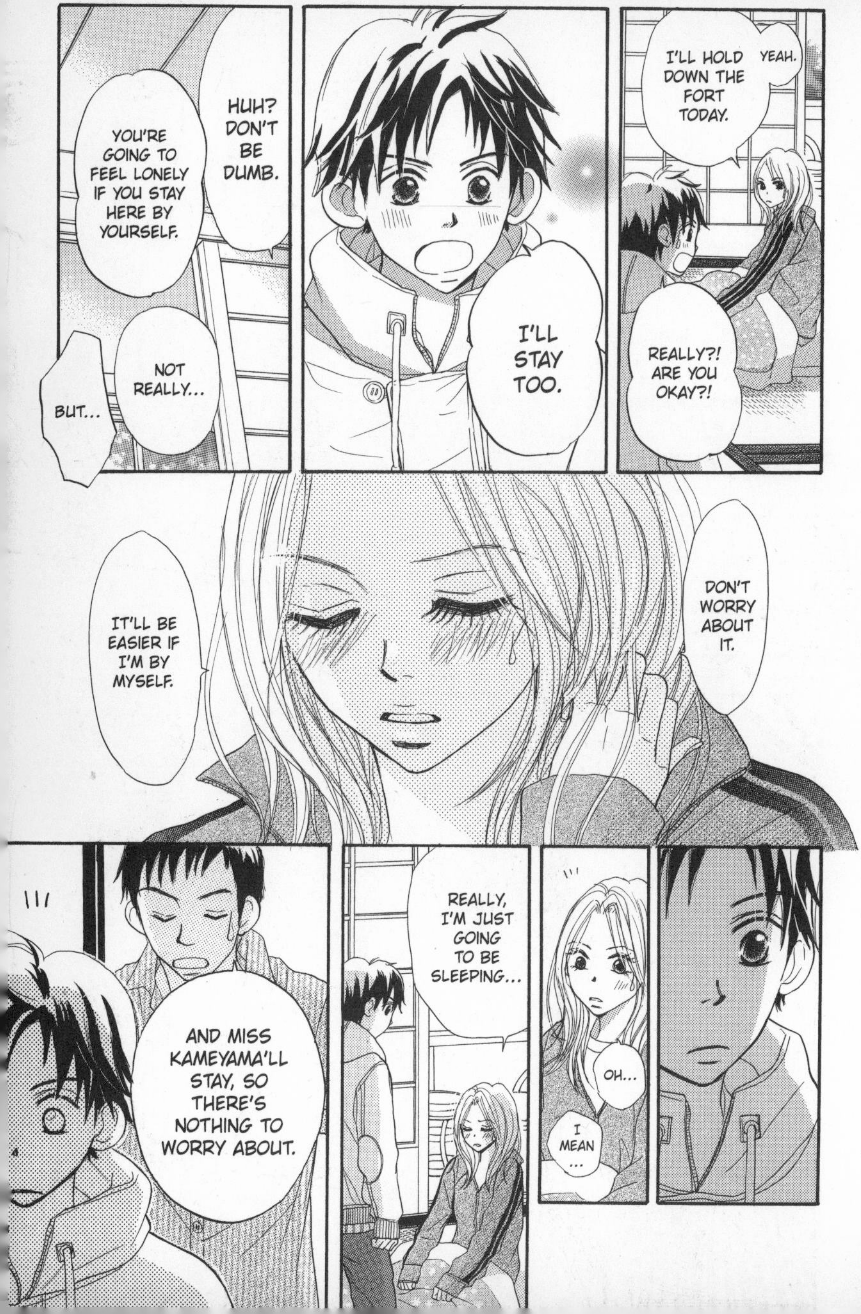
YEAH.
I'LL HOLD DOWN THE FORT TODAY.
REALLY?! ARE YOU OKAY?!
I'LL STAY TOO.
HUH? DON'T BE DUMB.
YOU'RE GOING TO FEEL LONELY IF YOU STAY HERE BY YOURSELF.
NOT REALLY...
BUT...
DON'T WORRY ABOUT IT.
IT'LL BE EASIER IF I'M BY MYSELF.
OH...
I MEAN ...
REALLY, I'M JUST GOING TO BE SLEEPING...
AND MISS KAMEYAMA'LL STAY, SO THERE'S NOTHING TO WORRY ABOUT.

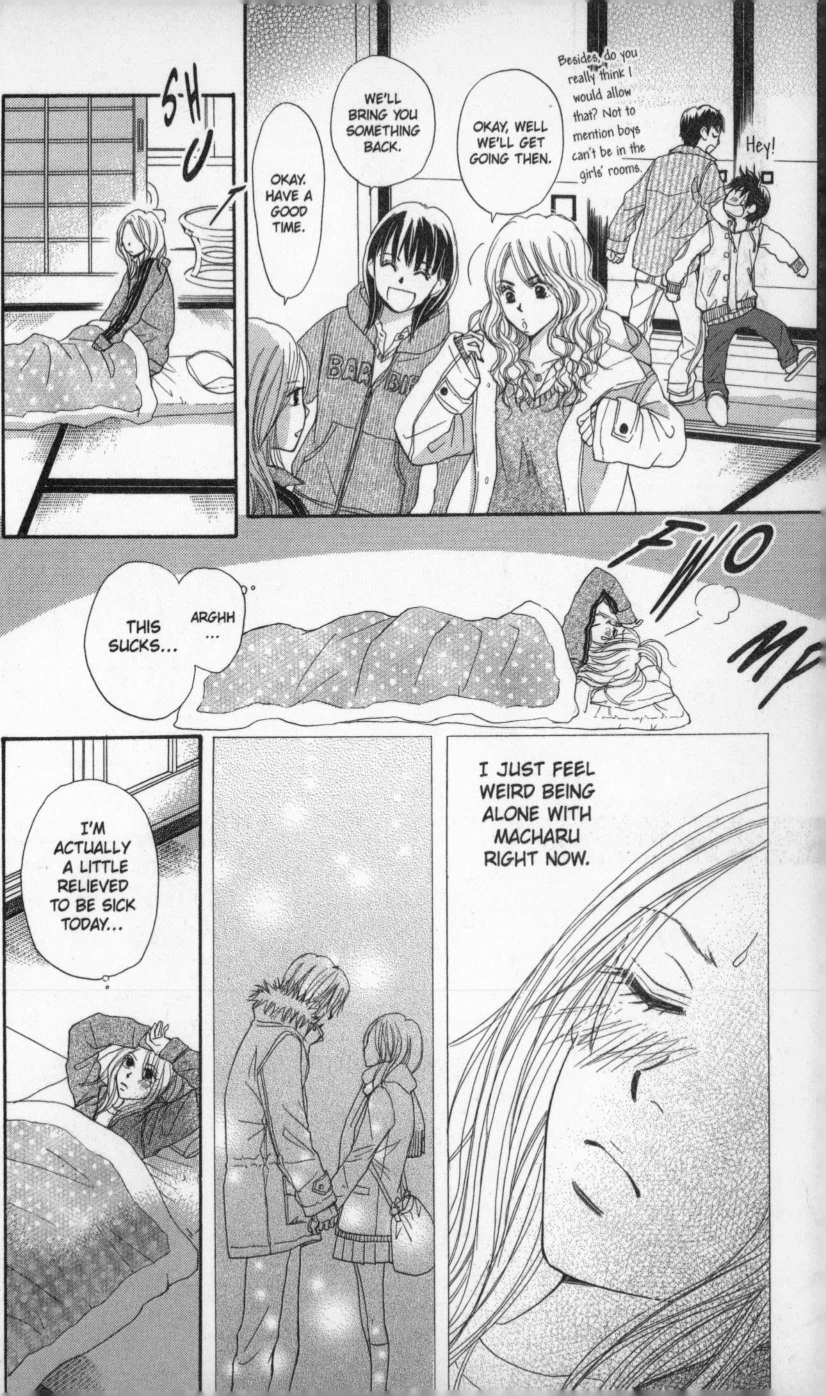
Besides, do you really think I would allow that? Not to mention boys can't be in the girls' rooms.
Hey!
OKAY, WELL WE'LL GET GOING THEN.
WE'LL BRING YOU SOMETHING BACK.
OKAY. HAVE A GOOD TIME.
S-H-U-T
FWOMP
ARGHH ...
THIS SUCKS...
I JUST FEEL WEIRD BEING ALONE WITH MACHARU RIGHT NOW.
I'M ACTUALLY A LITTLE RELIEVED TO BE SICK TODAY...

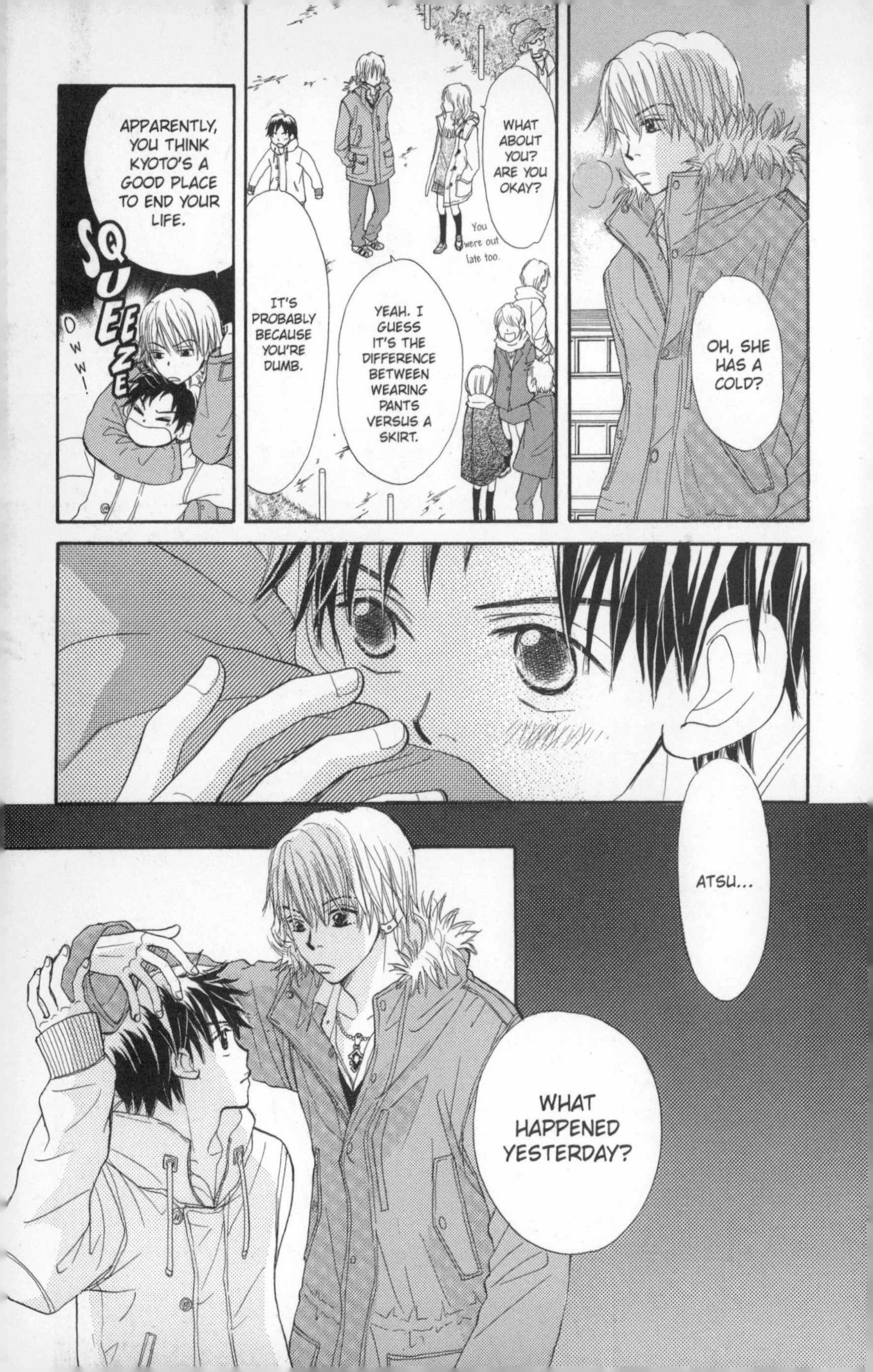
OH, SHE HAS A COLD?
WHAT ABOUT YOU? ARE YOU OKAY?
You were out late too.
YEAH. I GUESS IT'S THE DIFFERENCE BETWEEN WEARING PANTS VERSUS A SKIRT.
IT'S PROBABLY BECAUSE YOU'RE DUMB.
APPARENTLY, YOU THINK KYOTO'S A GOOD PLACE TO END YOUR LIFE.
SQUEEZE
OWW!
ATSU...
WHAT HAPPENED YESTERDAY?

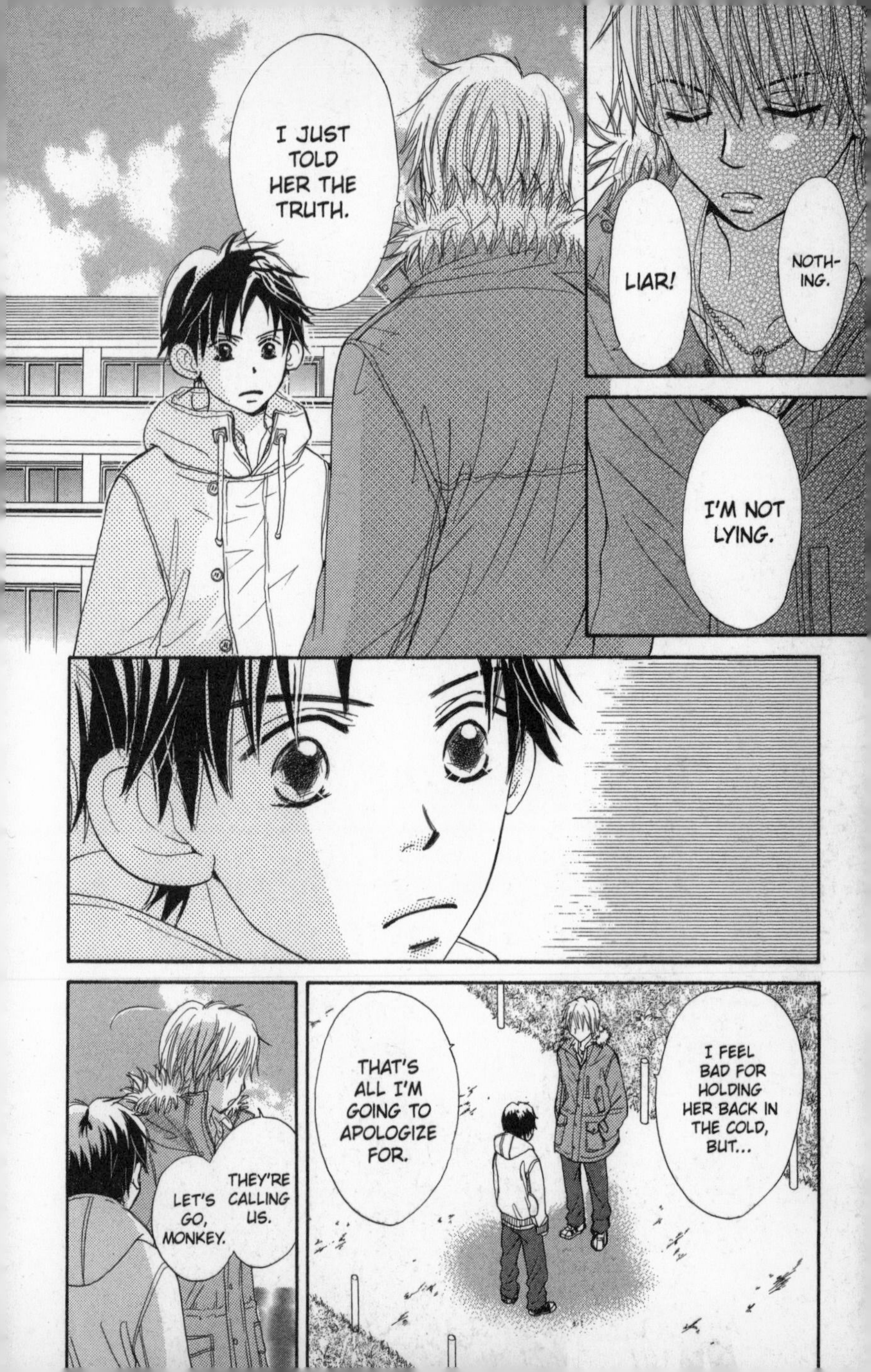
NOTH-ING.
LIAR!
I'M NOT LYING.
I JUST TOLD HER THE TRUTH.
I FEEL BAD FOR HOLDING HER BACK IN THE COLD, BUT...
THAT'S ALL I'M GOING TO APOLOGIZE FOR.
THEY'RE CALLING US.
LET'S GO, MONKEY.

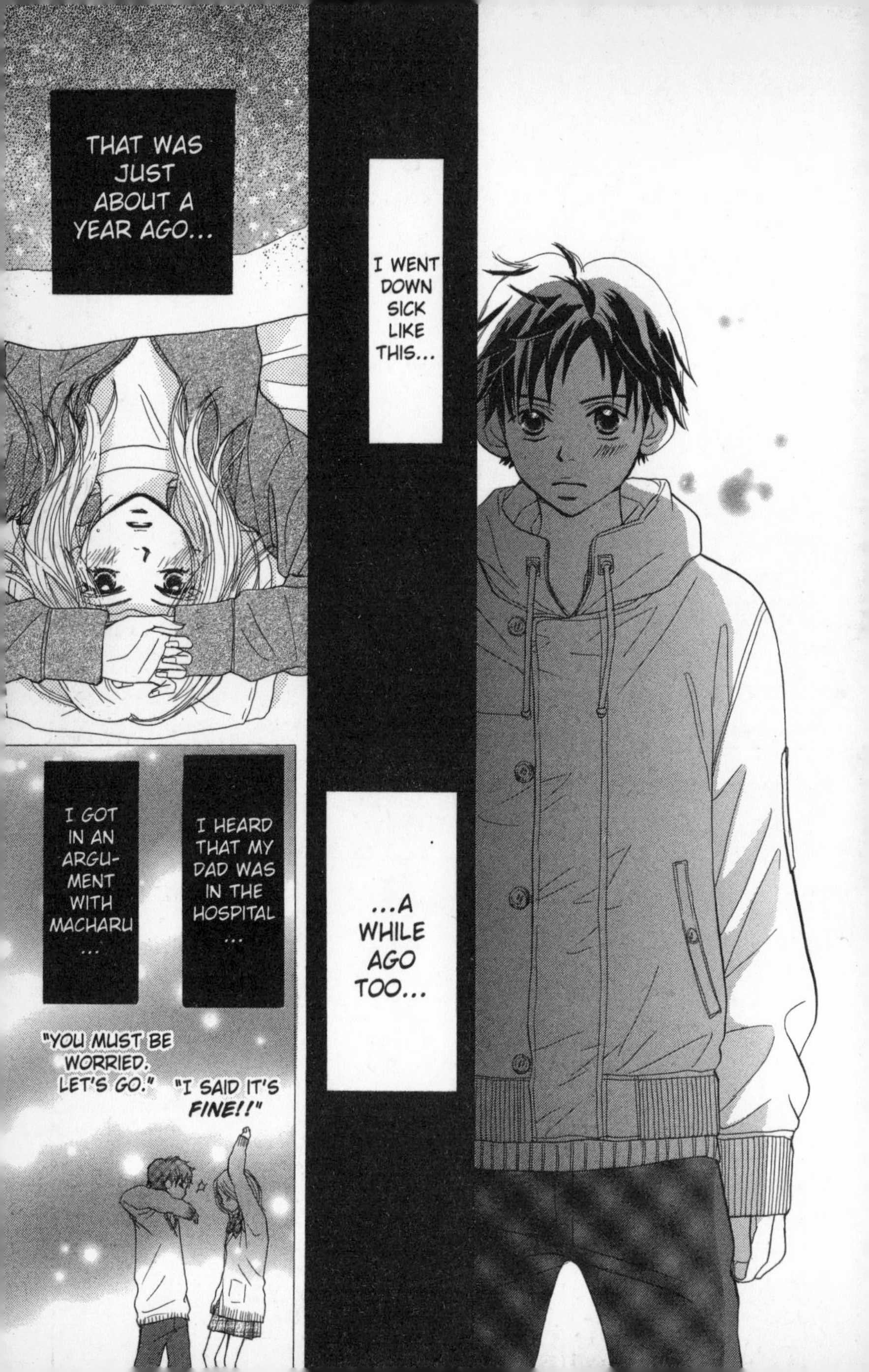
I WENT DOWN SICK LIKE THIS...
...A WHILE AGO TOO...
THAT WAS JUST ABOUT A YEAR AGO...
I HEARD THAT MY DAD WAS IN THE HOSPITAL...
I GOT IN AN ARGUMENT WITH MACHARU...
"YOU MUST BE WORRIED. LET'S GO."
"I SAID IT'S *FINE!!*"

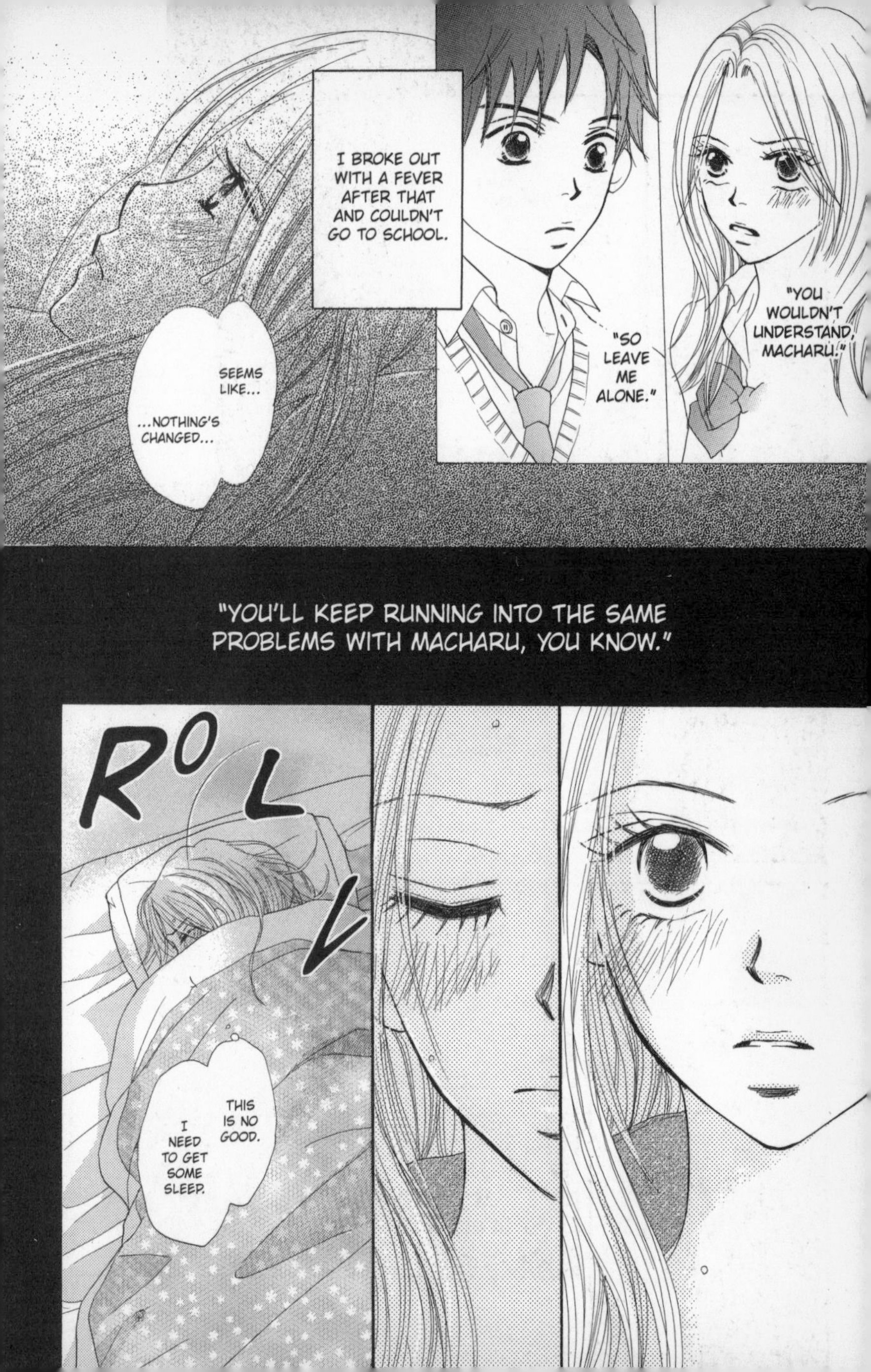
"YOU WOULDN'T UNDERSTAND, MACHARU."
"SO LEAVE ME ALONE."
I BROKE OUT WITH A FEVER AFTER THAT AND COULDN'T GO TO SCHOOL.
SEEMS LIKE... ...NOTHING'S CHANGED...
"YOU'LL KEEP RUNNING INTO THE SAME PROBLEMS WITH MACHARU, YOU KNOW."
ROLL
THIS IS NO GOOD. I NEED TO GET SOME SLEEP.

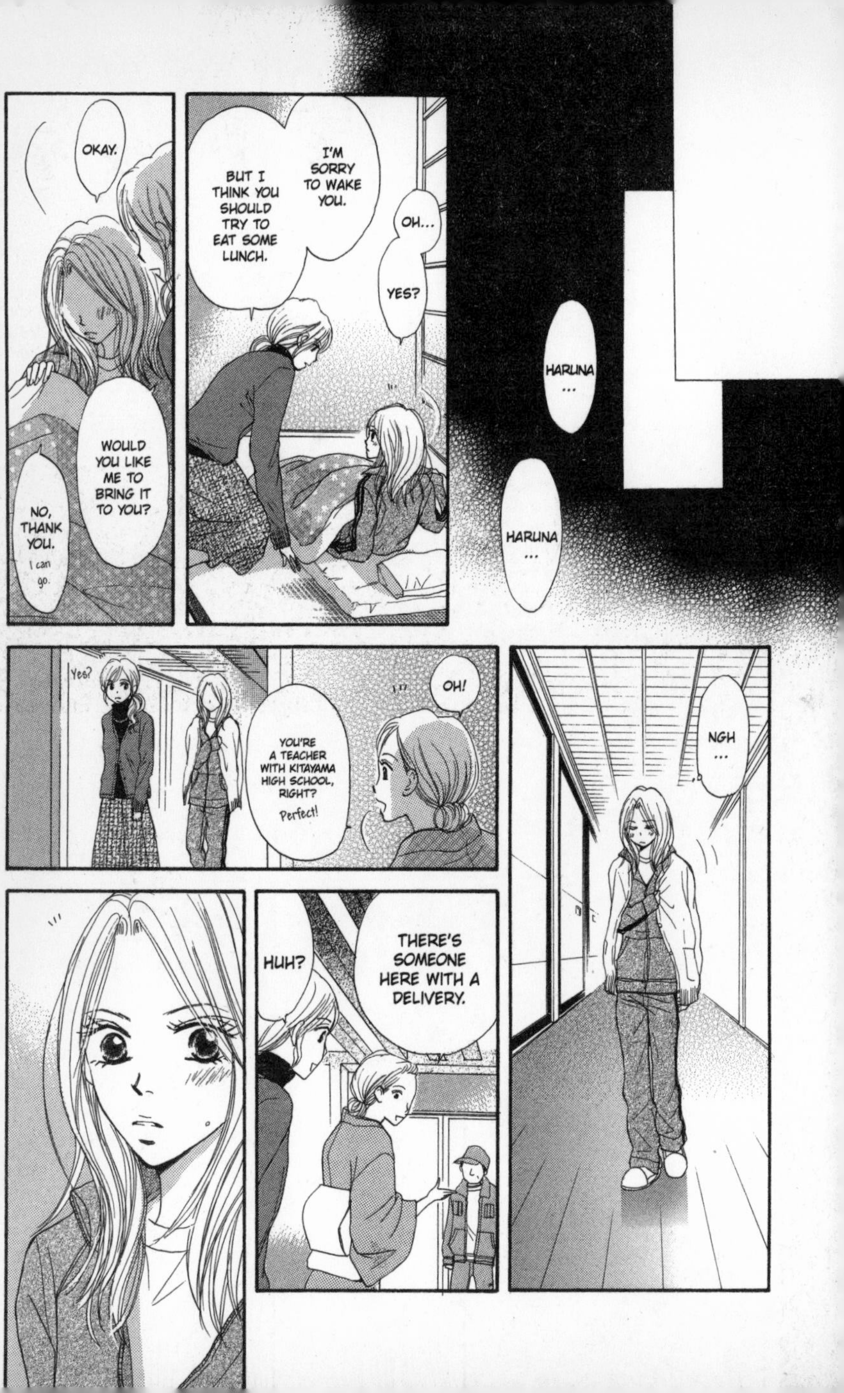
HARUNA...
HARUNA...
OH...
YES?
I'M SORRY TO WAKE YOU.
BUT I THINK YOU SHOULD TRY TO EAT SOME LUNCH.
OKAY.
WOULD YOU LIKE ME TO BRING IT TO YOU?
NO, THANK YOU.
I can go.
NGH...
OH!
YOU'RE A TEACHER WITH KITAYAMA HIGH SCHOOL, RIGHT?
Perfect!
Yes?
THERE'S SOMEONE HERE WITH A DELIVERY.
HUH?

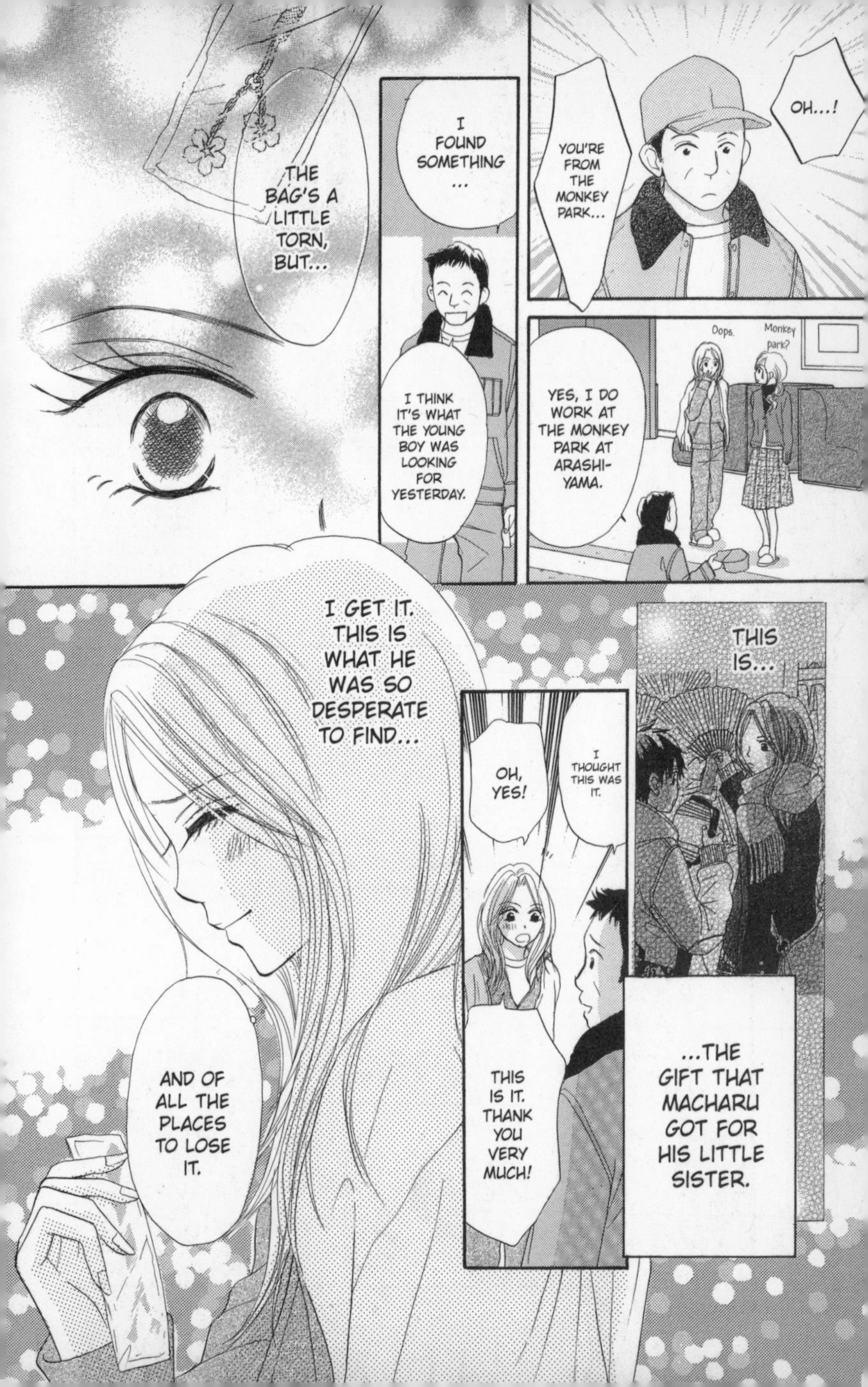
OH...!
YOU'RE FROM THE MONKEY PARK...
Monkey park?
Oops.
YES, I DO WORK AT THE MONKEY PARK AT ARASHI-YAMA.
I FOUND SOMETHING...
I THINK IT'S WHAT THE YOUNG BOY WAS LOOKING FOR YESTERDAY.
THE BAG'S A LITTLE TORN, BUT...
THIS IS...
...THE GIFT THAT MACHARU GOT FOR HIS LITTLE SISTER.
I THOUGHT THIS WAS IT.
OH, YES!
THIS IS IT. THANK YOU VERY MUCH!
I GET IT. THIS IS WHAT HE WAS SO DESPERATE TO FIND...
AND OF ALL THE PLACES TO LOSE IT.

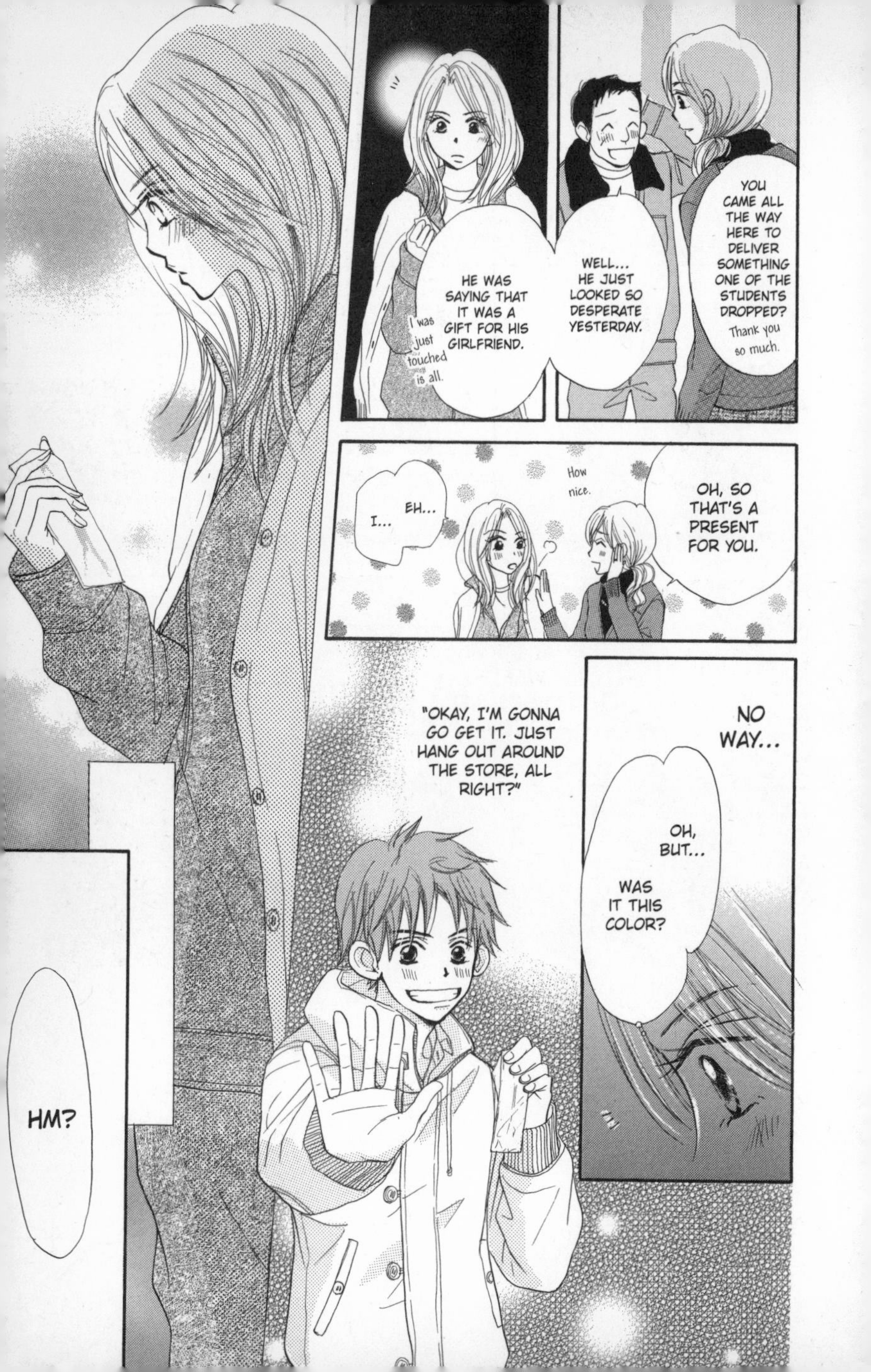
YOU CAME ALL THE WAY HERE TO DELIVER SOMETHING ONE OF THE STUDENTS DROPPED?
Thank you so much.
WELL... HE JUST LOOKED SO DESPERATE YESTERDAY.
HE WAS SAYING THAT IT WAS A GIFT FOR HIS GIRLFRIEND.
I was just touched is all.
OH, SO THAT'S A PRESENT FOR YOU.
How nice.
EH...
I...
NO WAY...
OH, BUT...
WAS IT THIS COLOR?
"OKAY, I'M GONNA GO GET IT. JUST HANG OUT AROUND THE STORE, ALL RIGHT?"
HM?

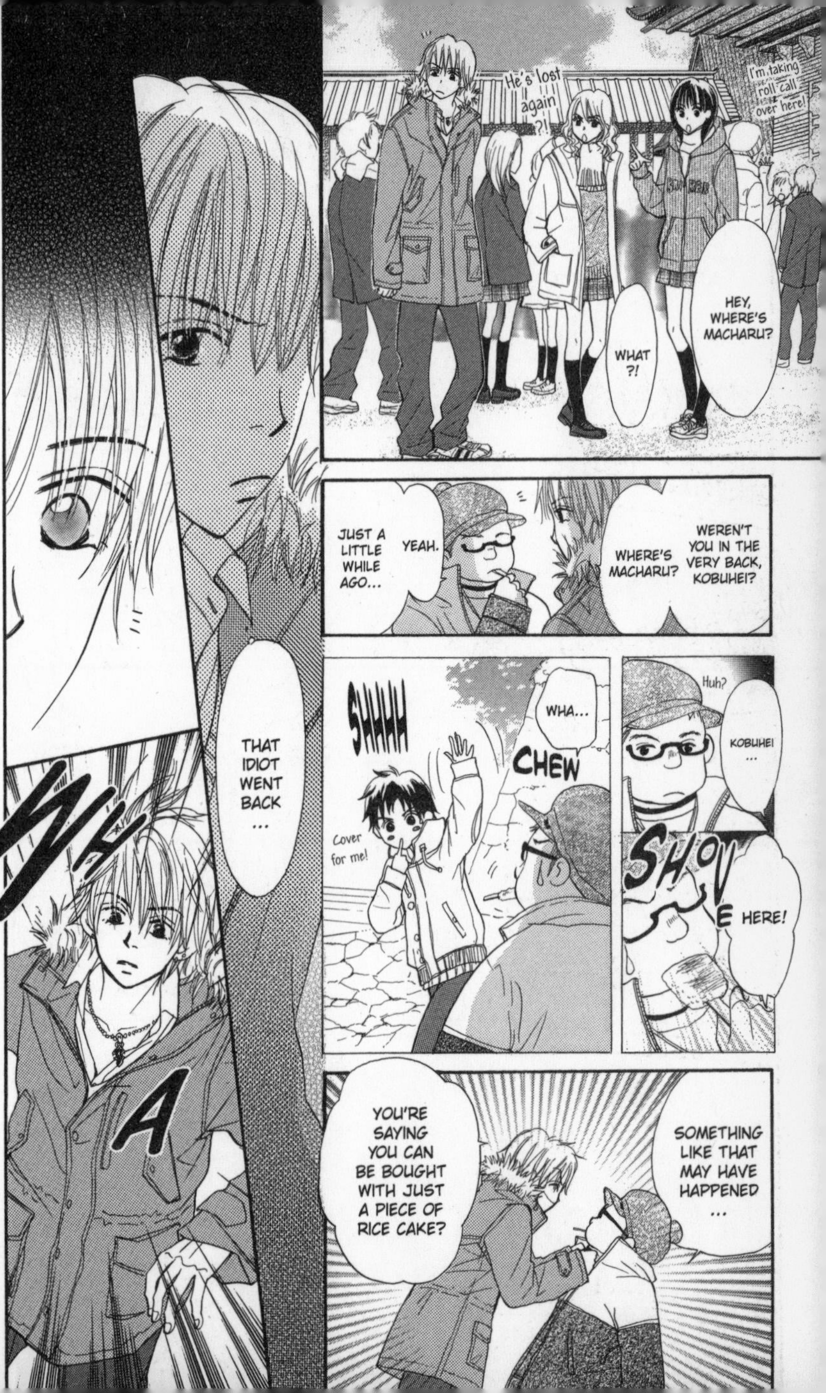
I'm taking roll call over here!
HEY, WHERE'S MACHARU?
He's lost again?!
WHAT ?!
WEREN'T YOU IN THE VERY BACK, KOBUHEI?
WHERE'S MACHARU?
YEAH.
JUST A LITTLE WHILE AGO...
Huh?
KOBUHEI ...
SHOVE
HERE!
WHA...
CHEW
SHHHH
Cover for me!
SOMETHING LIKE THAT MAY HAVE HAPPENED ...
YOU'RE SAYING YOU CAN BE BOUGHT WITH JUST A PIECE OF RICE CAKE?
THAT IDIOT WENT BACK ...
WHA
A

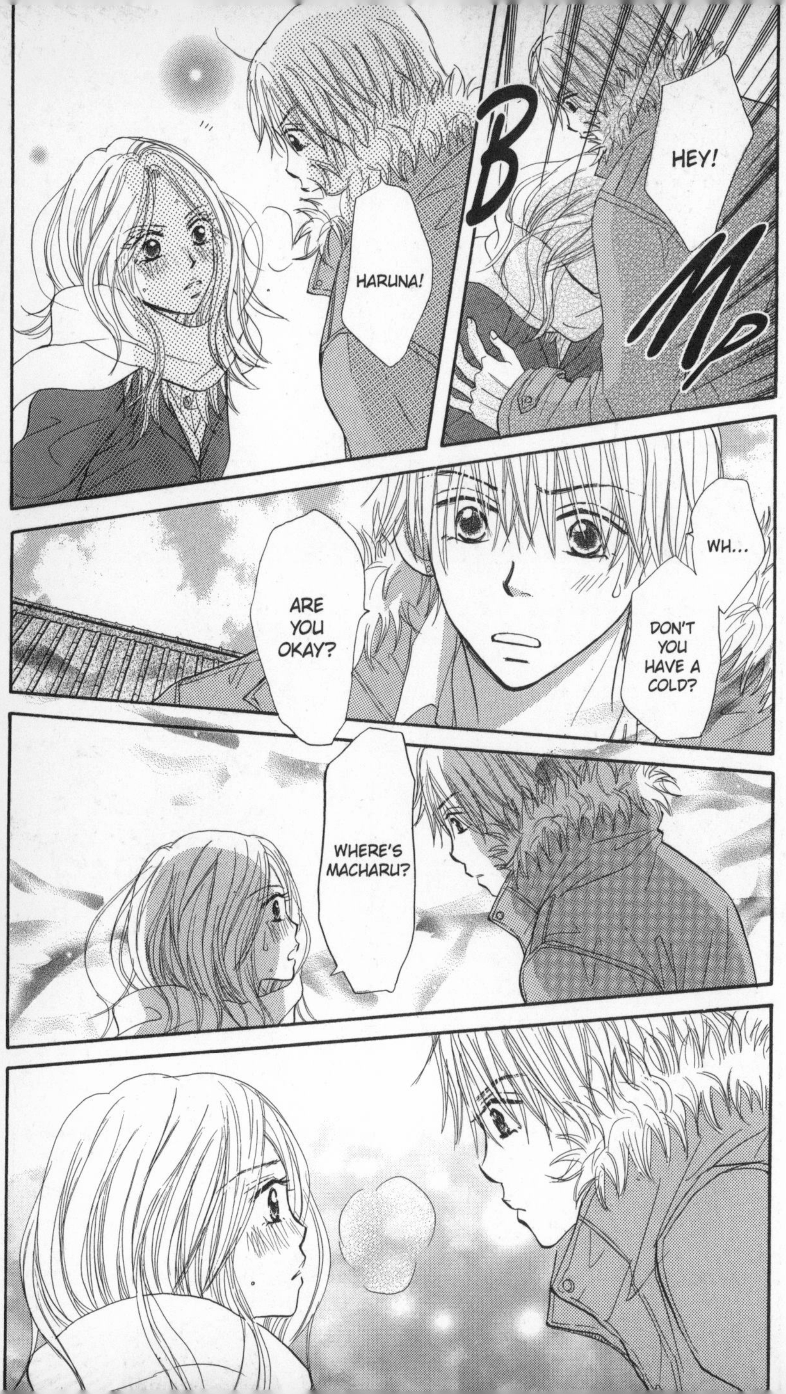
HEY!
BMP
HARUNA!
WH...
DON'T YOU HAVE A COLD?
ARE YOU OKAY?
WHERE'S MACHARU?

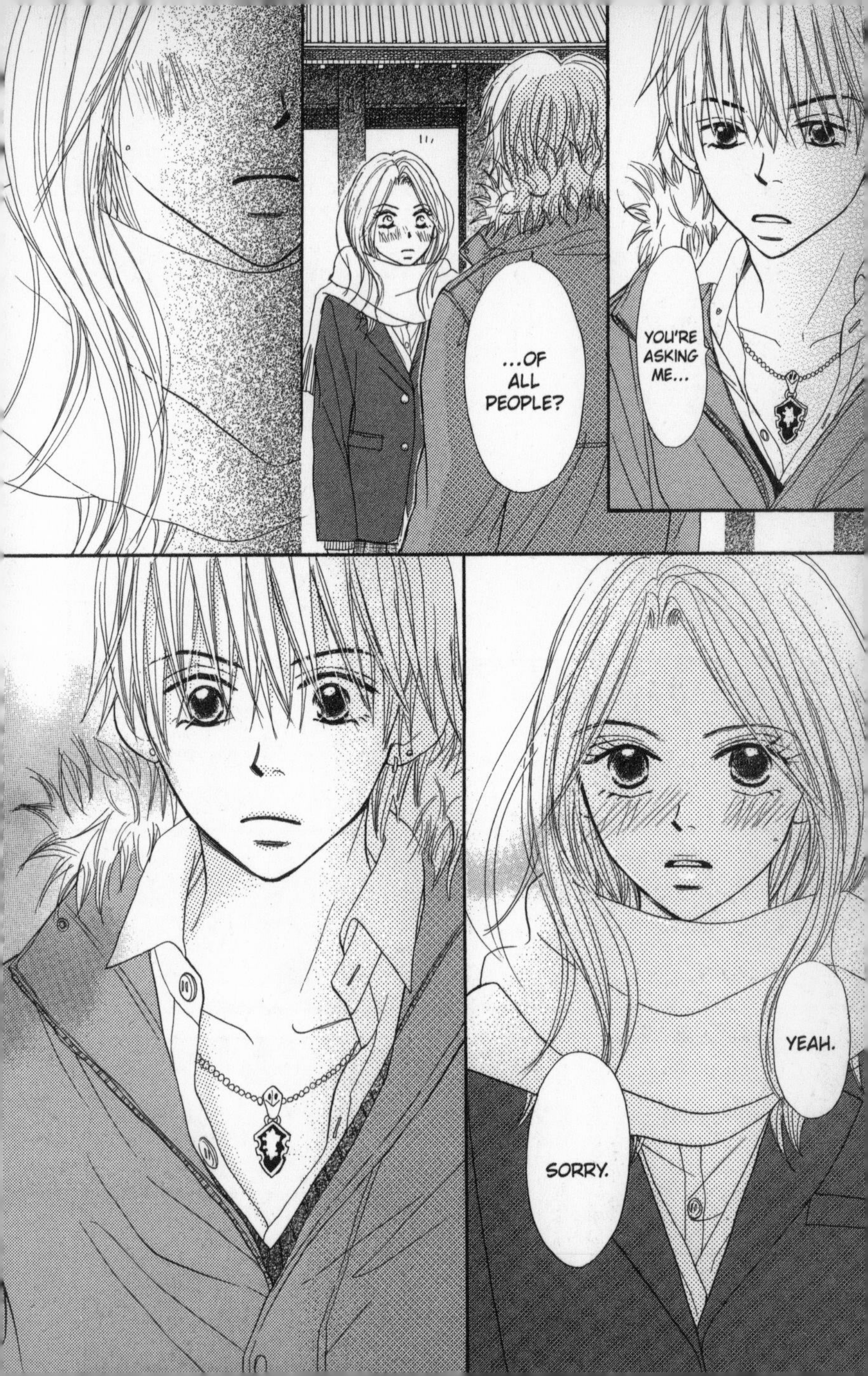
YOU'RE ASKING ME...
...OF ALL PEOPLE?
YEAH.
SORRY.

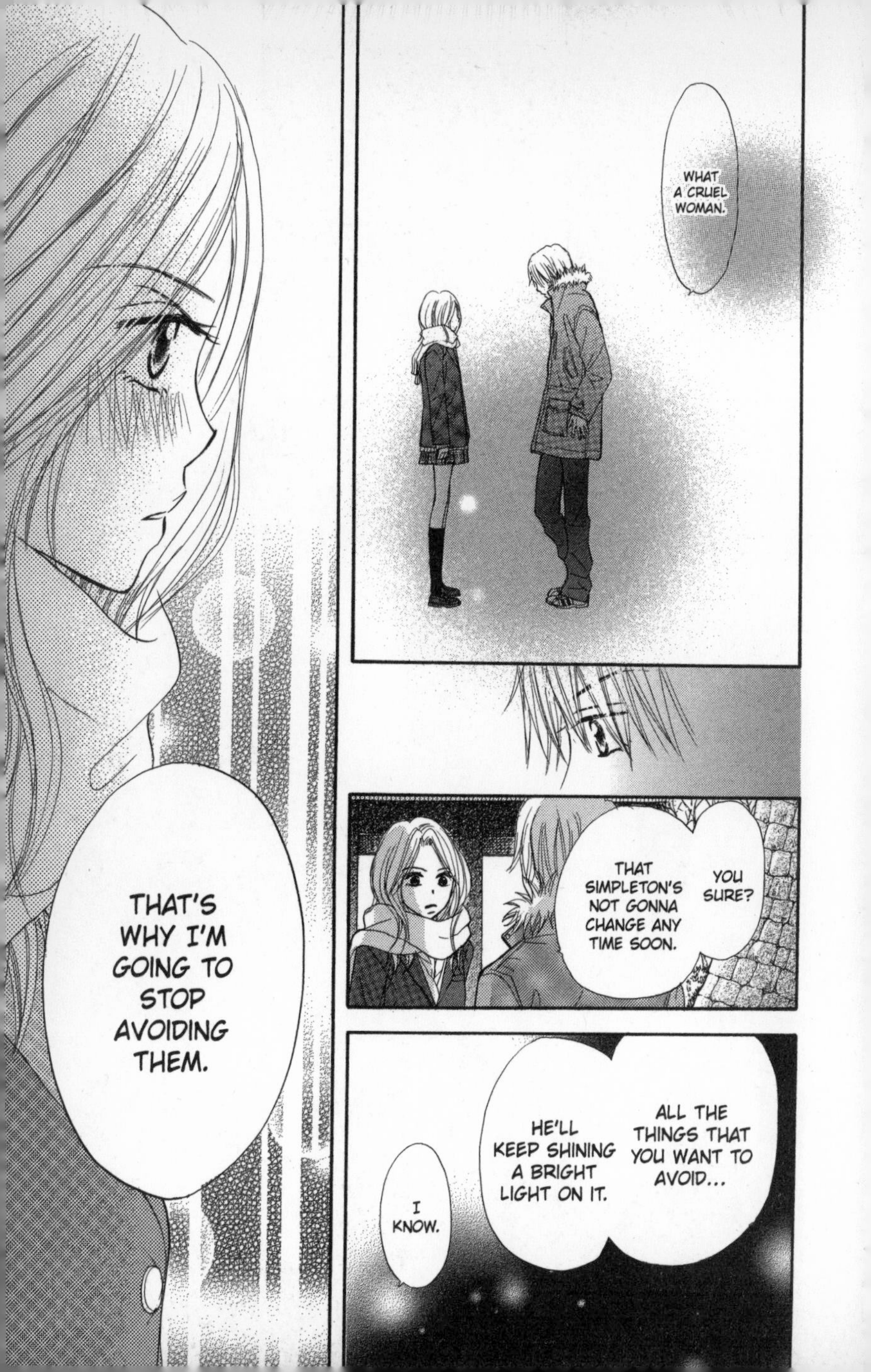
WHAT A CRUEL WOMAN.
YOU SURE?
THAT SIMPLETON'S NOT GONNA CHANGE ANY TIME SOON.
ALL THE THINGS THAT YOU WANT TO AVOID...
HE'LL KEEP SHINING A BRIGHT LIGHT ON IT.
I KNOW.
THAT'S WHY I'M GOING TO STOP AVOIDING THEM.

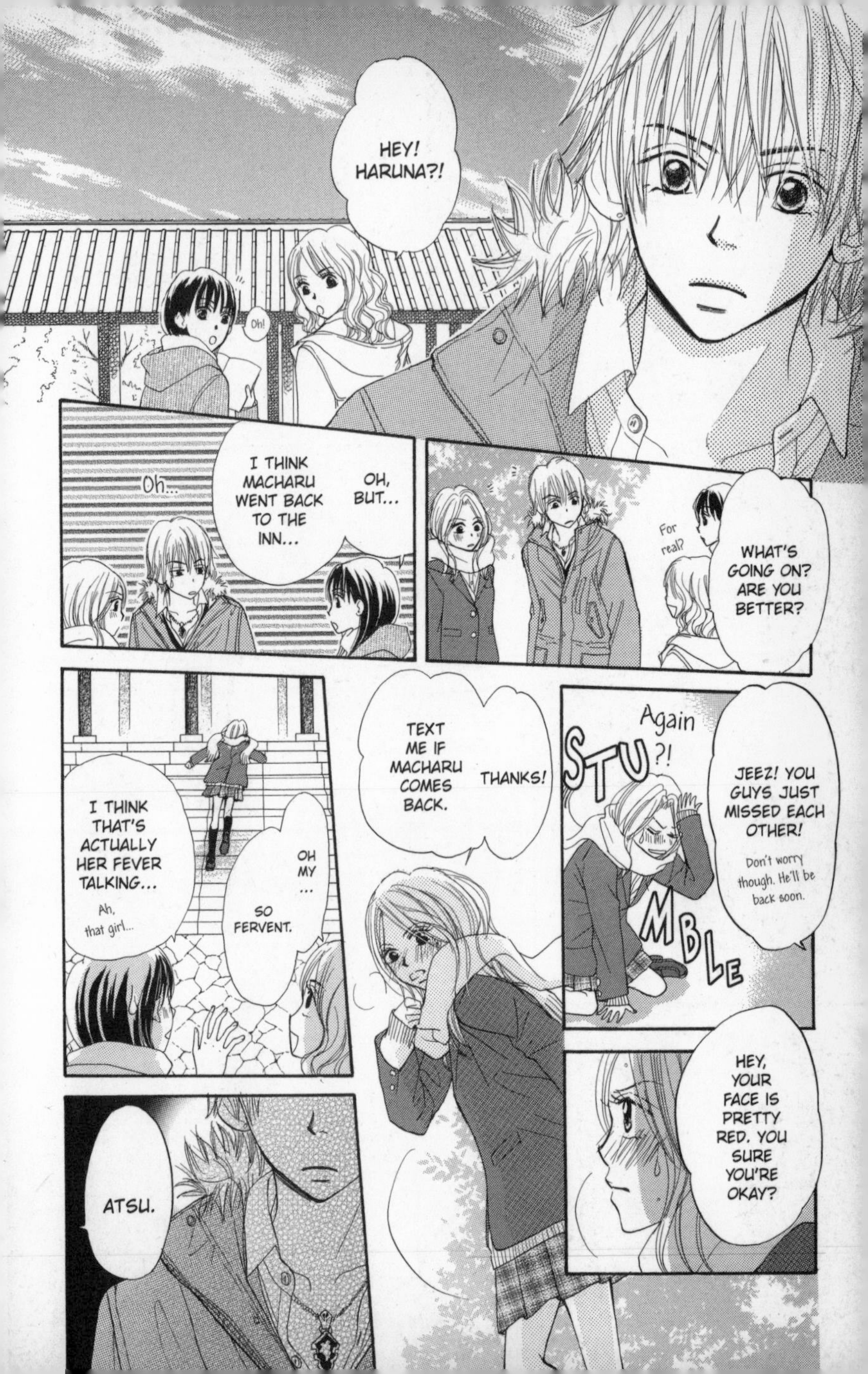
HEY! HARUNA?!
Oh!
WHAT'S GOING ON? ARE YOU BETTER?
For real?
OH, BUT...
I THINK MACHARU WENT BACK TO THE INN...
Oh...
Again ?!
STUMBLE
JEEZ! YOU GUYS JUST MISSED EACH OTHER!
Don't worry though. He'll be back soon.
HEY, YOUR FACE IS PRETTY RED. YOU SURE YOU'RE OKAY?
THANKS!
TEXT ME IF MACHARU COMES BACK.
OH MY ...
SO FERVENT.
I THINK THAT'S ACTUALLY HER FEVER TALKING...
Ah, that girl...
ATSU.

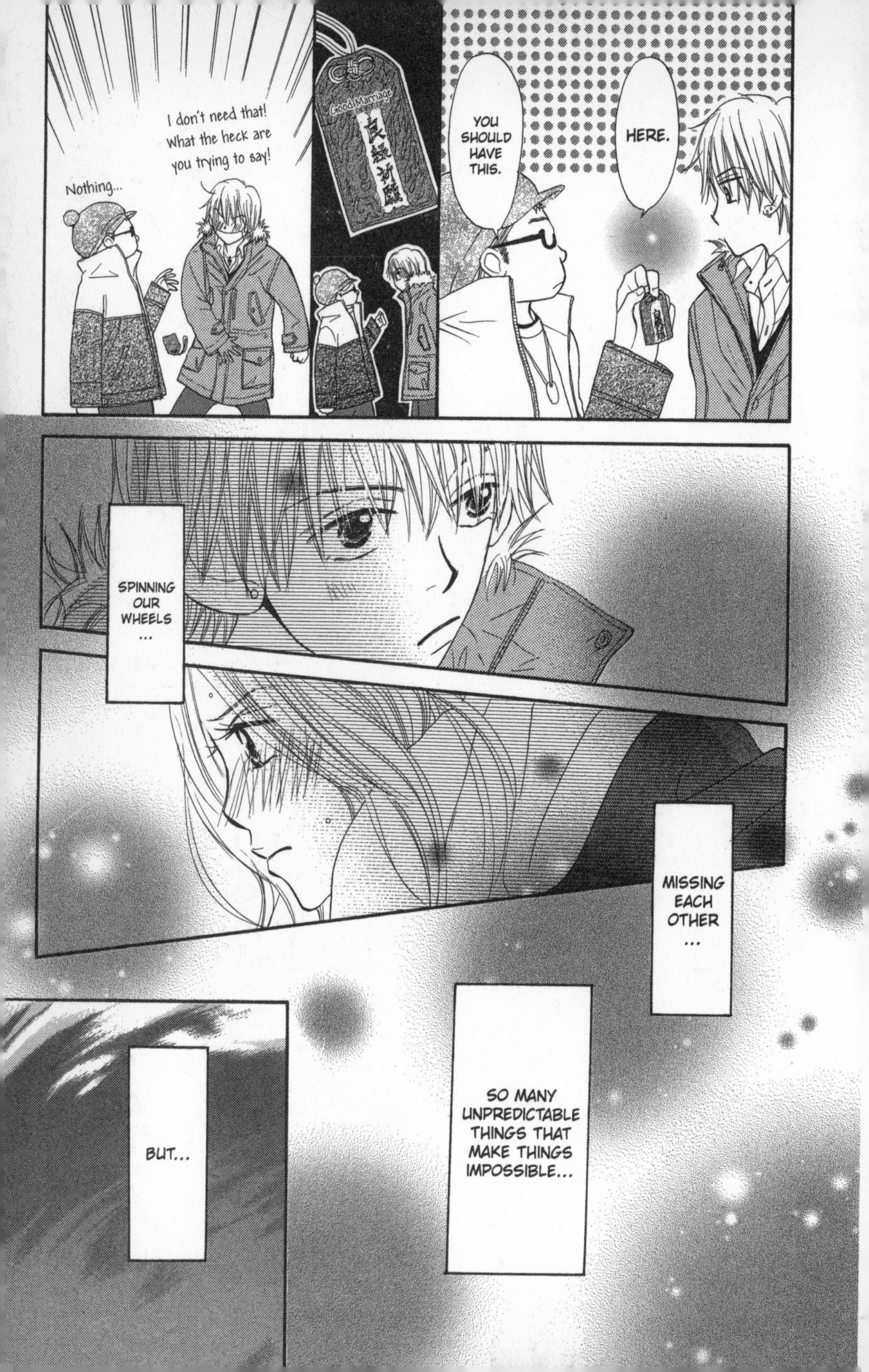
HERE.
YOU SHOULD HAVE THIS.
Good Marriage
良縁祈願
I don't need that! What the heck are you trying to say!
Nothing...
SPINNING OUR WHEELS ...
MISSING EACH OTHER ...
SO MANY UNPREDICTABLE THINGS THAT MAKE THINGS IMPOSSIBLE...
BUT...

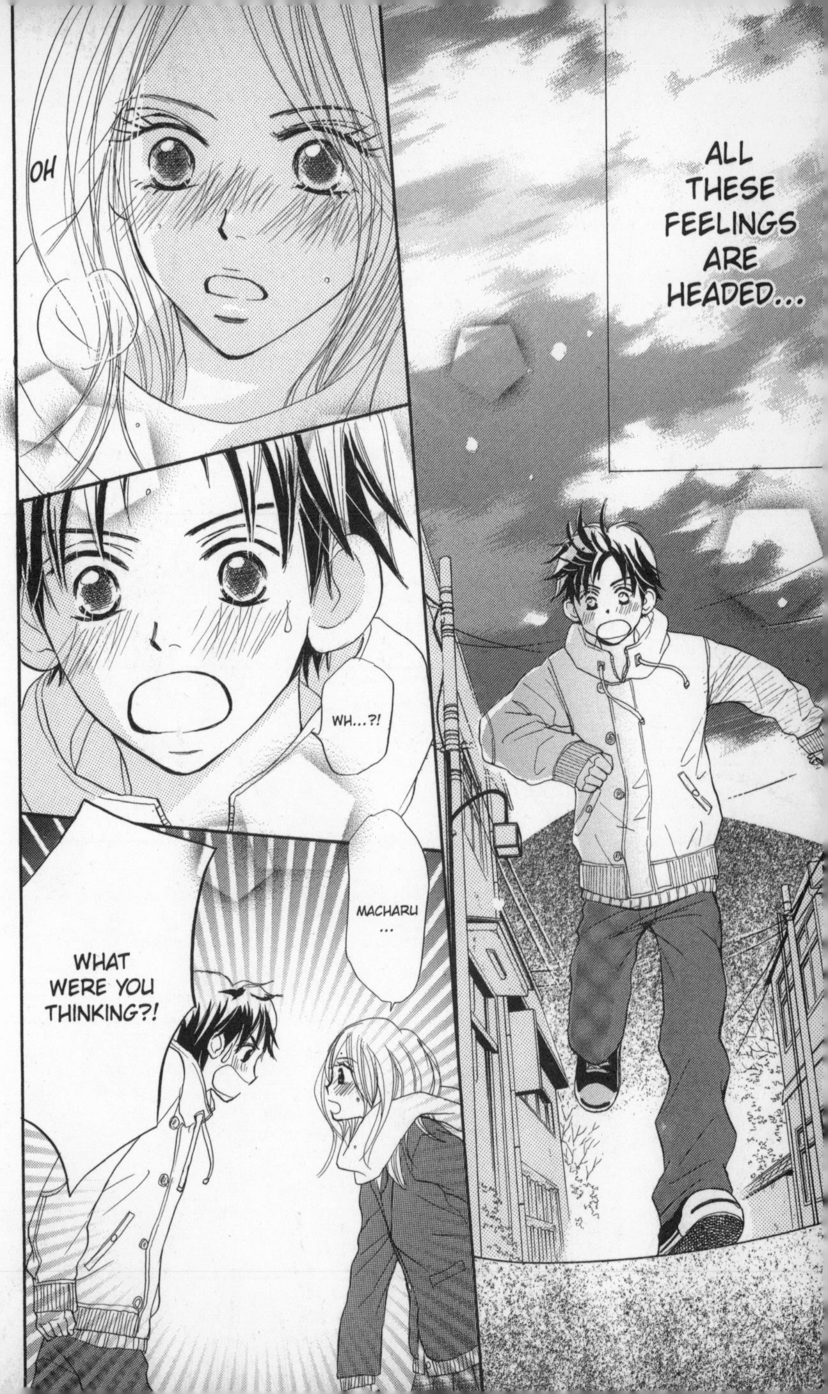
ALL THESE FEELINGS ARE HEADED...
OH
WH...?!
MACHARU ...
WHAT WERE YOU THINKING?!

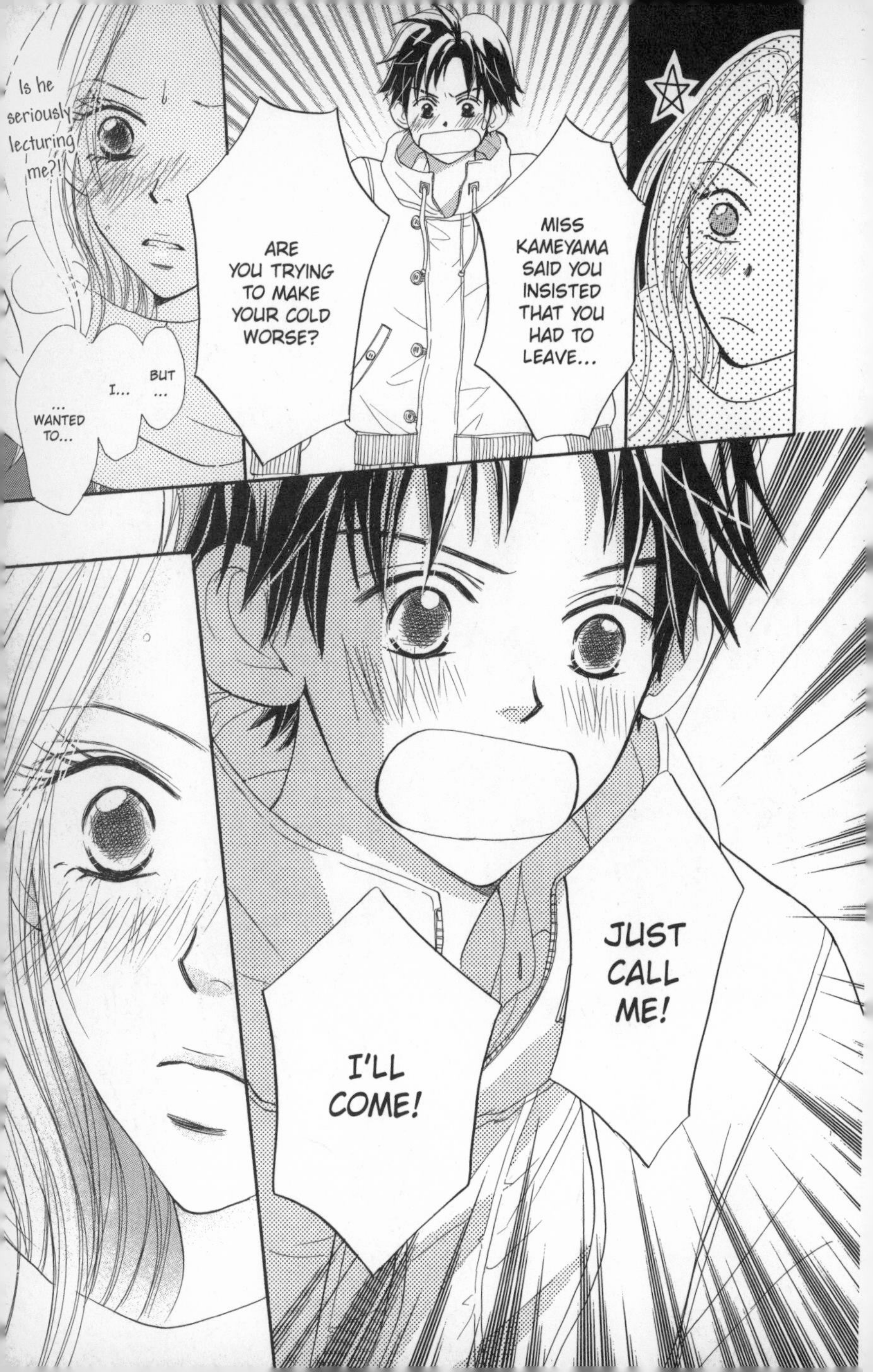
MISS KAMEYAMA SAID YOU INSISTED THAT YOU HAD TO LEAVE...
ARE YOU TRYING TO MAKE YOUR COLD WORSE?
Is he seriously lecturing me?!
BUT ...
I...
...WANTED TO...
JUST CALL ME!
I'LL COME!

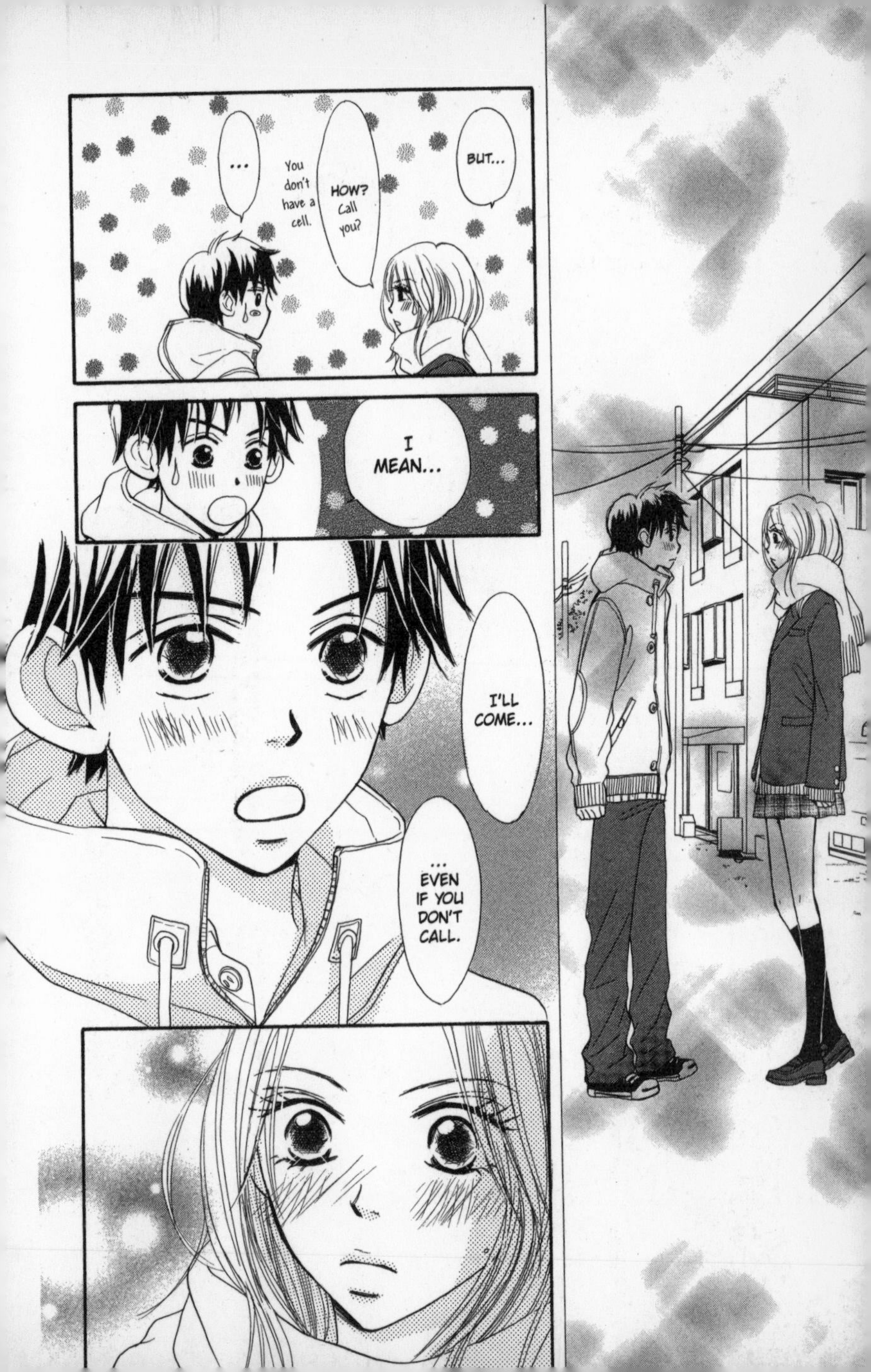
BUT...
HOW? Call you?
You don't have a cell.
...
I MEAN...
I'LL COME...
... EVEN IF YOU DON'T CALL.

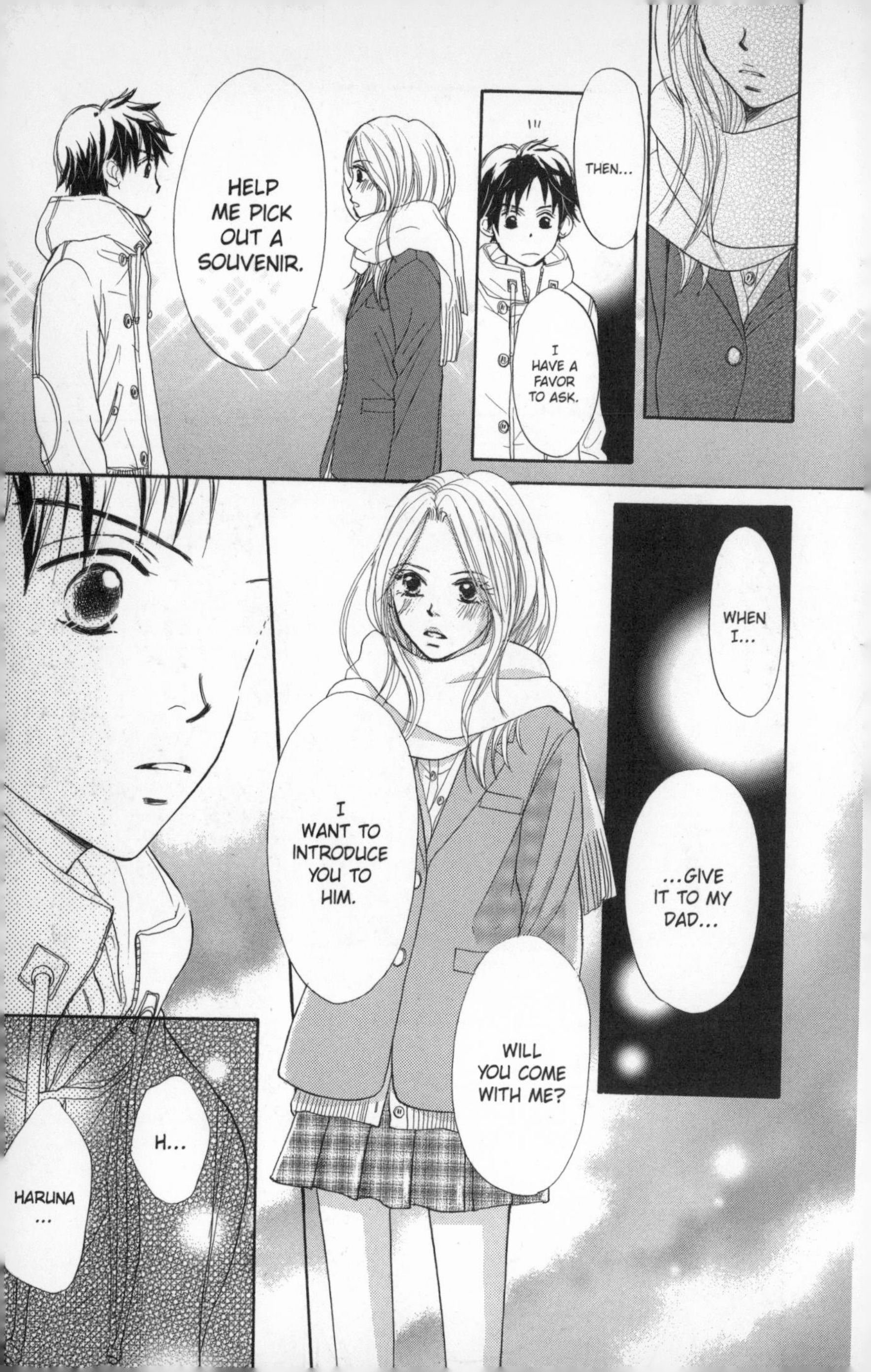
THEN...
I HAVE A FAVOR TO ASK.
HELP ME PICK OUT A SOUVENIR.
WHEN I...
...GIVE IT TO MY DAD...
I WANT TO INTRODUCE YOU TO HIM.
WILL YOU COME WITH ME?
H...
HARUNA ...

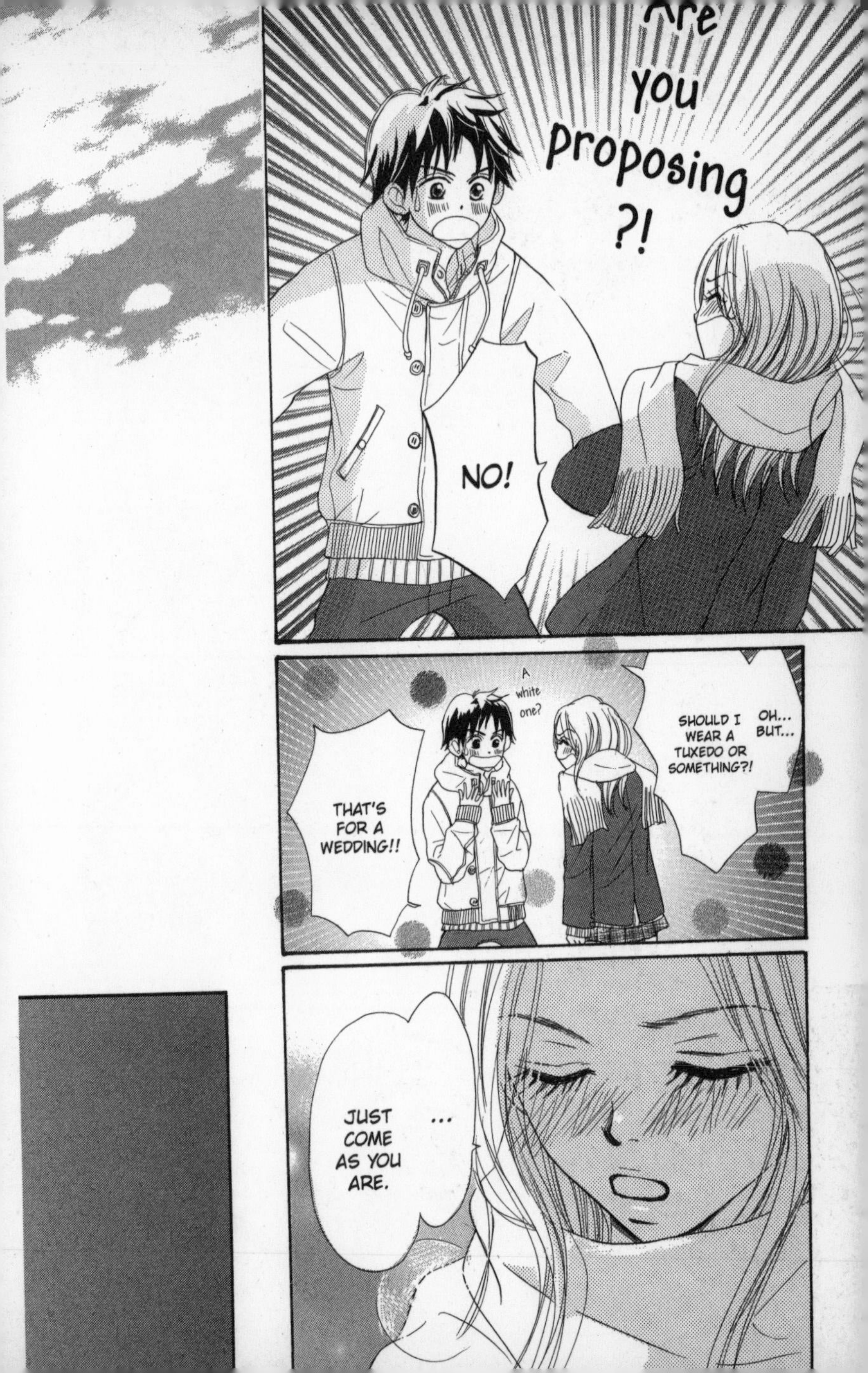

Are you Proposing ?!
NO!
OH... BUT...
SHOULD I WEAR A TUXEDO OR SOMETHING?!
A white one?
THAT'S FOR A WEDDING!!
...
JUST COME AS YOU ARE.

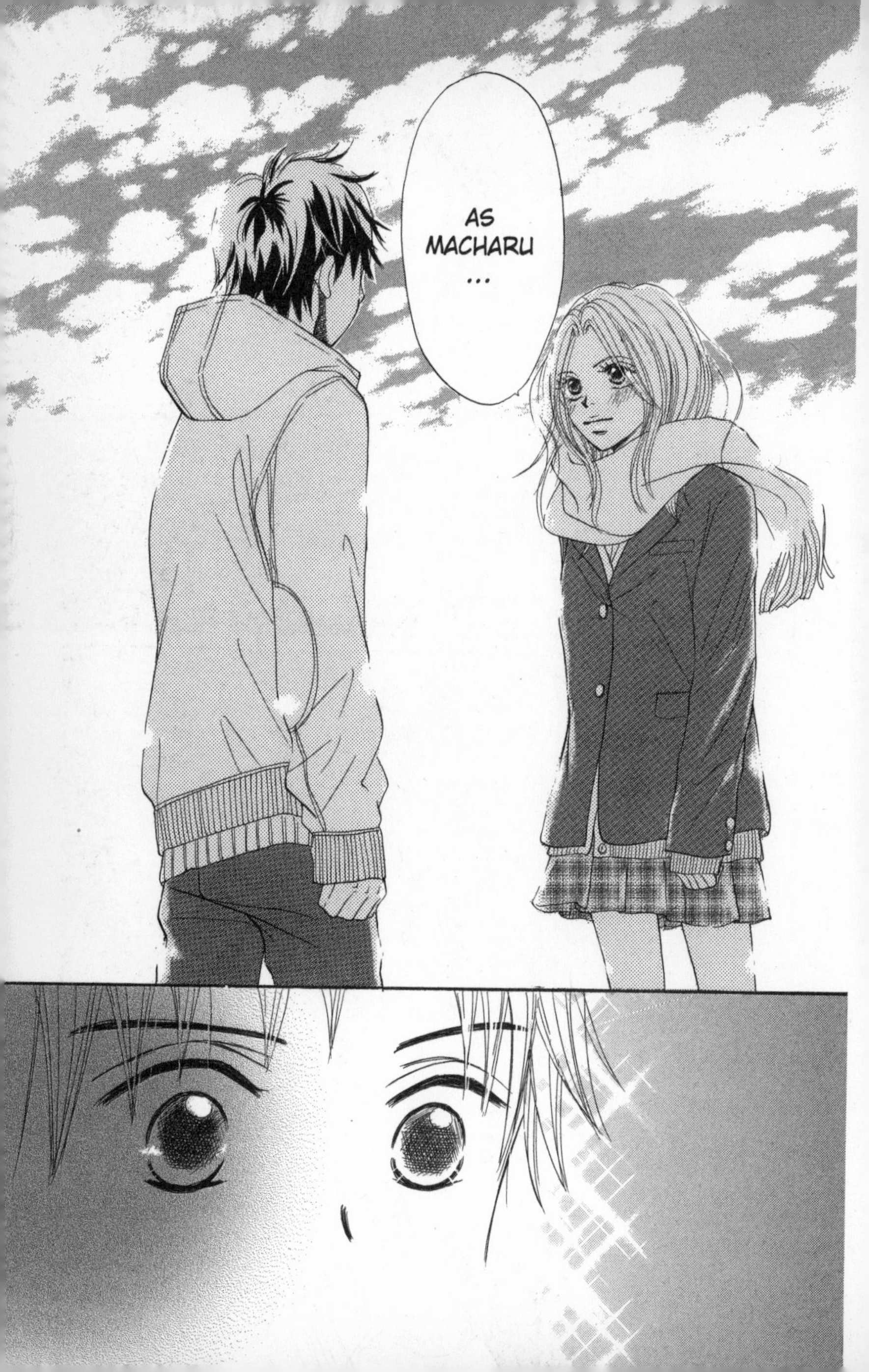
AS MACHARU ...

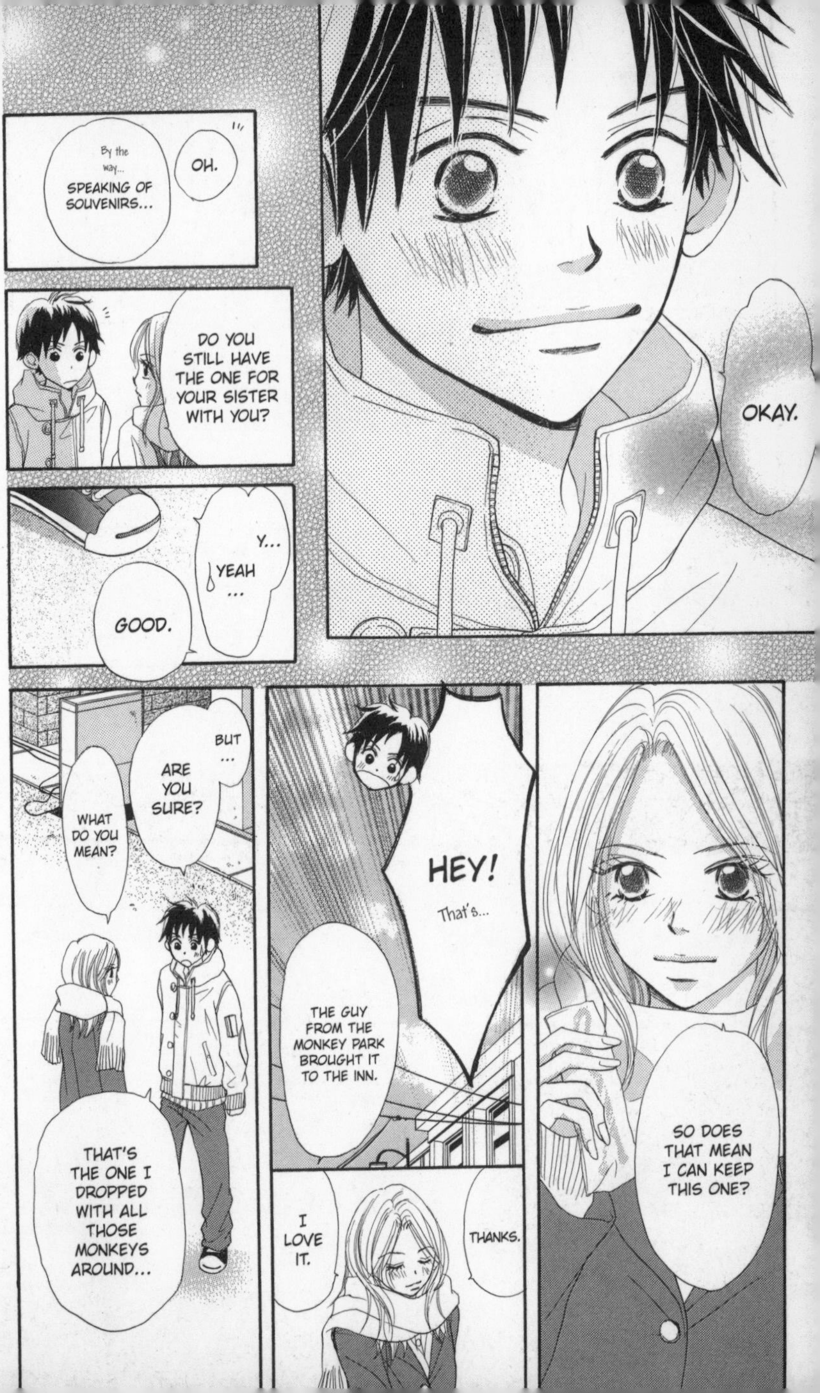
OKAY.
OH.
By the way...
SPEAKING OF SOUVENIRS...
DO YOU STILL HAVE THE ONE FOR YOUR SISTER WITH YOU?
Y... YEAH...
GOOD.
SO DOES THAT MEAN I CAN KEEP THIS ONE?
HEY!
That's...
THE GUY FROM THE MONKEY PARK BROUGHT IT TO THE INN.
THANKS.
I LOVE IT.
BUT...
ARE YOU SURE?
WHAT DO YOU MEAN?
THAT'S THE ONE I DROPPED WITH ALL THOSE MONKEYS AROUND...

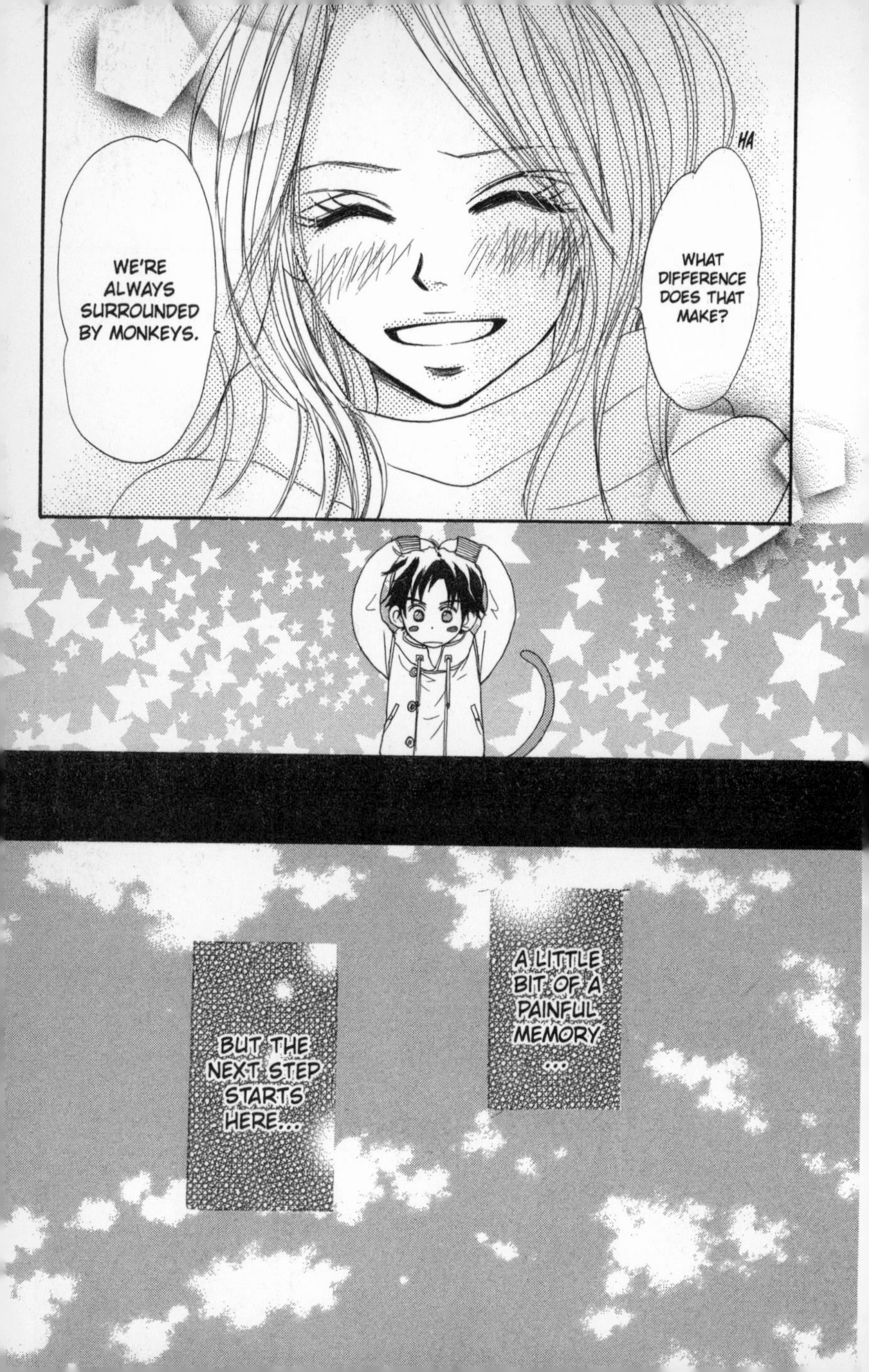
HA
WHAT DIFFERENCE DOES THAT MAKE?
WE'RE ALWAYS SURROUNDED BY MONKEYS.
A LITTLE BIT OF A PAINFUL MEMORY...
BUT THE NEXT STEP STARTS HERE...

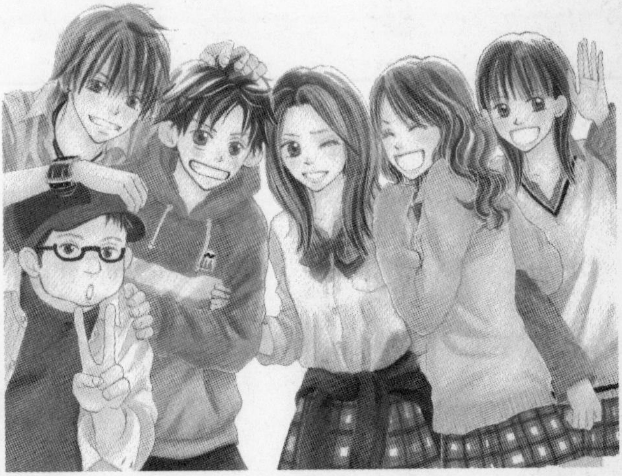
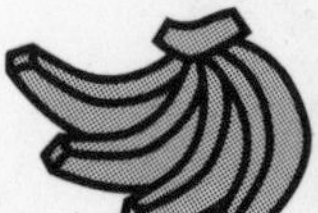

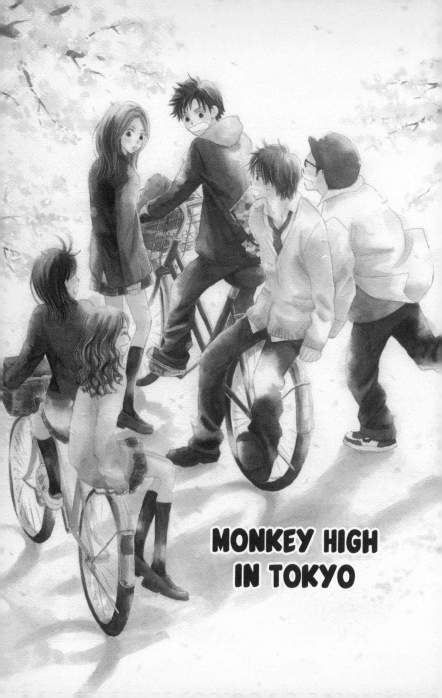

MONKEY HIGH
IN TOKYO

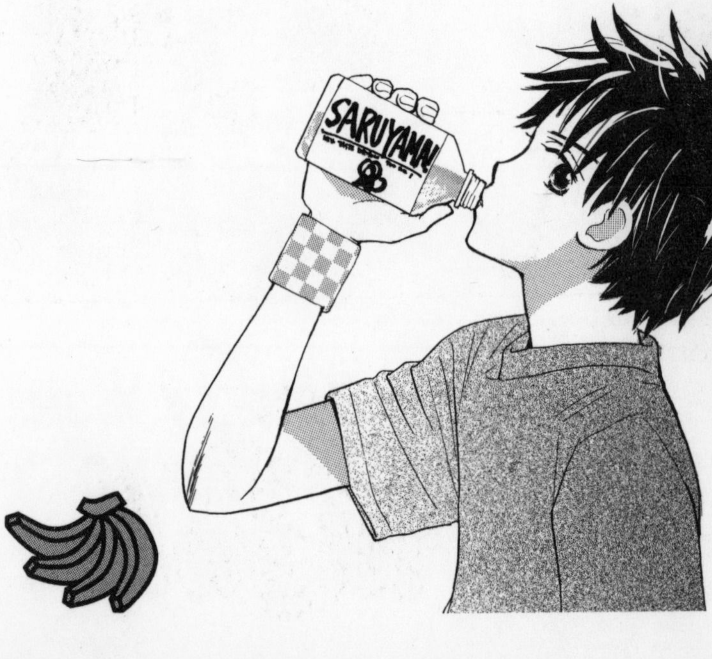
SARUYAMA!

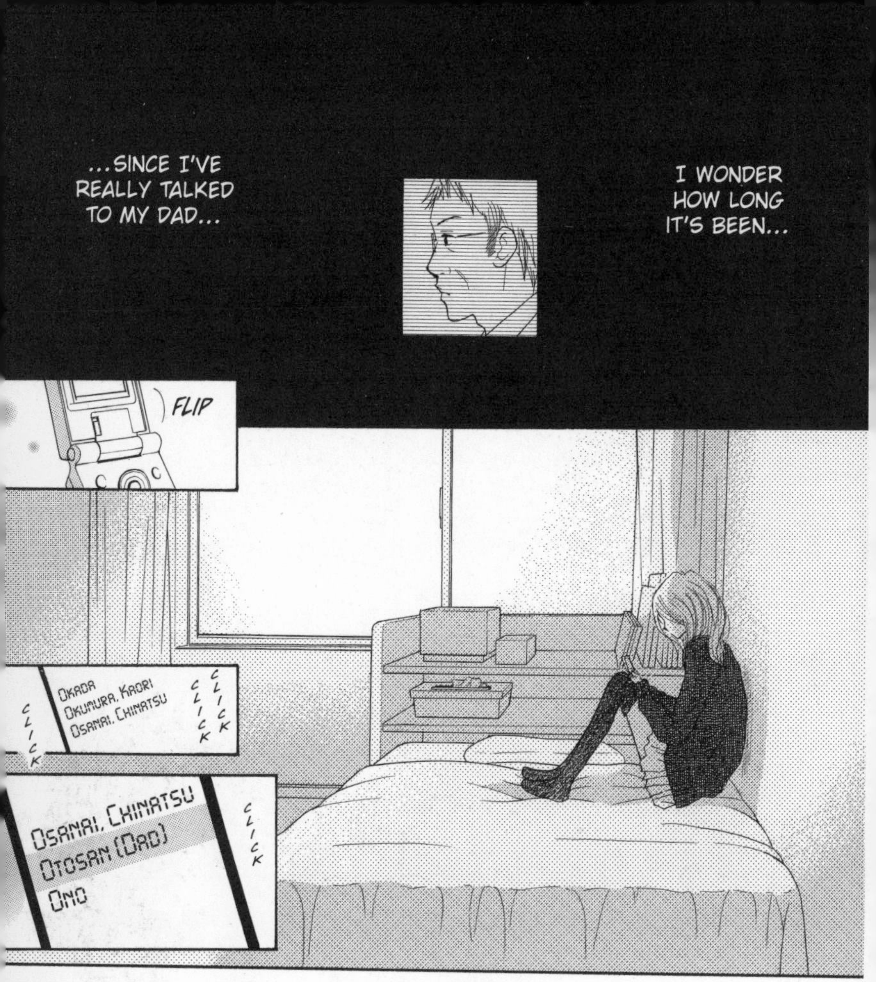
I WONDER HOW LONG IT'S BEEN...
...SINCE I'VE REALLY TALKED TO MY DAD...
FLIP
CLICK CLICK
Okada
Okumura, Kaori
Osanai, Chinatsu
CLICK
CLICK
Osanai, Chinatsu
Otosan (Dad)
Ono

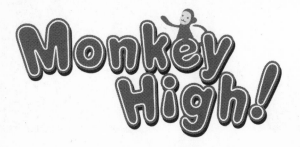

Monkey High!

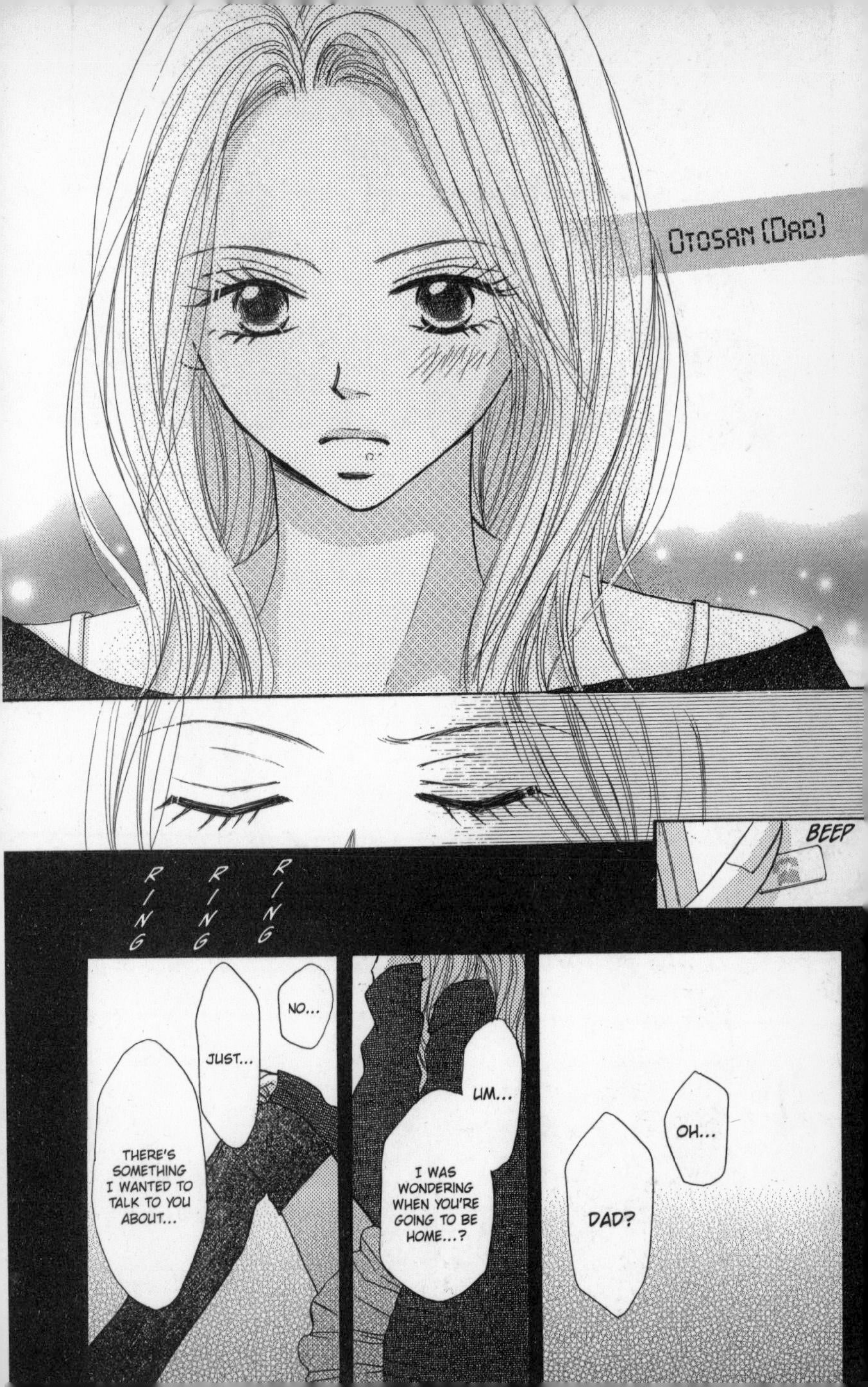
OTOSAN (DAD)
BEEP
RING RING RING
OH...
DAD?
UM...
I WAS WONDERING WHEN YOU'RE GOING TO BE HOME...?
NO...
JUST...
THERE'S SOMETHING I WANTED TO TALK TO YOU ABOUT...

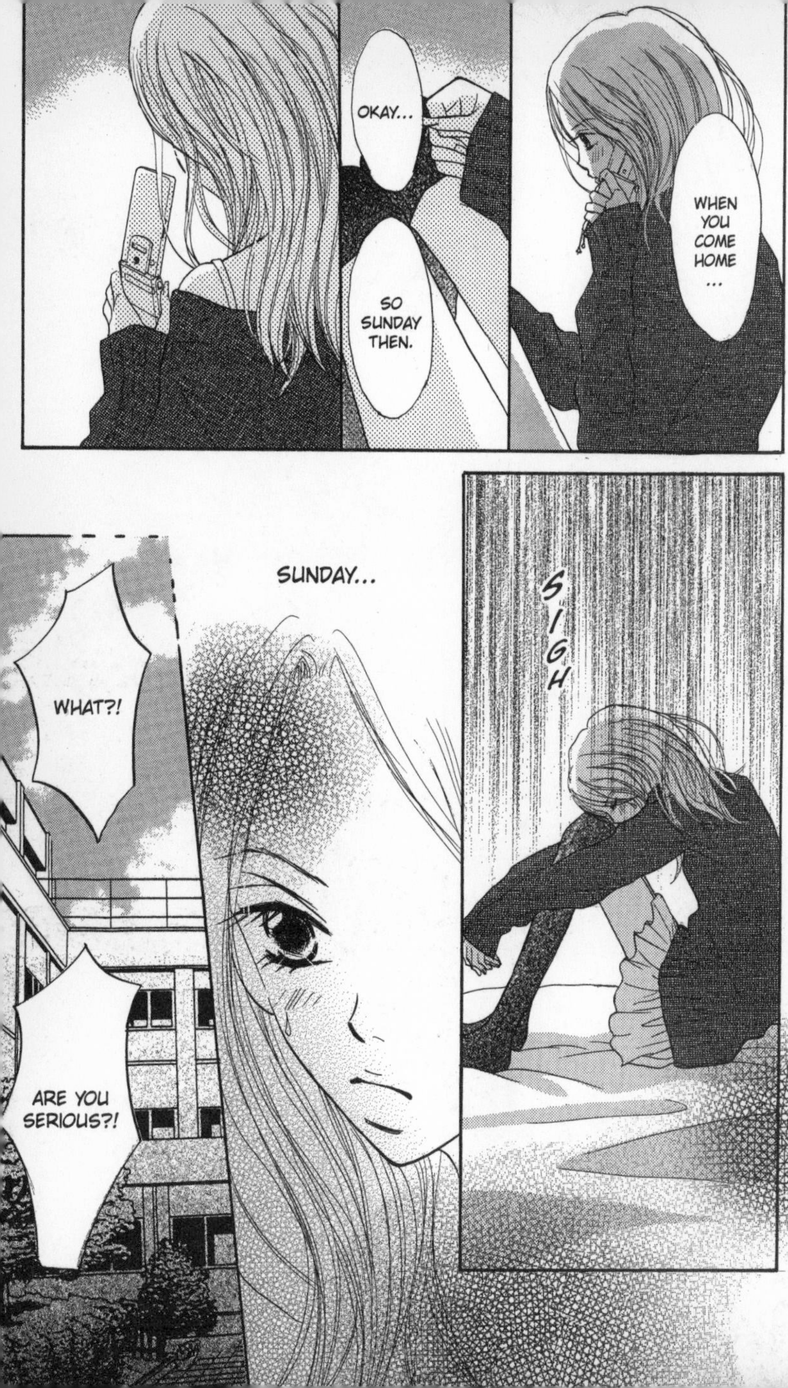
WHEN YOU COME HOME ...
OKAY...
SO SUNDAY THEN.
SIGH
SUNDAY...
WHAT?!
ARE YOU SERIOUS?!

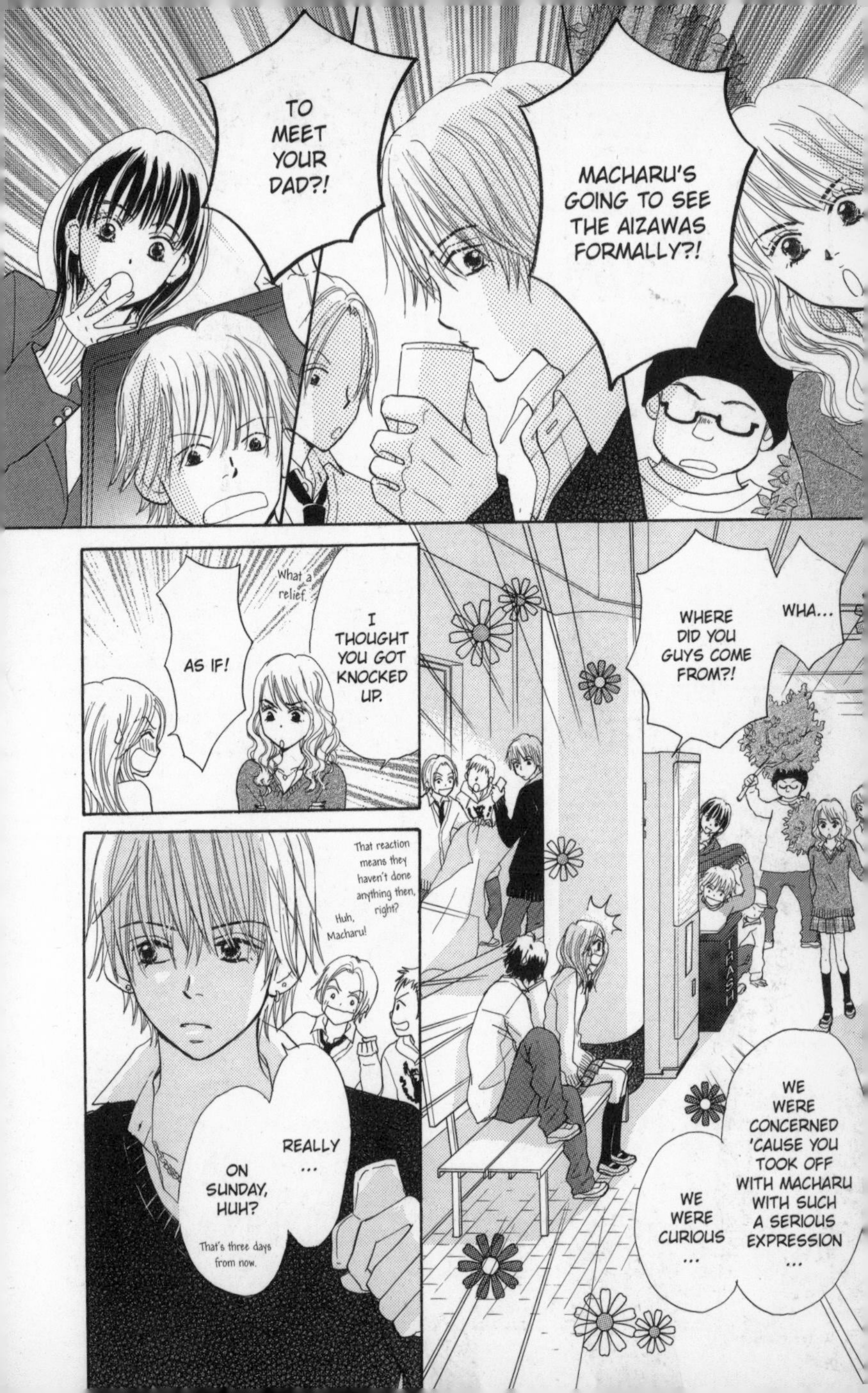
MACHARU'S GOING TO SEE THE AIZAWAS FORMALLY?!
TO MEET YOUR DAD?!
WHA...
WHERE DID YOU GUYS COME FROM?!
WE WERE CONCERNED 'CAUSE YOU TOOK OFF WITH MACHARU WITH SUCH A SERIOUS EXPRESSION ...
WE WERE CURIOUS ...
I THOUGHT YOU GOT KNOCKED UP.
What a relief.
AS IF!
That reaction means they haven't done anything then, right?
Huh, Macharu!
REALLY ...
ON SUNDAY, HUH?
That's three days from now.
TRASH

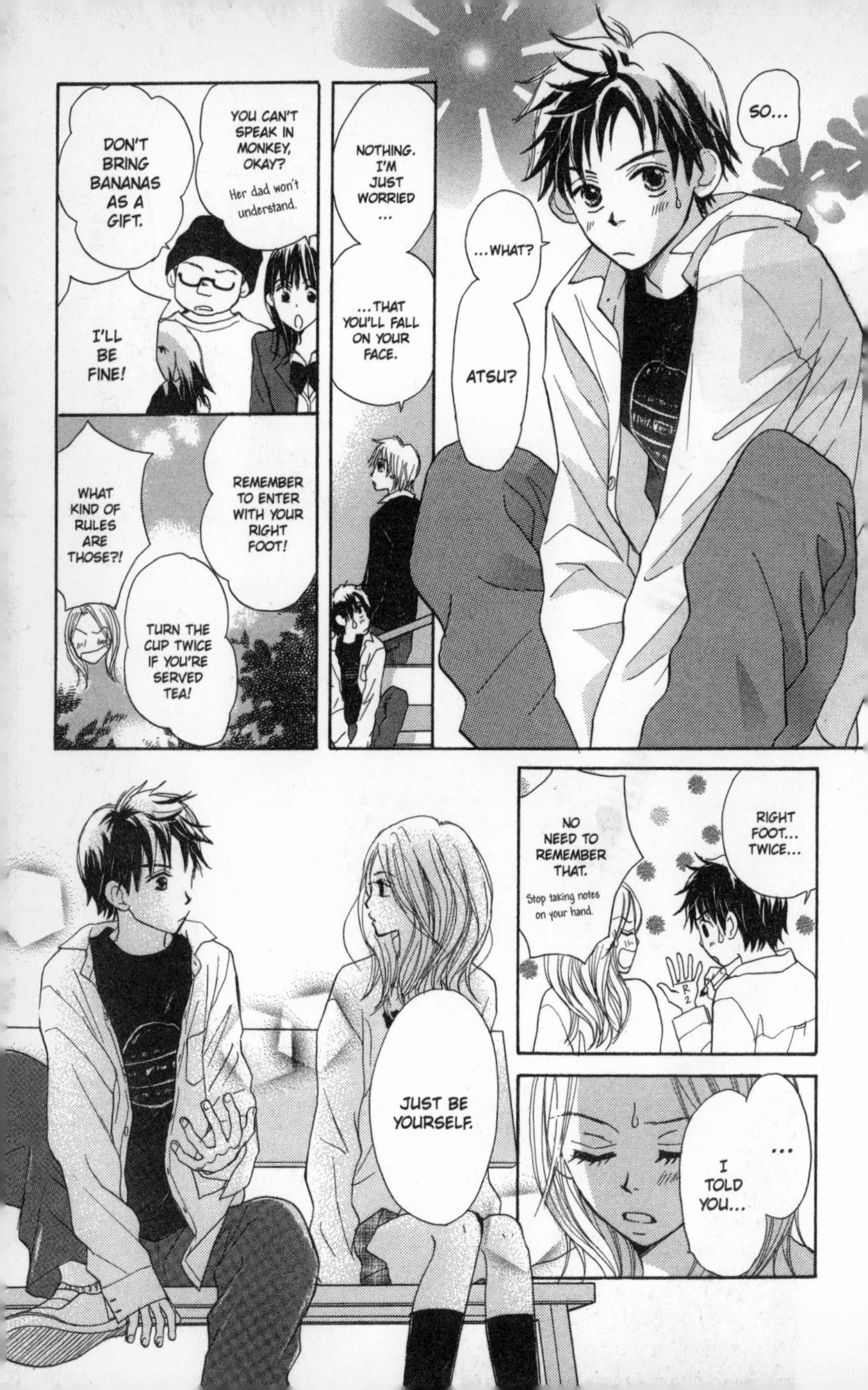
SO...
...WHAT?
ATSU?
NOTHING. I'M JUST WORRIED...
...THAT YOU'LL FALL ON YOUR FACE.
YOU CAN'T SPEAK IN MONKEY, OKAY?
Her dad won't understand.
DON'T BRING BANANAS AS A GIFT.
I'LL BE FINE!
REMEMBER TO ENTER WITH YOUR RIGHT FOOT!
WHAT KIND OF RULES ARE THOSE?!
TURN THE CUP TWICE IF YOU'RE SERVED TEA!
RIGHT FOOT... TWICE...
NO NEED TO REMEMBER THAT.
Stop taking notes on your hand.
... I TOLD YOU...
JUST BE YOURSELF.

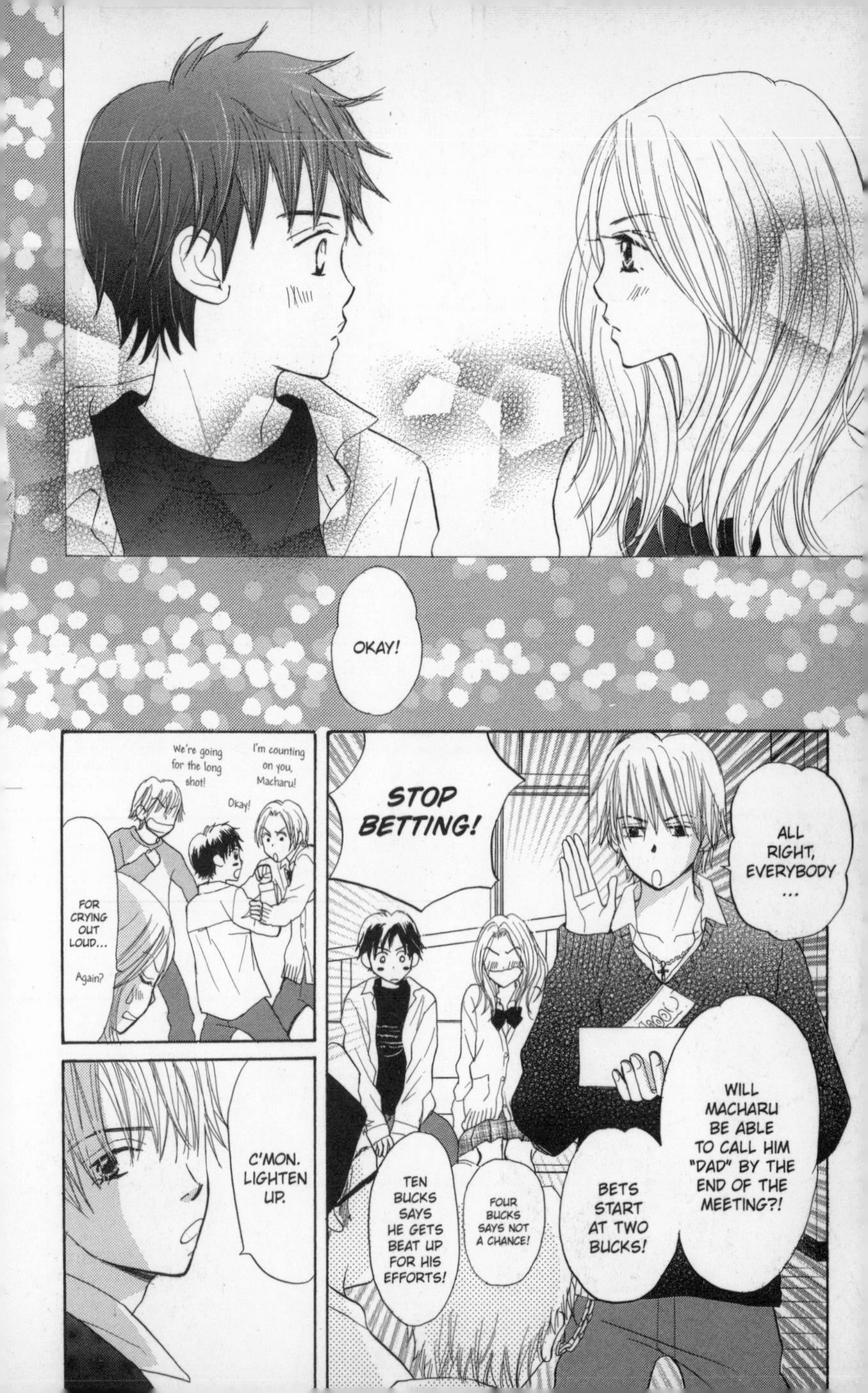
OKAY!
ALL RIGHT, EVERYBODY ...
WILL MACHARU BE ABLE TO CALL HIM "DAD" BY THE END OF THE MEETING?!
BETS START AT TWO BUCKS!
FOUR BUCKS SAYS NOT A CHANCE!
TEN BUCKS SAYS HE GETS BEAT UP FOR HIS EFFORTS!
STOP BETTING!
I'm counting on you, Macharu!
We're going for the long shot!
Okay!
FOR CRYING OUT LOUD...
Again?
C'MON. LIGHTEN UP.

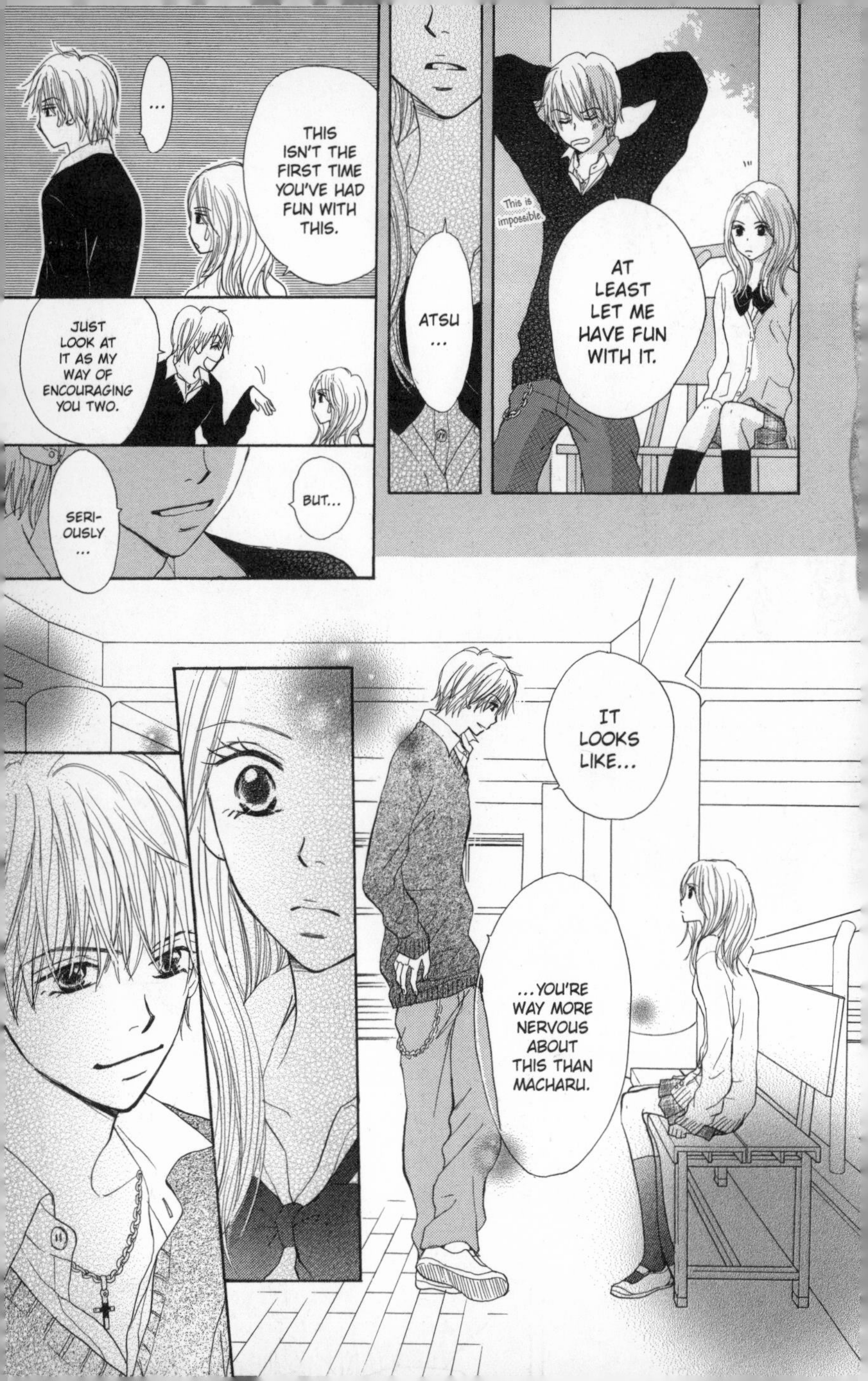
This is impossible.
AT LEAST LET ME HAVE FUN WITH IT.
ATSU...
...
THIS ISN'T THE FIRST TIME YOU'VE HAD FUN WITH THIS.
JUST LOOK AT IT AS MY WAY OF ENCOURAGING YOU TWO.
BUT...
SERI-OUSLY...
IT LOOKS LIKE...
...YOU'RE WAY MORE NERVOUS ABOUT THIS THAN MACHARU.

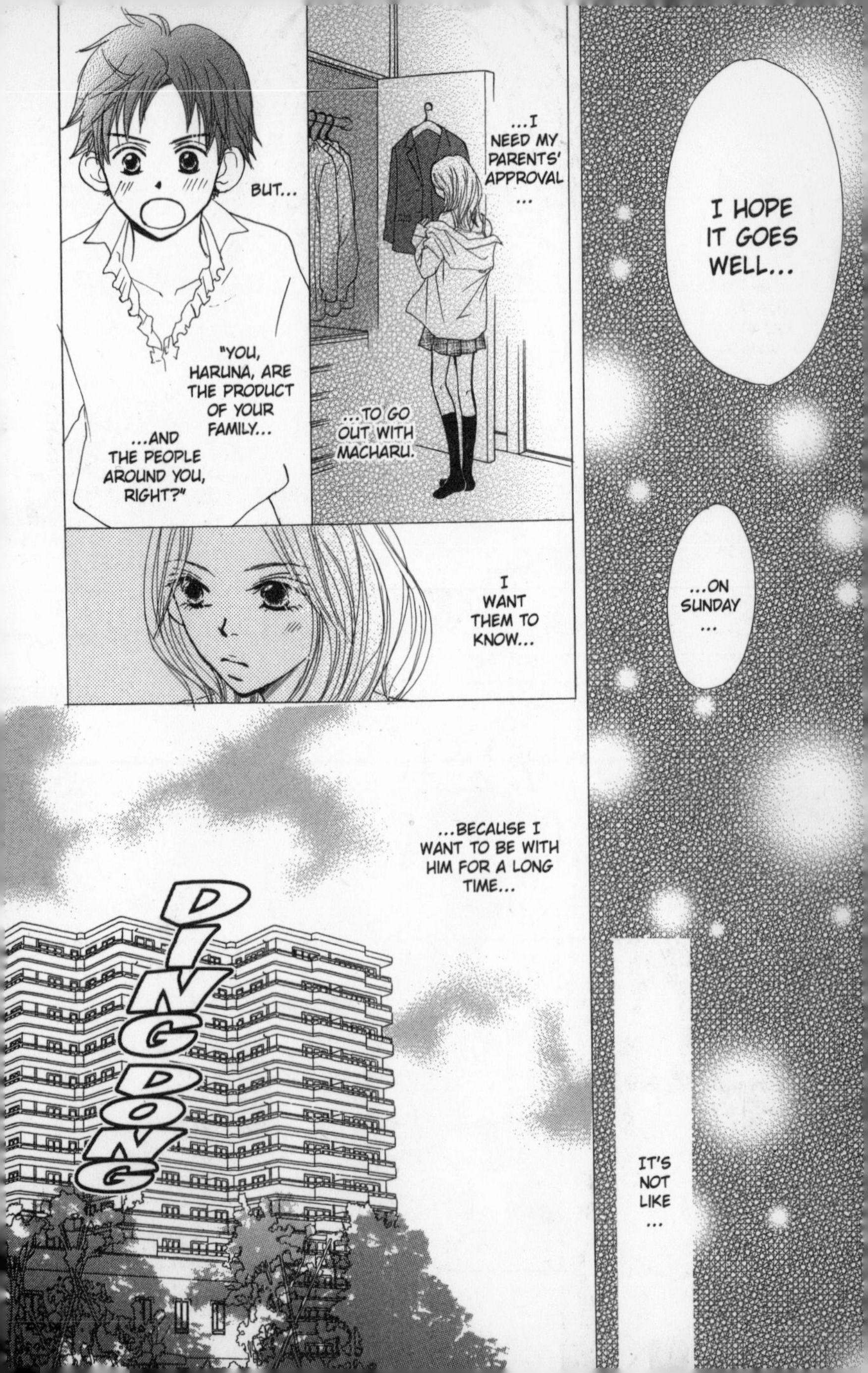
I HOPE IT GOES WELL...
...ON SUNDAY ...
IT'S NOT LIKE ...
...I NEED MY PARENTS' APPROVAL ...
...TO GO OUT WITH MACHARU.
BUT...
"YOU, HARUNA, ARE THE PRODUCT OF YOUR FAMILY...
...AND THE PEOPLE AROUND YOU, RIGHT?"
I WANT THEM TO KNOW...
...BECAUSE I WANT TO BE WITH HIM FOR A LONG TIME...
DING DONG

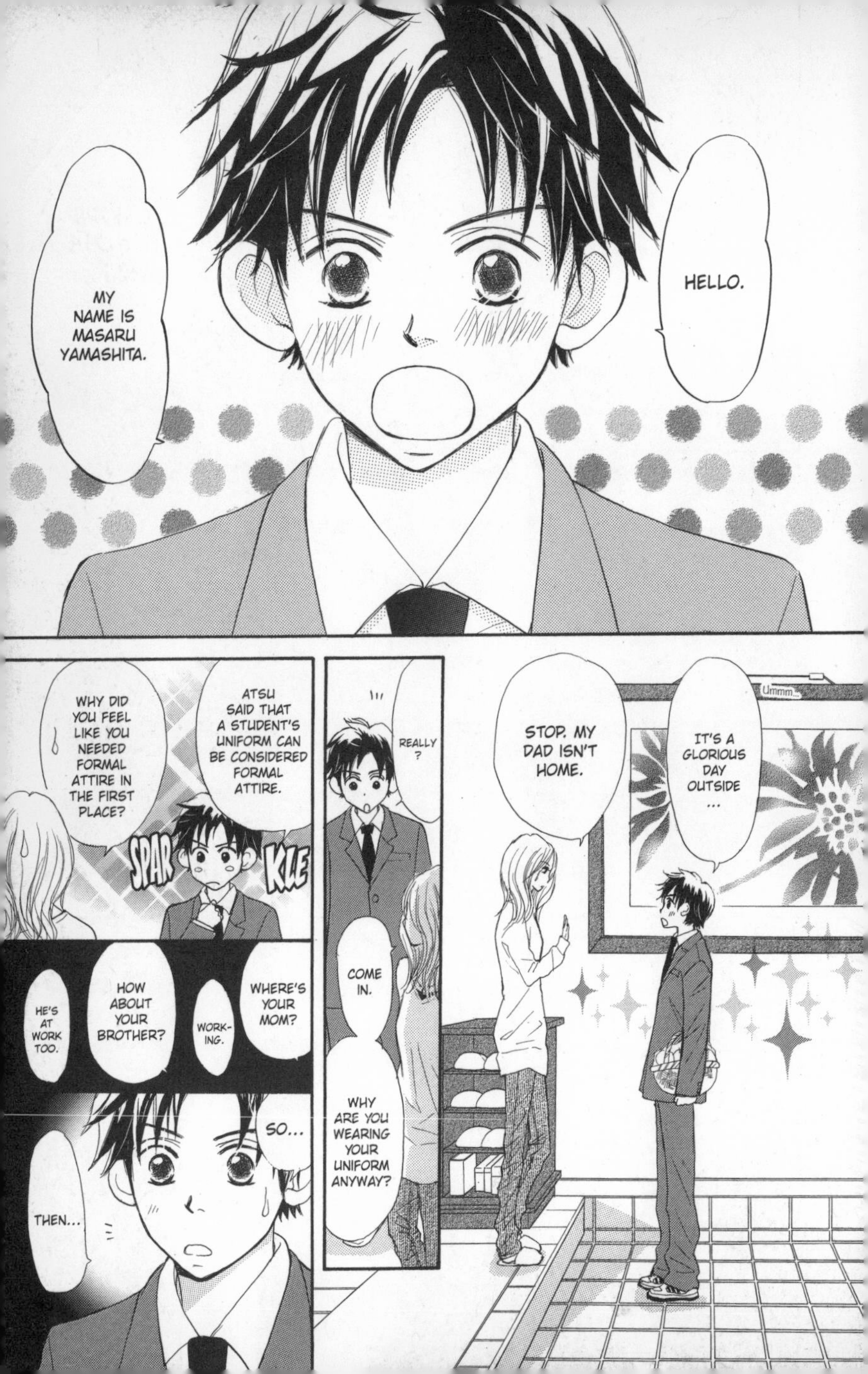
HELLO.
MY NAME IS MASARU YAMASHITA.
Ummm...
IT'S A GLORIOUS DAY OUTSIDE ...
STOP. MY DAD ISN'T HOME.
REALLY?
COME IN.
WHY ARE YOU WEARING YOUR UNIFORM ANYWAY?
ATSU SAID THAT A STUDENT'S UNIFORM CAN BE CONSIDERED FORMAL ATTIRE.
WHY DID YOU FEEL LIKE YOU NEEDED FORMAL ATTIRE IN THE FIRST PLACE?
SPAR
KLE
WHERE'S YOUR MOM?
WORKING.
HOW ABOUT YOUR BROTHER?
HE'S AT WORK TOO.
SO...
THEN...

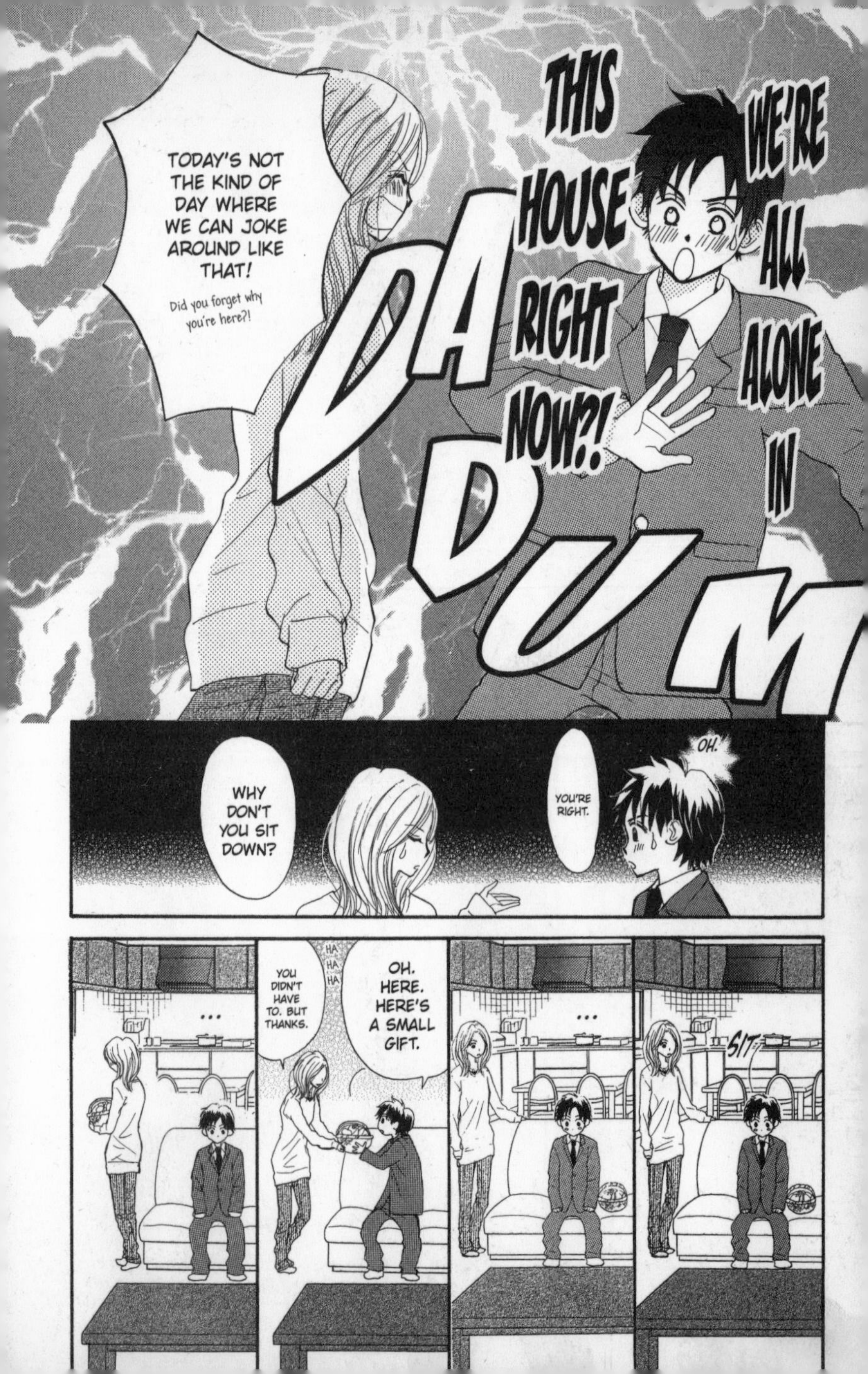
WE'RE ALL ALONE IN
THIS HOUSE RIGHT NOW?!
DA DUM
TODAY'S NOT THE KIND OF DAY WHERE WE CAN JOKE AROUND LIKE THAT!
Did you forget why you're here?!
OH.
YOU'RE RIGHT.
WHY DON'T YOU SIT DOWN?
SIT
...
OH. HERE. HERE'S A SMALL GIFT.
HA HA HA
YOU DIDN'T HAVE TO. BUT THANKS.
...

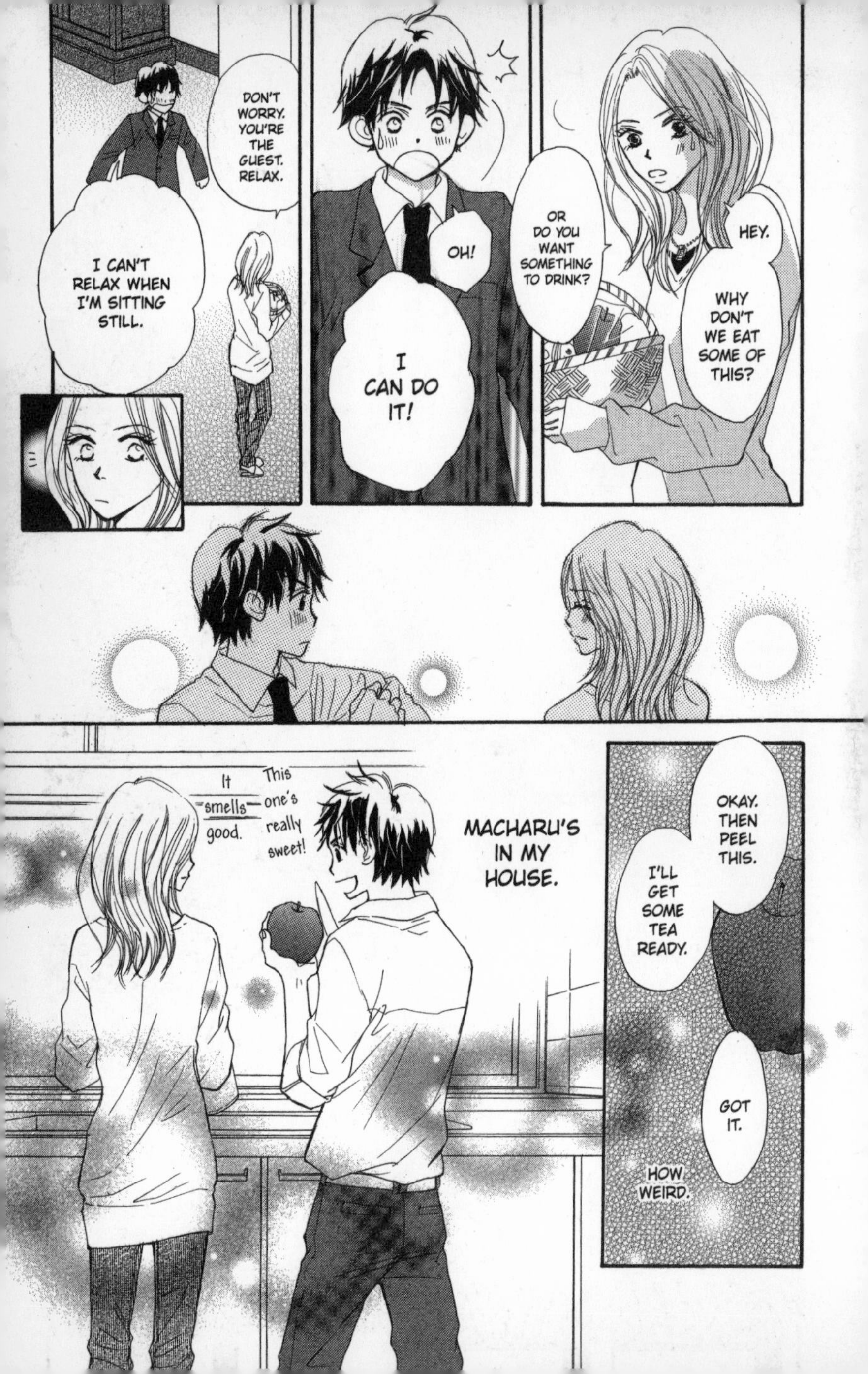
HEY.
WHY DON'T WE EAT SOME OF THIS?
OR DO YOU WANT SOMETHING TO DRINK?
OH!
I CAN DO IT!
DON'T WORRY. YOU'RE THE GUEST. RELAX.
I CAN'T RELAX WHEN I'M SITTING STILL.
OKAY. THEN PEEL THIS.
I'LL GET SOME TEA READY.
GOT IT.
HOW WEIRD.
MACHARU'S IN MY HOUSE.
This one's really sweet!
It smells good.

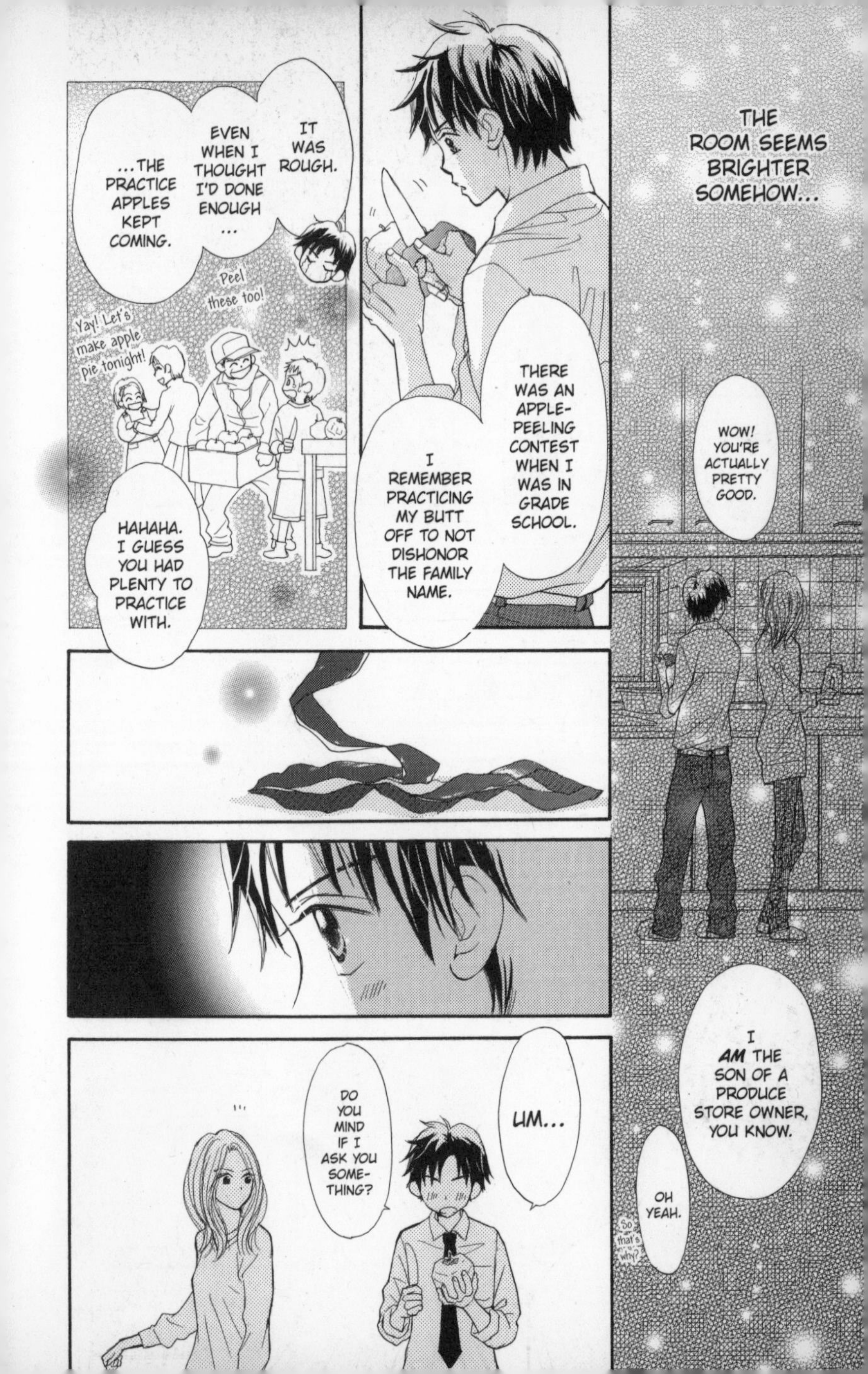
THE ROOM SEEMS BRIGHTER SOMEHOW...
WOW! YOU'RE ACTUALLY PRETTY GOOD.
I AM THE SON OF A PRODUCE STORE OWNER, YOU KNOW.
OH YEAH.
So that's why?
THERE WAS AN APPLE-PEELING CONTEST WHEN I WAS IN GRADE SCHOOL.
I REMEMBER PRACTICING MY BUTT OFF TO NOT DISHONOR THE FAMILY NAME.
IT WAS ROUGH.
EVEN WHEN I THOUGHT I'D DONE ENOUGH...
...THE PRACTICE APPLES KEPT COMING.
Peel these too!
Yay! Let's make apple pie tonight!
HAHAHA. I GUESS YOU HAD PLENTY TO PRACTICE WITH.
UM...
DO YOU MIND IF I ASK YOU SOMETHING?

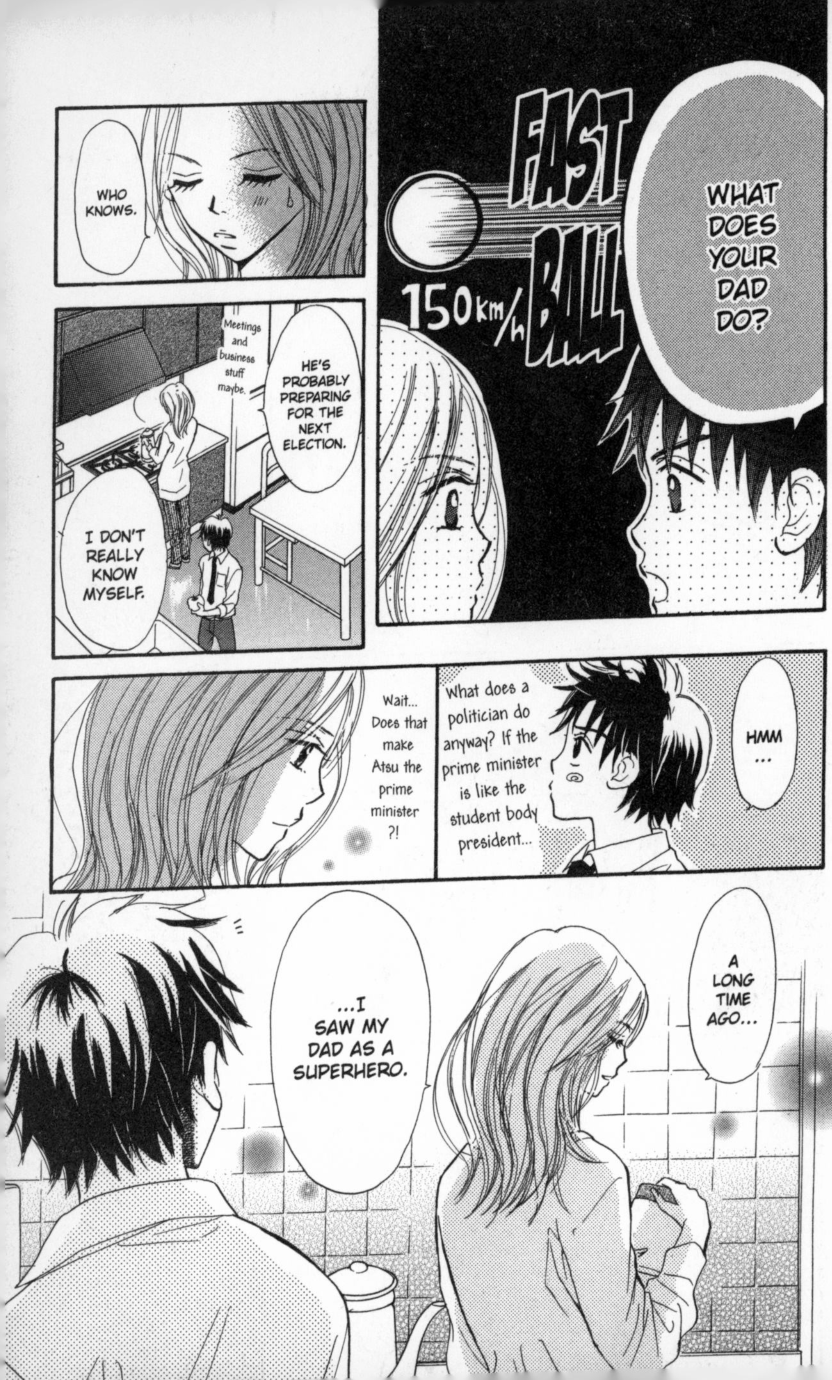
WHAT DOES YOUR DAD DO?
FAST BALL
150km/h
WHO KNOWS.
HE'S PROBABLY PREPARING FOR THE NEXT ELECTION.
Meetings and business stuff maybe.
I DON'T REALLY KNOW MYSELF.
HMM...
What does a politician do anyway? If the prime minister is like the student body president...
Wait... Does that make Atsu the prime minister?!
A LONG TIME AGO...
...I SAW MY DAD AS A SUPERHERO.

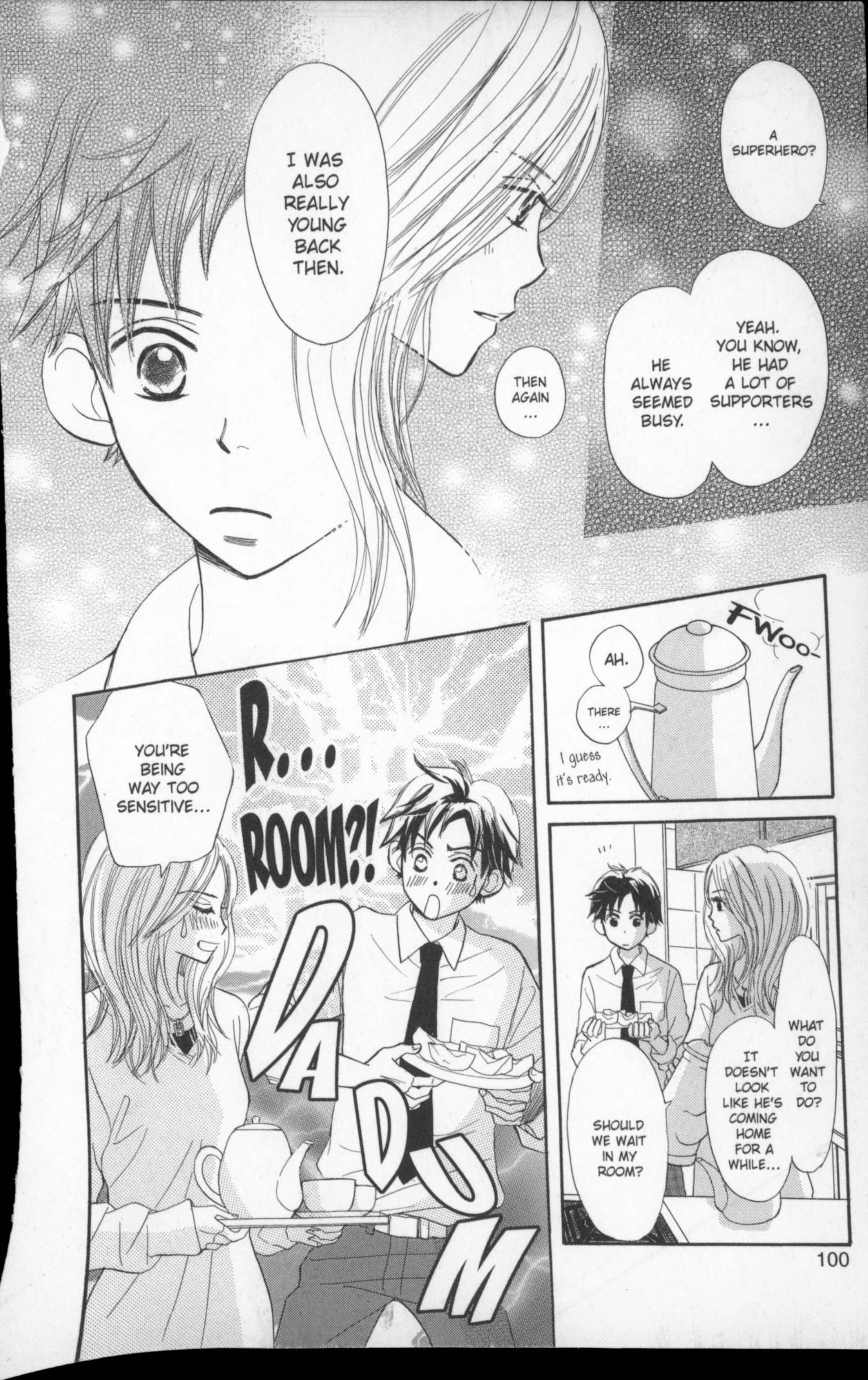

A SUPERHERO?
YEAH. YOU KNOW, HE HAD A LOT OF SUPPORTERS...
HE ALWAYS SEEMED BUSY.
THEN AGAIN...
I WAS ALSO REALLY YOUNG BACK THEN.
FWOO-
AH.
THERE...
I guess it's ready.
WHAT DO YOU WANT TO DO?
IT DOESN'T LOOK LIKE HE'S COMING HOME FOR A WHILE...
SHOULD WE WAIT IN MY ROOM?
R... ROOM?!
DADUM
YOU'RE BEING WAY TOO SENSITIVE...

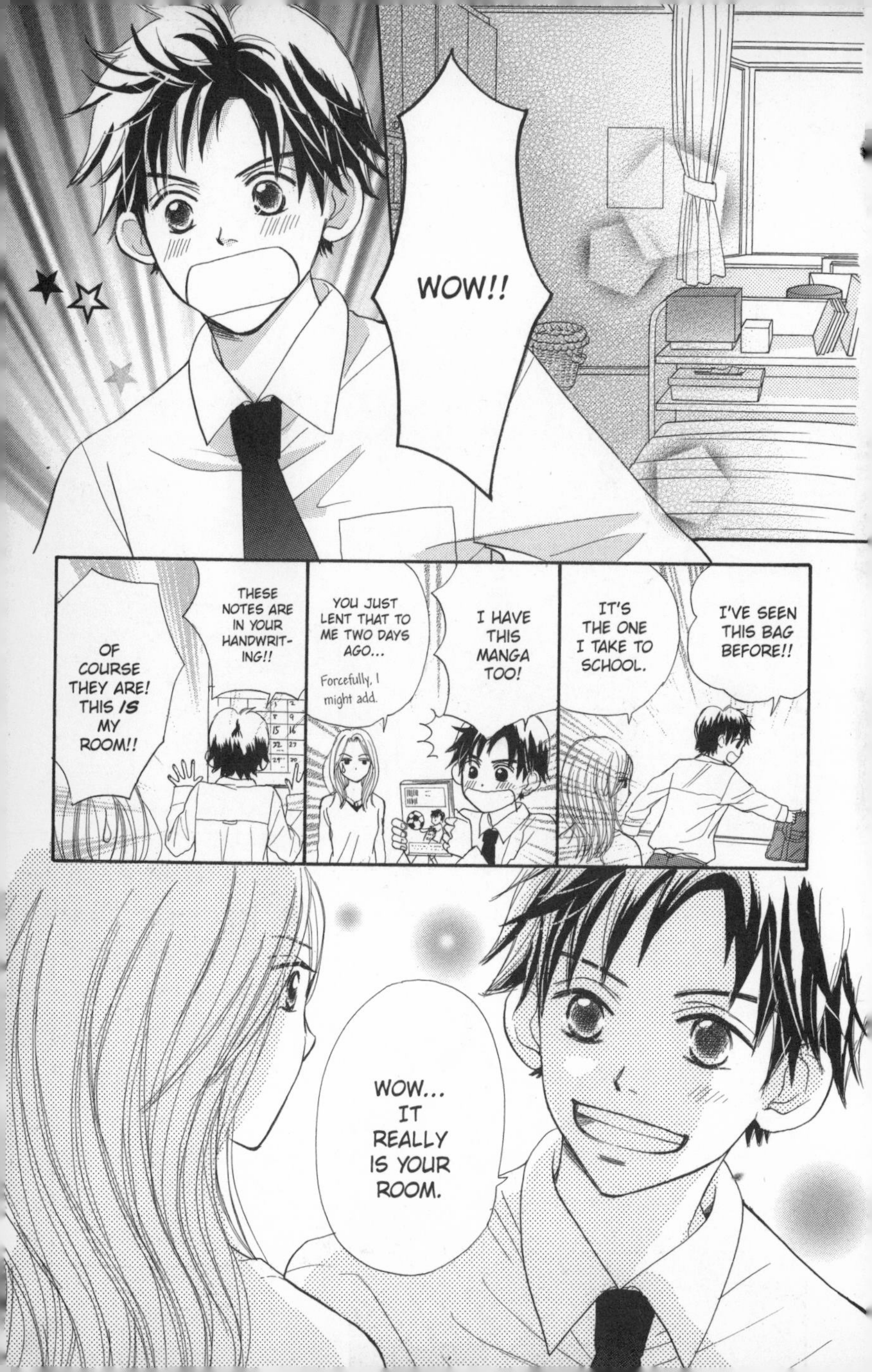
WOW!!
I'VE SEEN THIS BAG BEFORE!!
IT'S THE ONE I TAKE TO SCHOOL.
I HAVE THIS MANGA TOO!
YOU JUST LENT THAT TO ME TWO DAYS AGO...
Forcefully, I might add.
THESE NOTES ARE IN YOUR HANDWRITING!!
OF COURSE THEY ARE! THIS *IS* MY ROOM!!
WOW... IT REALLY IS YOUR ROOM.

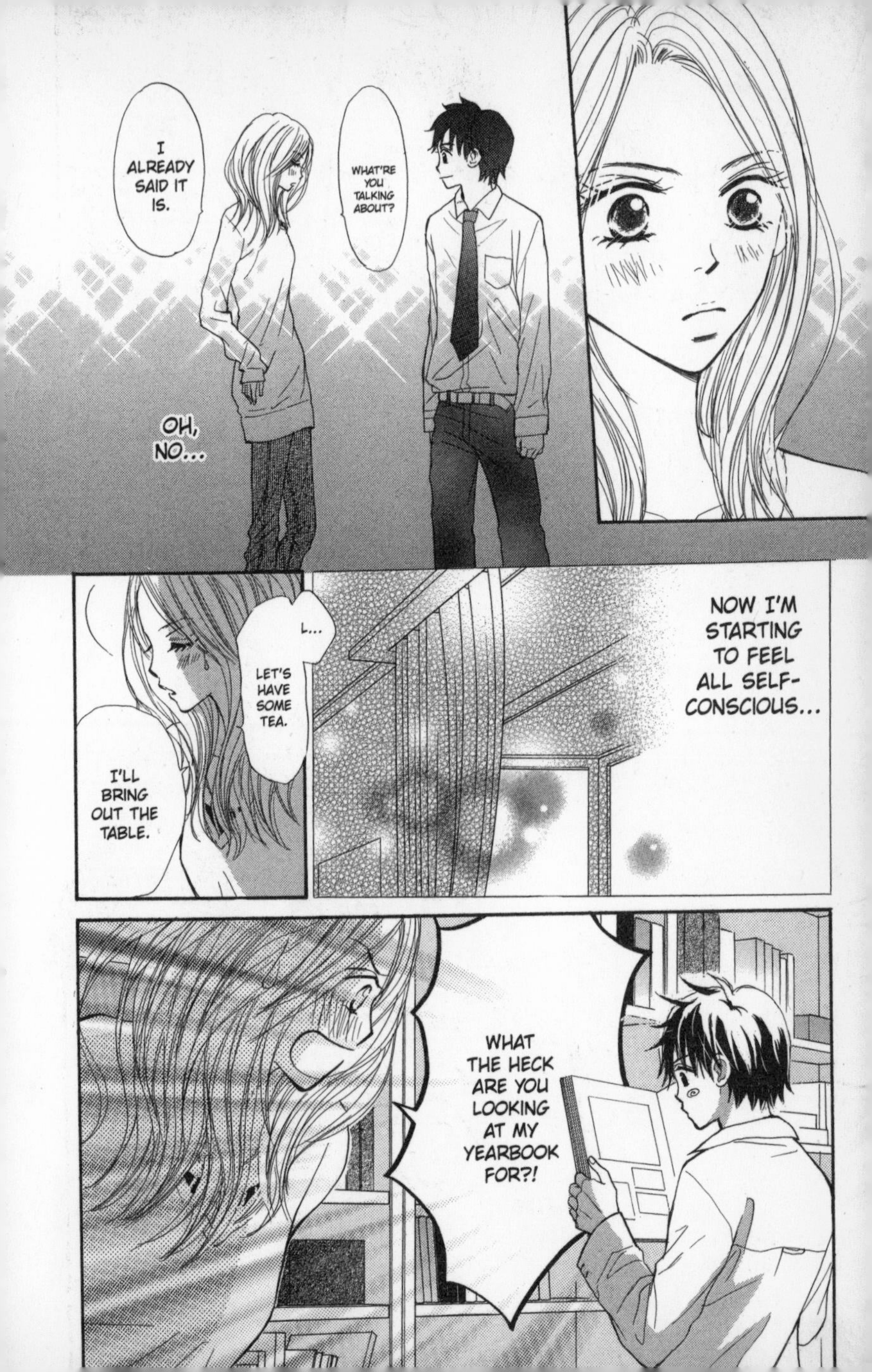
WHAT'RE YOU TALKING ABOUT?
I ALREADY SAID IT IS.
OH, NO...
NOW I'M STARTING TO FEEL ALL SELF-CONSCIOUS...
I...
LET'S HAVE SOME TEA.
I'LL BRING OUT THE TABLE.
WHAT THE HECK ARE YOU LOOKING AT MY YEARBOOK FOR?!

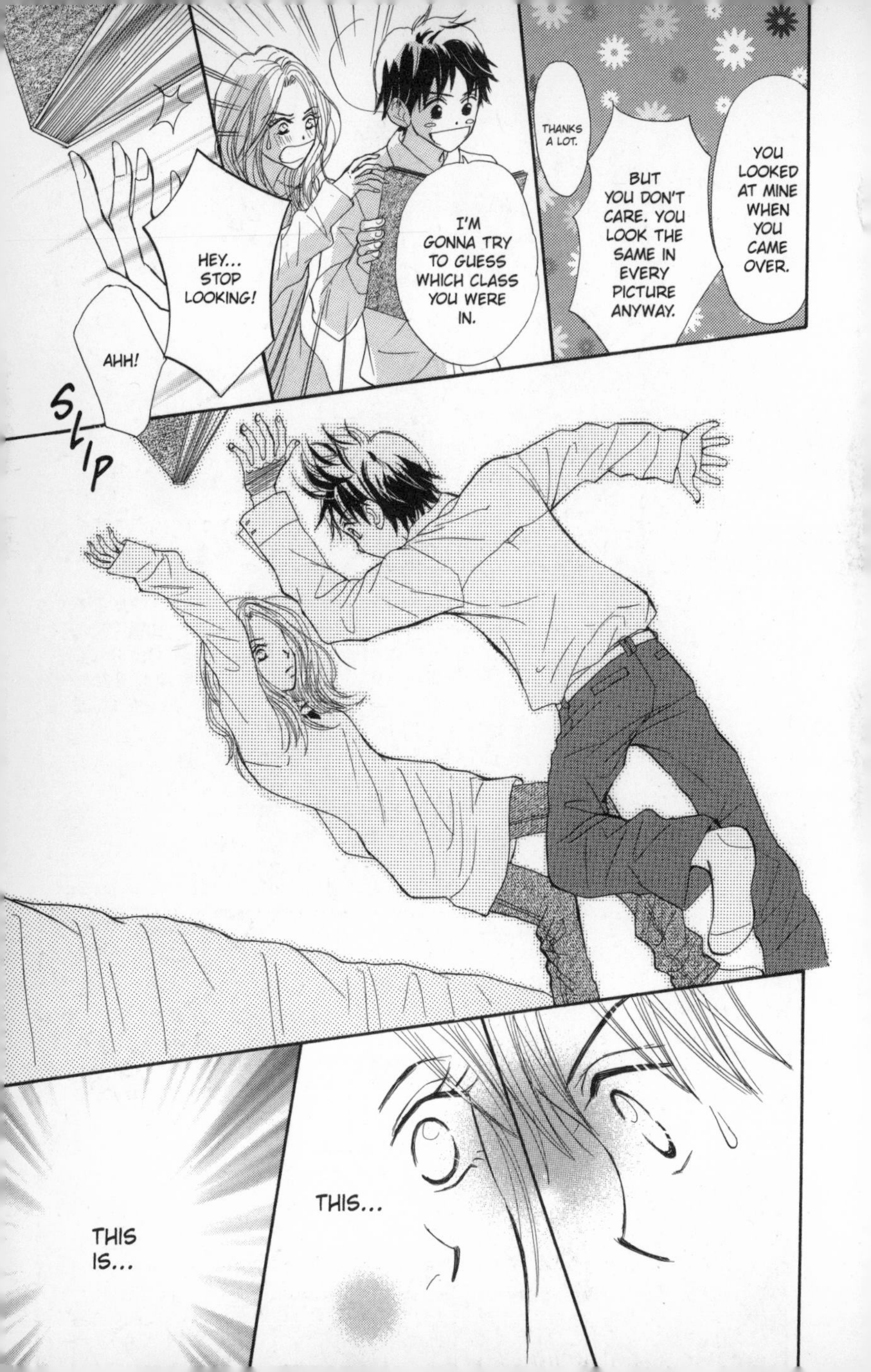
YOU LOOKED AT MINE WHEN YOU CAME OVER.
BUT YOU DON'T CARE. YOU LOOK THE SAME IN EVERY PICTURE ANYWAY.
THANKS A LOT.
I'M GONNA TRY TO GUESS WHICH CLASS YOU WERE IN.
HEY... STOP LOOKING!
AHH!
SLIP
THIS...
THIS IS...

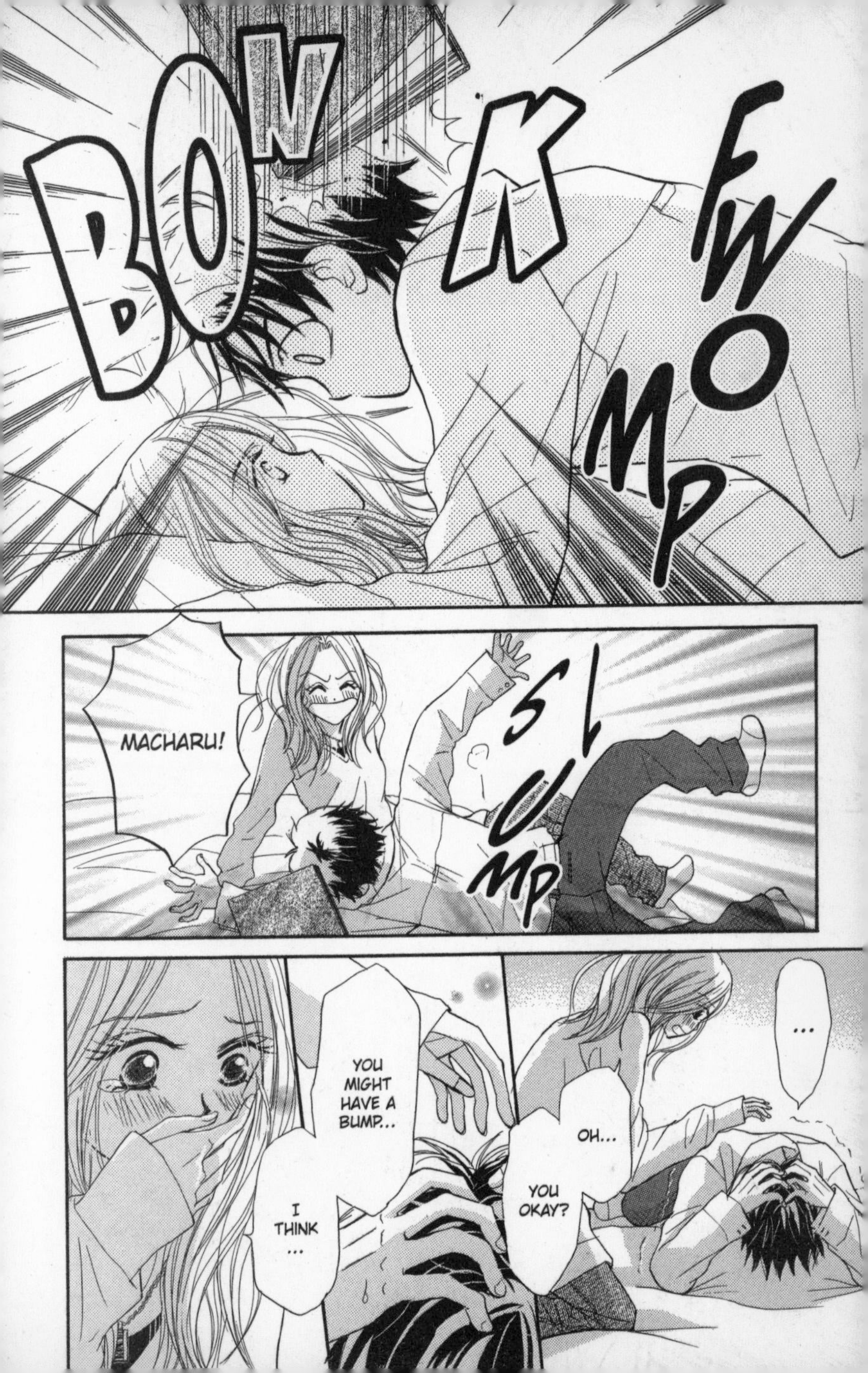
FWOMP
BONK
SLUMP
MACHARU!
...
OH...
YOU OKAY?
YOU MIGHT HAVE A BUMP...
I THINK ...

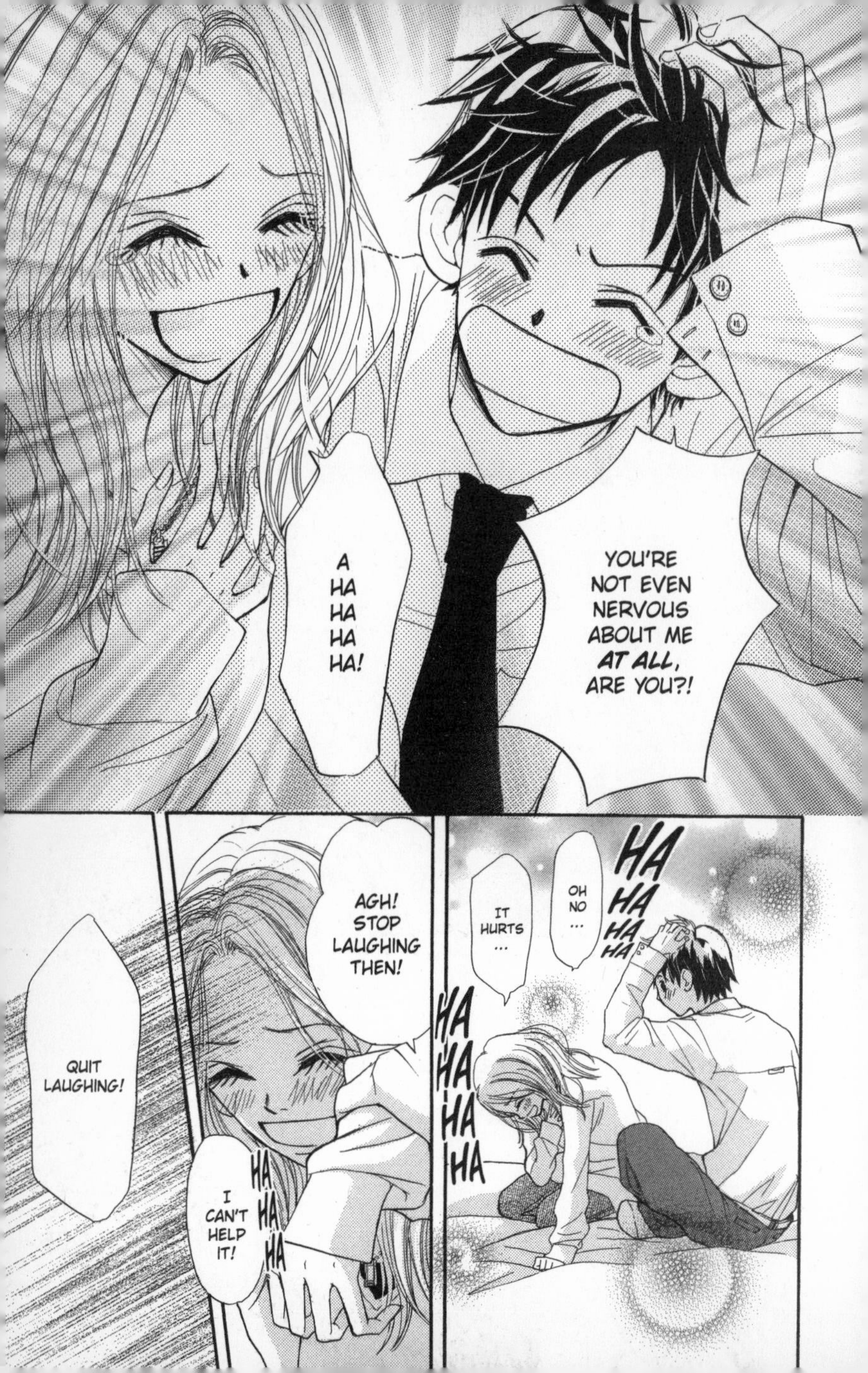
YOU'RE NOT EVEN NERVOUS ABOUT ME *AT ALL*, ARE YOU?!
A HA HA HA HA!
HA HA HA HA
OH NO ...
IT HURTS ...
HA HA HA HA HA
AGH! STOP LAUGHING THEN!
I CAN'T HELP IT!
HA HA HA
QUIT LAUGHING!

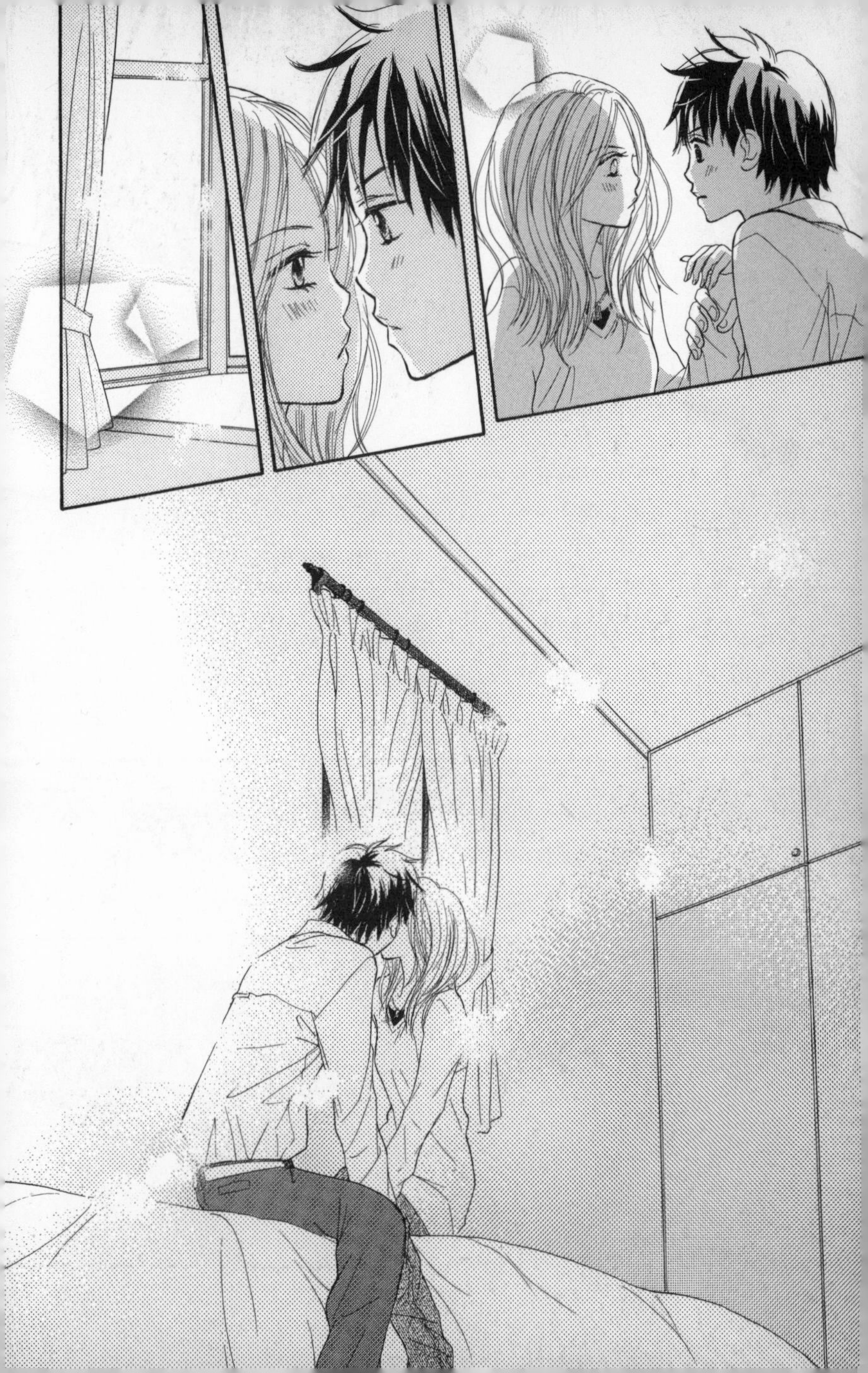

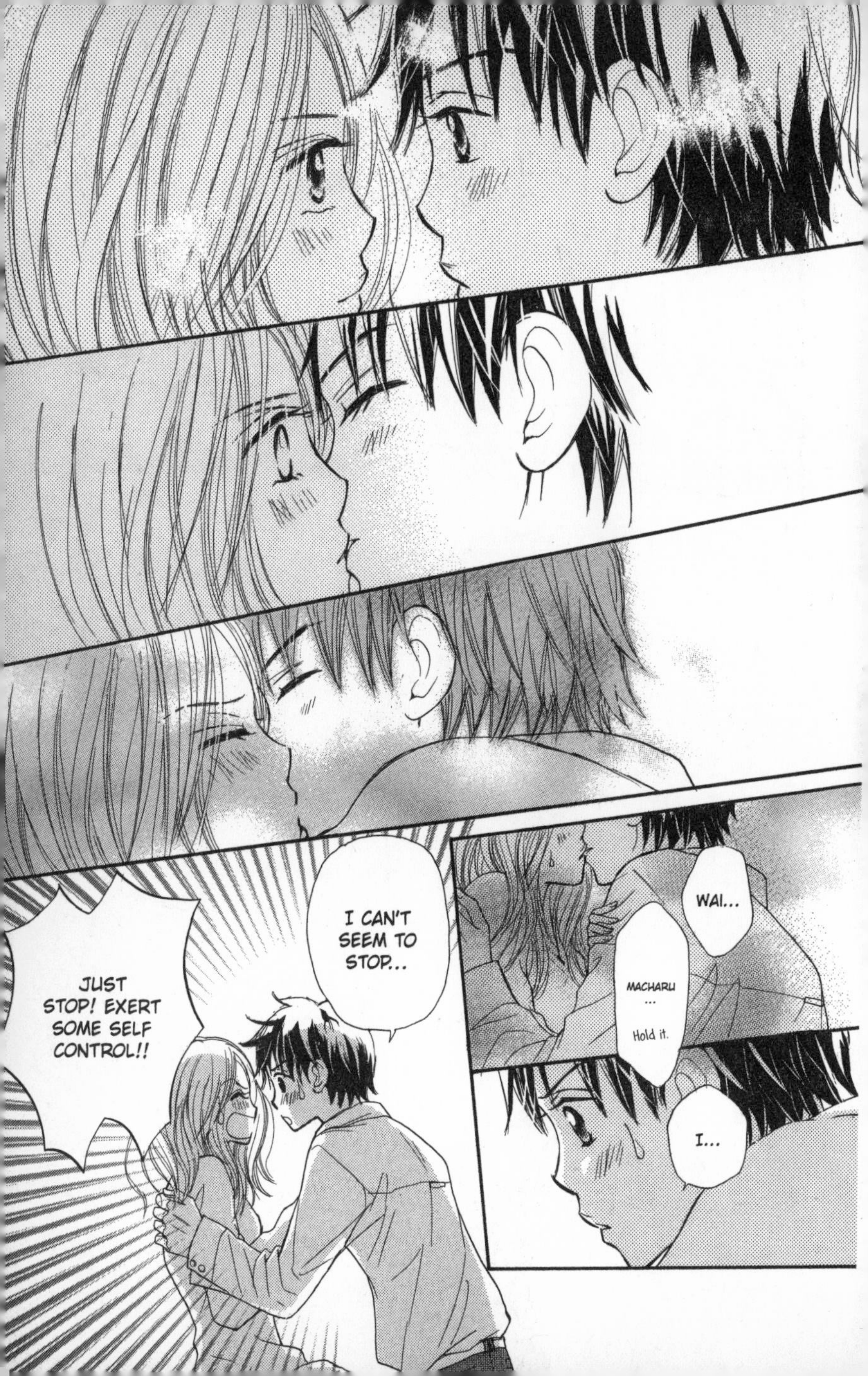
WAI...
MACHARU ... Hold it.
I...
I CAN'T SEEM TO STOP...
JUST STOP! EXERT SOME SELF CONTROL!!

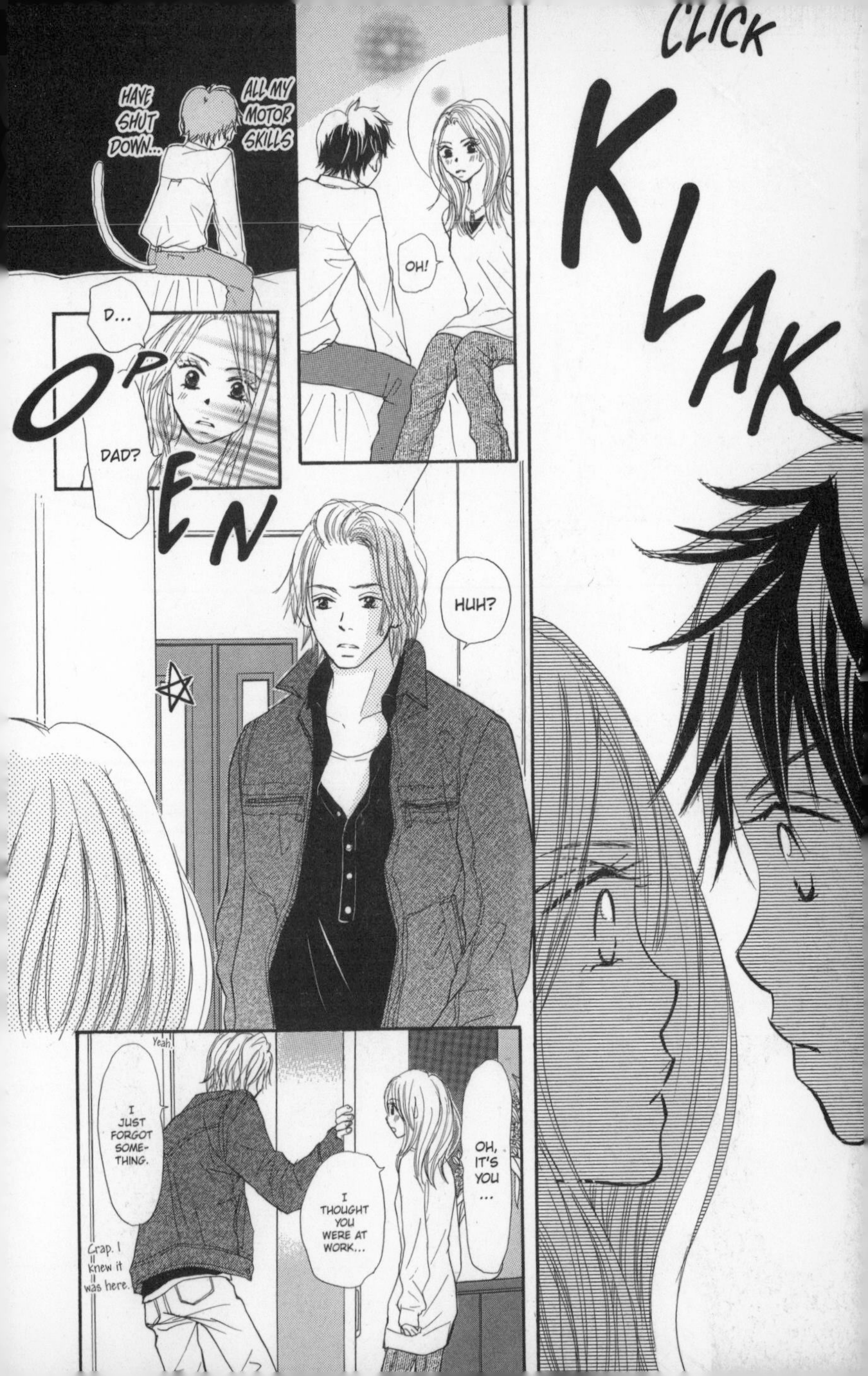
CLICK
KLAK
OH!
ALL MY MOTOR SKILLS
HAVE SHUT DOWN...
D...
DAD?
OPEN
HUH?
OH, IT'S YOU...
I THOUGHT YOU WERE AT WORK...
Yeah.
I JUST FORGOT SOMETHING.
Crap. I knew it was here.

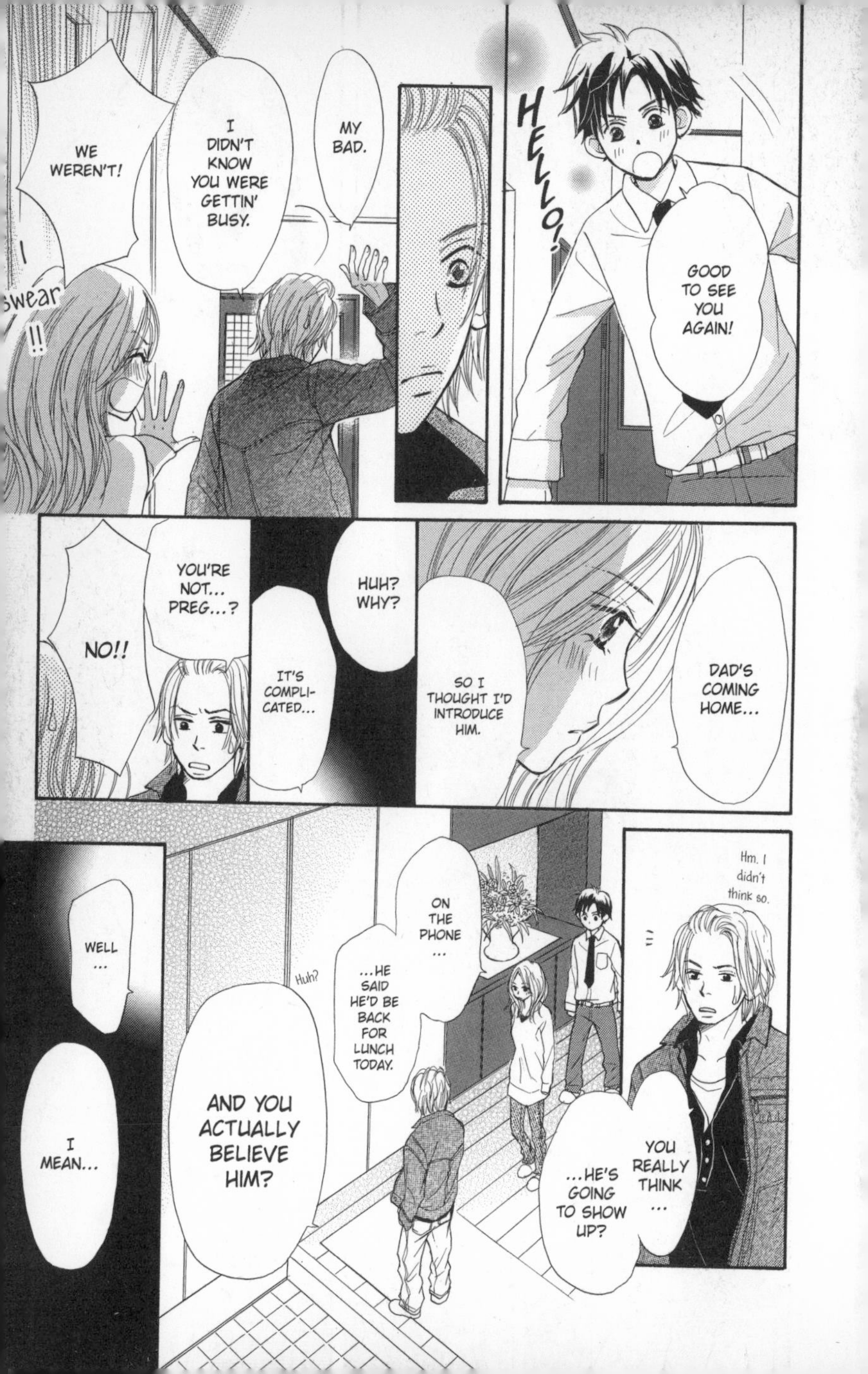
HELLO!
GOOD TO SEE YOU AGAIN!
MY BAD.
I DIDN'T KNOW YOU WERE GETTIN' BUSY.
WE WEREN'T!
I swear!!
DAD'S COMING HOME...
SO I THOUGHT I'D INTRODUCE HIM.
HUH? WHY?
IT'S COMPLI-CATED...
YOU'RE NOT... PREG...?
NO!!
Hm. I didn't think so.
YOU REALLY THINK...
...HE'S GOING TO SHOW UP?
ON THE PHONE...
...HE SAID HE'D BE BACK FOR LUNCH TODAY.
Huh?
AND YOU ACTUALLY BELIEVE HIM?
WELL...
I MEAN...

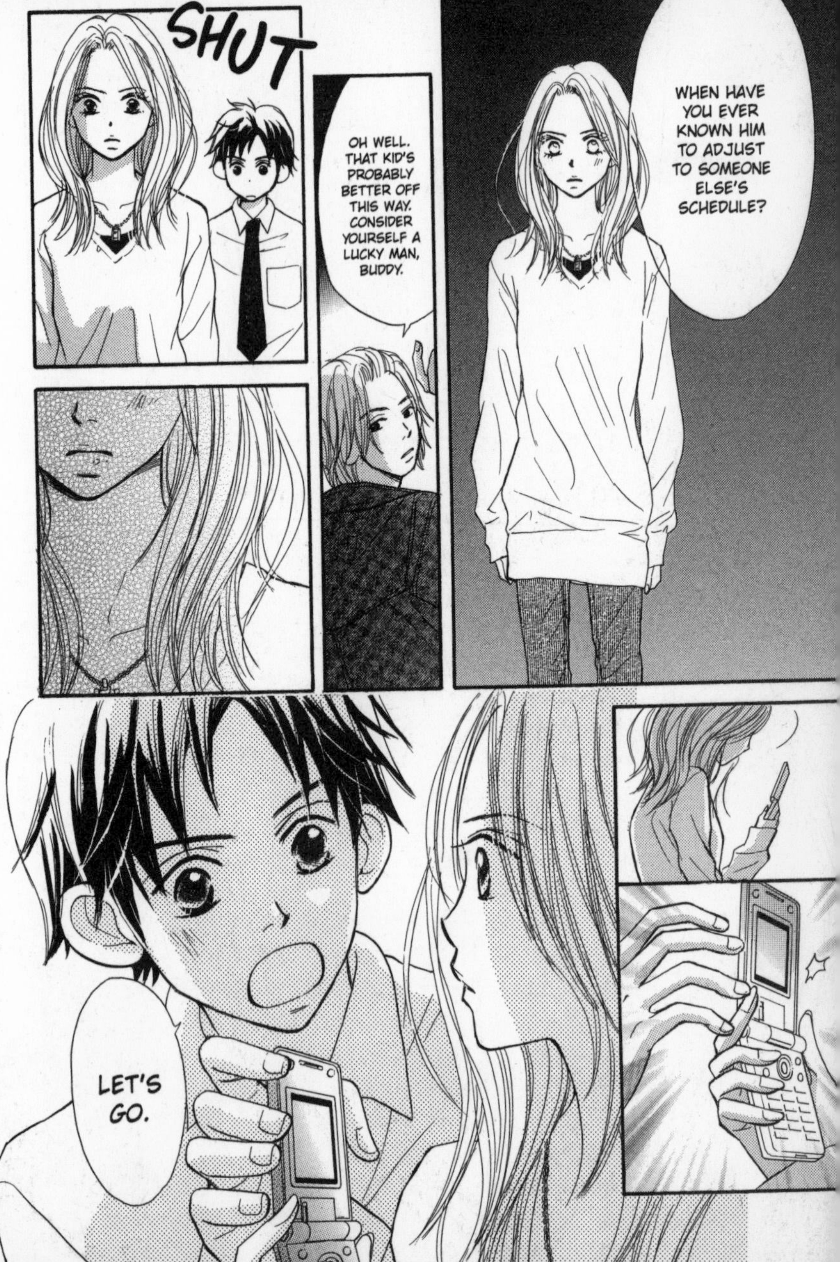
WHEN HAVE YOU EVER KNOWN HIM TO ADJUST TO SOMEONE ELSE'S SCHEDULE?
OH WELL. THAT KID'S PROBABLY BETTER OFF THIS WAY. CONSIDER YOURSELF A LUCKY MAN, BUDDY.
SHUT
LET'S GO.

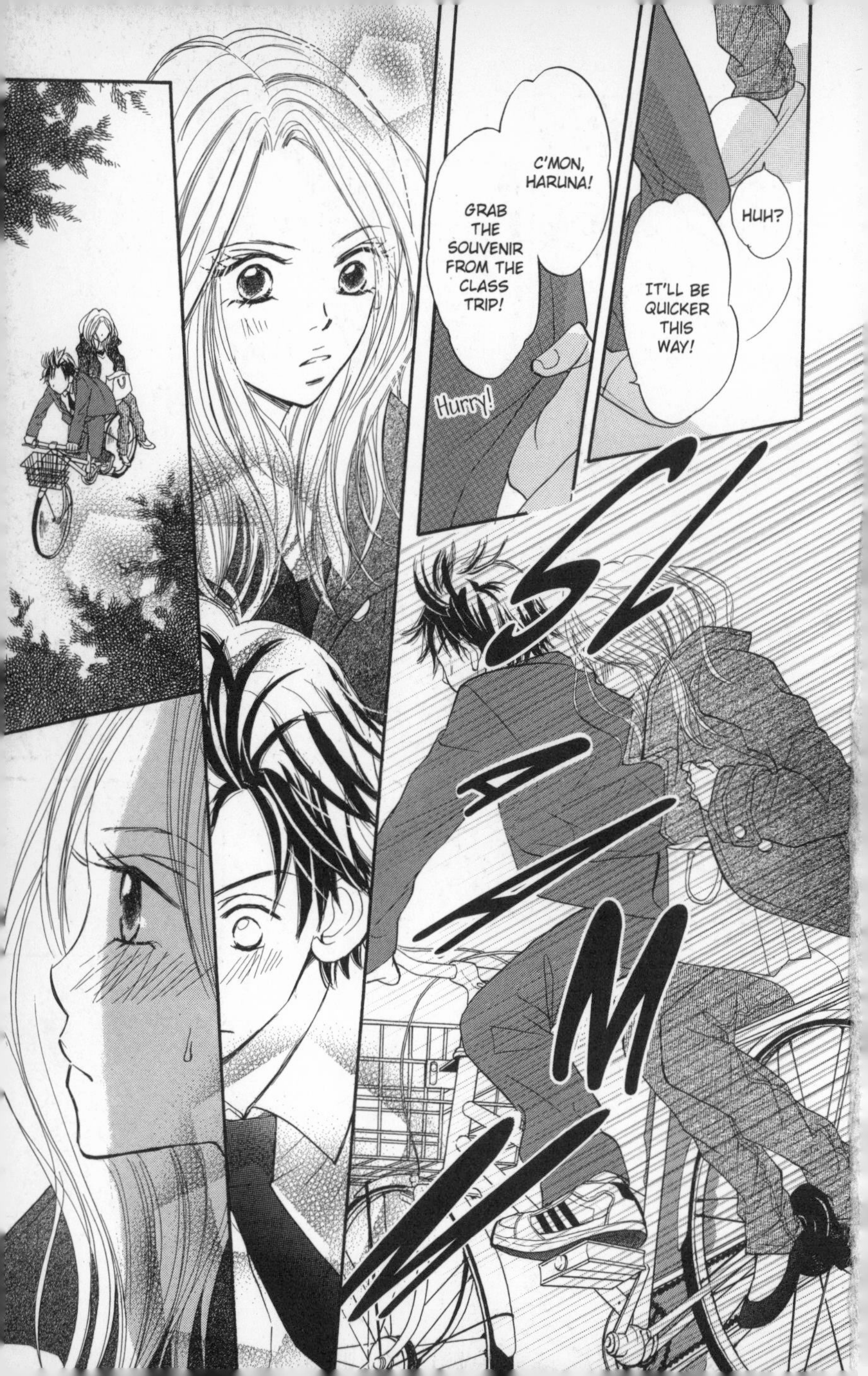
HUH?
IT'LL BE QUICKER THIS WAY!
C'MON, HARUNA!
GRAB THE SOUVENIR FROM THE CLASS TRIP!
Hurry!
SLAM

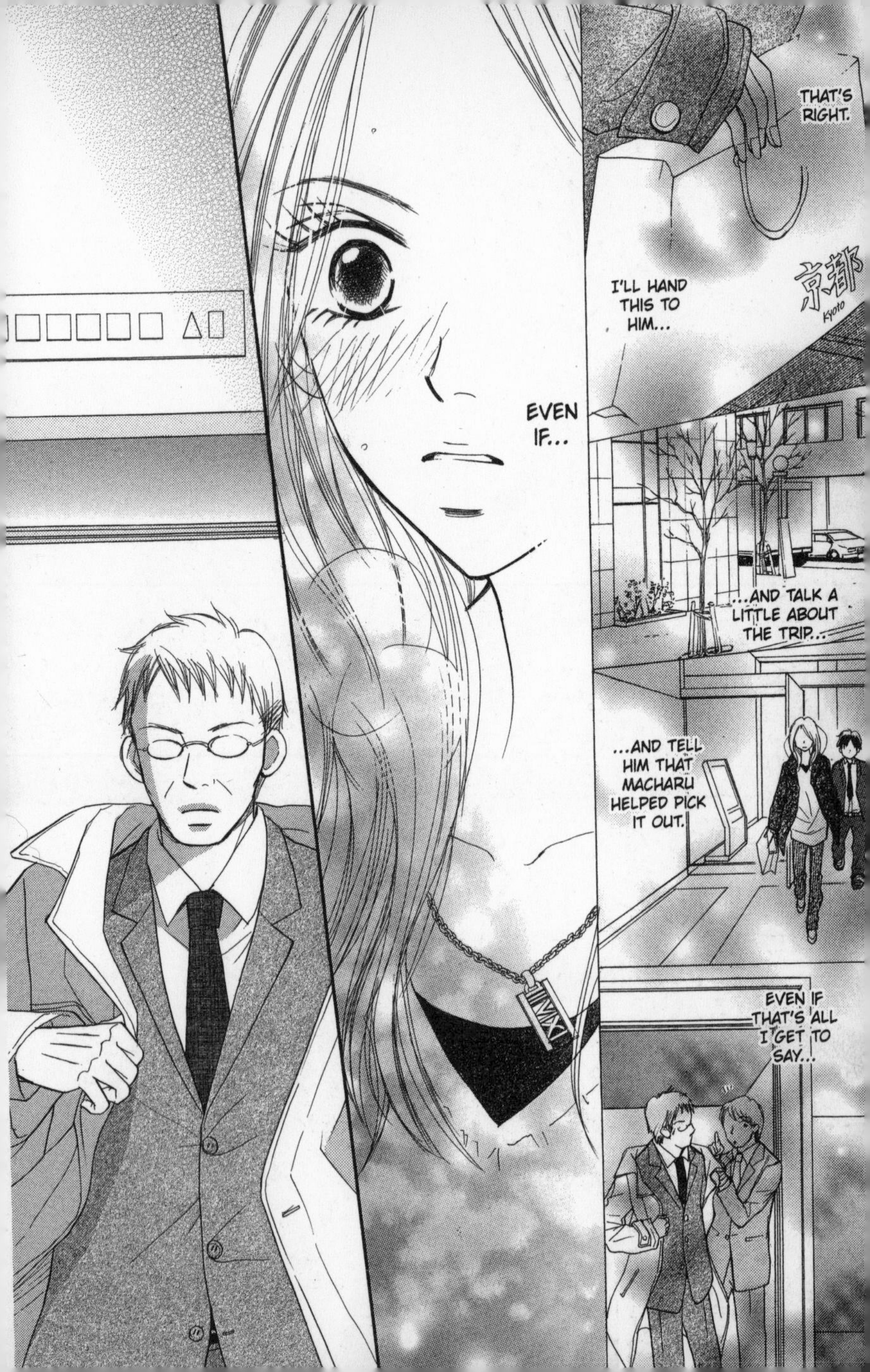
THAT'S RIGHT.
京都
Kyoto
I'LL HAND THIS TO HIM...
...AND TALK A LITTLE ABOUT THE TRIP...
...AND TELL HIM THAT MACHARU HELPED PICK IT OUT.
EVEN IF THAT'S ALL I GET TO SAY...
EVEN IF...

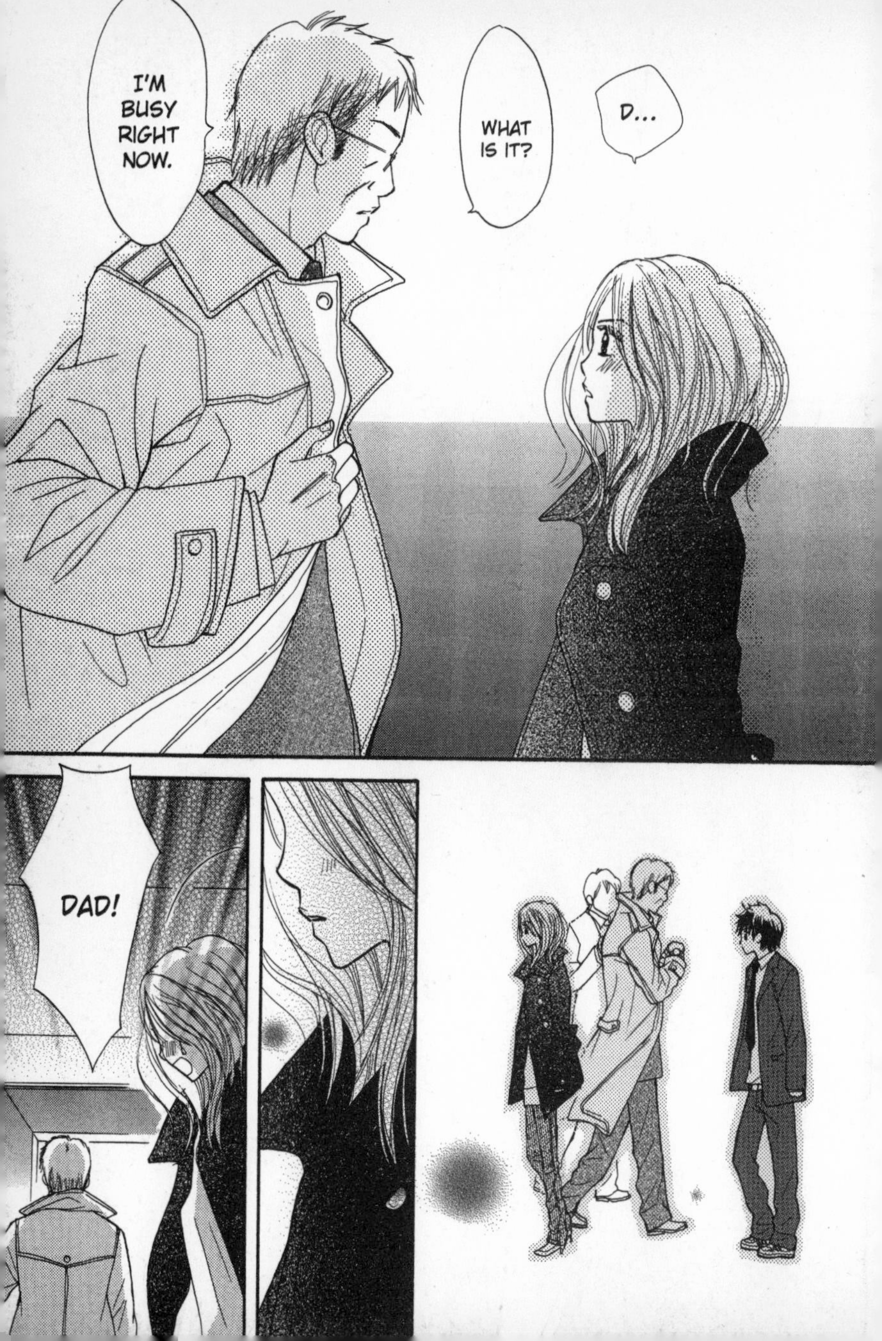
D...
WHAT IS IT?
I'M BUSY RIGHT NOW.
DAD!

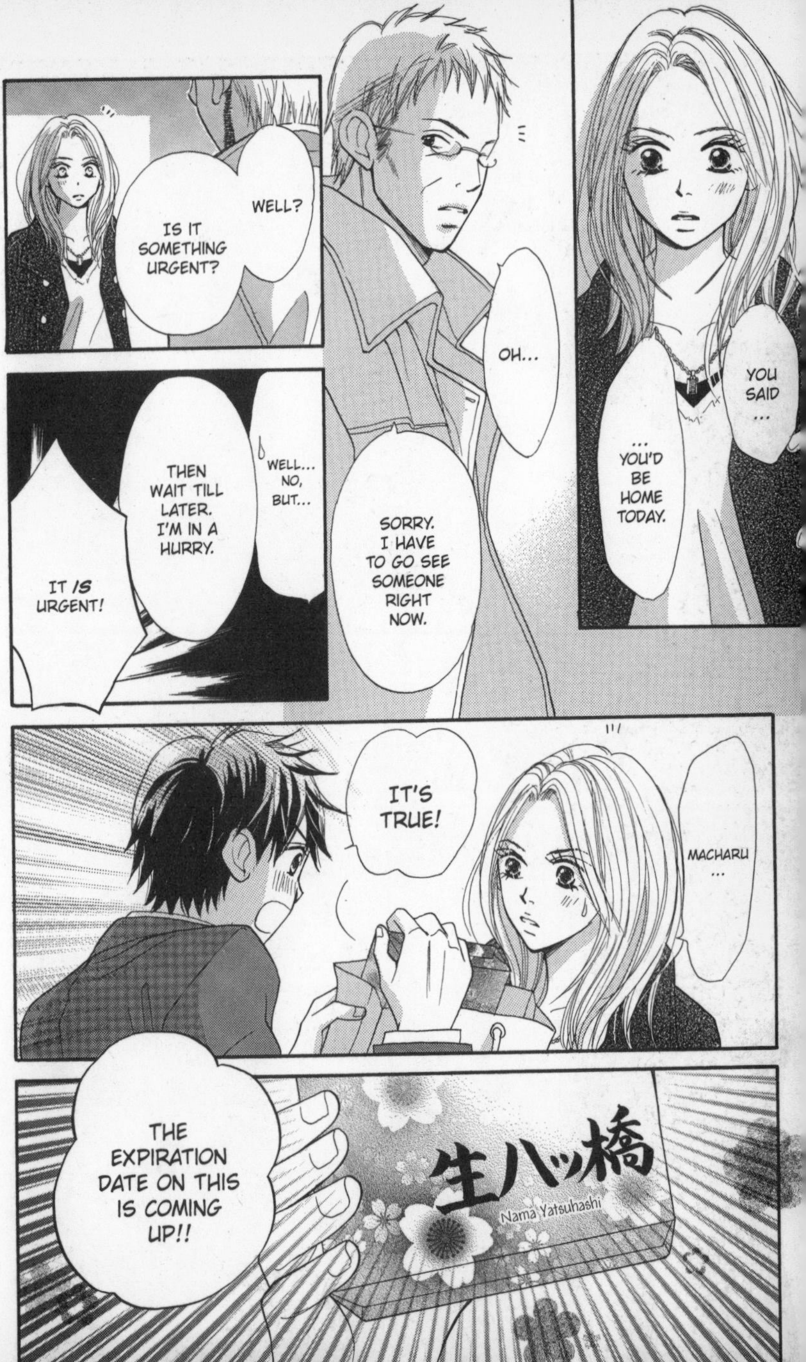
YOU SAID...
...YOU'D BE HOME TODAY.
OH...
SORRY. I HAVE TO GO SEE SOMEONE RIGHT NOW.
WELL?
IS IT SOMETHING URGENT?
WELL... NO, BUT...
THEN WAIT TILL LATER. I'M IN A HURRY.
IT *IS* URGENT!
MACHARU...
IT'S TRUE!
THE EXPIRATION DATE ON THIS IS COMING UP!!
生八ッ橋
Nama Yatsuhashi

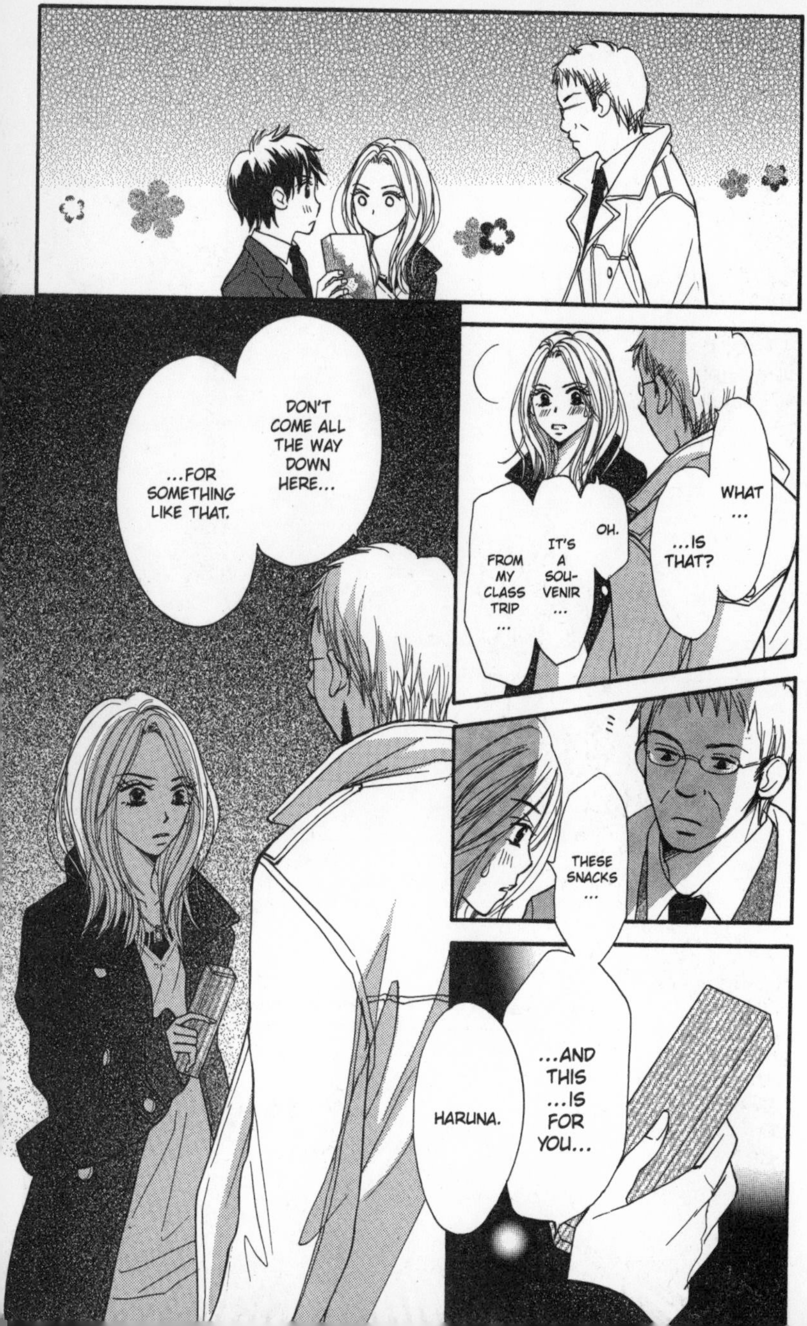
WHAT... ...IS THAT?
OH.
IT'S A SOU-VENIR... FROM MY CLASS TRIP...
THESE SNACKS...
...AND THIS ...IS FOR YOU...
HARUNA.
DON'T COME ALL THE WAY DOWN HERE...
...FOR SOMETHING LIKE THAT.

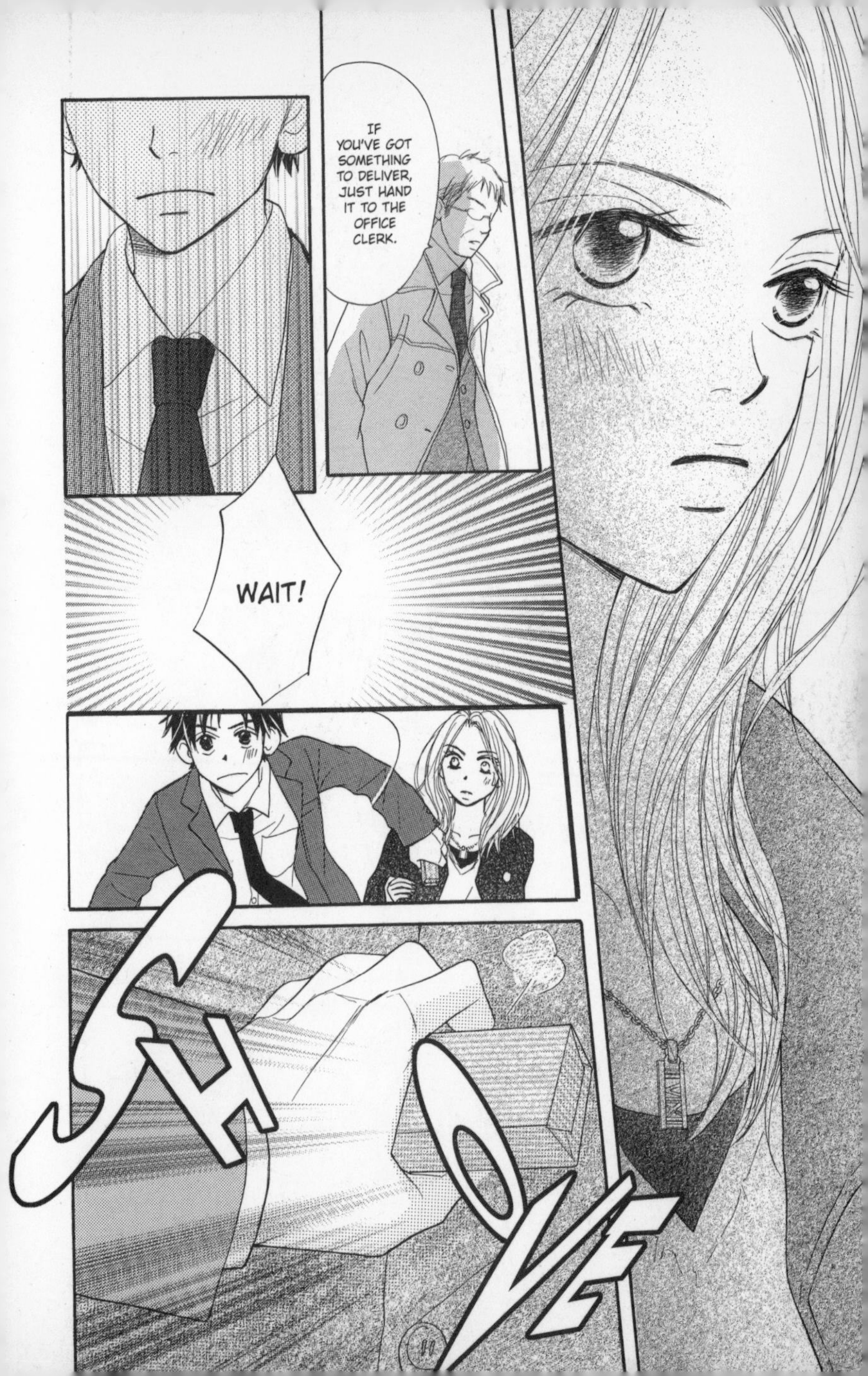
IF YOU'VE GOT SOMETHING TO DELIVER, JUST HAND IT TO THE OFFICE CLERK.
WAIT!
SHOVE

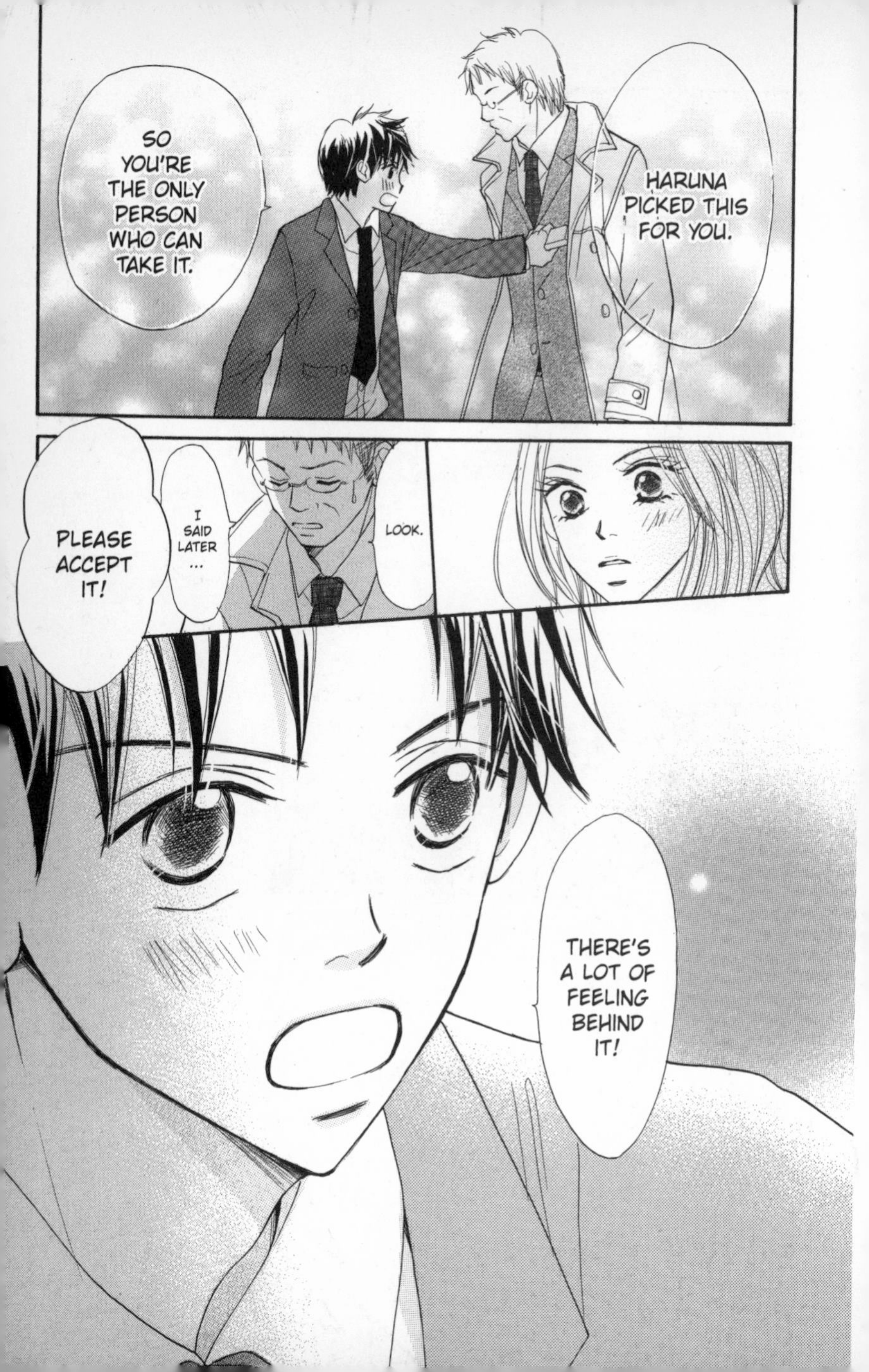
HARUNA PICKED THIS FOR YOU.
SO YOU'RE THE ONLY PERSON WHO CAN TAKE IT.
LOOK.
I SAID LATER ...
PLEASE ACCEPT IT!
THERE'S A LOT OF FEELING BEHIND IT!

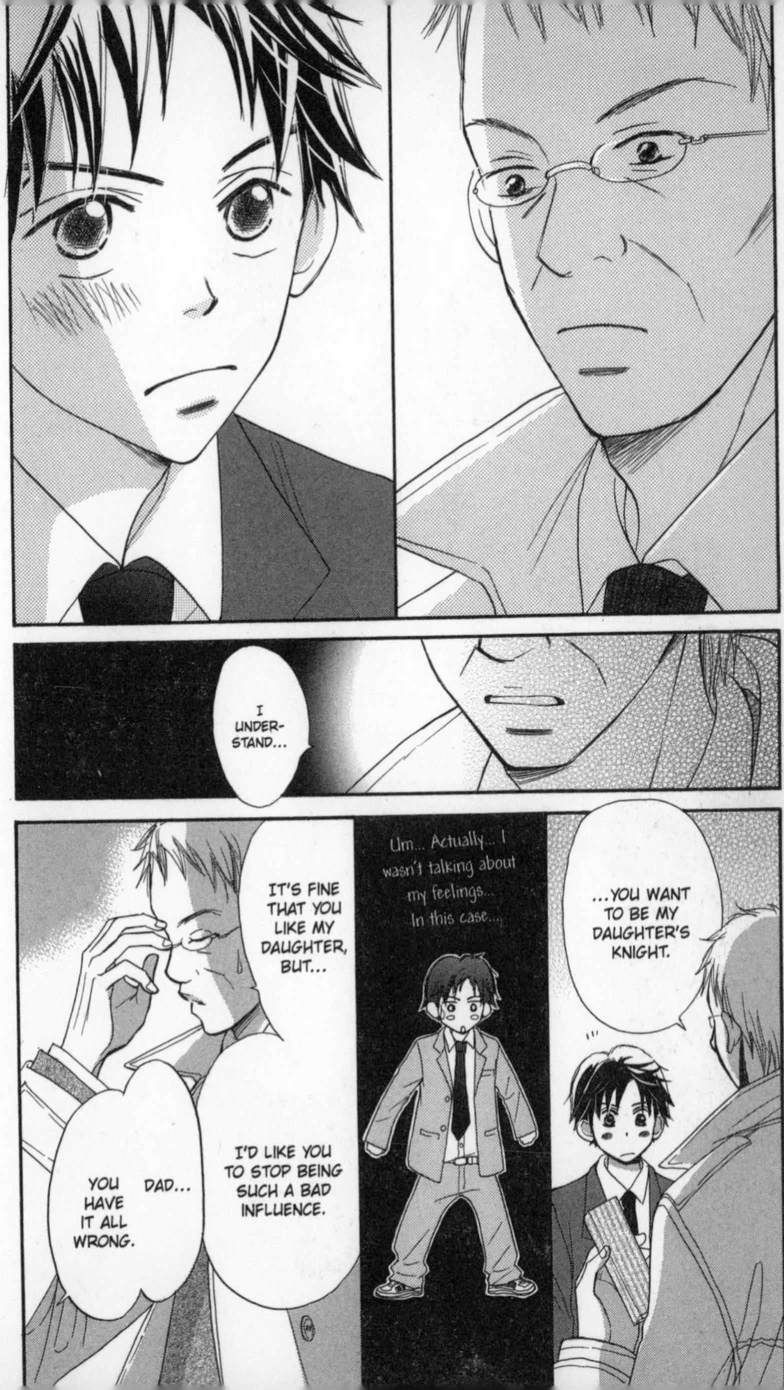
I UNDERSTAND...
...YOU WANT TO BE MY DAUGHTER'S KNIGHT.
Um... Actually... I wasn't talking about my feelings... In this case...
IT'S FINE THAT YOU LIKE MY DAUGHTER, BUT...
I'D LIKE YOU TO STOP BEING SUCH A BAD INFLUENCE.
DAD...
YOU HAVE IT ALL WRONG.

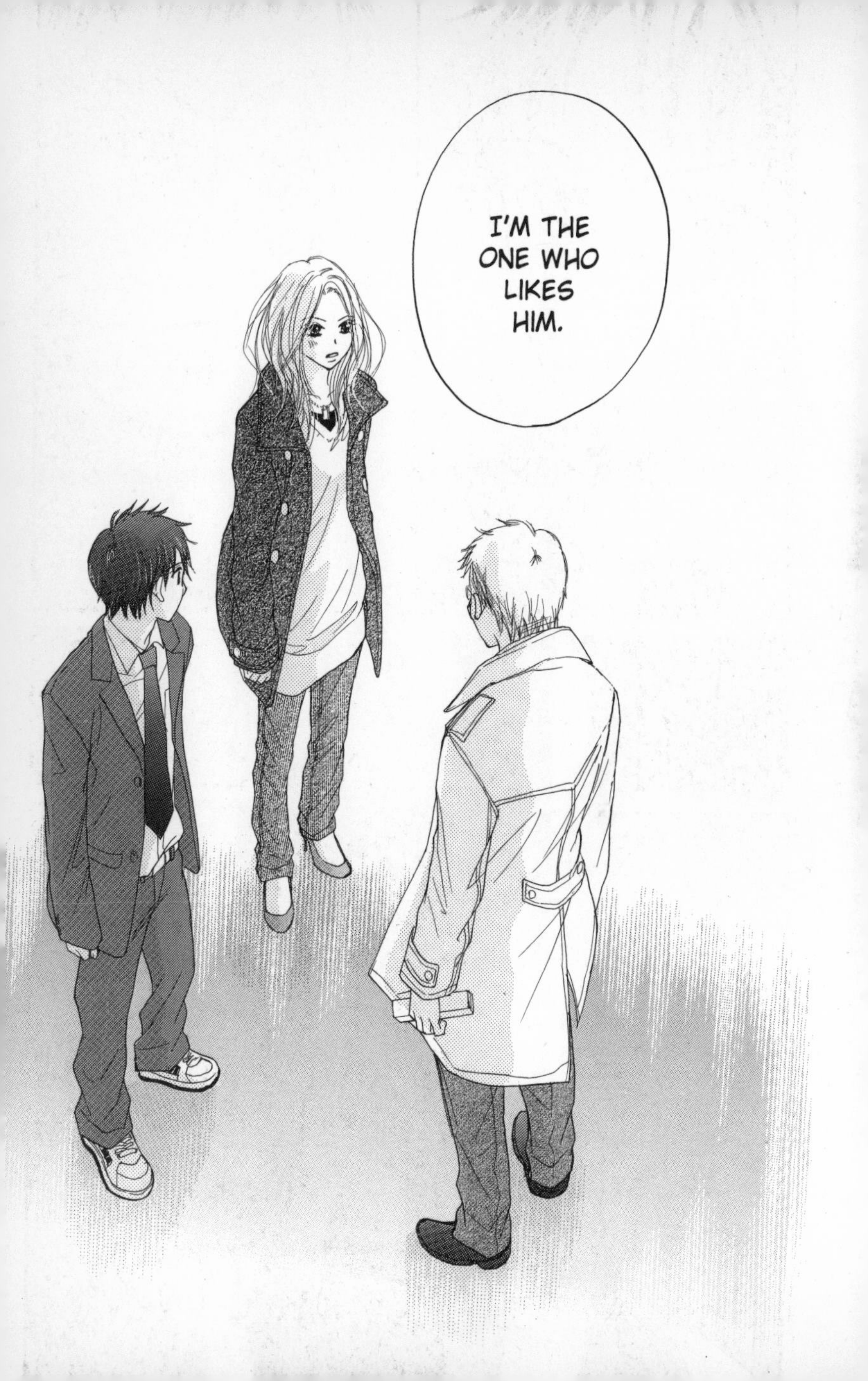
I'M THE ONE WHO LIKES HIM.

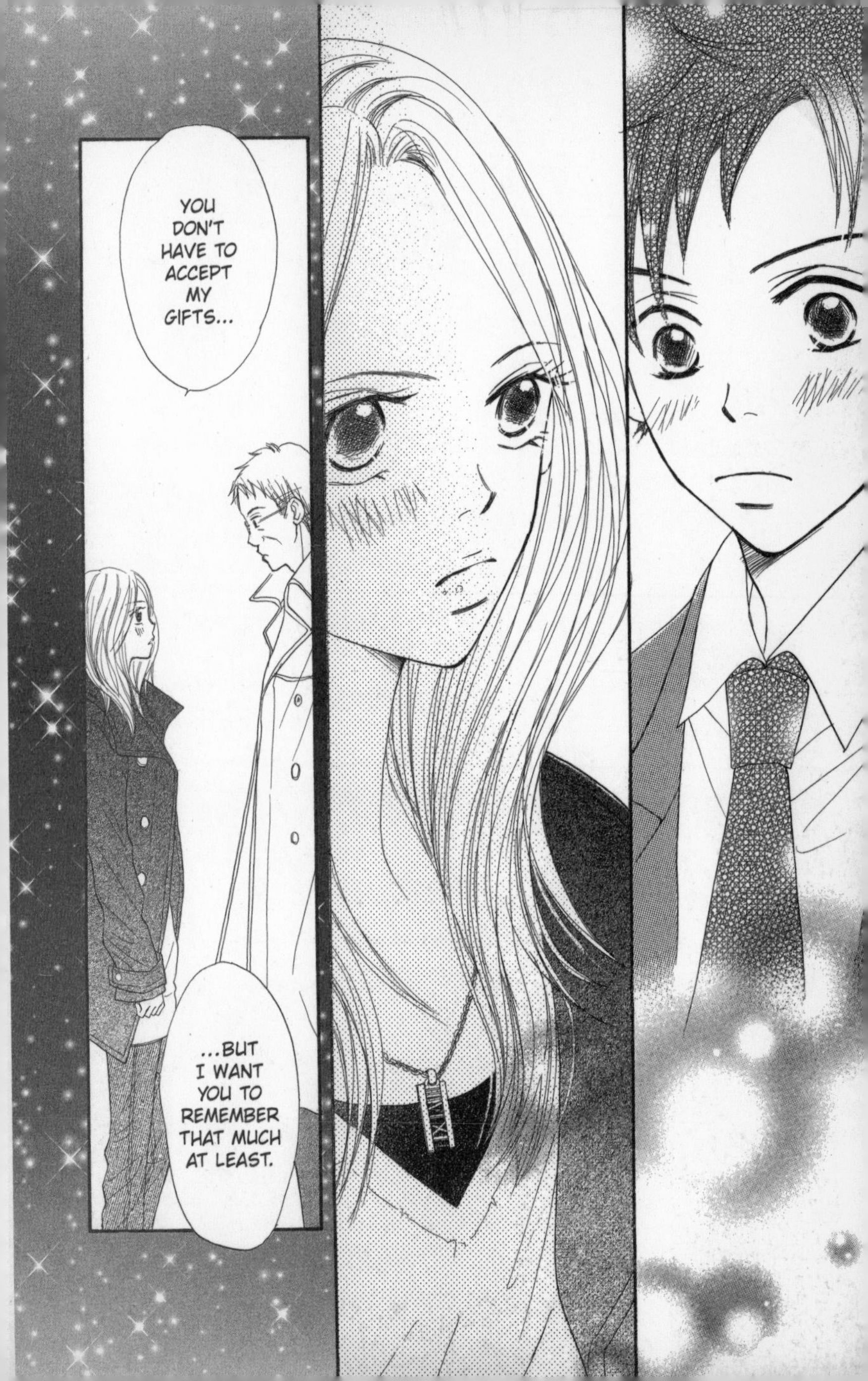
YOU DON'T HAVE TO ACCEPT MY GIFTS...
...BUT I WANT YOU TO REMEMBER THAT MUCH AT LEAST.

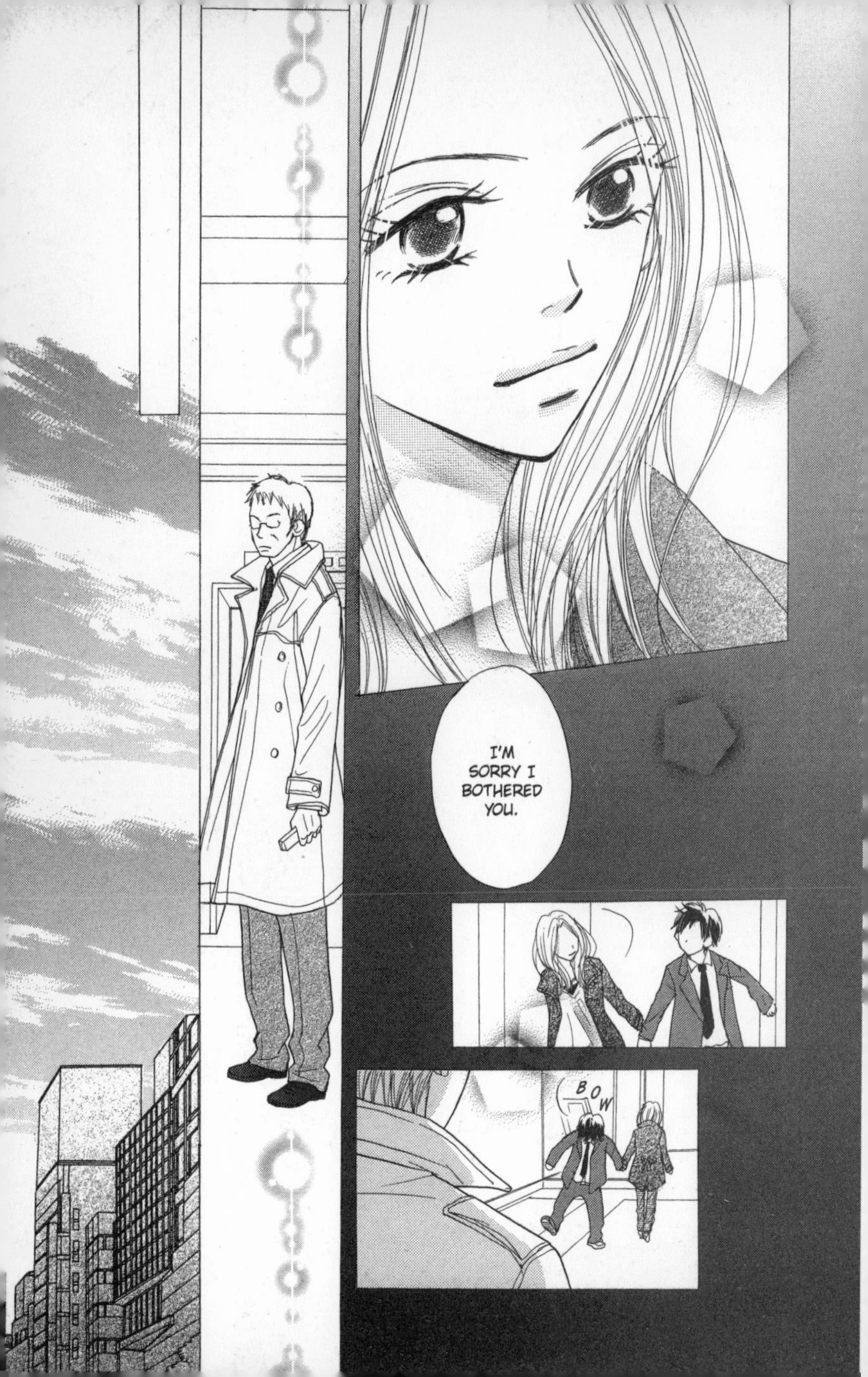
I'M SORRY I BOTHERED YOU.
BOW

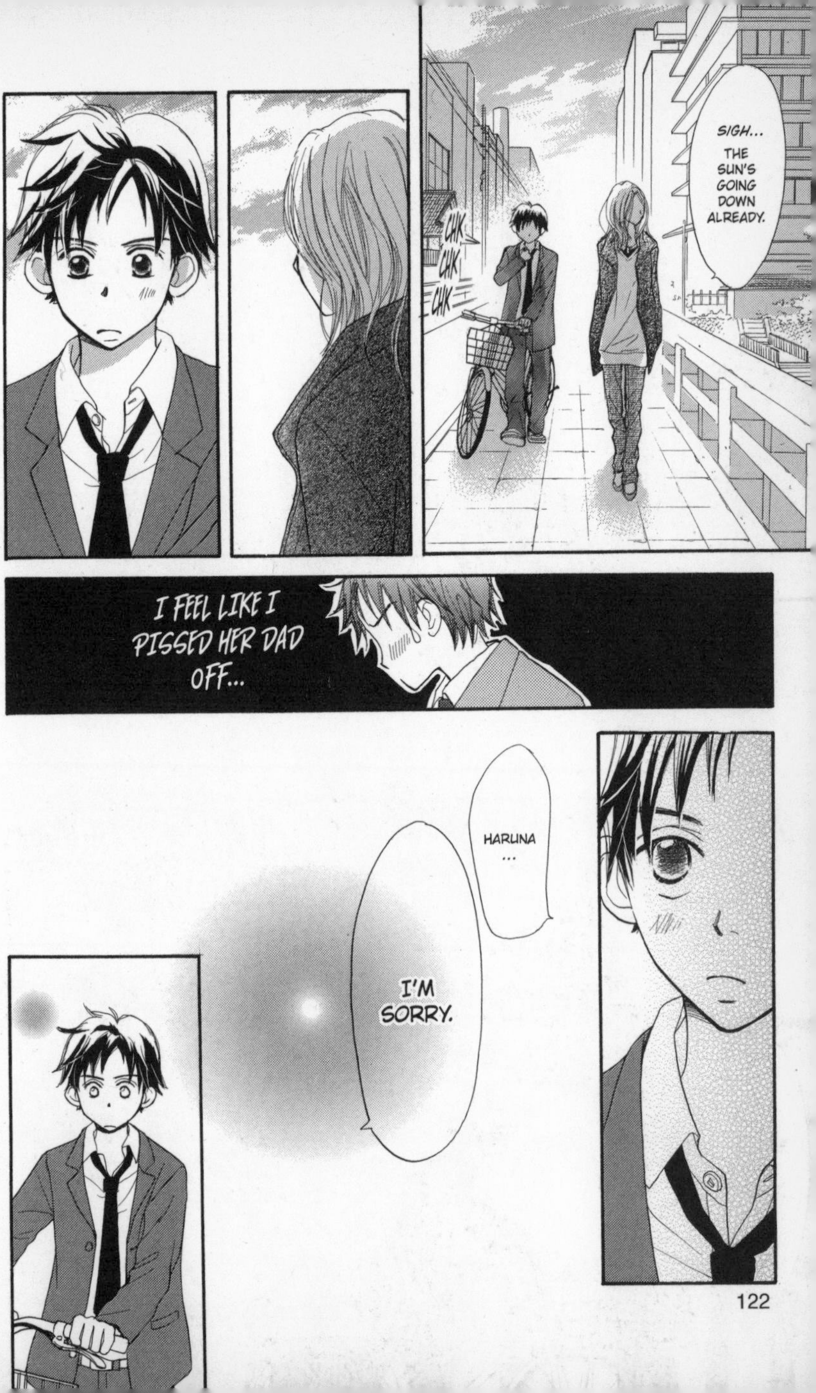
SIGH... THE SUN'S GOING DOWN ALREADY.
CHK CHK CHK
I FEEL LIKE I PISSED HER DAD OFF...
HARUNA ...
I'M SORRY.

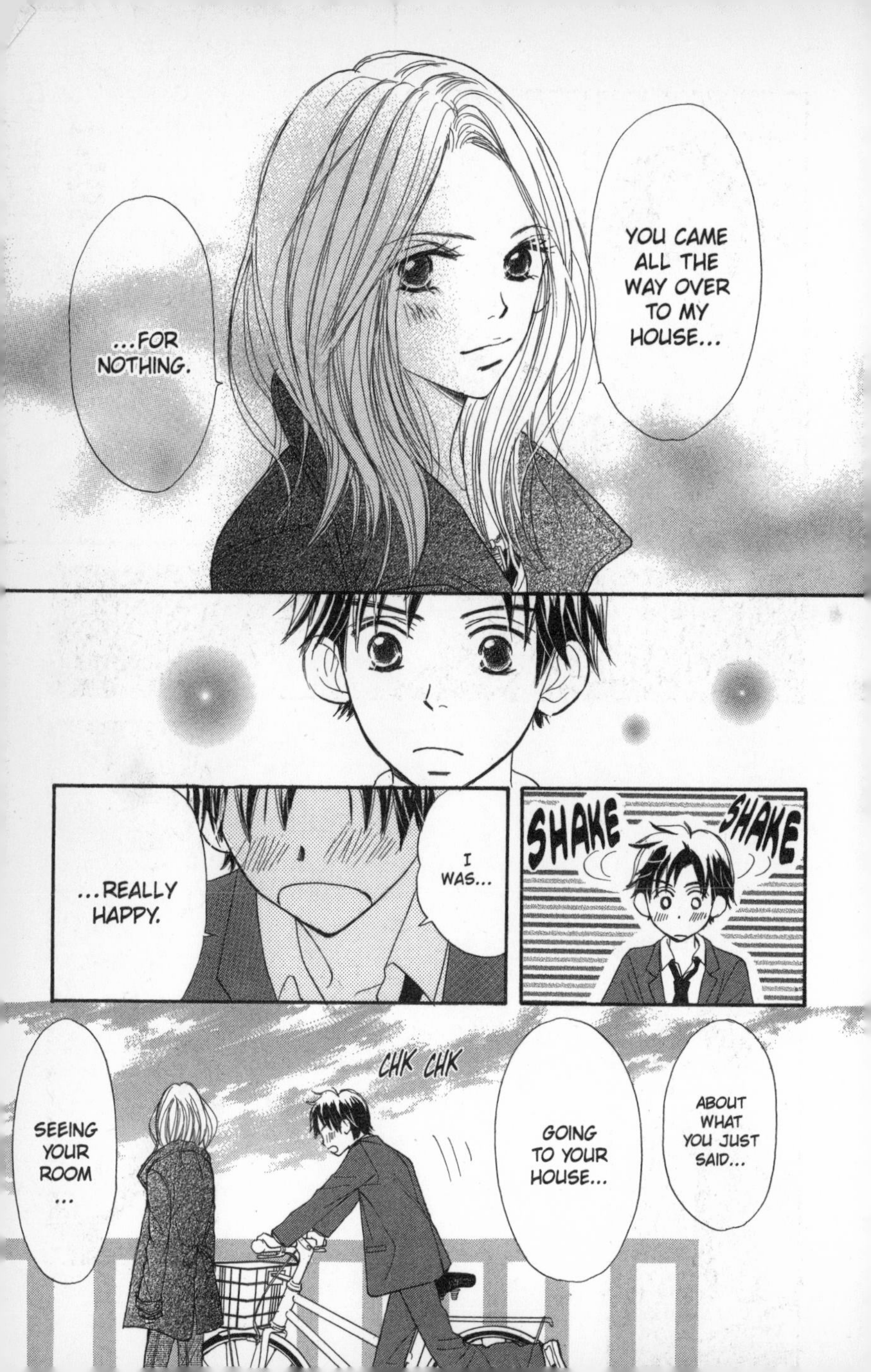
YOU CAME ALL THE WAY OVER TO MY HOUSE...
...FOR NOTHING.
I WAS...
...REALLY HAPPY.
SHAKE
SHAKE
CHK CHK
ABOUT WHAT YOU JUST SAID...
GOING TO YOUR HOUSE...
SEEING YOUR ROOM ...

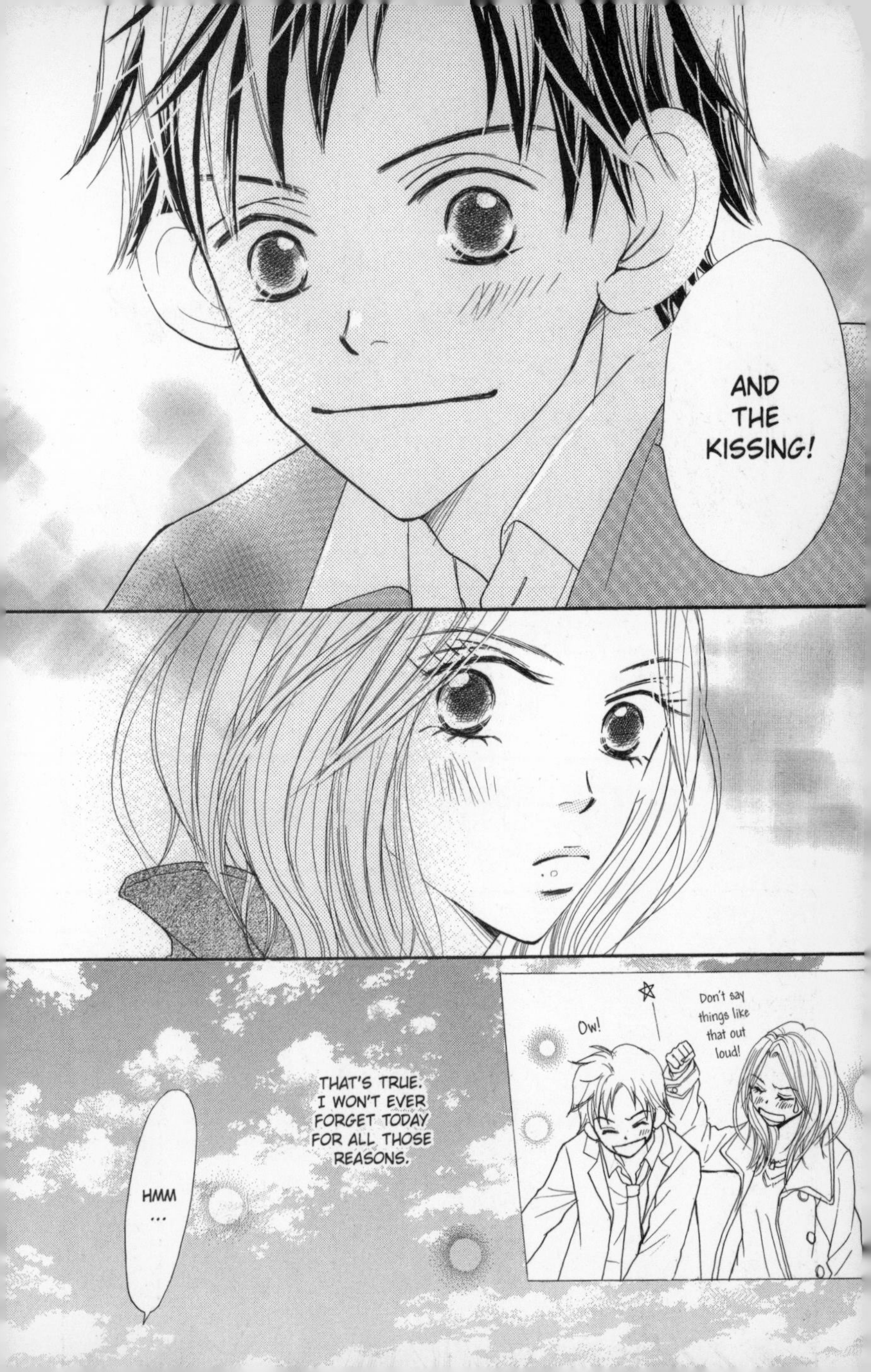
AND THE KISSING!
Don't say things like that out loud!
Ow!
THAT'S TRUE. I WON'T EVER FORGET TODAY FOR ALL THOSE REASONS.
HMM ...

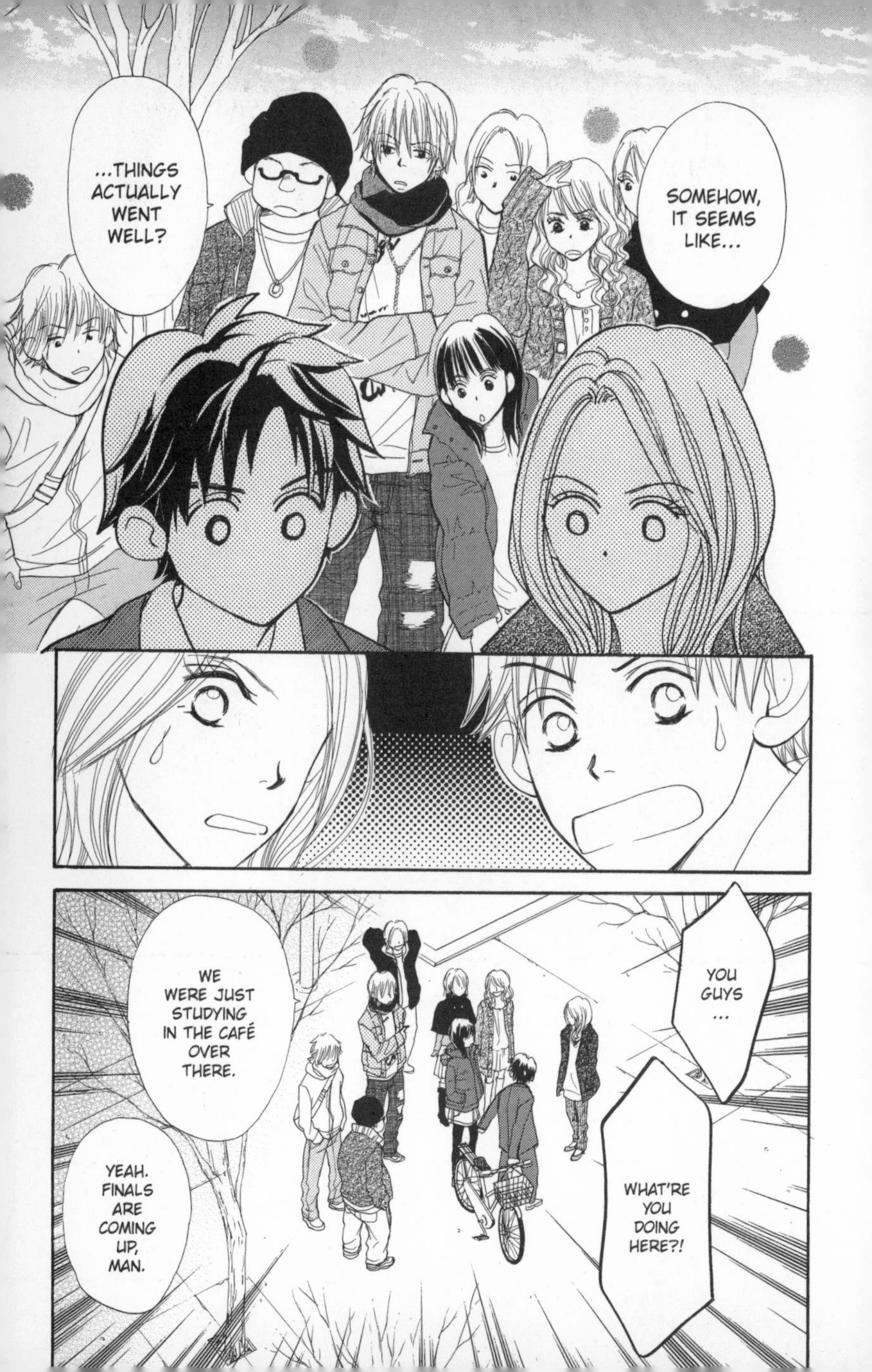
SOMEHOW, IT SEEMS LIKE...
...THINGS ACTUALLY WENT WELL?
YOU GUYS ...
WHAT'RE YOU DOING HERE?!
WE WERE JUST STUDYING IN THE CAFÉ OVER THERE.
YEAH. FINALS ARE COMING UP, MAN.

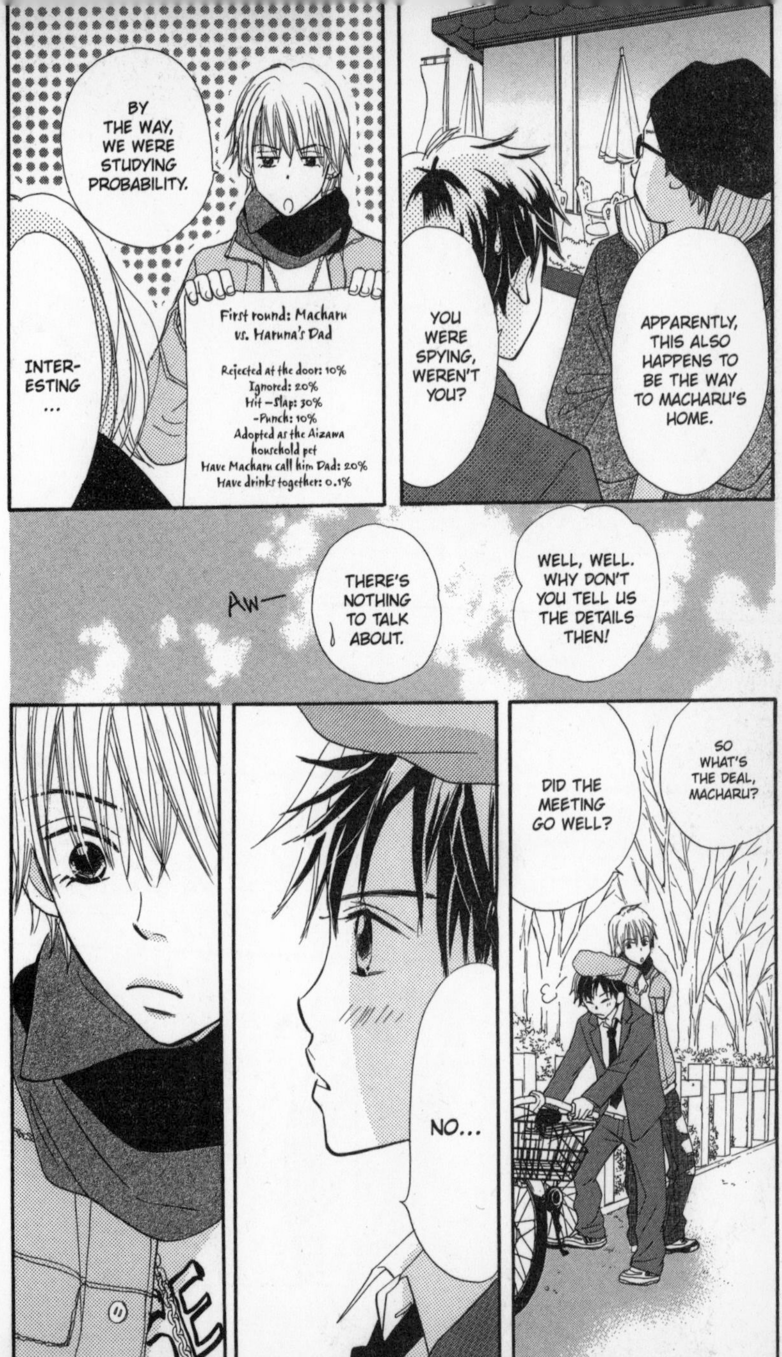
APPARENTLY, THIS ALSO HAPPENS TO BE THE WAY TO MACHARU'S HOME.
YOU WERE SPYING, WEREN'T YOU?
BY THE WAY, WE WERE STUDYING PROBABILITY.
First round: Macharu vs. Haruna's Dad
Rejected at the door: 10%
Ignored: 20%
Hit –Slap: 30%
–Punch: 10%
Adopted as the Aizawa household pet
Have Macharu call him Dad: 20%
Have drinks together: 0.1%
INTER-ESTING...
WELL, WELL. WHY DON'T YOU TELL US THE DETAILS THEN!
THERE'S NOTHING TO TALK ABOUT.
AW—
SO WHAT'S THE DEAL, MACHARU?
DID THE MEETING GO WELL?
NO...

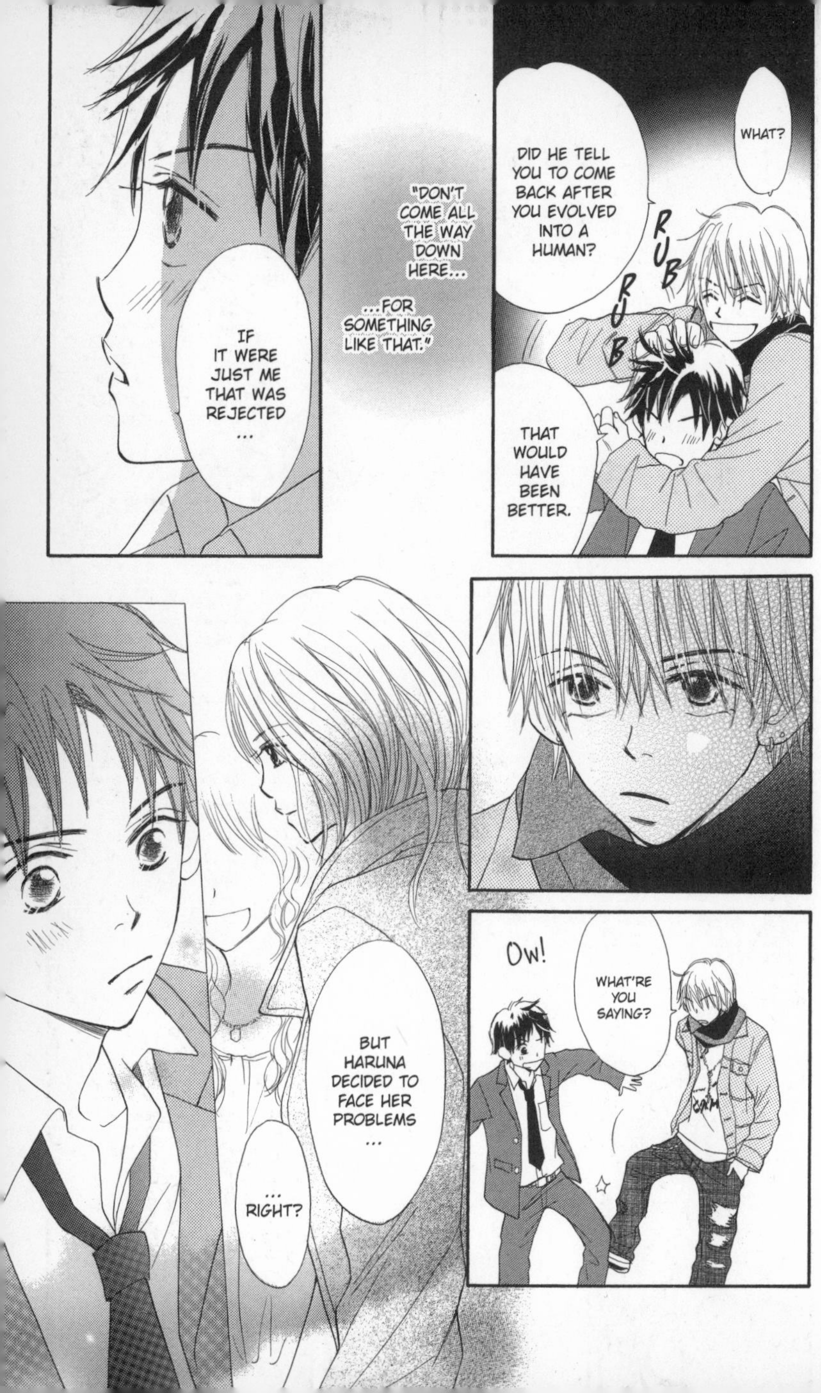
WHAT?
DID HE TELL YOU TO COME BACK AFTER YOU EVOLVED INTO A HUMAN?
RUB
RUB
THAT WOULD HAVE BEEN BETTER.
"DON'T COME ALL THE WAY DOWN HERE...
...FOR SOMETHING LIKE THAT."
IF IT WERE JUST ME THAT WAS REJECTED...
Ow!
WHAT'RE YOU SAYING?
BUT HARUNA DECIDED TO FACE HER PROBLEMS...
...RIGHT?

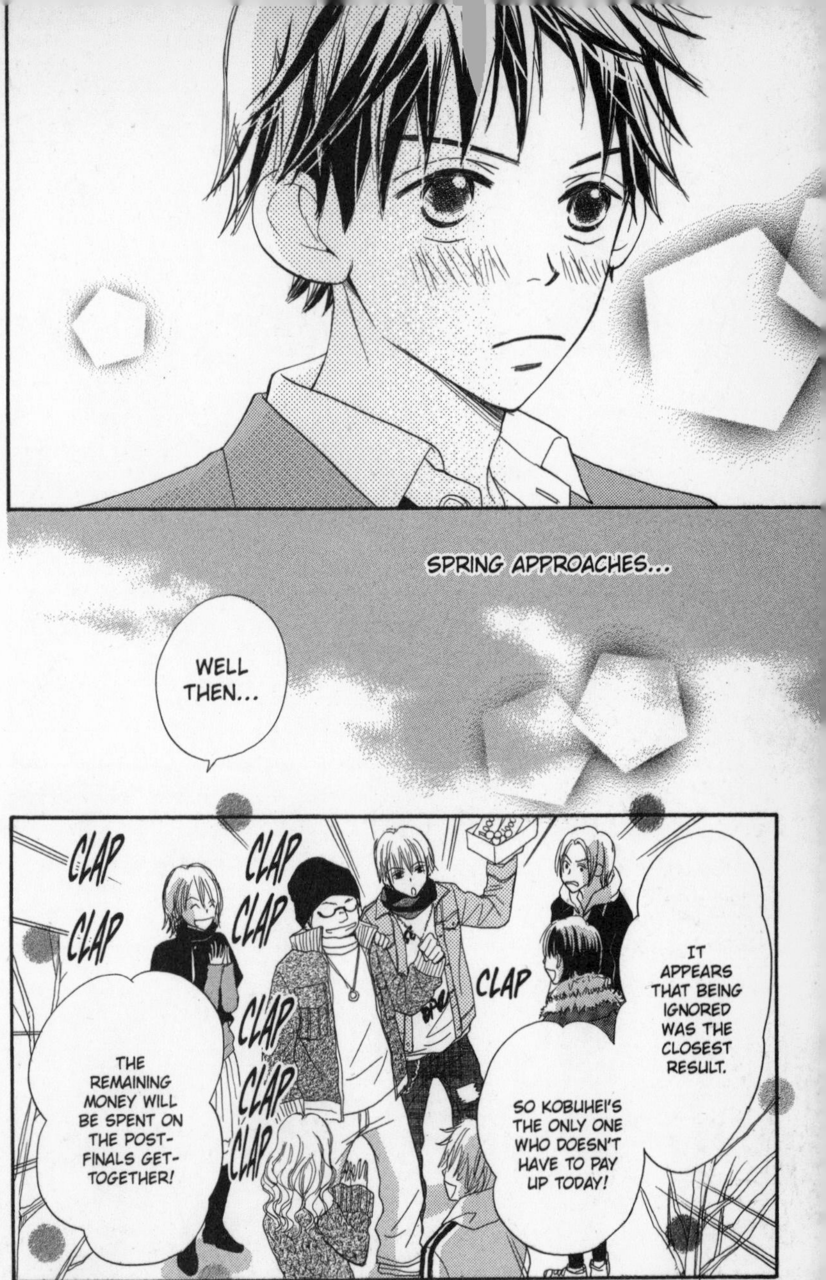
SPRING APPROACHES...
WELL THEN...
IT APPEARS THAT BEING IGNORED WAS THE CLOSEST RESULT.
CLAP
SO KOBUHEI'S THE ONLY ONE WHO DOESN'T HAVE TO PAY UP TODAY!
CLAP
CLAP
CLAP
CLAP
CLAP
CLAP
CLAP
THE REMAINING MONEY WILL BE SPENT ON THE POST-FINALS GET-TOGETHER!

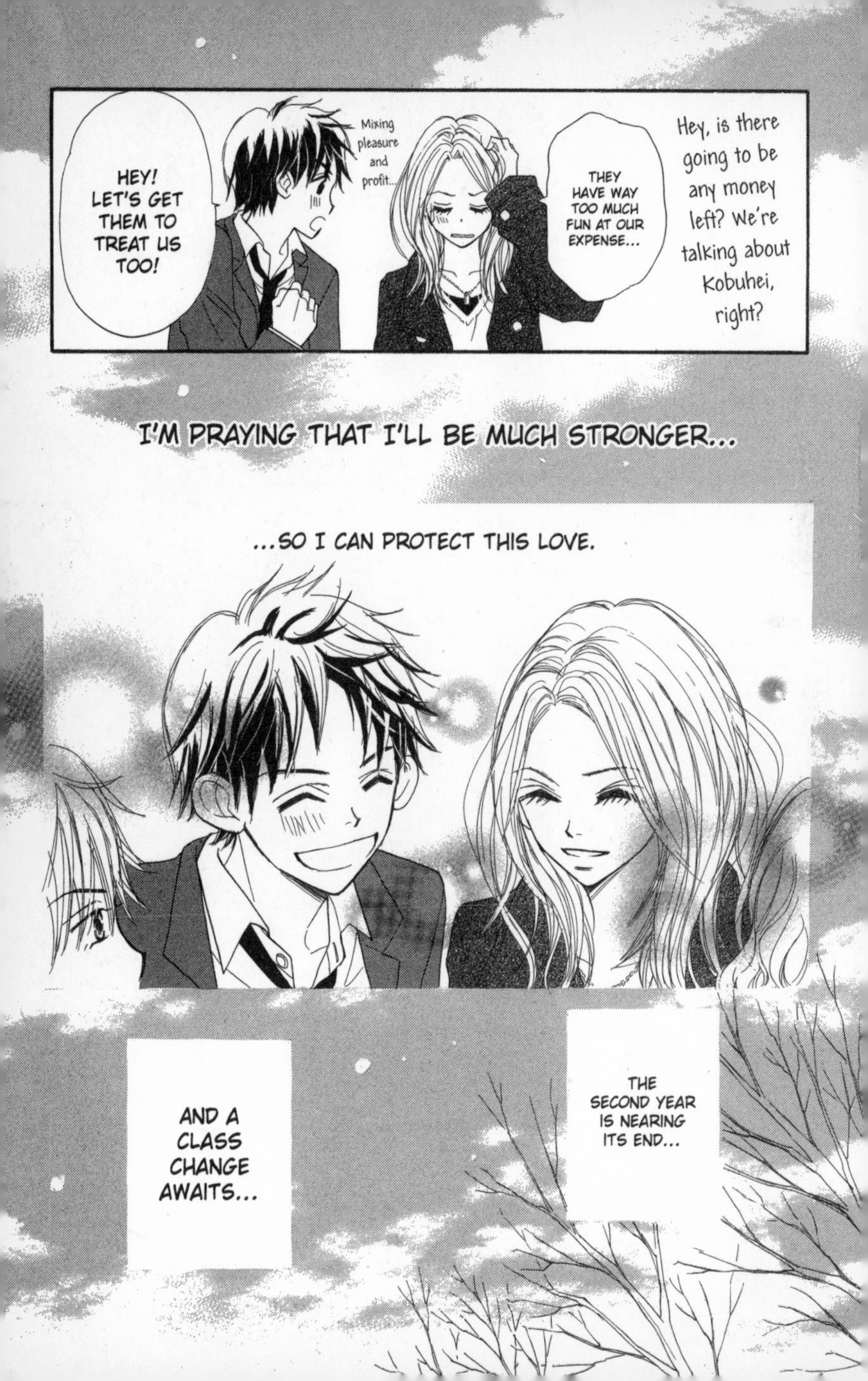
Hey, is there going to be any money left? We're talking about Kobuhei, right?
THEY HAVE WAY TOO MUCH FUN AT OUR EXPENSE...
Mixing pleasure and profit...
HEY! LET'S GET THEM TO TREAT US TOO!
I'M PRAYING THAT I'LL BE MUCH STRONGER...
...SO I CAN PROTECT THIS LOVE.
THE SECOND YEAR IS NEARING ITS END...
AND A CLASS CHANGE AWAITS...

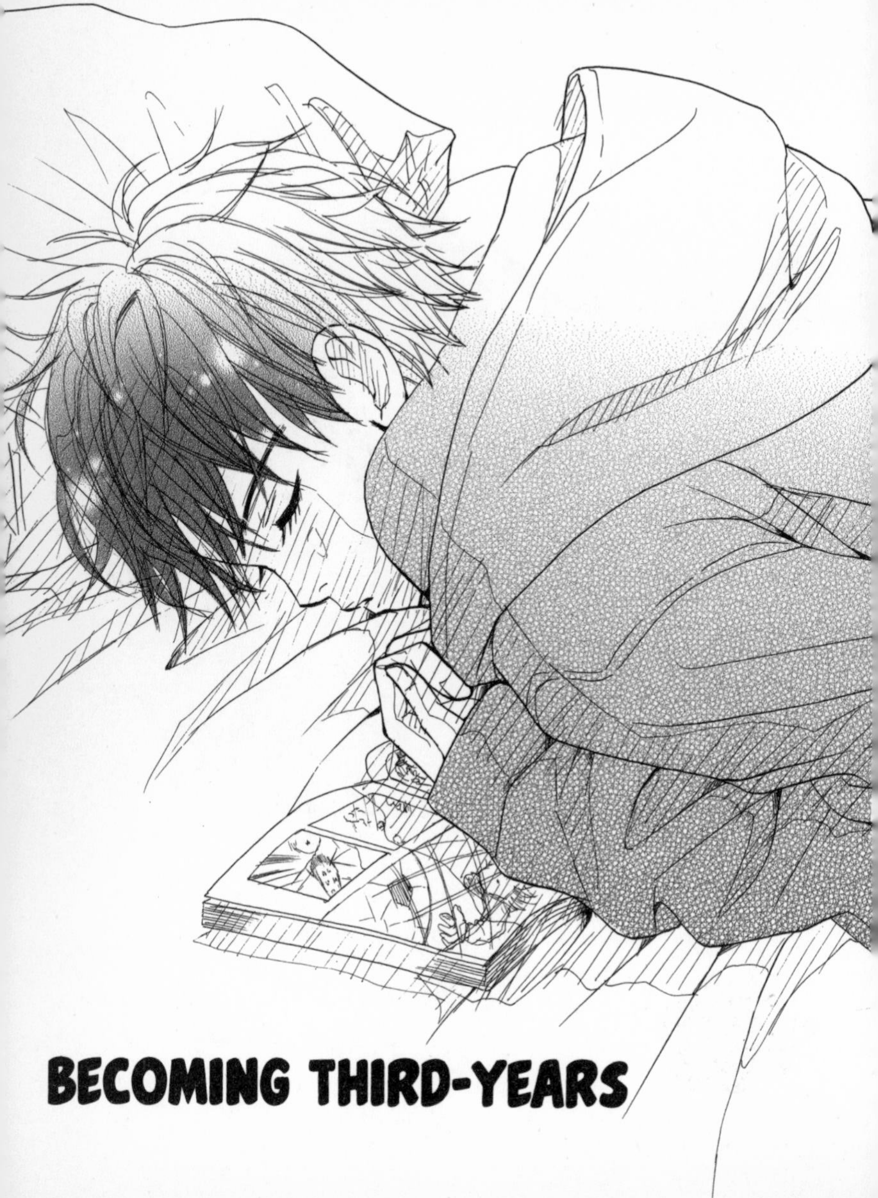

BECOMING THIRD-YEARS

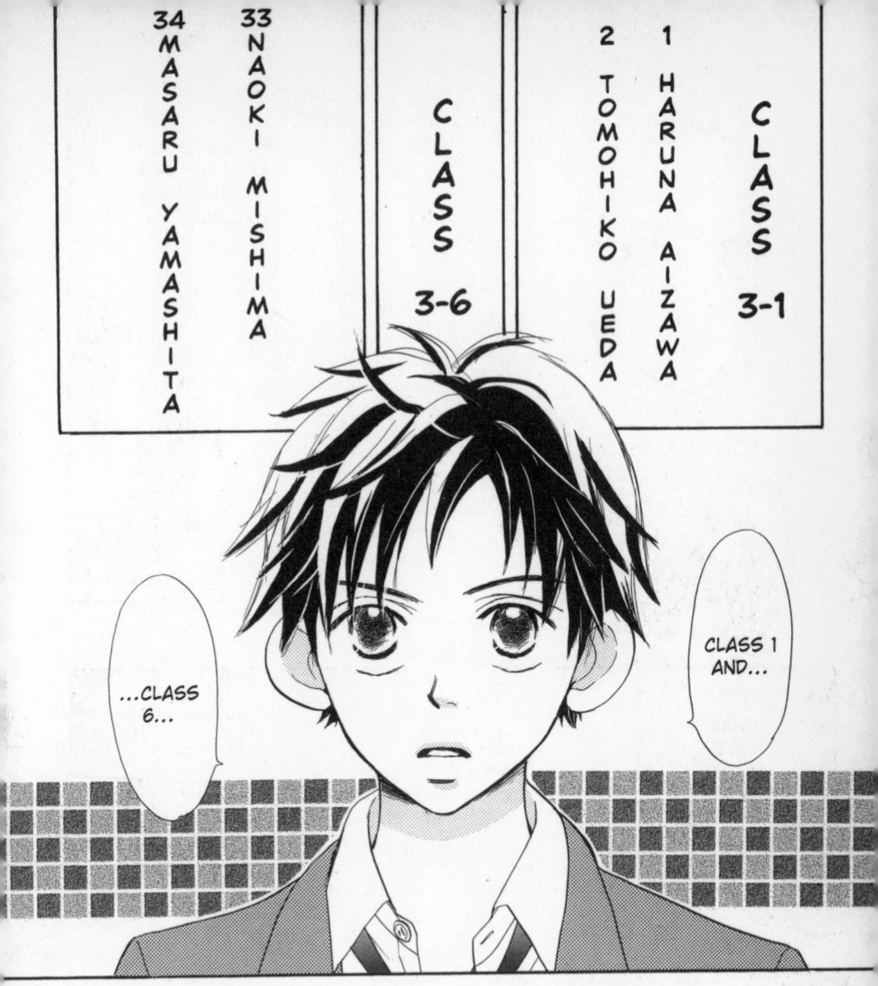
CLASS 3-1
1 HARUNA AIZAWA
2 TOMOHIKO UEDA
CLASS 3-6
33 NAOKI MISHIMA
34 MASARU YAMASHITA
CLASS 1 AND...
...CLASS 6...

Monkey High!

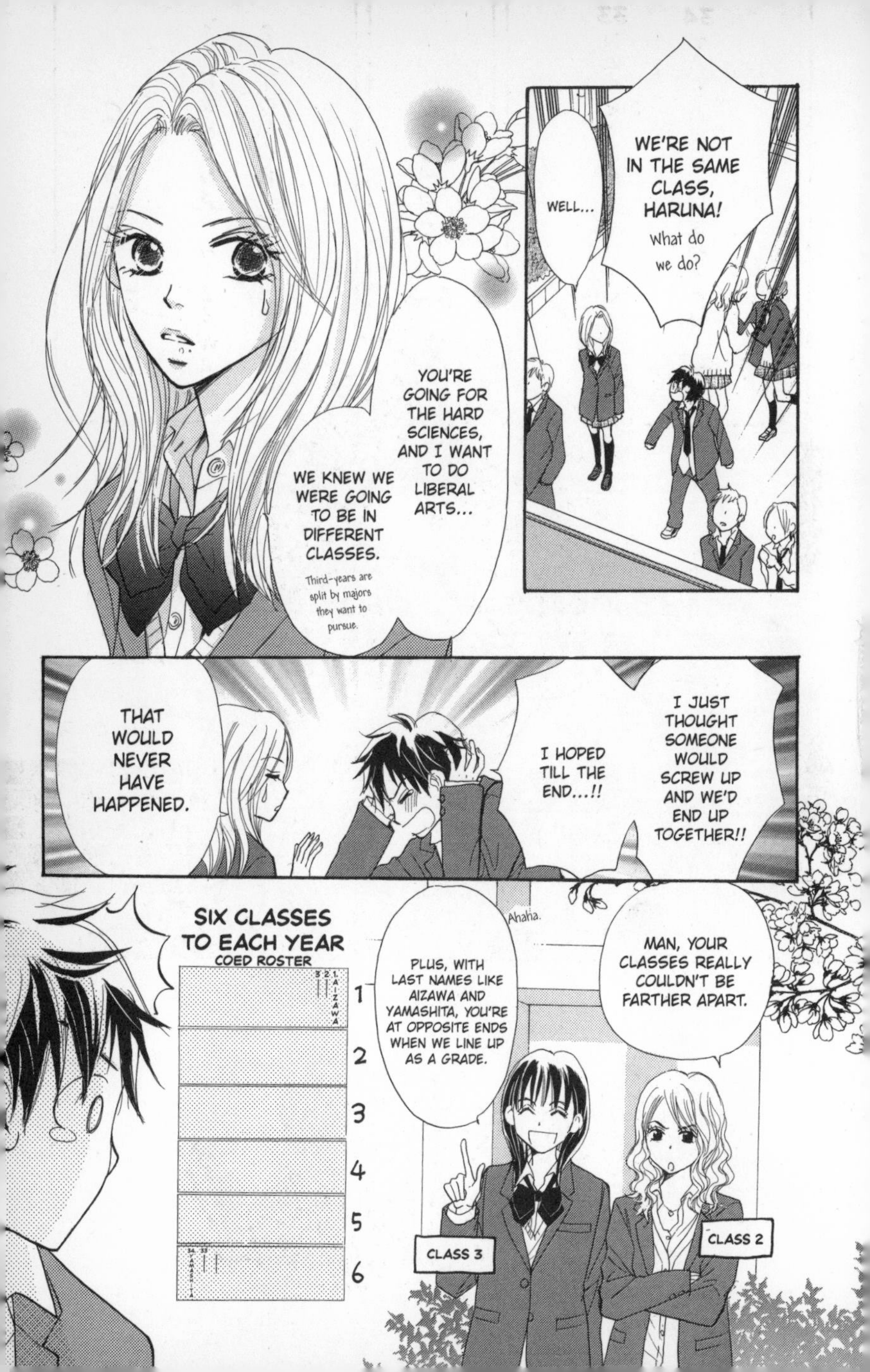
WE'RE NOT IN THE SAME CLASS, HARUNA!
What do we do?
WELL...
YOU'RE GOING FOR THE HARD SCIENCES, AND I WANT TO DO LIBERAL ARTS...
WE KNEW WE WERE GOING TO BE IN DIFFERENT CLASSES.
Third-years are split by majors they want to pursue.
I JUST THOUGHT SOMEONE WOULD SCREW UP AND WE'D END UP TOGETHER!!
I HOPED TILL THE END...!!
THAT WOULD NEVER HAVE HAPPENED.
MAN, YOUR CLASSES REALLY COULDN'T BE FARTHER APART.
Ahaha.
PLUS, WITH LAST NAMES LIKE AIZAWA AND YAMASHITA, YOU'RE AT OPPOSITE ENDS WHEN WE LINE UP AS A GRADE.
CLASS 2
CLASS 3
SIX CLASSES TO EACH YEAR
COED ROSTER
1
2
3
4
5
6

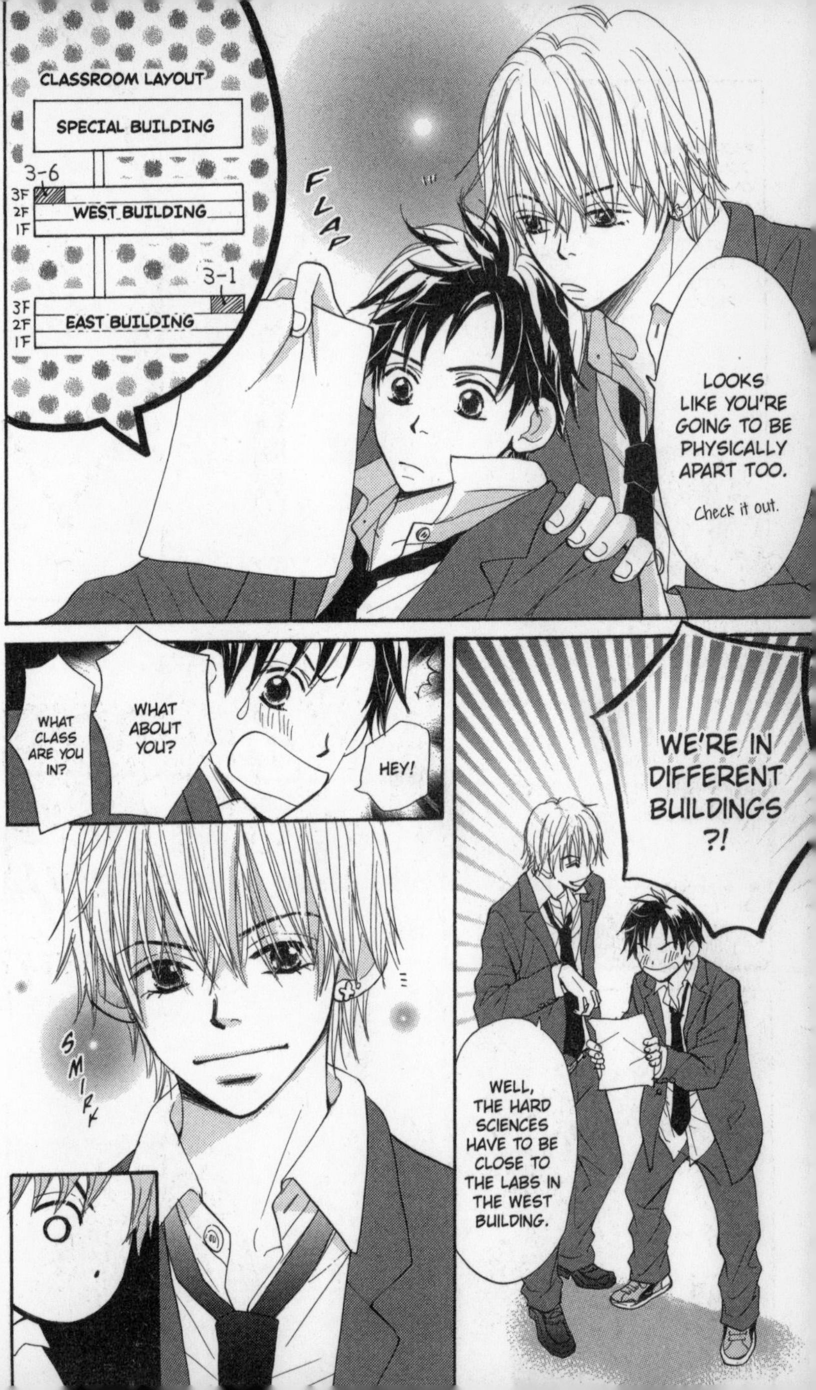
LOOKS LIKE YOU'RE GOING TO BE PHYSICALLY APART TOO.
Check it out.
FLAP
CLASSROOM LAYOUT
SPECIAL BUILDING
3-6
3F
2F
1F
WEST BUILDING
3-1
3F
2F
1F
EAST BUILDING
WE'RE IN DIFFERENT BUILDINGS ?!
WELL, THE HARD SCIENCES HAVE TO BE CLOSE TO THE LABS IN THE WEST BUILDING.
HEY!
WHAT ABOUT YOU?
WHAT CLASS ARE YOU IN?
SMIRK

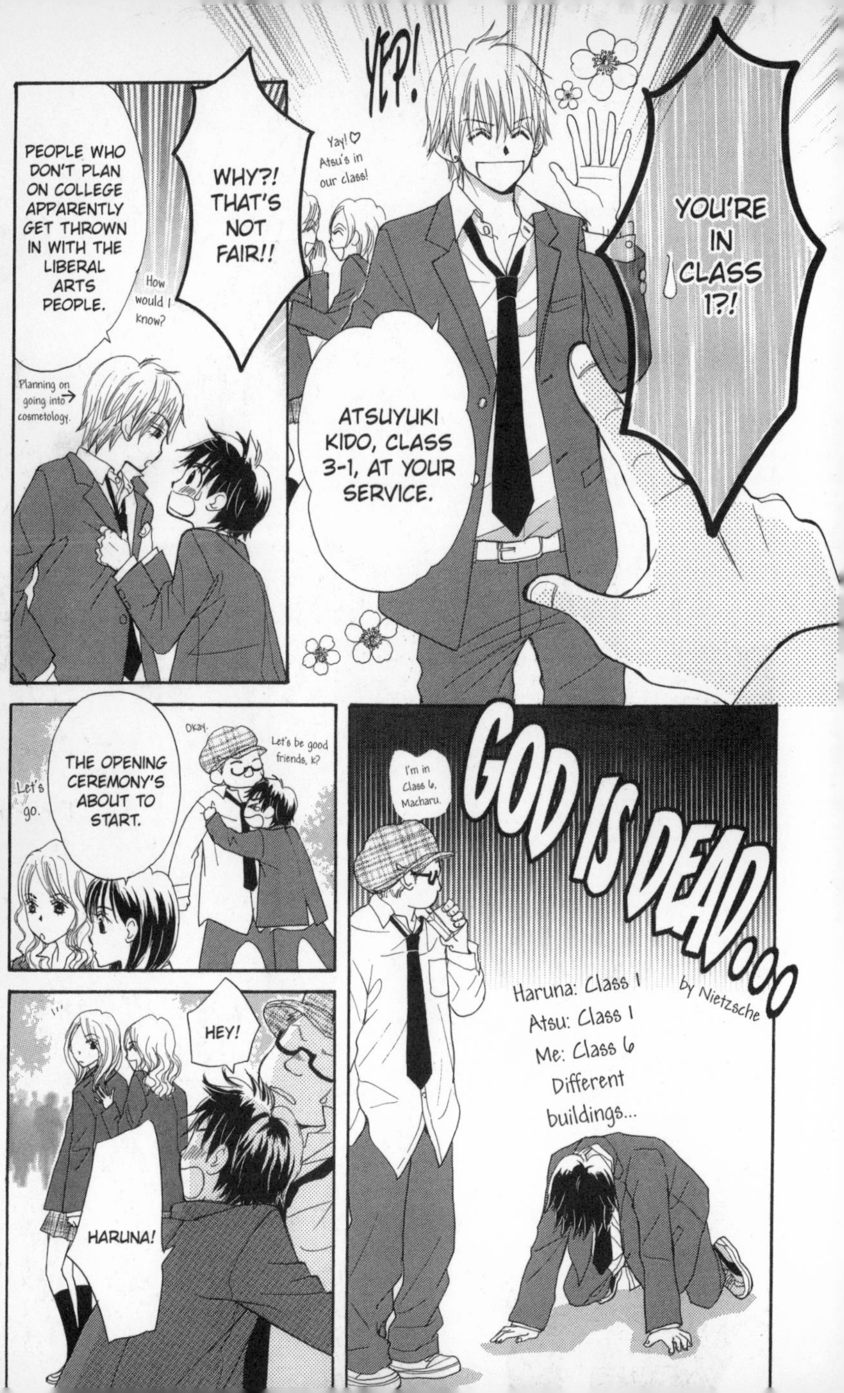
YOU'RE IN CLASS 1?!
YEP!
ATSUYUKI KIDO, CLASS 3-1, AT YOUR SERVICE.
Yay! ♡ Atsu's in our class!
WHY?! THAT'S NOT FAIR!!
PEOPLE WHO DON'T PLAN ON COLLEGE APPARENTLY GET THROWN IN WITH THE LIBERAL ARTS PEOPLE.
How would I know?
Planning on going into cosmetology. →
I'm in Class 6, Macharu.
GOD IS DEAD...
by Nietzsche
Haruna: Class 1
Atsu: Class 1
Me: Class 6
Different buildings...
Let's be good friends, k?
Okay.
THE OPENING CEREMONY'S ABOUT TO START.
Let's go.
HEY!
HARUNA!

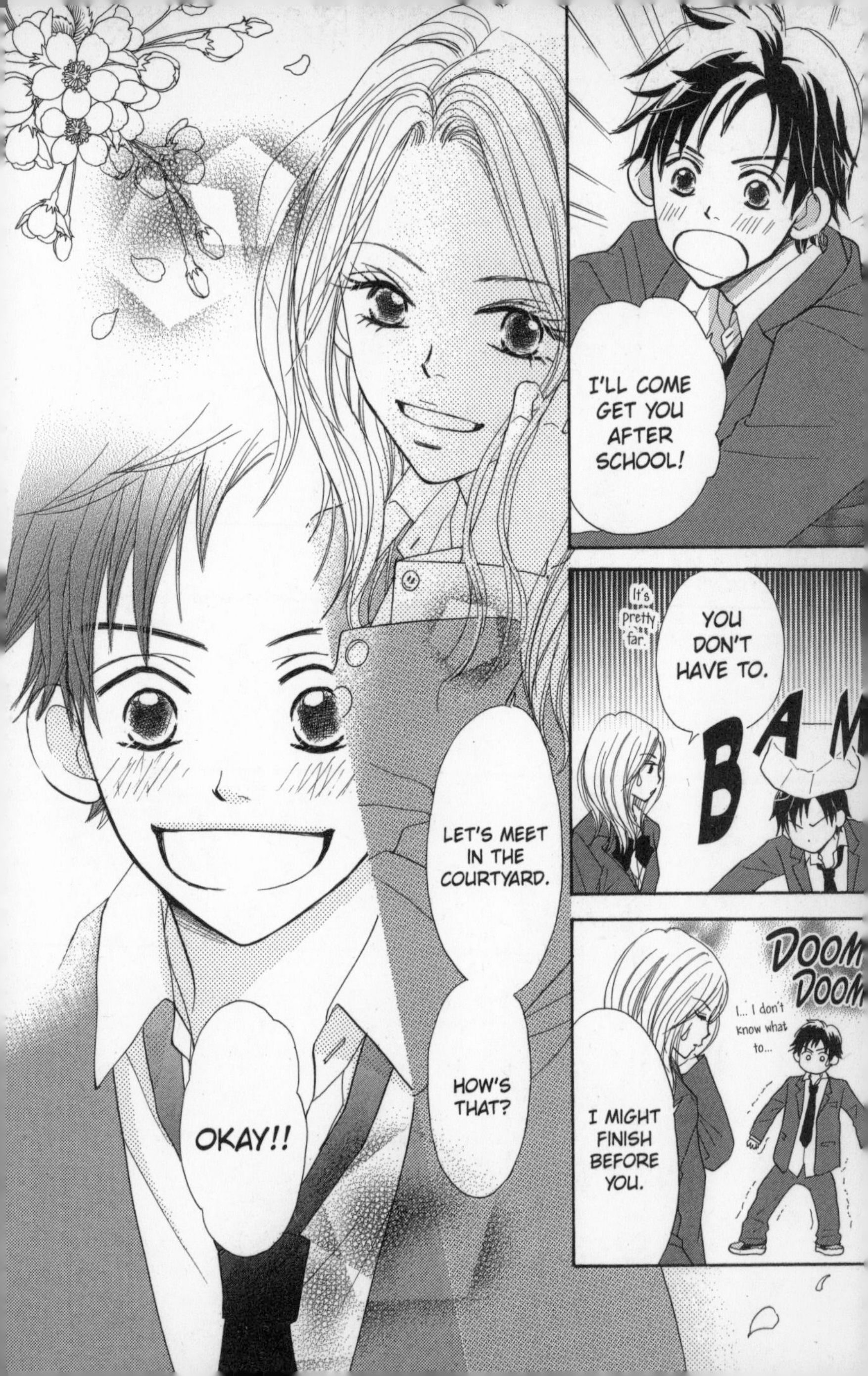
I'LL COME GET YOU AFTER SCHOOL!
YOU DON'T HAVE TO.
It's pretty far.
BAM
DOOM DOOM
I MIGHT FINISH BEFORE YOU.
I... I don't know what to...
LET'S MEET IN THE COURTYARD.
HOW'S THAT?
OKAY!!

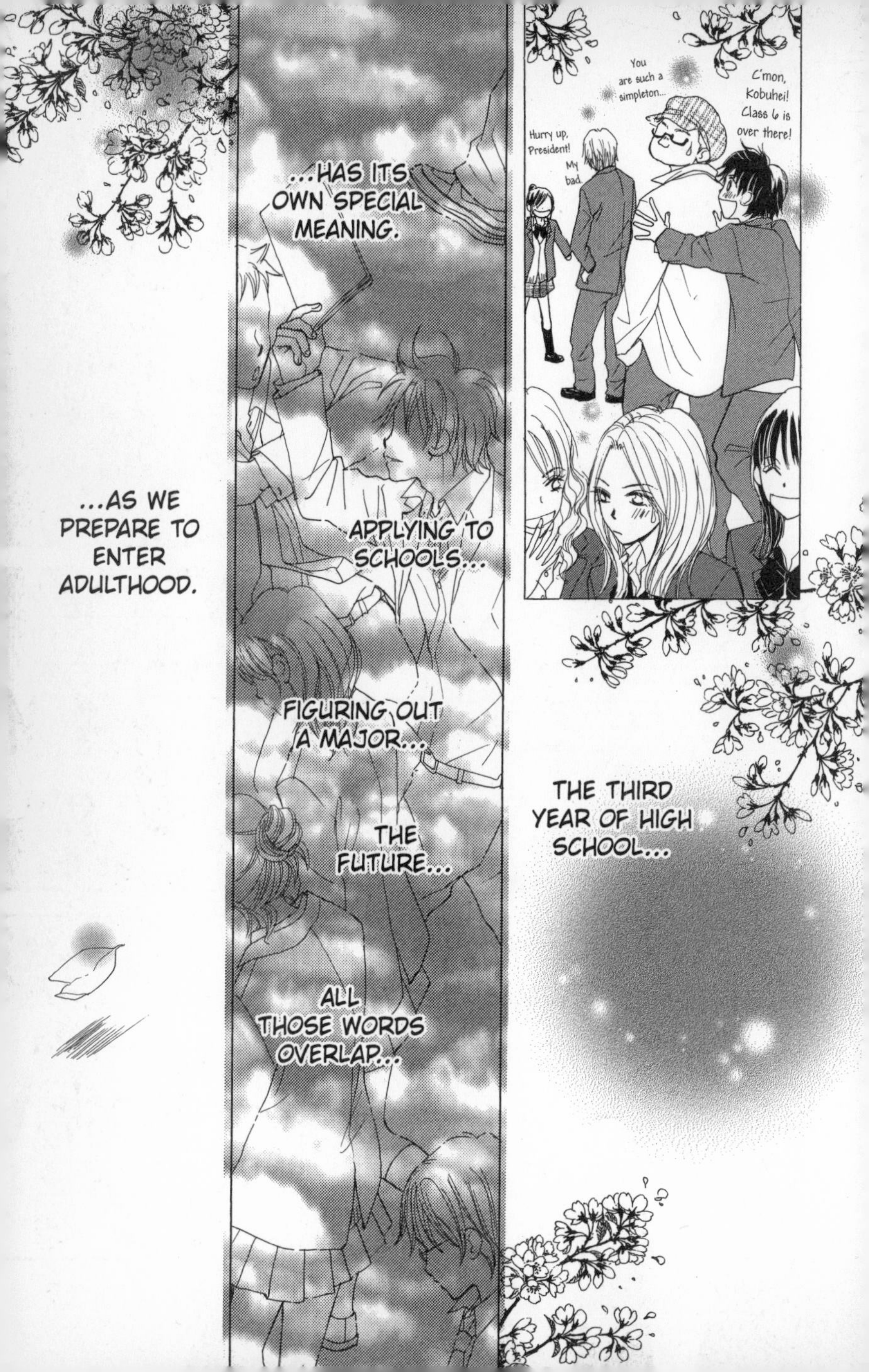

C'mon, Kobuhei! Class 6 is over there!
You are such a simpleton...
My bad.
Hurry up, President!
THE THIRD YEAR OF HIGH SCHOOL...
...HAS ITS OWN SPECIAL MEANING.
APPLYING TO SCHOOLS...
FIGURING OUT A MAJOR...
THE FUTURE...
ALL THOSE WORDS OVERLAP...
...AS WE PREPARE TO ENTER ADULTHOOD.

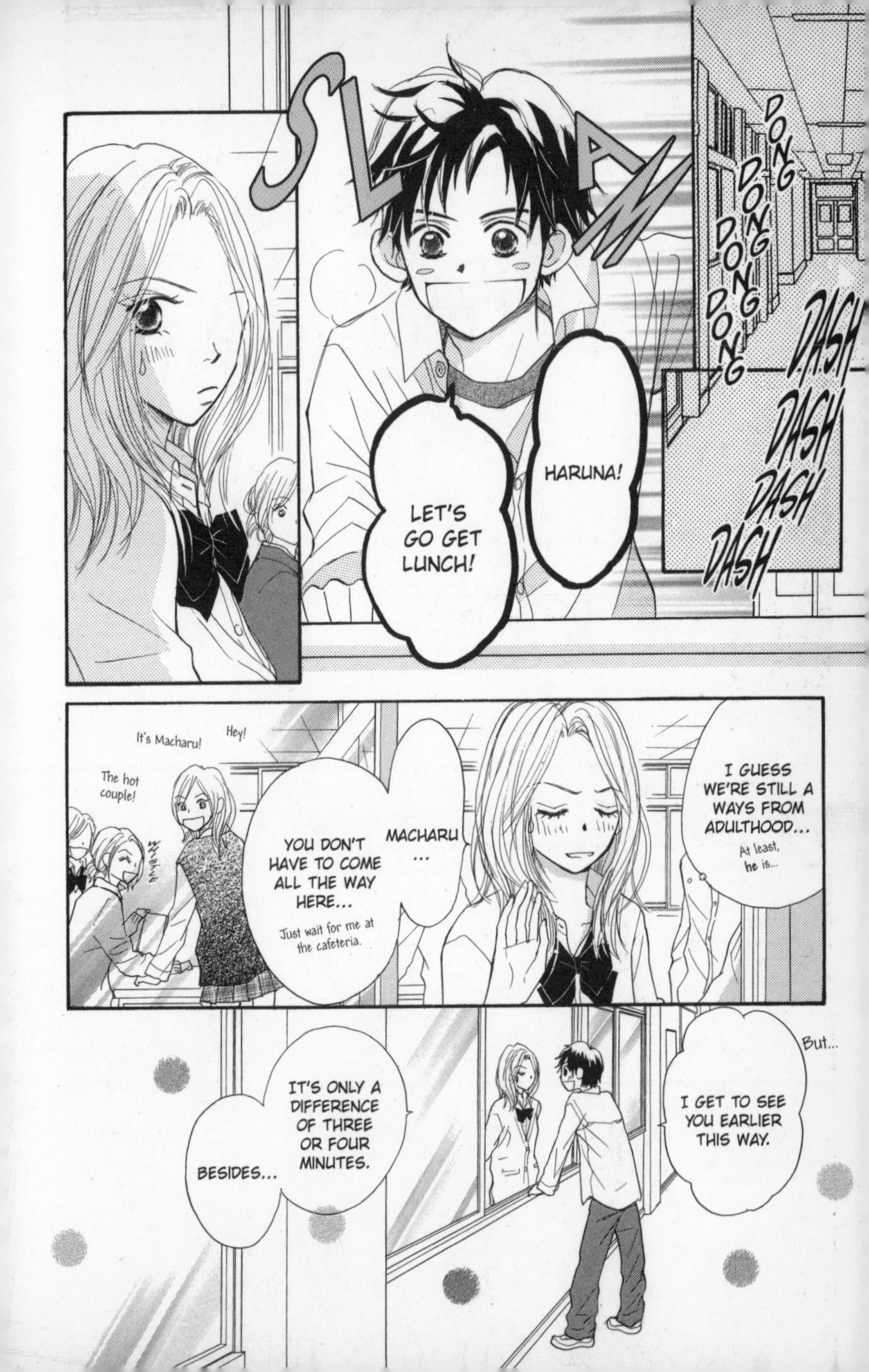
DONG DONG DONG DONG DONG
DASH DASH DASH DASH DASH
SLAM
HARUNA!
LET'S GO GET LUNCH!
I GUESS WE'RE STILL A WAYS FROM ADULTHOOD...
At least, he is...
MACHARU ...
YOU DON'T HAVE TO COME ALL THE WAY HERE...
Just wait for me at the cafeteria.
Hey!
It's Macharu!
The hot couple!
But...
I GET TO SEE YOU EARLIER THIS WAY.
IT'S ONLY A DIFFERENCE OF THREE OR FOUR MINUTES.
BESIDES...

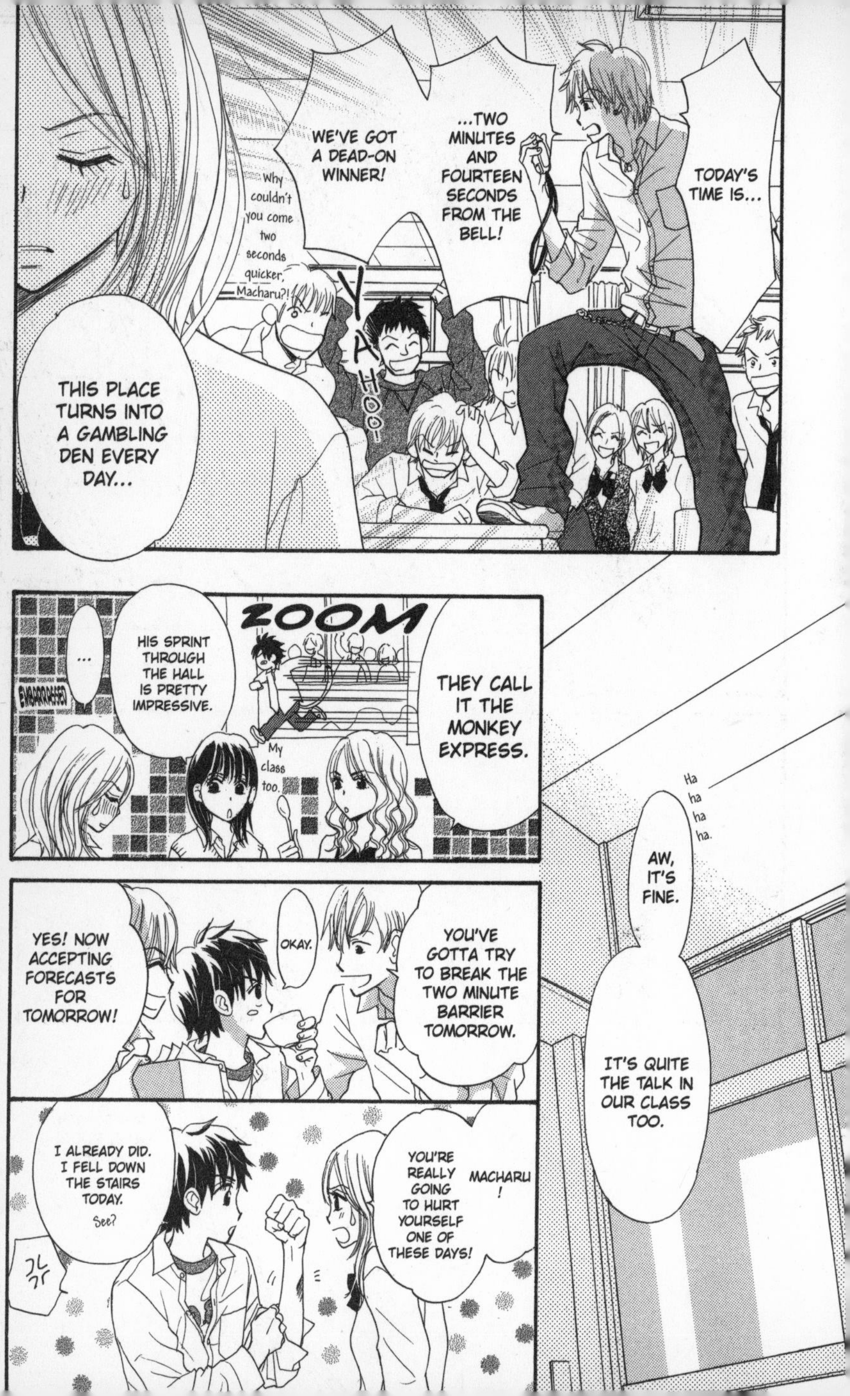
TODAY'S TIME IS...
...TWO MINUTES AND FOURTEEN SECONDS FROM THE BELL!
WE'VE GOT A DEAD-ON WINNER!
Why couldn't you come two seconds quicker, Macharu?!
YAHOO!
THIS PLACE TURNS INTO A GAMBLING DEN EVERY DAY...
Ha ha ha ha.
AW, IT'S FINE.
IT'S QUITE THE TALK IN OUR CLASS TOO.
THEY CALL IT THE MONKEY EXPRESS.
ZOOM
My class too.
HIS SPRINT THROUGH THE HALL IS PRETTY IMPRESSIVE.
...
EMBARRASSED
YOU'VE GOTTA TRY TO BREAK THE TWO MINUTE BARRIER TOMORROW.
OKAY.
YES! NOW ACCEPTING FORECASTS FOR TOMORROW!
MACHARU!
YOU'RE REALLY GOING TO HURT YOURSELF ONE OF THESE DAYS!
I ALREADY DID. I FELL DOWN THE STAIRS TODAY.
See?

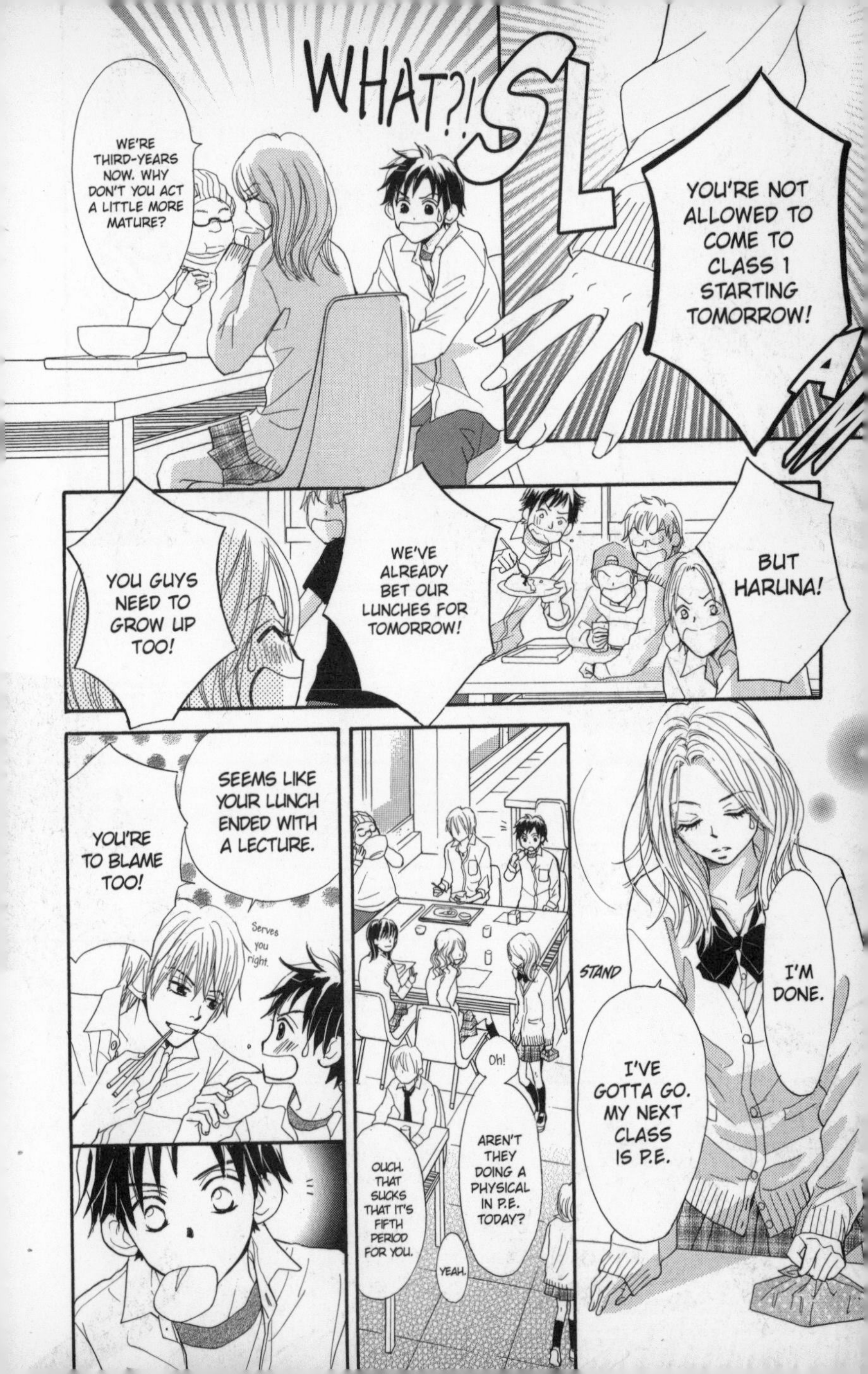
SL
AM
YOU'RE NOT ALLOWED TO COME TO CLASS 1 STARTING TOMORROW!
WHAT?!
WE'RE THIRD-YEARS NOW. WHY DON'T YOU ACT A LITTLE MORE MATURE?
BUT HARUNA!
WE'VE ALREADY BET OUR LUNCHES FOR TOMORROW!
YOU GUYS NEED TO GROW UP TOO!
STAND
I'M DONE.
I'VE GOTTA GO. MY NEXT CLASS IS P.E.
Oh!
AREN'T THEY DOING A PHYSICAL IN P.E. TODAY?
OUCH. THAT SUCKS THAT IT'S FIFTH PERIOD FOR YOU.
YEAH.
SEEMS LIKE YOUR LUNCH ENDED WITH A LECTURE.
Serves you right.
YOU'RE TO BLAME TOO!

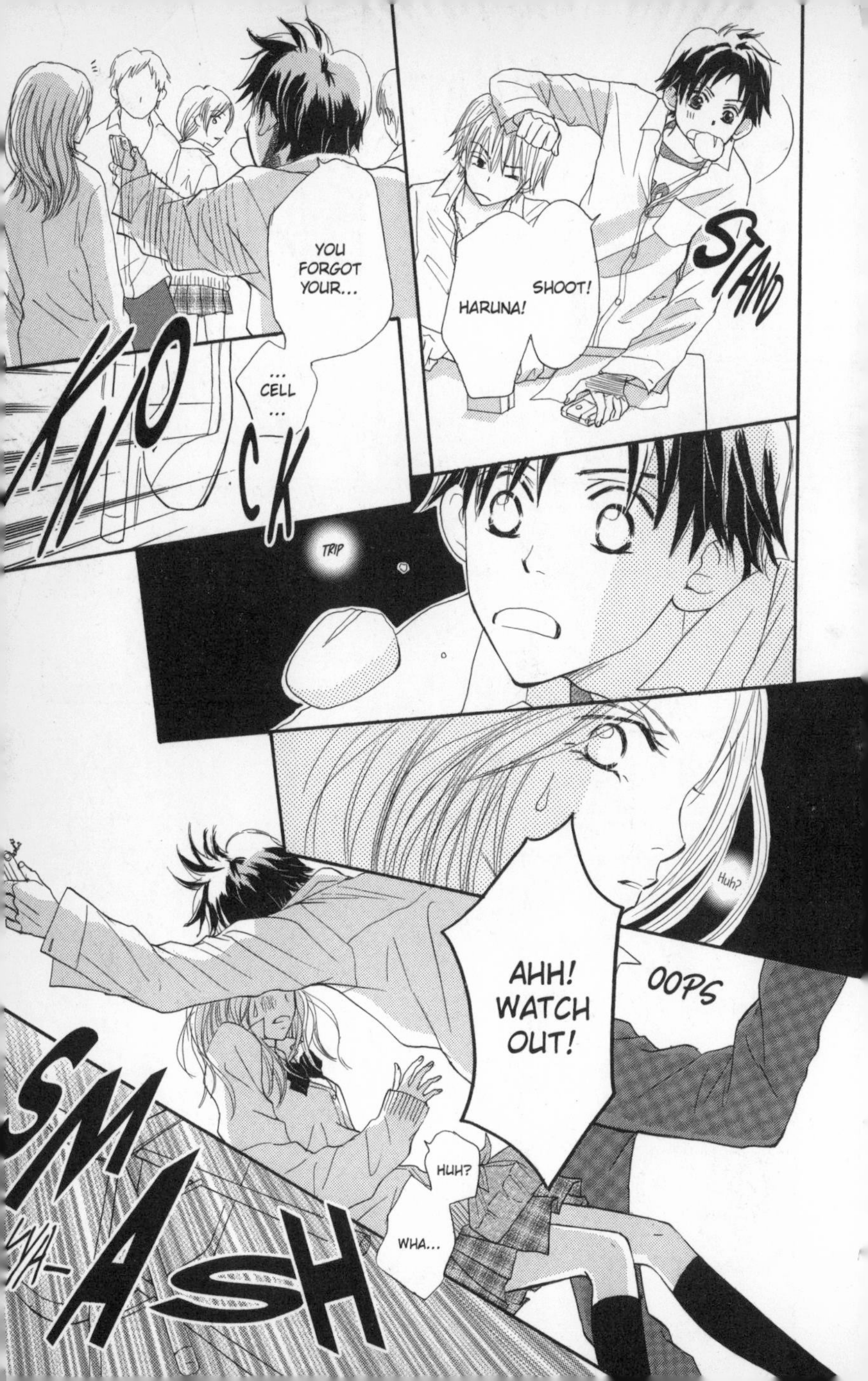
STAND
SHOOT!
HARUNA!
YOU FORGOT YOUR...
... CELL ...
KNOCK
TRIP
Huh?
OOPS
AHH! WATCH OUT!
HUH?
WHA...
SMAA-ASH

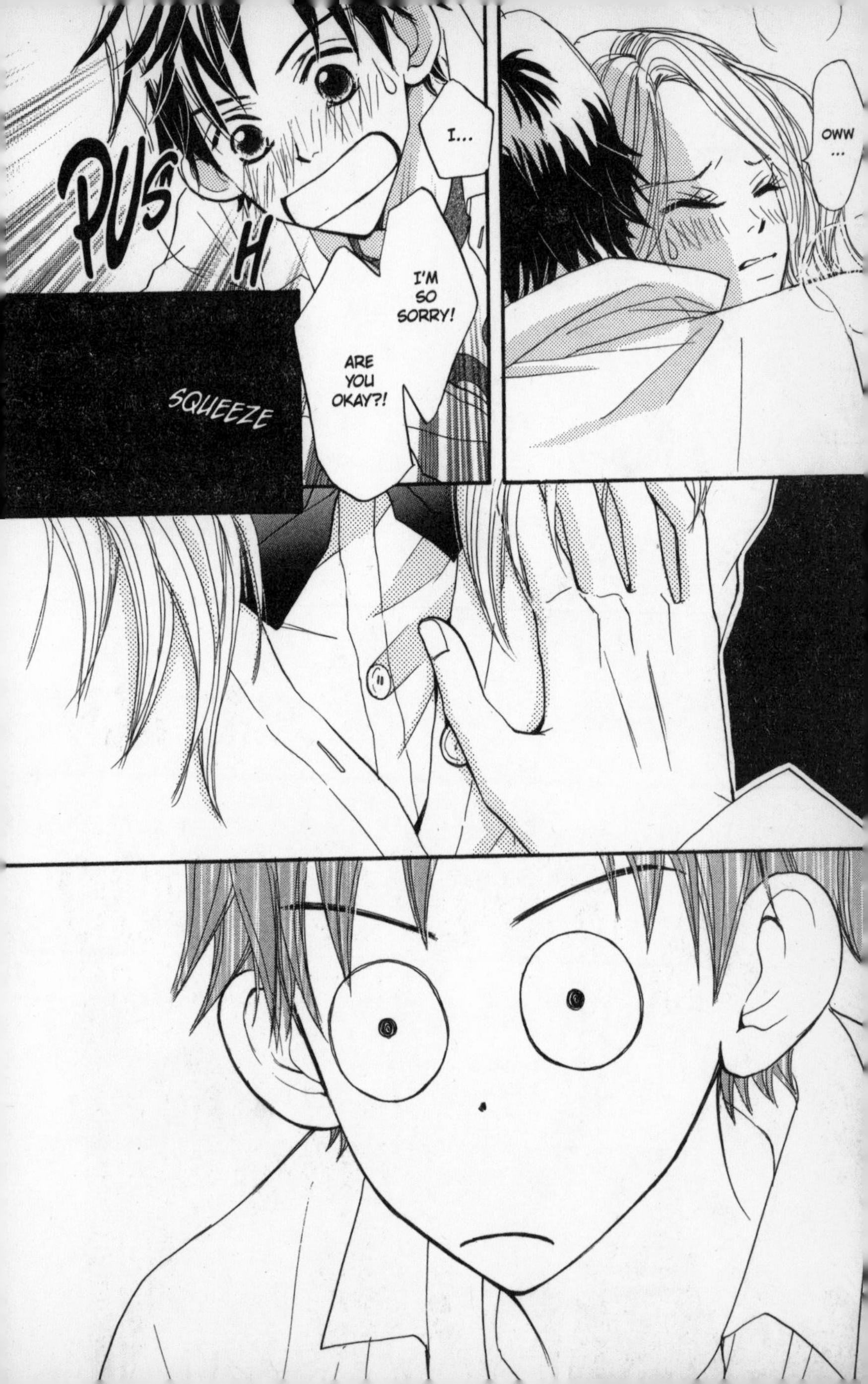
OWW ...
I...
I'M SO SORRY! ARE YOU OKAY?!
PUSH
SQUEEZE

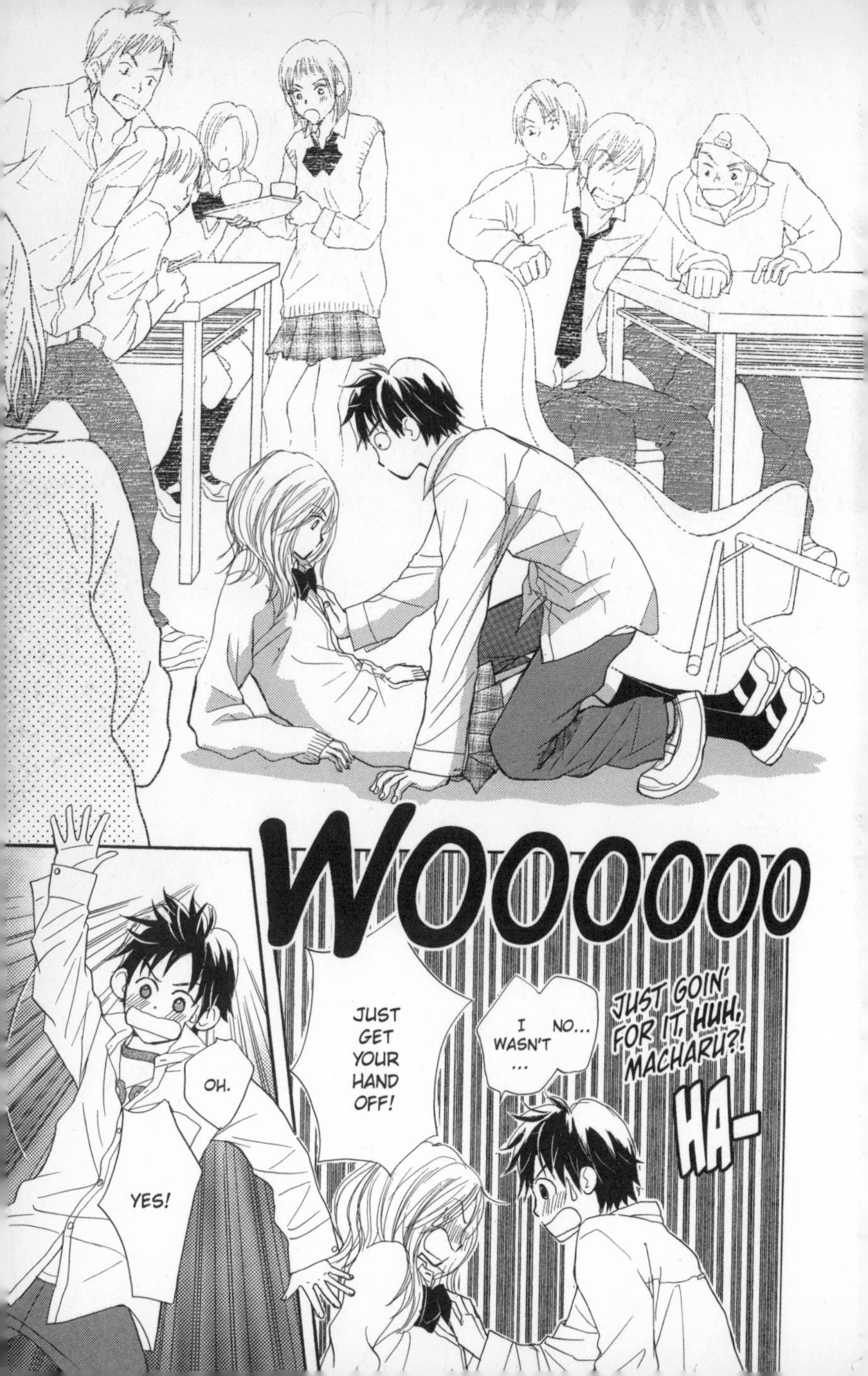
JUST GOIN' FOR IT, HUH, MACHARU?!
HA-
WOOOOOO
I WASN'T ... NO...
JUST GET YOUR HAND OFF!
OH.
YES!

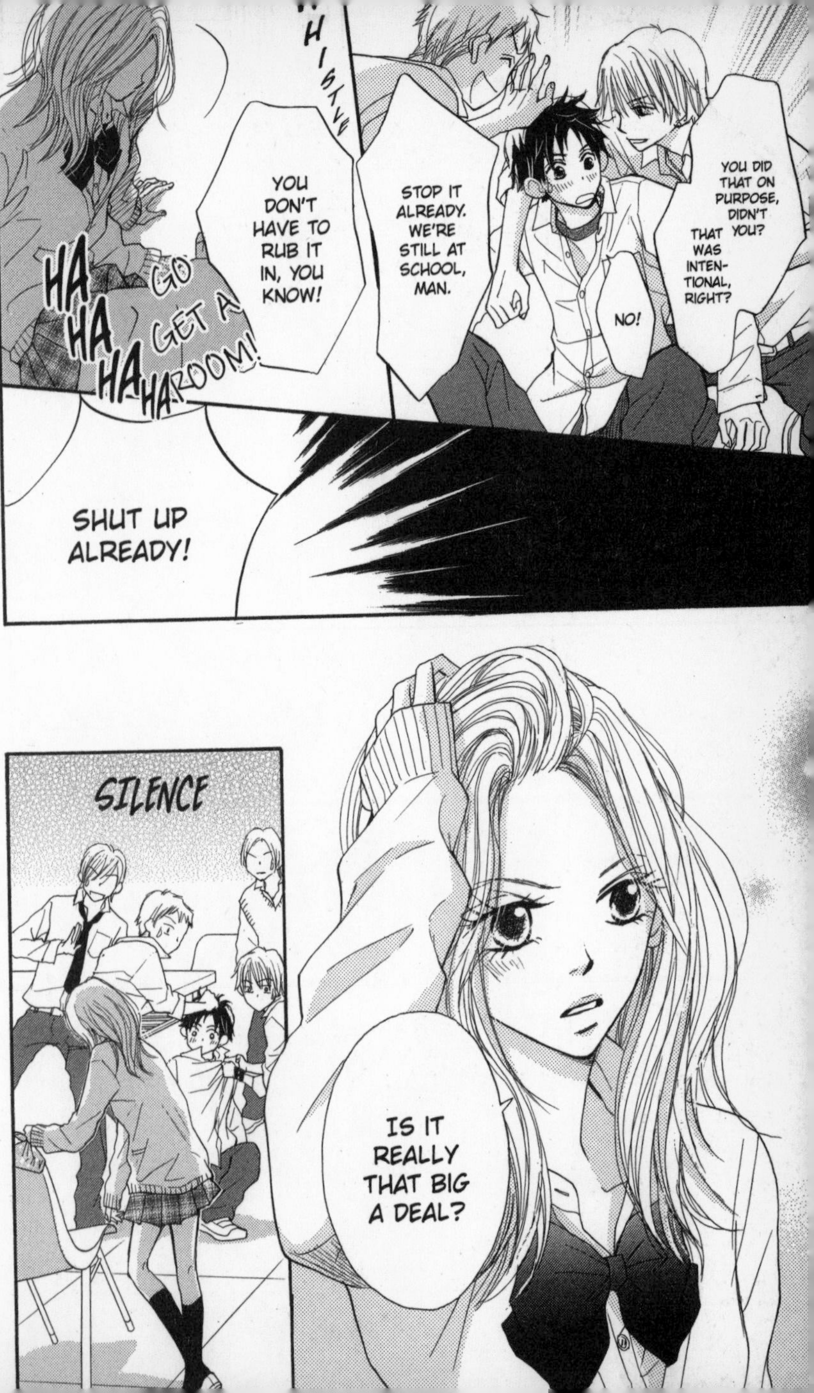
YOU DID THAT ON PURPOSE, DIDN'T YOU?
THAT WAS INTEN-TIONAL, RIGHT?
NO!
STOP IT ALREADY. WE'RE STILL AT SCHOOL, MAN.
YOU DON'T HAVE TO RUB IT IN, YOU KNOW!
GO GET A ROOM!
HA HA HA HA HA HA
SHUT UP ALREADY!
IS IT REALLY THAT BIG A DEAL?
SILENCE

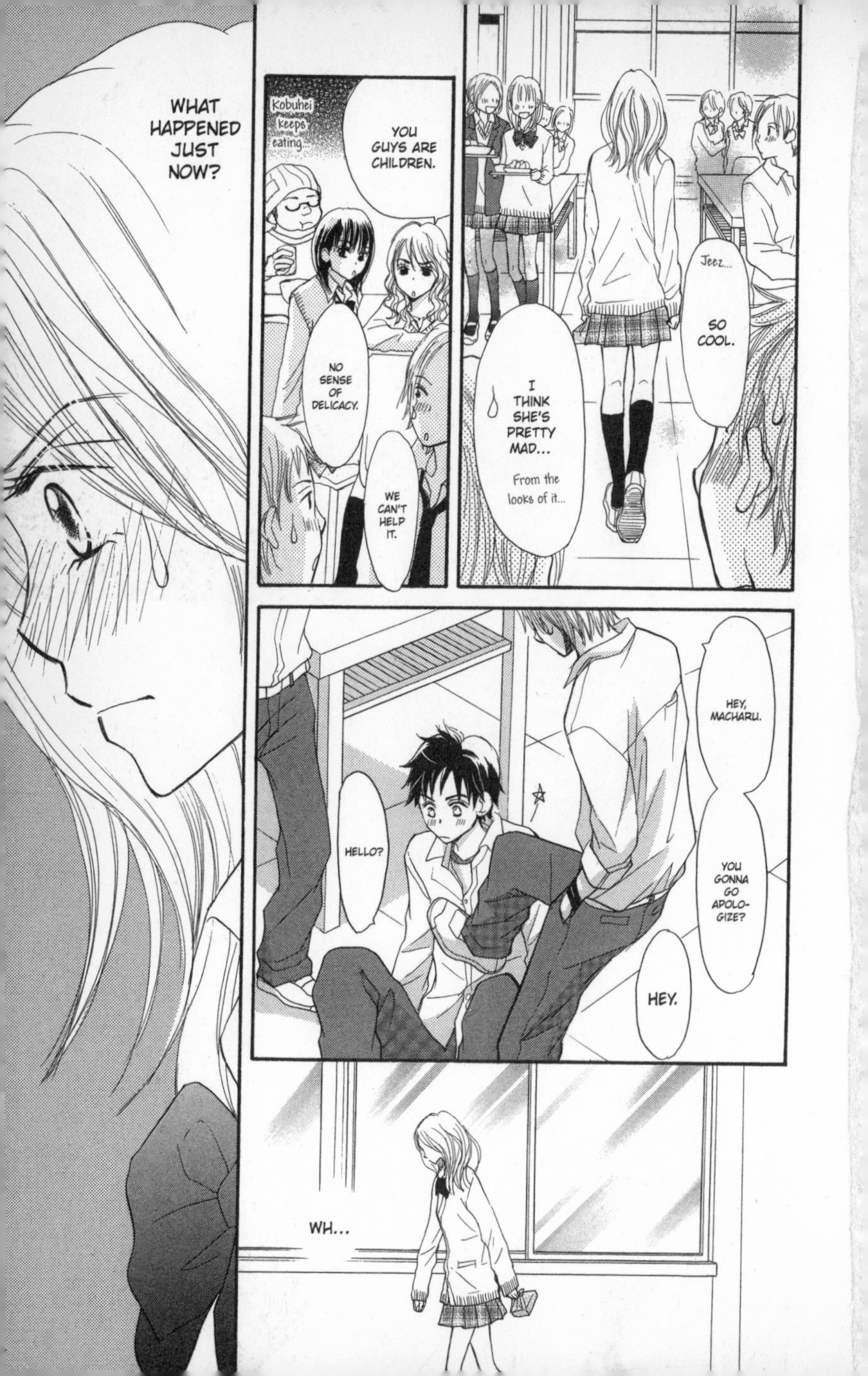
Jeez...
SO COOL.
I THINK SHE'S PRETTY MAD...
From the looks of it...
YOU GUYS ARE CHILDREN.
Kobuhei keeps eating...
NO SENSE OF DELICACY.
WE CAN'T HELP IT.
HEY, MACHARU.
YOU GONNA GO APOLOGIZE?
HEY.
HELLO?
WH...
WHAT HAPPENED JUST NOW?

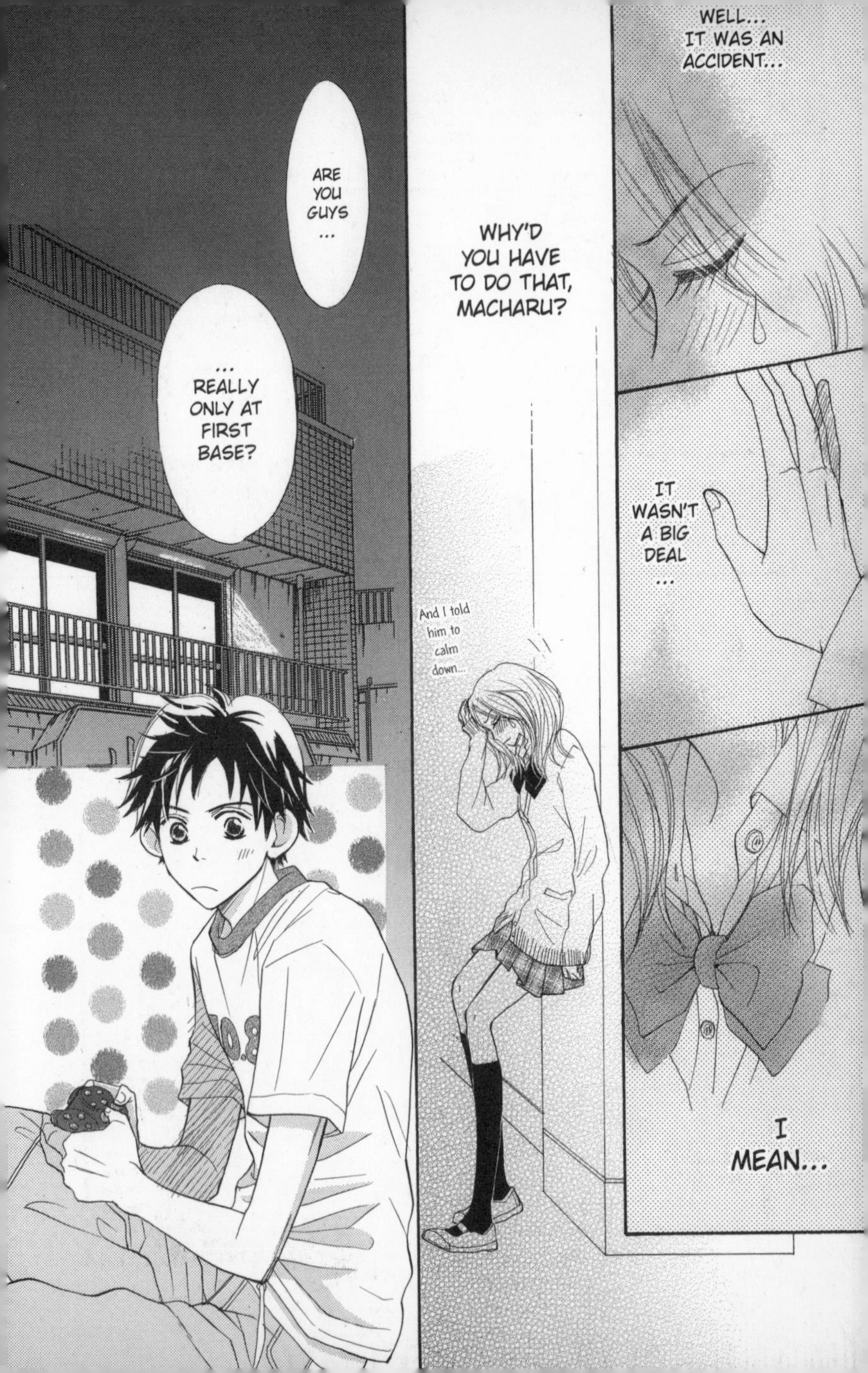
WELL... IT WAS AN ACCIDENT...
IT WASN'T A BIG DEAL ...
I MEAN...
WHY'D YOU HAVE TO DO THAT, MACHARU?
And I told him to calm down...
ARE YOU GUYS ...
... REALLY ONLY AT FIRST BASE?

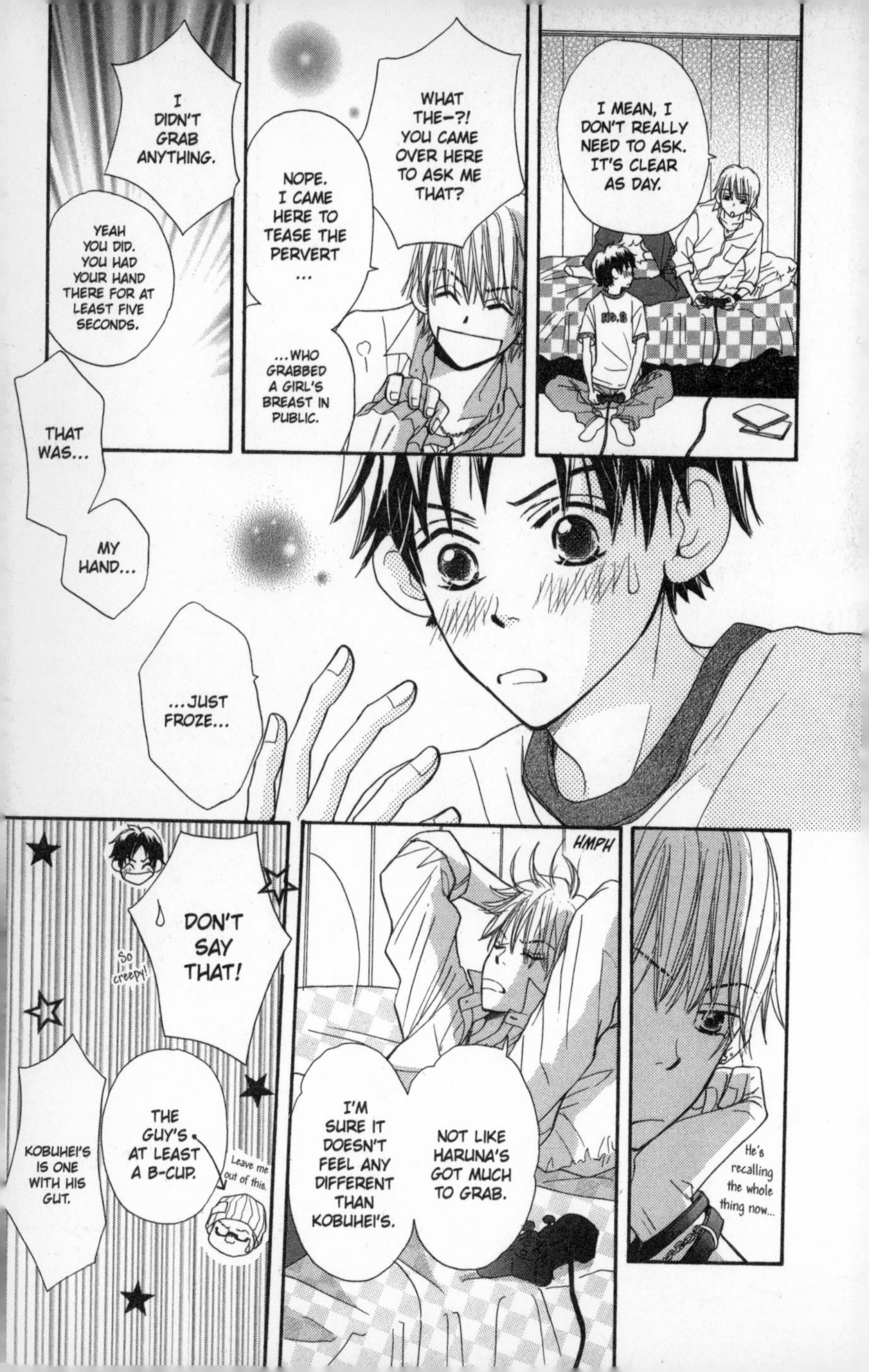
I MEAN, I DON'T REALLY NEED TO ASK. IT'S CLEAR AS DAY.
WHAT THE-?! YOU CAME OVER HERE TO ASK ME THAT?
NOPE. I CAME HERE TO TEASE THE PERVERT ...
...WHO GRABBED A GIRL'S BREAST IN PUBLIC.
I DIDN'T GRAB ANYTHING.
YEAH YOU DID. YOU HAD YOUR HAND THERE FOR AT LEAST FIVE SECONDS.
THAT WAS...
MY HAND...
...JUST FROZE...
He's recalling the whole thing now...
HMPH
NOT LIKE HARUNA'S GOT MUCH TO GRAB.
I'M SURE IT DOESN'T FEEL ANY DIFFERENT THAN KOBUHEI'S.
DON'T SAY THAT!
So creepy!
THE GUY'S AT LEAST A B-CUP.
Leave me out of this.
KOBUHEI'S IS ONE WITH HIS GUT.

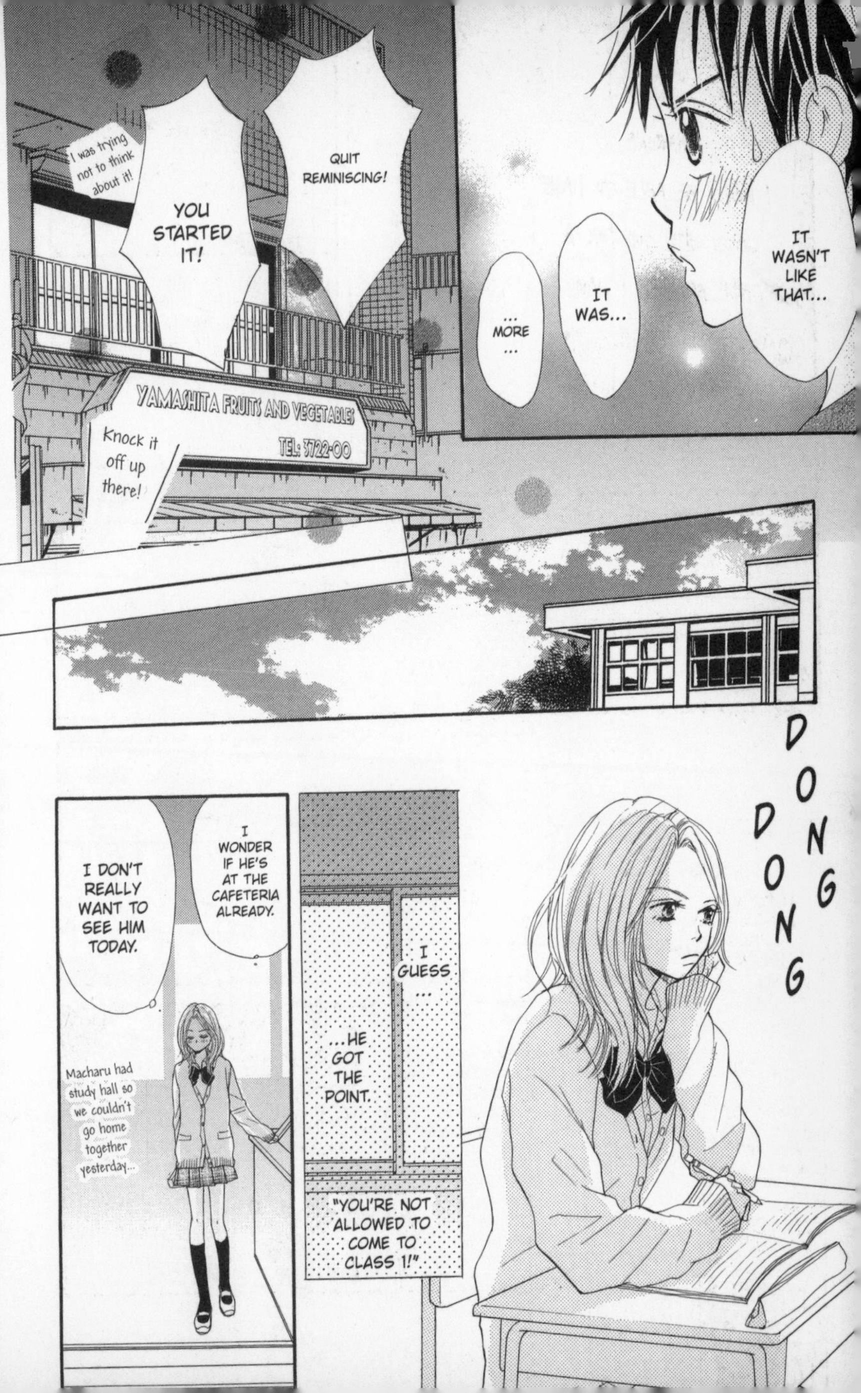

IT WASN'T LIKE THAT...
IT WAS...
...MORE...
QUIT REMINISCING!
YOU STARTED IT!
I was trying not to think about it!
YAMASHITA FRUITS AND VEGETABLES
TEL: 3722-00
Knock it off up there!
DONG DONG
I GUESS...
...HE GOT THE POINT.
"YOU'RE NOT ALLOWED TO COME TO CLASS 1!"
I WONDER IF HE'S AT THE CAFETERIA ALREADY.
I DON'T REALLY WANT TO SEE HIM TODAY.
Macharu had study hall so we couldn't go home together yesterday...

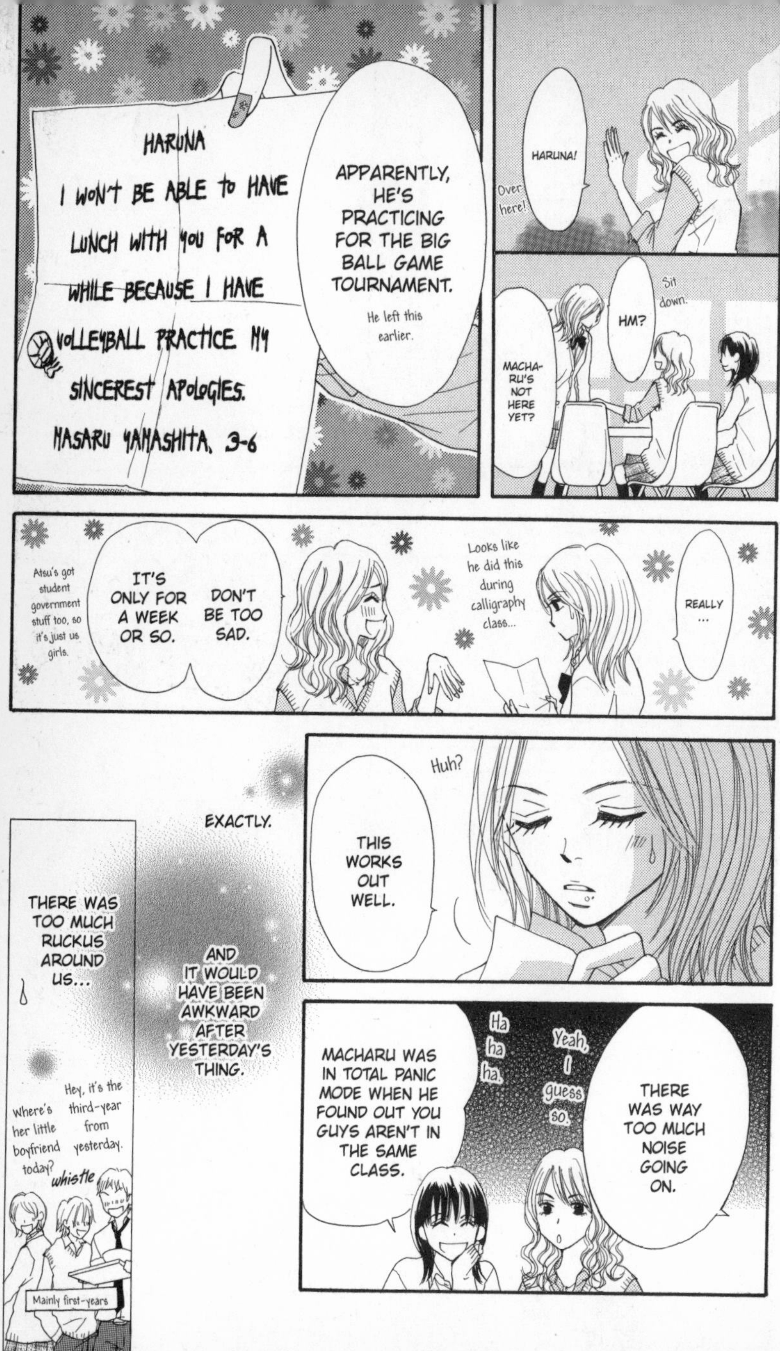
HARUNA!
Over here!
Sit down.
HM?
MACHARU'S NOT HERE YET?
HARUNA
I WON'T BE ABLE TO HAVE LUNCH WITH YOU FOR A WHILE BECAUSE I HAVE VOLLEYBALL PRACTICE. MY SINCEREST APOLOGIES.
MASARU YAMASHITA, 3-6
APPARENTLY, HE'S PRACTICING FOR THE BIG BALL GAME TOURNAMENT.
He left this earlier.
REALLY...
Looks like he did this during calligraphy class...
IT'S ONLY FOR A WEEK OR SO.
DON'T BE TOO SAD.
Atsu's got student government stuff too, so it's just us girls.
Huh?
THIS WORKS OUT WELL.
THERE WAS WAY TOO MUCH NOISE GOING ON.
Yeah, I guess so.
Ha ha ha.
MACHARU WAS IN TOTAL PANIC MODE WHEN HE FOUND OUT YOU GUYS AREN'T IN THE SAME CLASS.
EXACTLY.
THERE WAS TOO MUCH RUCKUS AROUND US...
AND IT WOULD HAVE BEEN AWKWARD AFTER YESTERDAY'S THING.
Hey, it's the third-year from yesterday.
Where's her little boyfriend today?
whistle
Mainly first-years

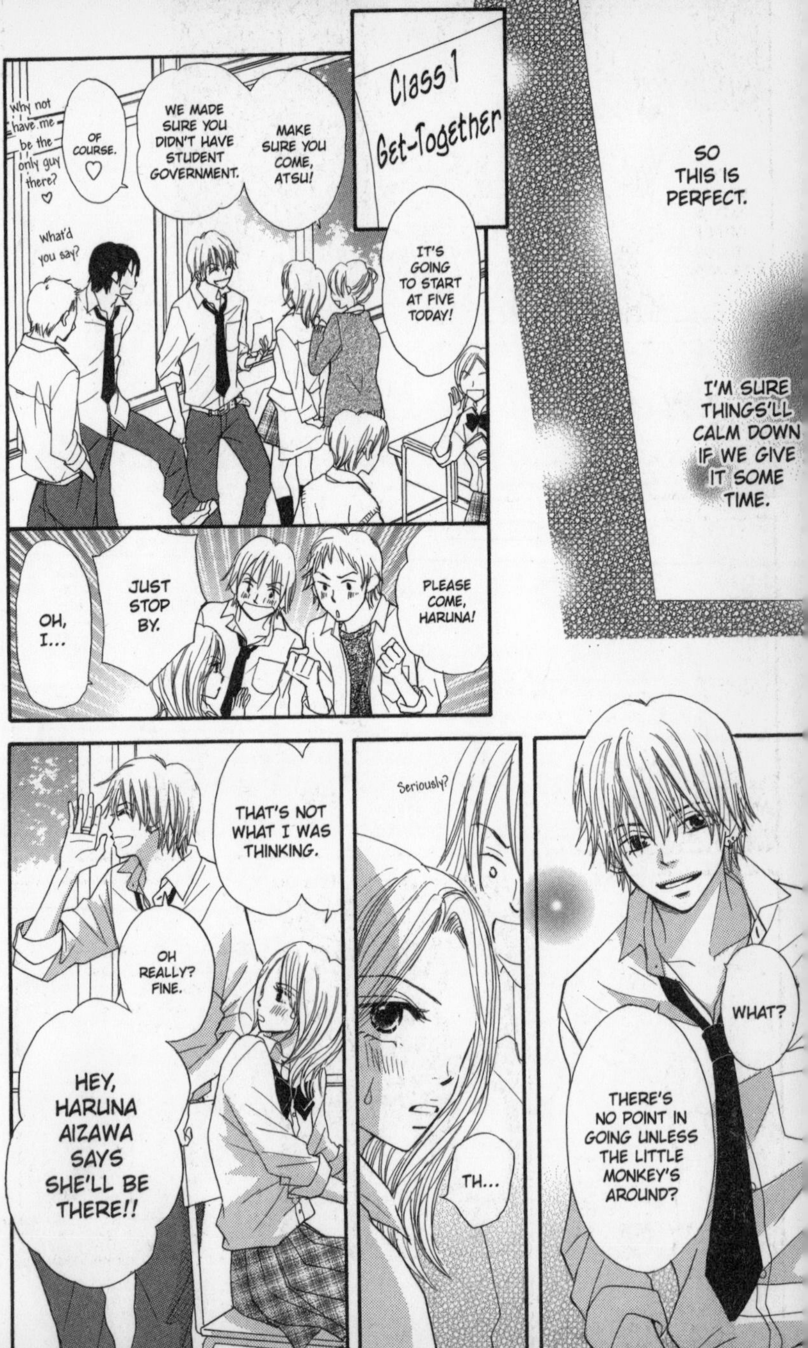
SO THIS IS PERFECT.
I'M SURE THINGS'LL CALM DOWN IF WE GIVE IT SOME TIME.
Class 1 Get-Together
IT'S GOING TO START AT FIVE TODAY!
MAKE SURE YOU COME, ATSU!
WE MADE SURE YOU DIDN'T HAVE STUDENT GOVERNMENT.
OF COURSE. ♡
Why not have me be the only guy there? ♡
What'd you say?
PLEASE COME, HARUNA!
JUST STOP BY.
OH, I...
WHAT?
THERE'S NO POINT IN GOING UNLESS THE LITTLE MONKEY'S AROUND?
Seriously?
TH...
THAT'S NOT WHAT I WAS THINKING.
OH REALLY? FINE.
HEY, HARUNA AIZAWA SAYS SHE'LL BE THERE!!

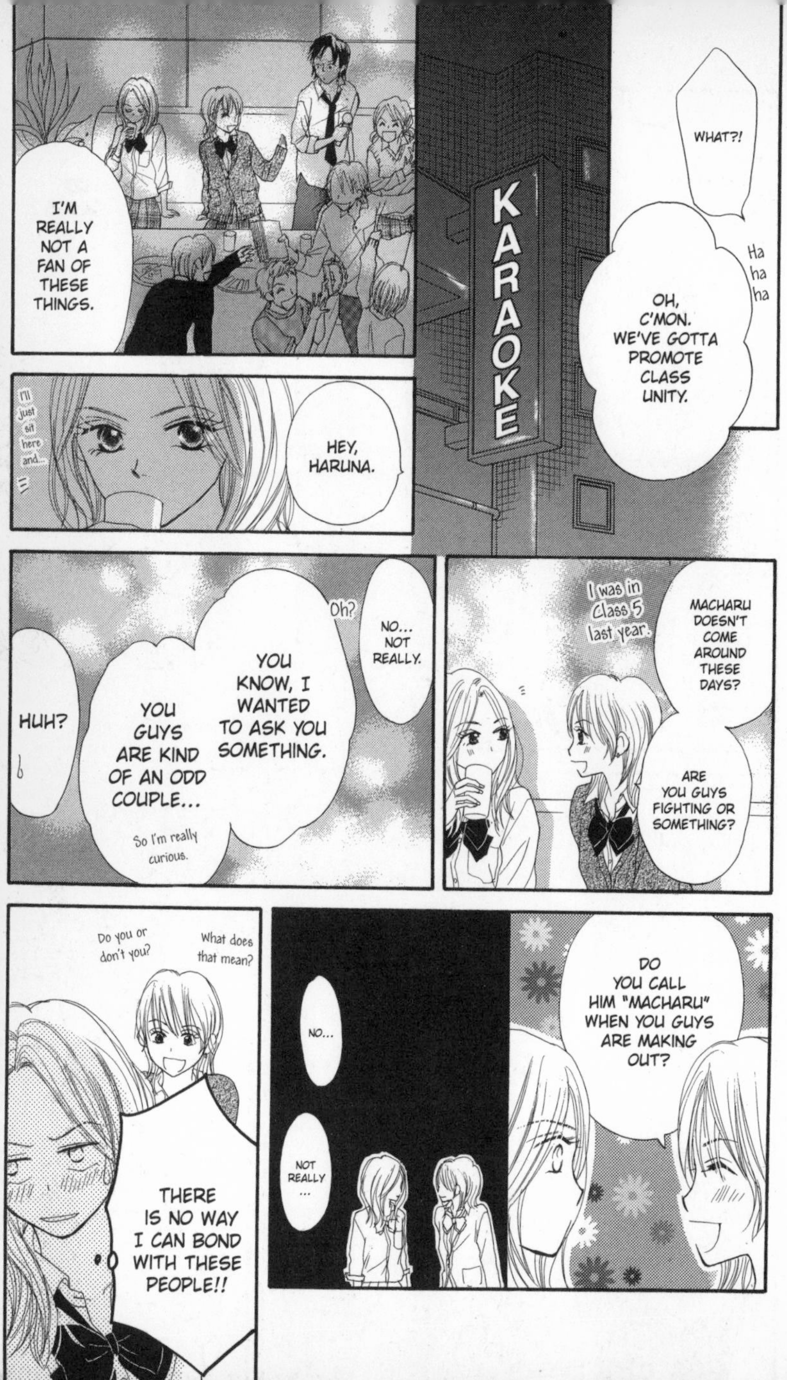
WHAT?!
Ha ha ha
OH, C'MON. WE'VE GOTTA PROMOTE CLASS UNITY.
KARAOKE
I'M REALLY NOT A FAN OF THESE THINGS.
HEY, HARUNA.
I'll just sit here and...
MACHARU DOESN'T COME AROUND THESE DAYS?
I was in Class 5 last year.
ARE YOU GUYS FIGHTING OR SOMETHING?
NO... NOT REALLY.
Oh?
YOU KNOW, I WANTED TO ASK YOU SOMETHING.
YOU GUYS ARE KIND OF AN ODD COUPLE...
So I'm really curious.
HUH?
DO YOU CALL HIM "MACHARU" WHEN YOU GUYS ARE MAKING OUT?
NO...
NOT REALLY ...
What does that mean?
Do you or don't you?
THERE IS NO WAY I CAN BOND WITH THESE PEOPLE!!

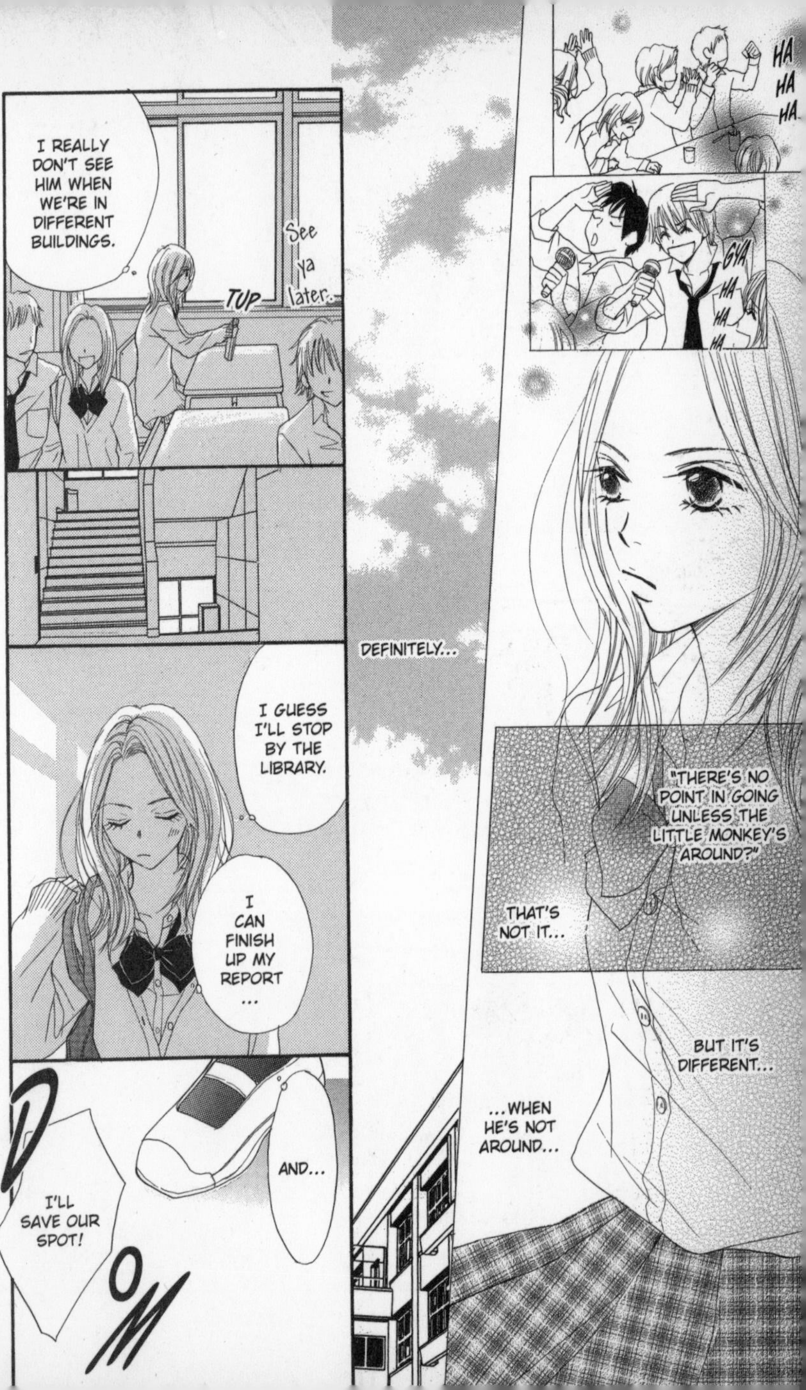
HA HA HA
GYA HA HA HA HA
"THERE'S NO POINT IN GOING UNLESS THE LITTLE MONKEY'S AROUND?"
THAT'S NOT IT...
BUT IT'S DIFFERENT...
...WHEN HE'S NOT AROUND...
DEFINITELY...
I REALLY DON'T SEE HIM WHEN WE'RE IN DIFFERENT BUILDINGS.
See ya later.
TUP
I GUESS I'LL STOP BY THE LIBRARY.
I CAN FINISH UP MY REPORT ...
AND...
I'LL SAVE OUR SPOT!
DOM

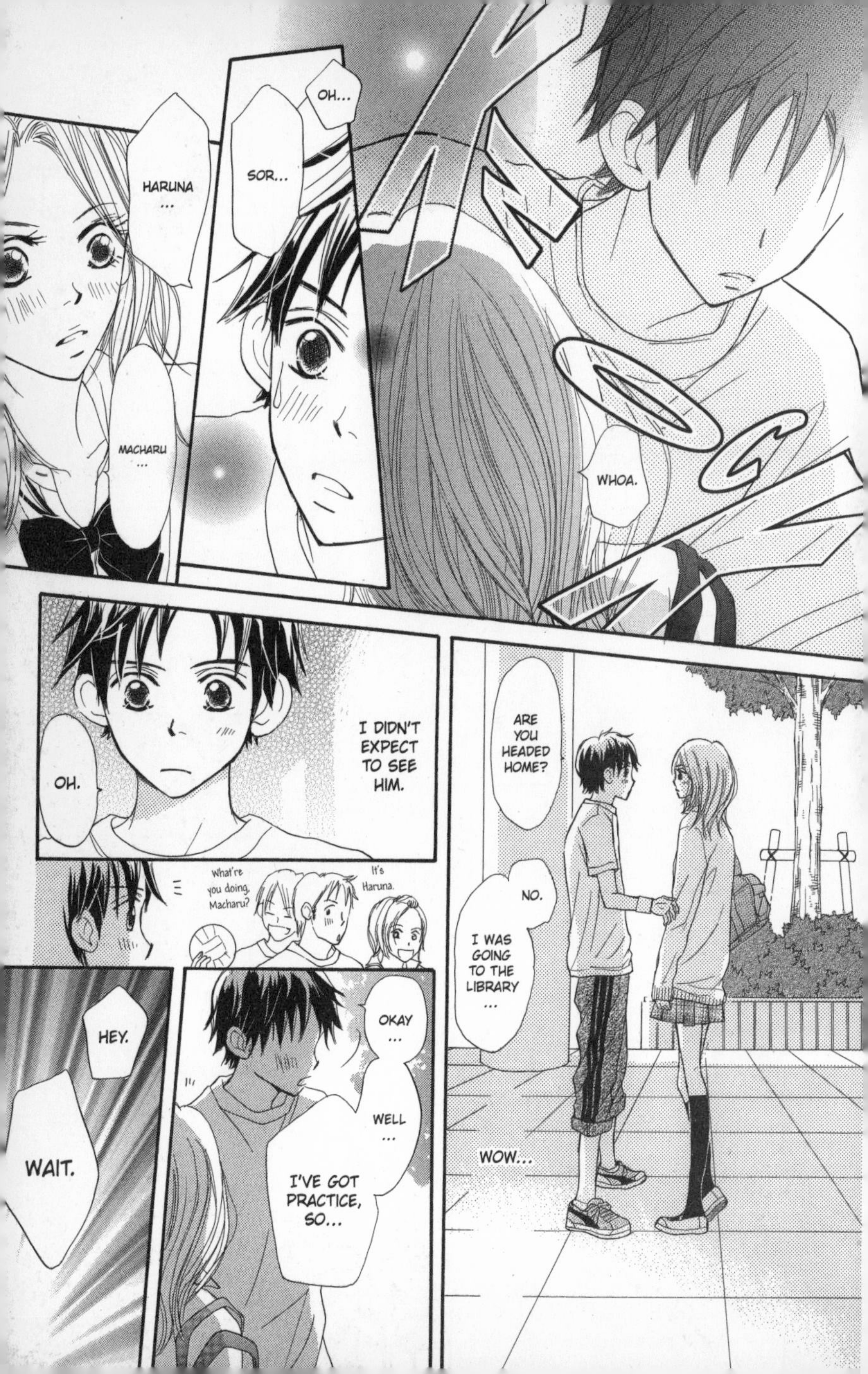
WHOA.
OH...
SOR...
HARUNA ...
MACHARU ...
ARE YOU HEADED HOME?
NO.
I WAS GOING TO THE LIBRARY ...
WOW...
I DIDN'T EXPECT TO SEE HIM.
OH.
It's Haruna.
What're you doing, Macharu?
OKAY ...
WELL ...
I'VE GOT PRACTICE, SO...
HEY.
WAIT.

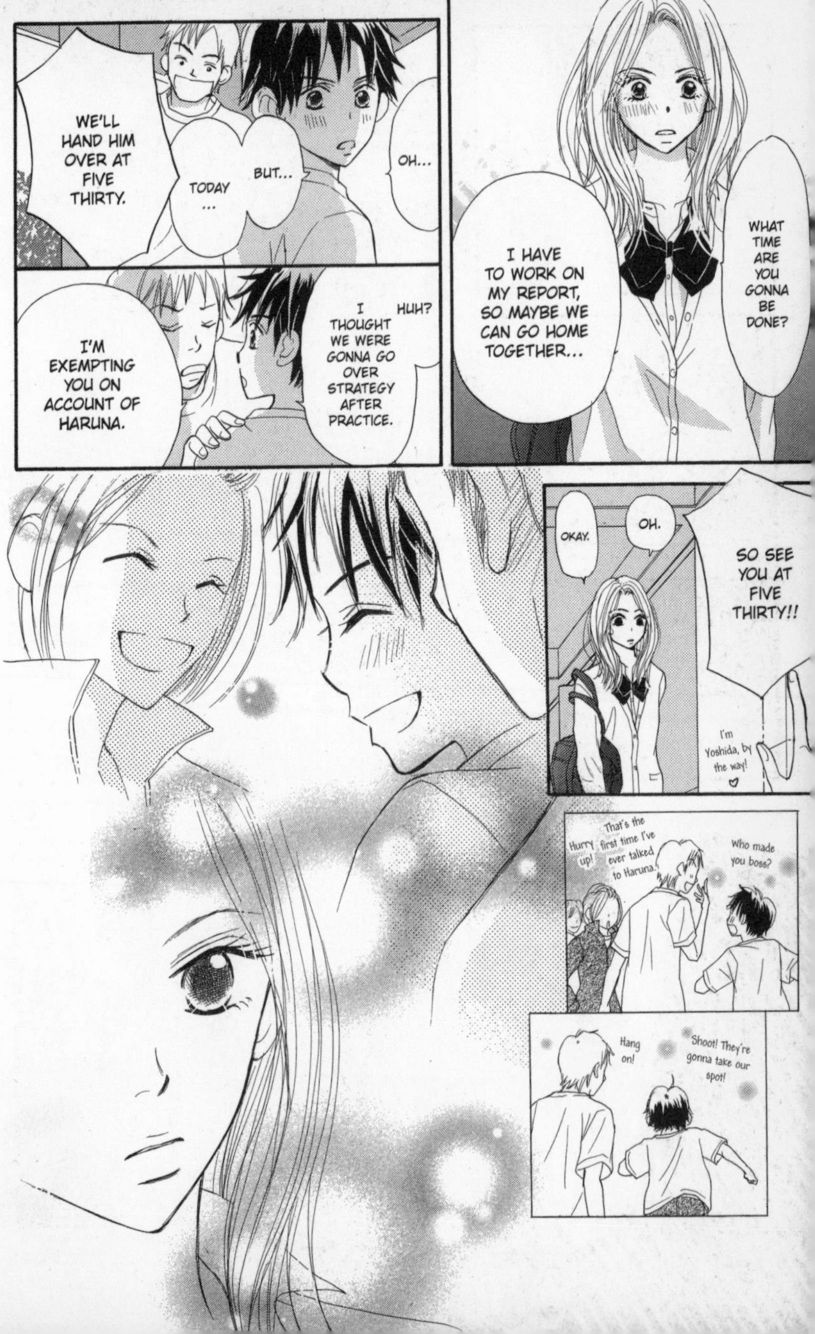
WHAT TIME ARE YOU GONNA BE DONE?
I HAVE TO WORK ON MY REPORT, SO MAYBE WE CAN GO HOME TOGETHER...
OH...
BUT...
TODAY...
WE'LL HAND HIM OVER AT FIVE THIRTY.
HUH?
I THOUGHT WE WERE GONNA GO OVER STRATEGY AFTER PRACTICE.
I'M EXEMPTING YOU ON ACCOUNT OF HARUNA.
SO SEE YOU AT FIVE THIRTY!!
I'm Yoshida, by the way! ♡
OH.
OKAY.
Who made you boss?
That's the first time I've ever talked to Haruna!
Hurry up!
Shoot! They're gonna take our spot!
Hang on!

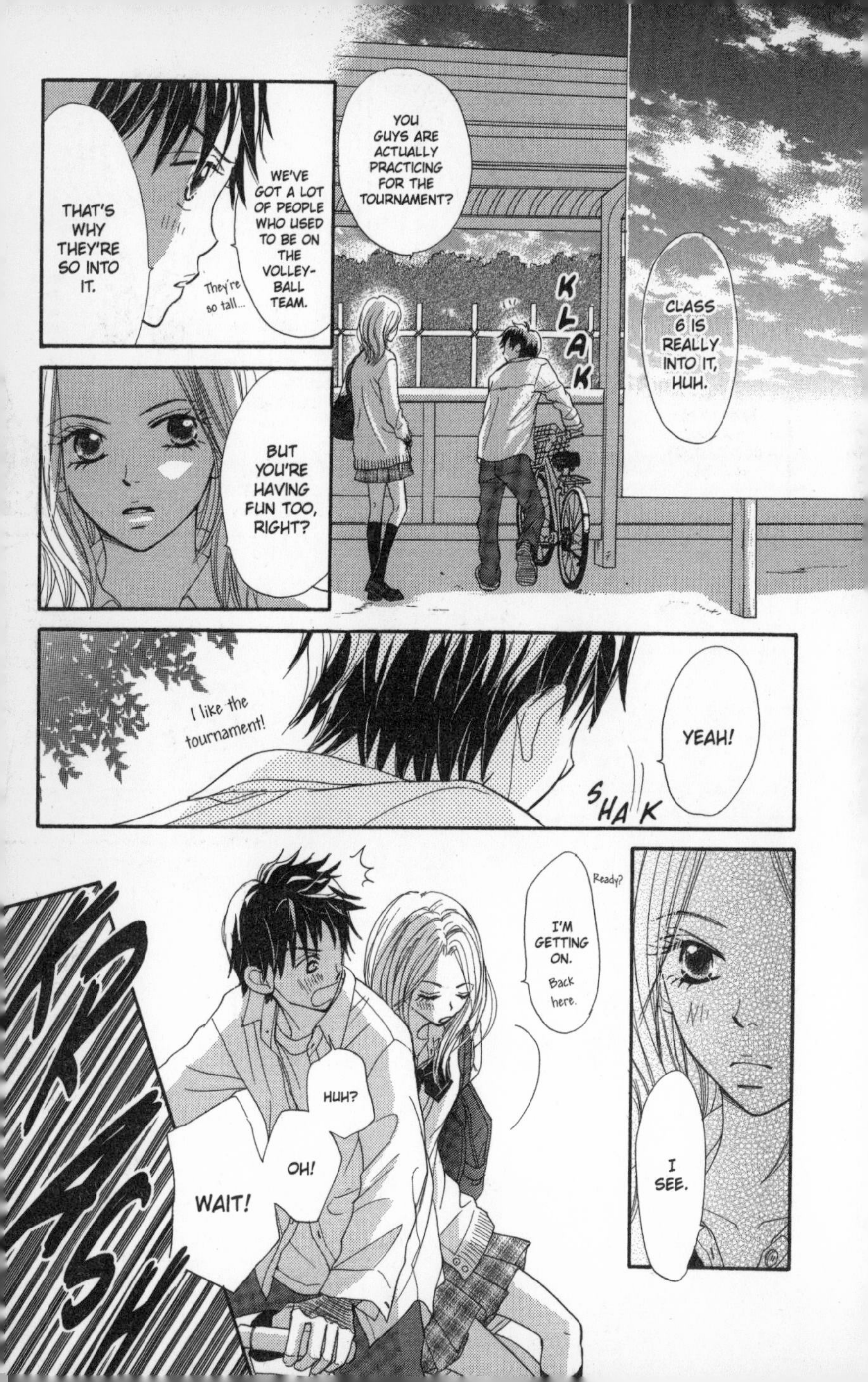
CLASS 6 IS REALLY INTO IT, HUH.
YOU GUYS ARE ACTUALLY PRACTICING FOR THE TOURNAMENT?
KLAK
WE'VE GOT A LOT OF PEOPLE WHO USED TO BE ON THE VOLLEY-BALL TEAM.
They're so tall...
THAT'S WHY THEY'RE SO INTO IT.
BUT YOU'RE HAVING FUN TOO, RIGHT?
YEAH!
SHAK
I like the tournament!
I SEE.
Ready?
I'M GETTING ON.
Back here.
HUH?
OH!
WAIT!

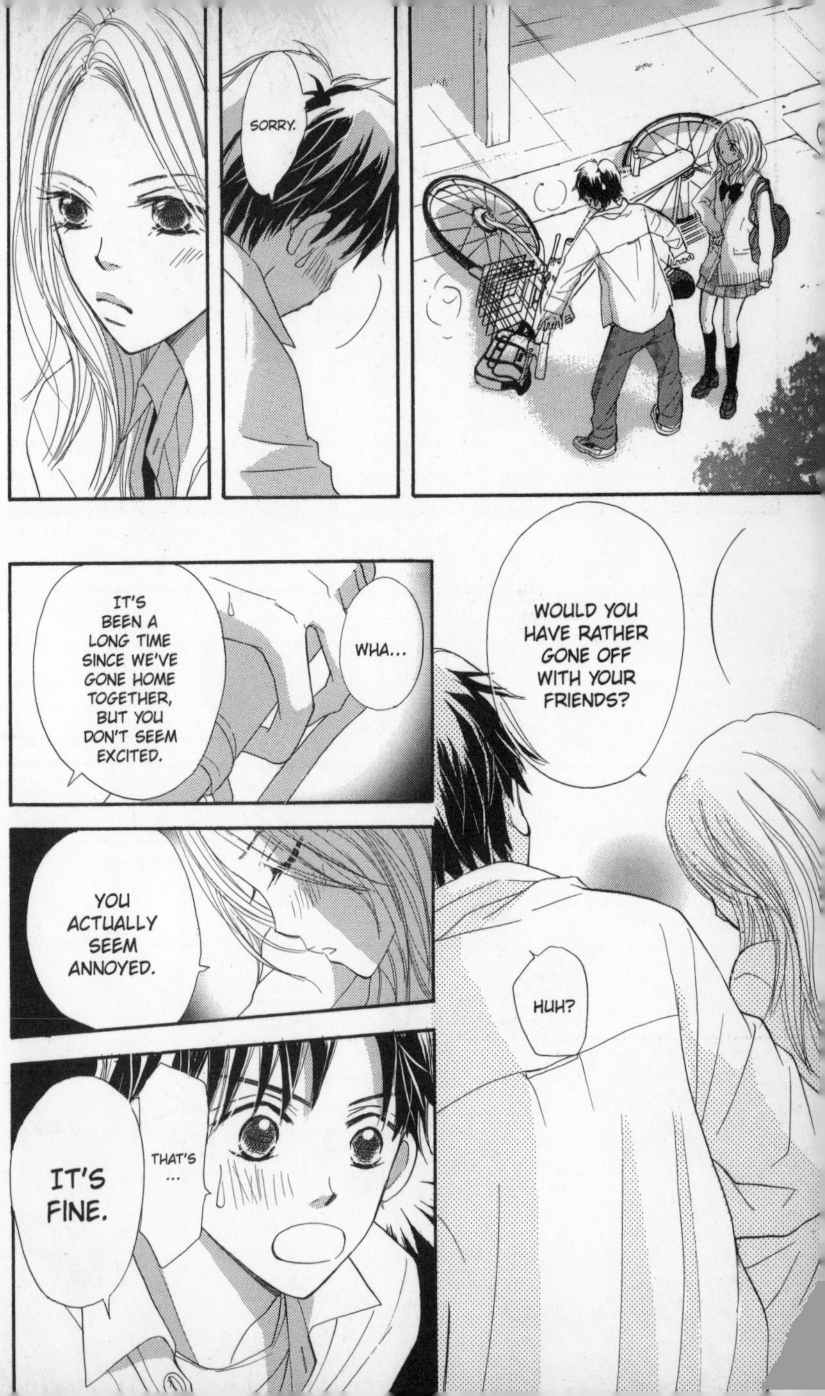
SORRY.
WOULD YOU HAVE RATHER GONE OFF WITH YOUR FRIENDS?
HUH?
WHA...
IT'S BEEN A LONG TIME SINCE WE'VE GONE HOME TOGETHER, BUT YOU DON'T SEEM EXCITED.
YOU ACTUALLY SEEM ANNOYED.
THAT'S...
IT'S FINE.

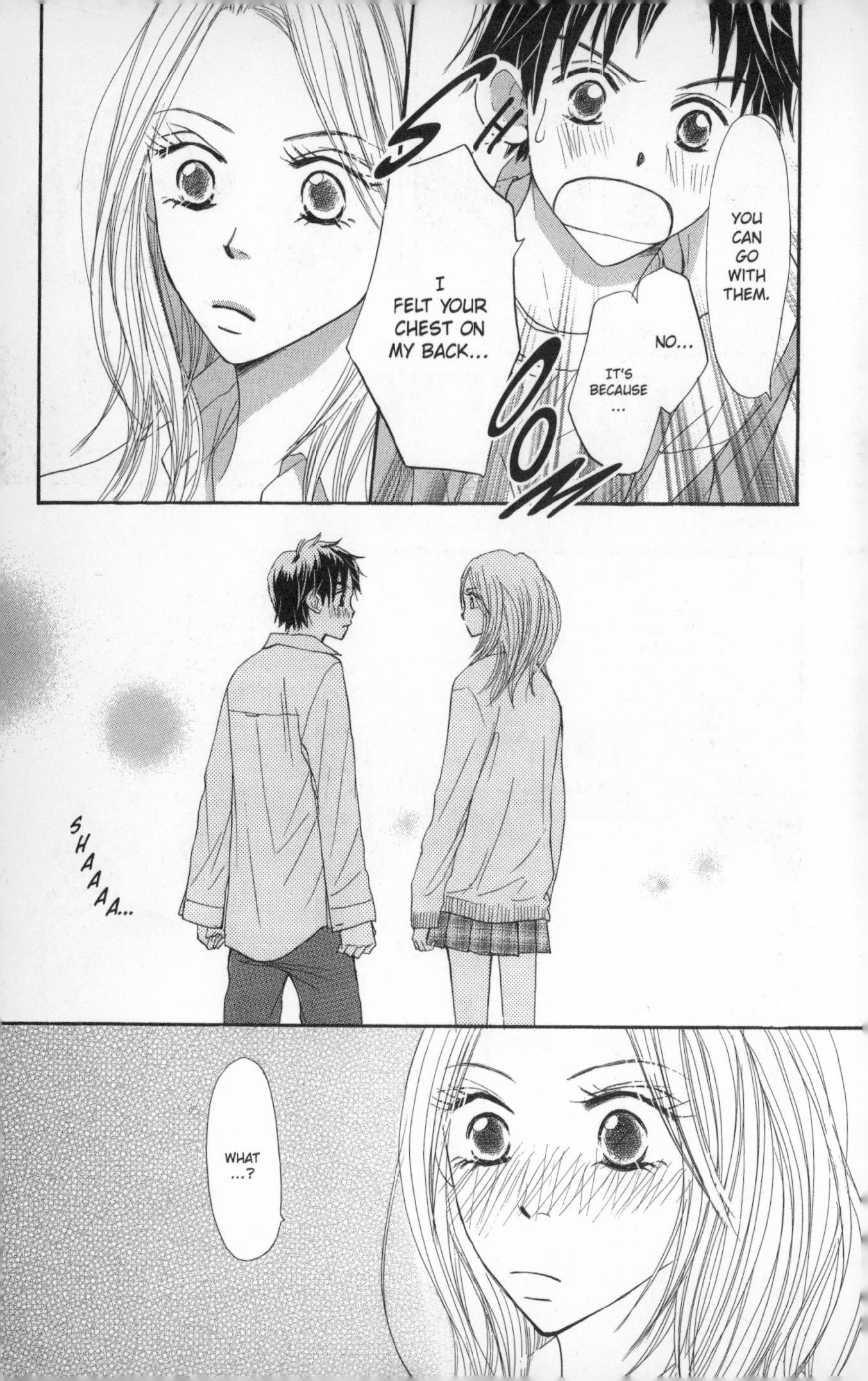
YOU CAN GO WITH THEM.
NO...
IT'S BECAUSE ...
I FELT YOUR CHEST ON MY BACK...
SHOOOM
SHAAAA...
WHAT ...?

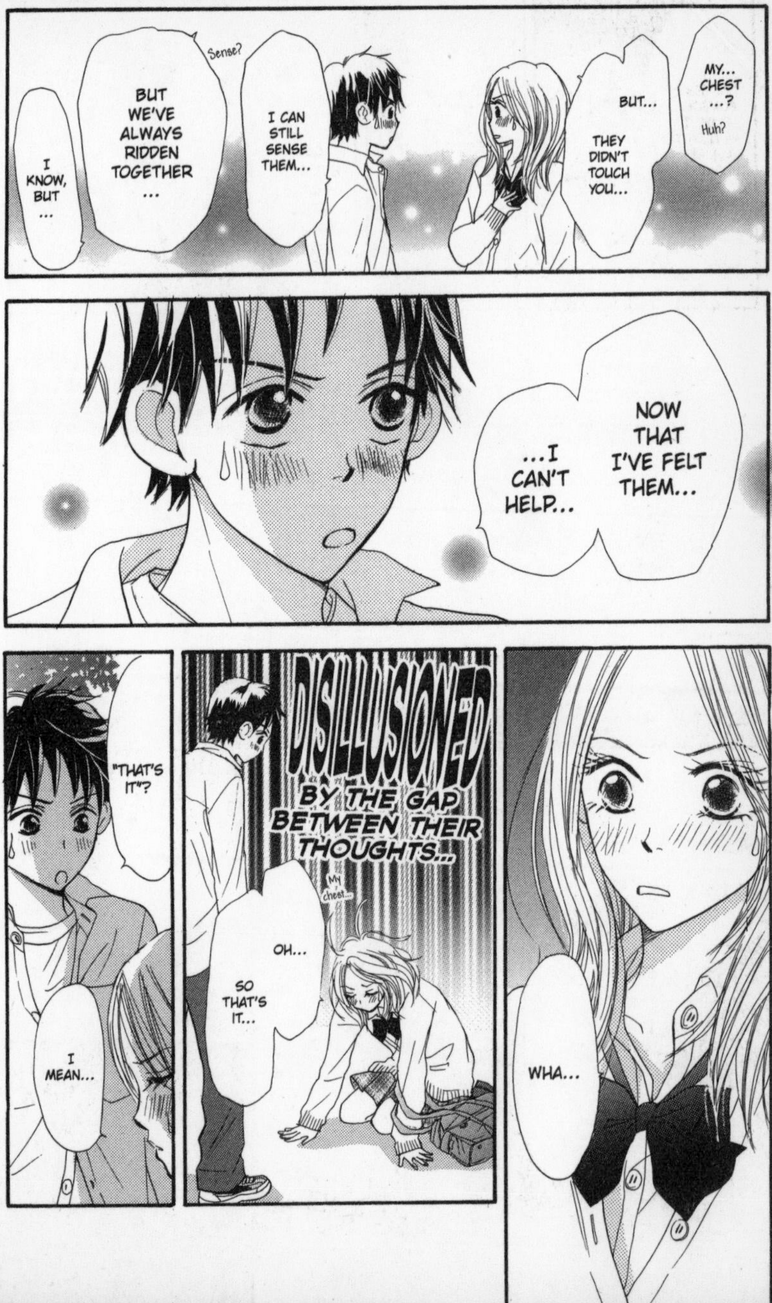
MY... CHEST ...?
Huh?
BUT...
THEY DIDN'T TOUCH YOU...
I CAN STILL SENSE THEM...
Sense?
BUT WE'VE ALWAYS RIDDEN TOGETHER ...
I KNOW, BUT ...
NOW THAT I'VE FELT THEM...
...I CAN'T HELP...
WHA...
DISILLUSIONED
BY THE GAP BETWEEN THEIR THOUGHTS...
My chest...
OH...
SO THAT'S IT...
"THAT'S IT"?
I MEAN...

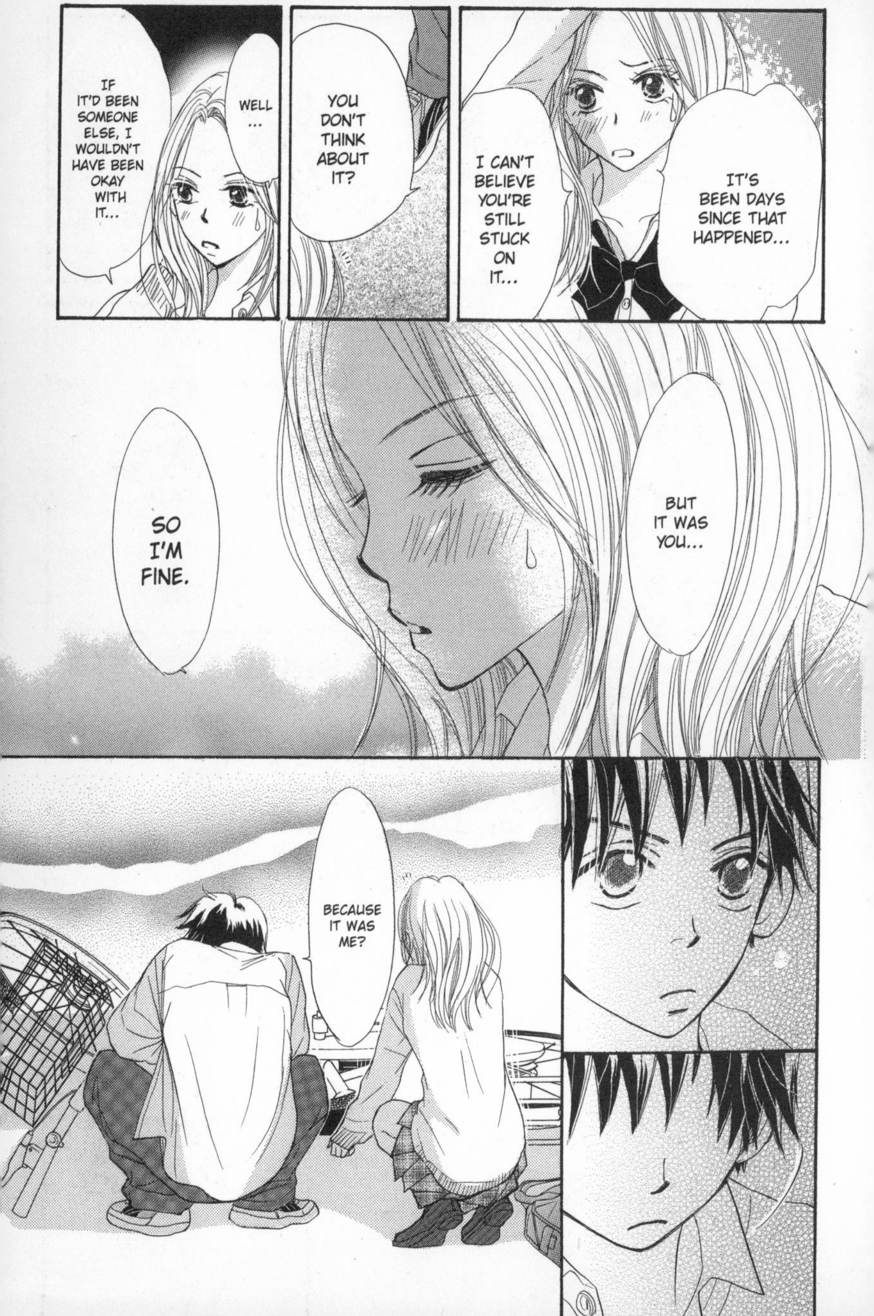
IT'S BEEN DAYS SINCE THAT HAPPENED...
I CAN'T BELIEVE YOU'RE STILL STUCK ON IT...
YOU DON'T THINK ABOUT IT?
WELL...
IF IT'D BEEN SOMEONE ELSE, I WOULDN'T HAVE BEEN OKAY WITH IT...
BUT IT WAS YOU...
SO I'M FINE.
BECAUSE IT WAS ME?

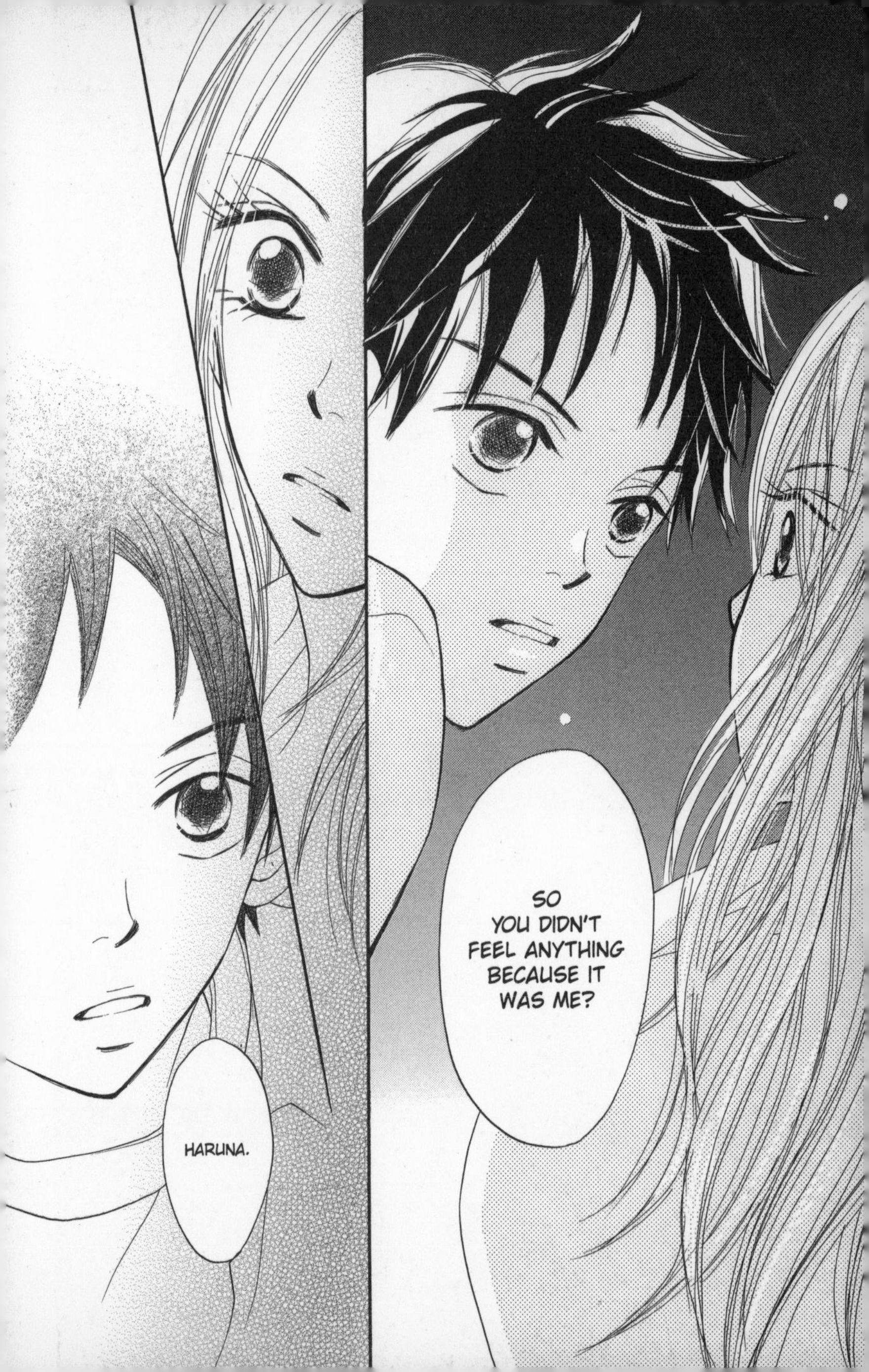
SO YOU DIDN'T FEEL ANYTHING BECAUSE IT WAS ME?
HARUNA.

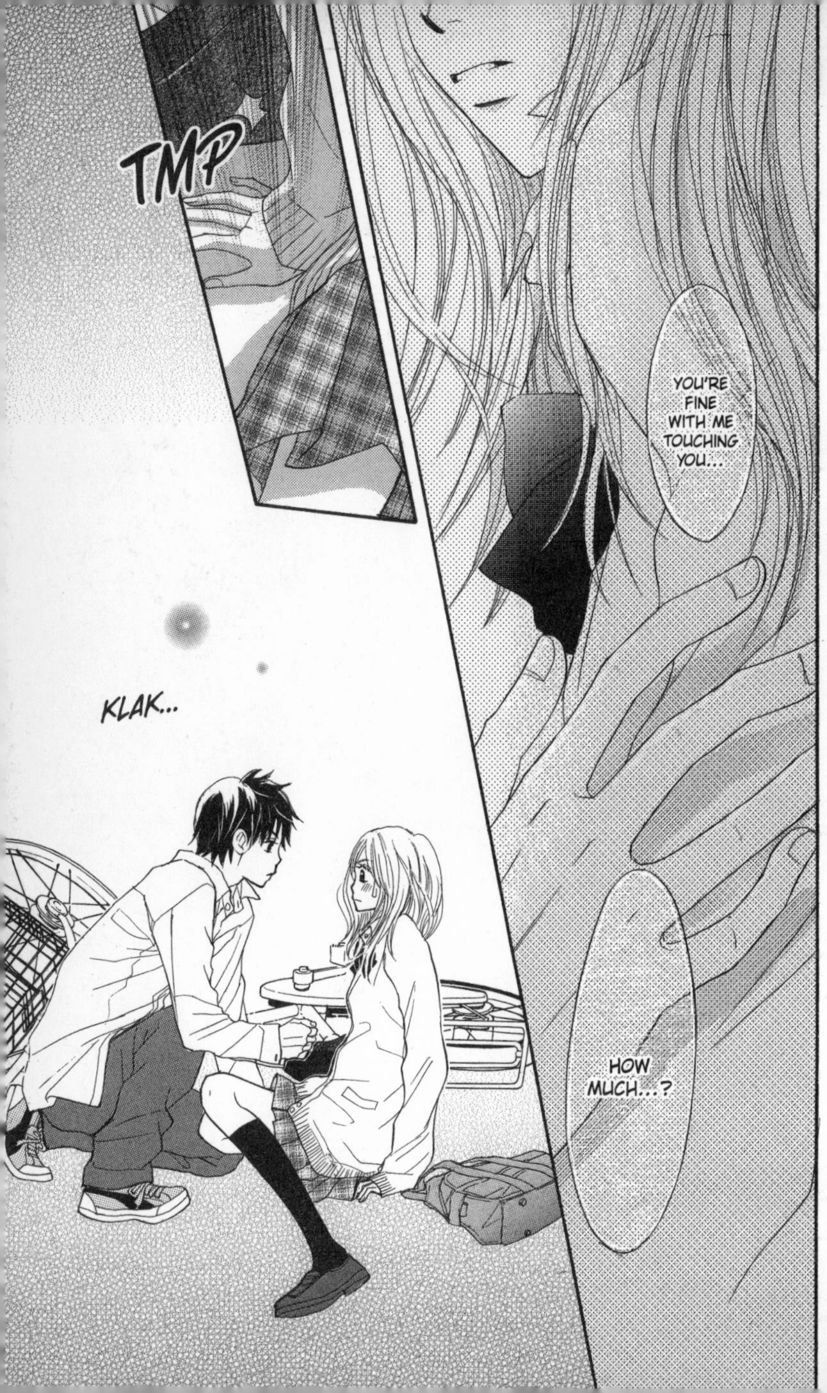
YOU'RE FINE WITH ME TOUCHING YOU...
HOW MUCH...?
TMP
KLAK...

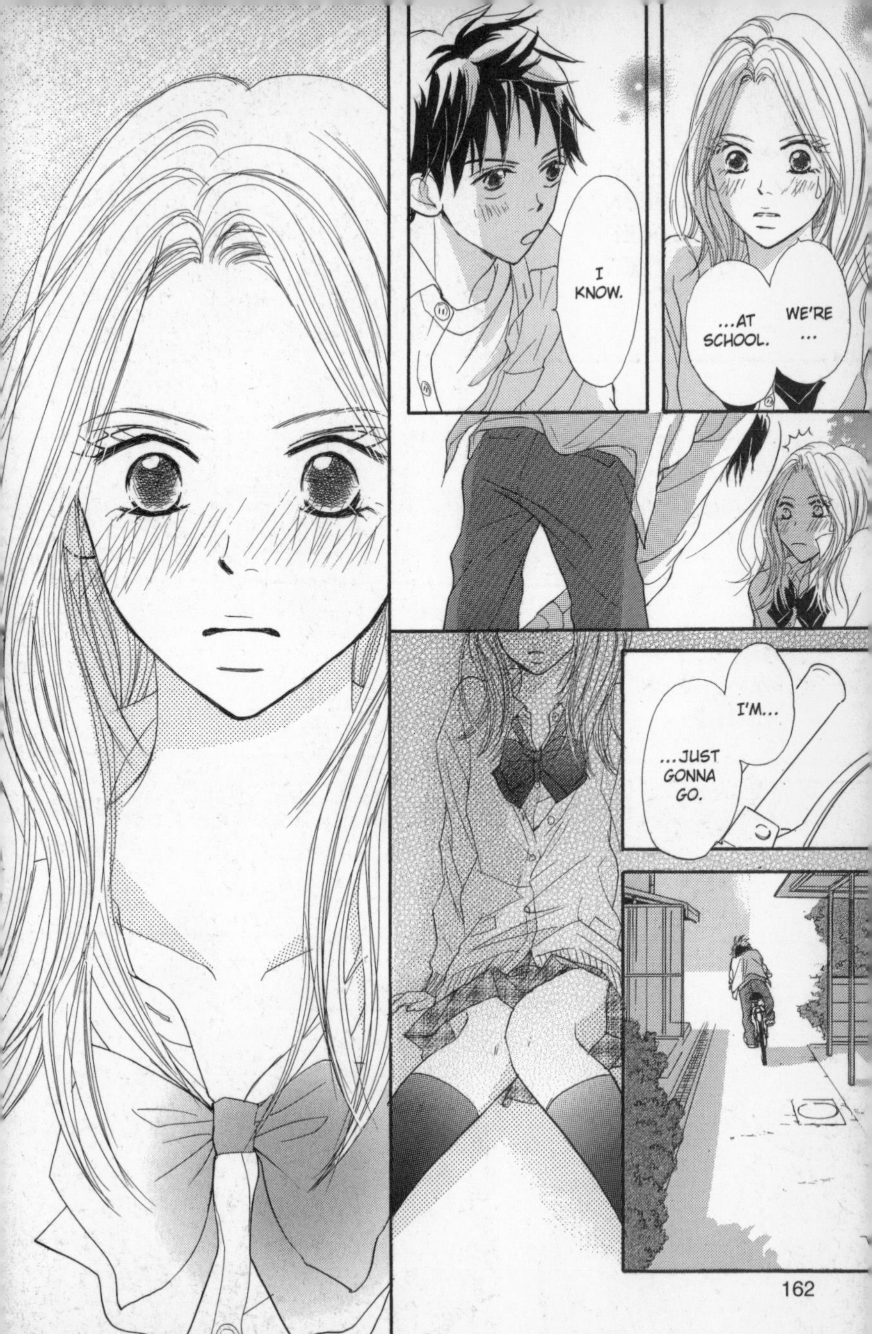
WE'RE ...
...AT SCHOOL.
I KNOW.
I'M...
...JUST GONNA GO.

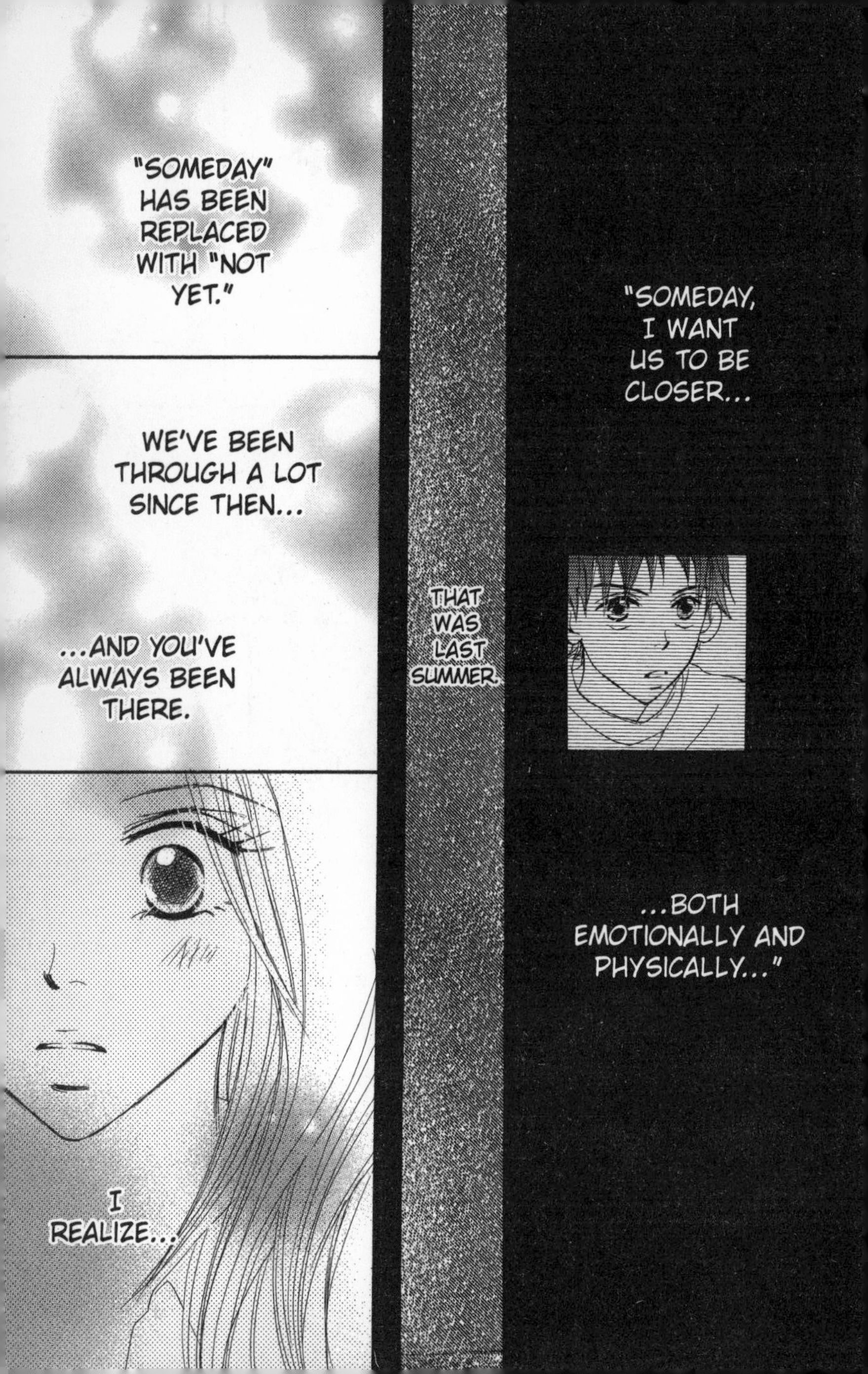
"SOMEDAY, I WANT US TO BE CLOSER...
...BOTH EMOTIONALLY AND PHYSICALLY..."
THAT WAS LAST SUMMER.
"SOMEDAY" HAS BEEN REPLACED WITH "NOT YET."
WE'VE BEEN THROUGH A LOT SINCE THEN...
...AND YOU'VE ALWAYS BEEN THERE.
I REALIZE...

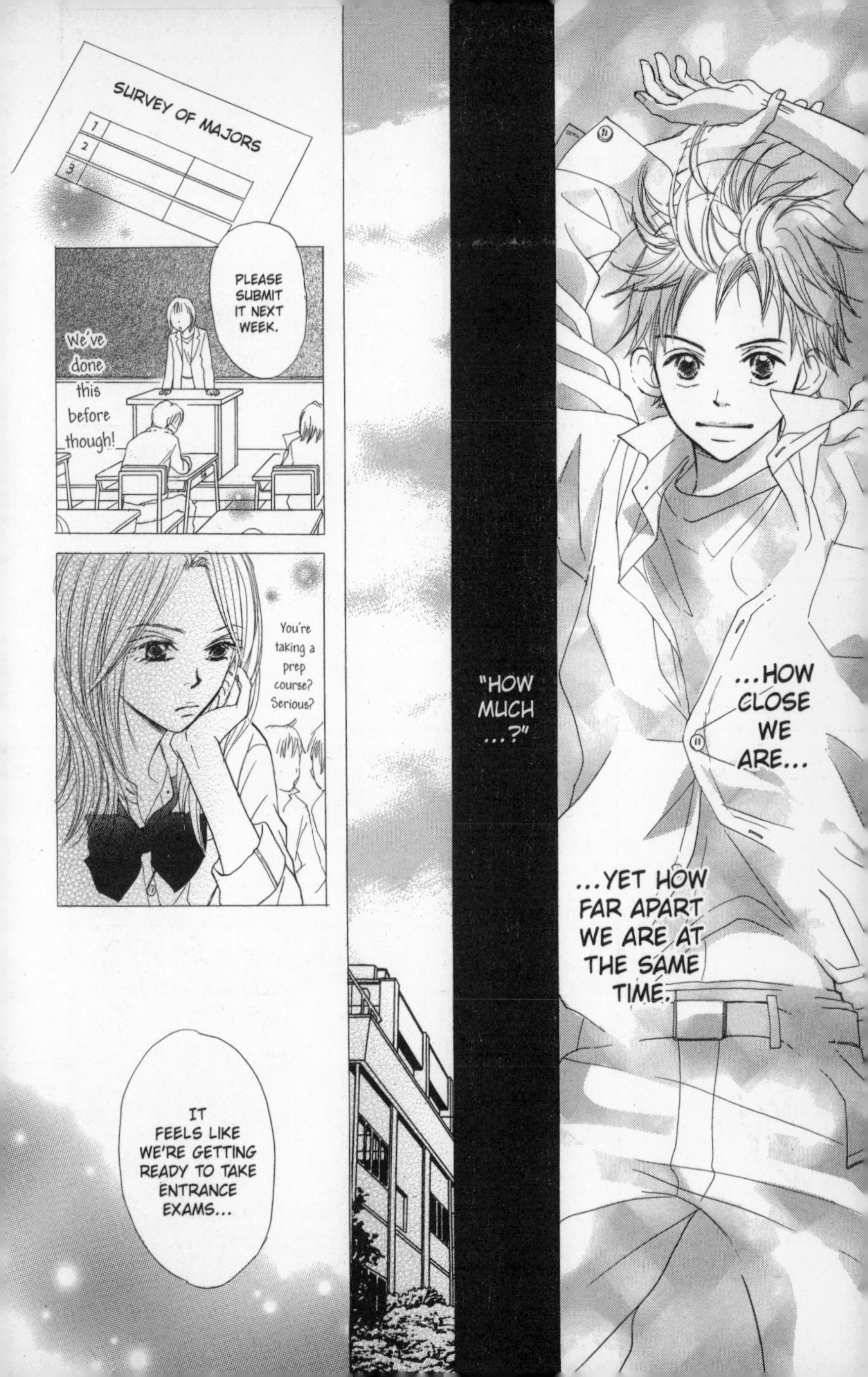
...HOW CLOSE WE ARE...
...YET HOW FAR APART WE ARE AT THE SAME TIME.
"HOW MUCH ...?"
SURVEY OF MAJORS
1
2
3
PLEASE SUBMIT IT NEXT WEEK.
We've done this before though!
You're taking a prep course? Serious?
IT FEELS LIKE WE'RE GETTING READY TO TAKE ENTRANCE EXAMS...

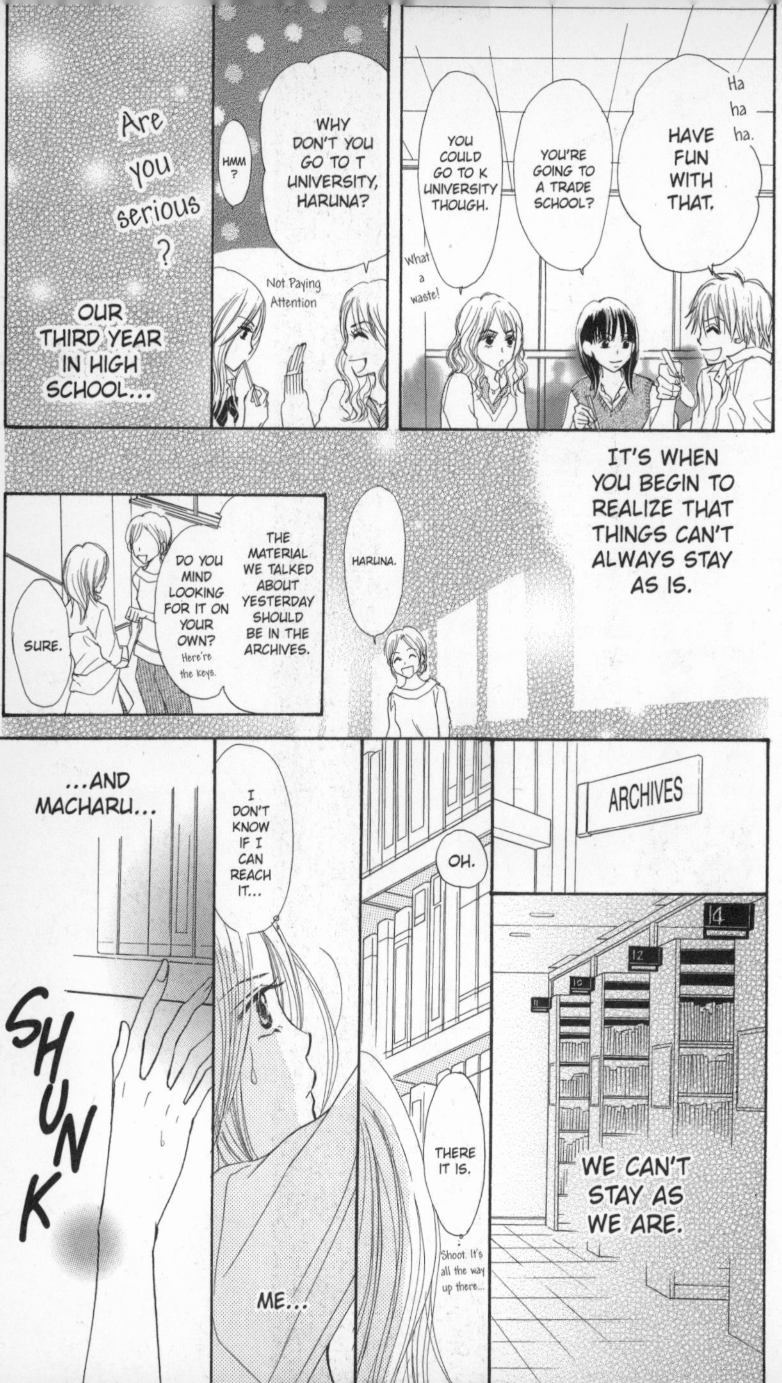
Ha ha ha.
HAVE FUN WITH THAT.
YOU'RE GOING TO A TRADE SCHOOL?
YOU COULD GO TO K UNIVERSITY THOUGH.
What a waste!
WHY DON'T YOU GO TO T UNIVERSITY, HARUNA?
HMM?
Not Paying Attention
Are you serious?
OUR THIRD YEAR IN HIGH SCHOOL...
IT'S WHEN YOU BEGIN TO REALIZE THAT THINGS CAN'T ALWAYS STAY AS IS.
HARUNA.
THE MATERIAL WE TALKED ABOUT YESTERDAY SHOULD BE IN THE ARCHIVES.
DO YOU MIND LOOKING FOR IT ON YOUR OWN?
Here're the keys.
SURE.
ARCHIVES
14
12
10
11
WE CAN'T STAY AS WE ARE.
OH.
THERE IT IS.
Shoot. It's all the way up there...
I DON'T KNOW IF I CAN REACH IT...
ME...
...AND MACHARU...
SHUNK

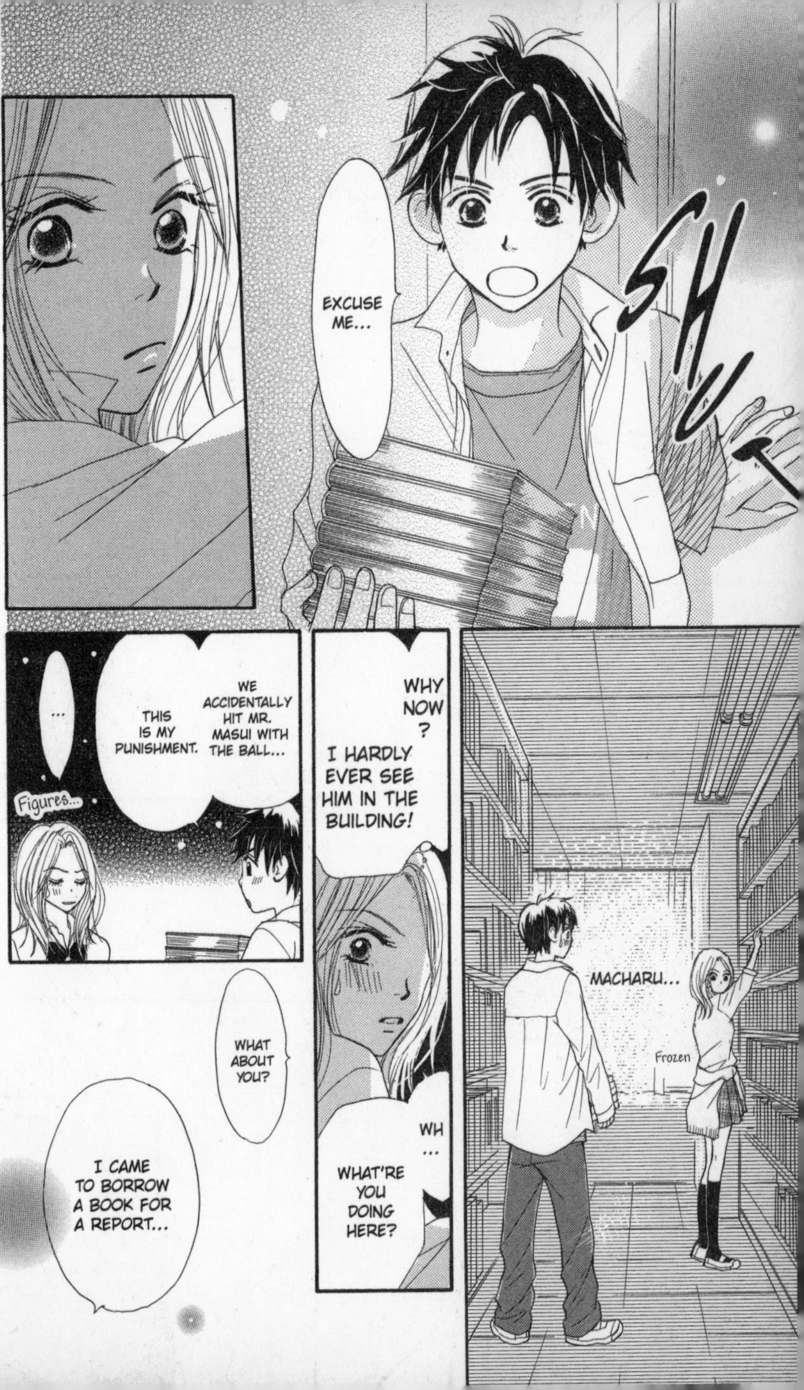
SHUT
EXCUSE ME...
MACHARU...
Frozen
WHY NOW?
I HARDLY EVER SEE HIM IN THE BUILDING!
WH...
WHAT'RE YOU DOING HERE?
WE ACCIDENTALLY HIT MR. MASUI WITH THE BALL...
THIS IS MY PUNISHMENT.
...
Figures...
WHAT ABOUT YOU?
I CAME TO BORROW A BOOK FOR A REPORT...

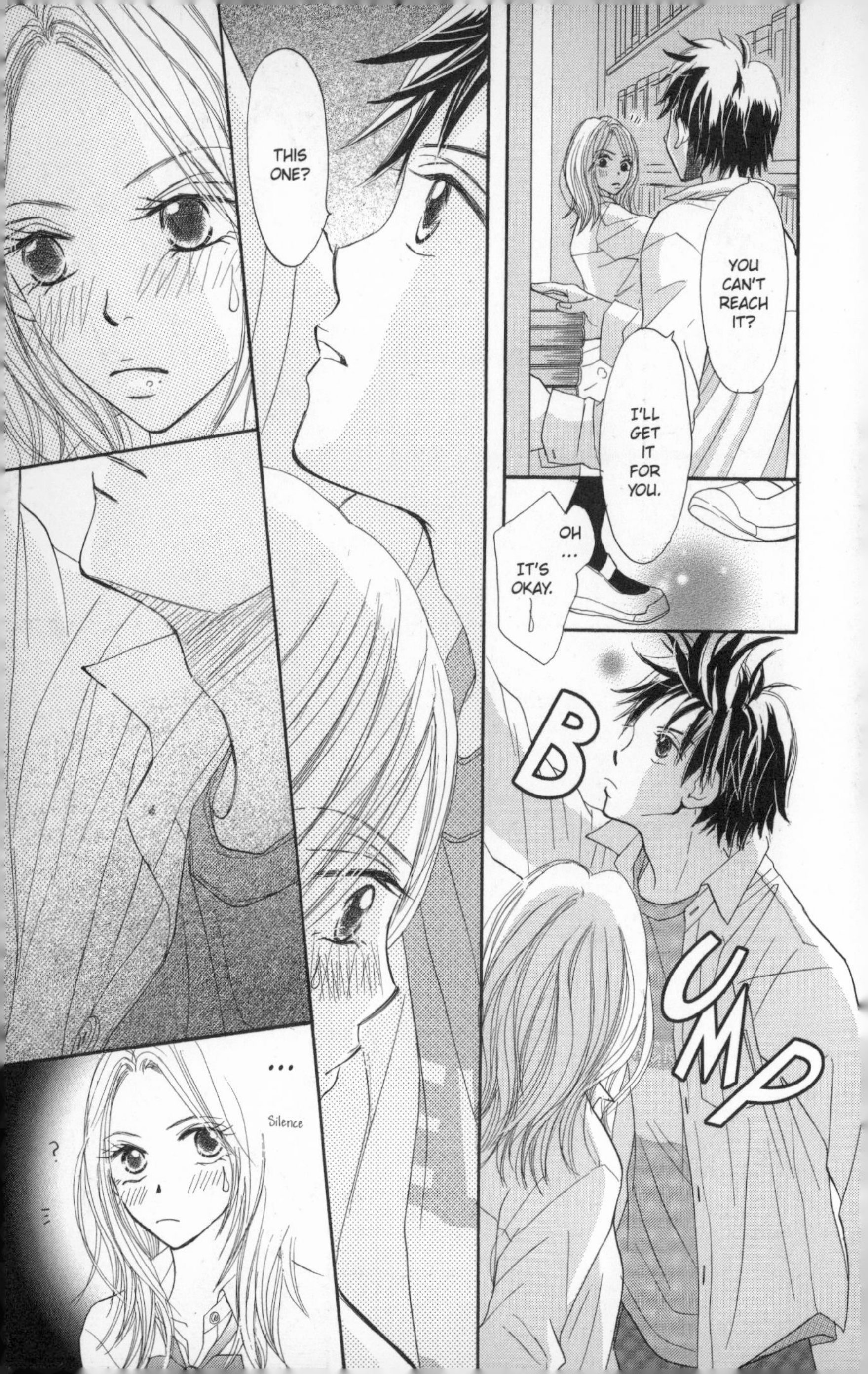
YOU CAN'T REACH IT?
I'LL GET IT FOR YOU.
OH ... IT'S OKAY.
BUMP
THIS ONE?
...
Silence
?

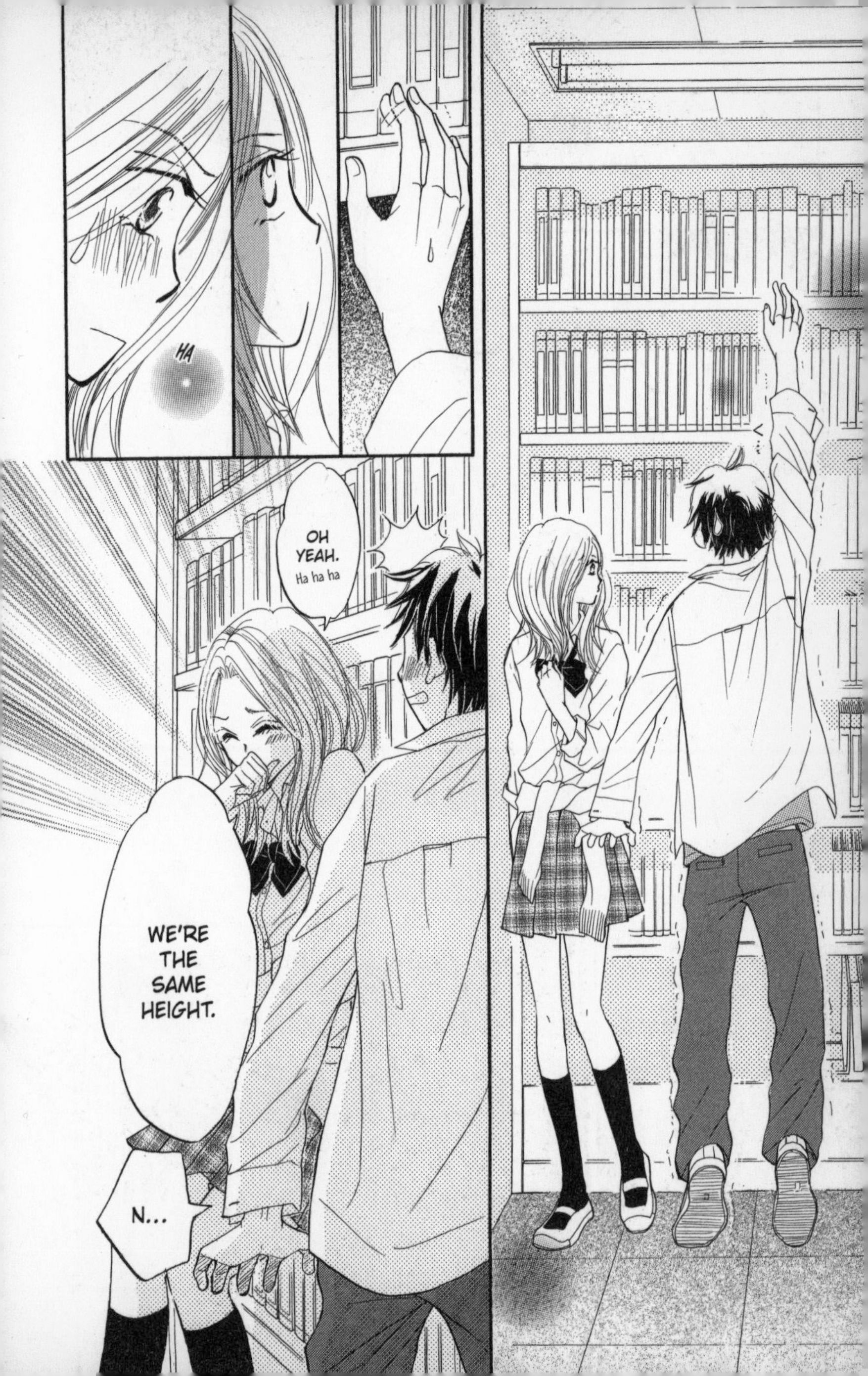
HA
OH YEAH.
Ha ha ha
WE'RE THE SAME HEIGHT.
N...

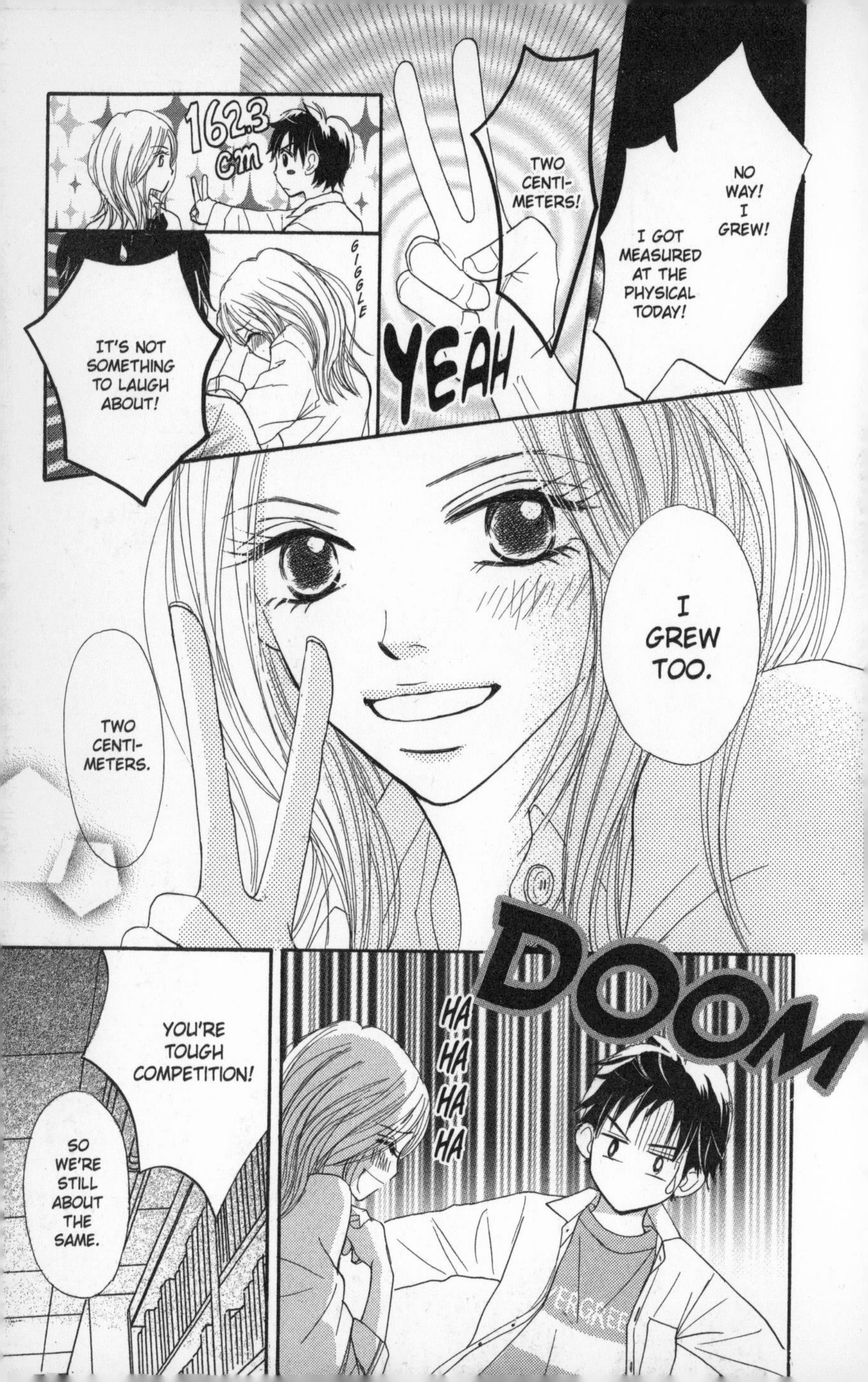
NO WAY! I GREW!
I GOT MEASURED AT THE PHYSICAL TODAY!
TWO CENTI-METERS!
YEAH
162.3 cm
GIGGLE
IT'S NOT SOMETHING TO LAUGH ABOUT!
I GREW TOO.
TWO CENTI-METERS.
DOOM
HA HA HA HA HA
YOU'RE TOUGH COMPETITION!
SO WE'RE STILL ABOUT THE SAME.

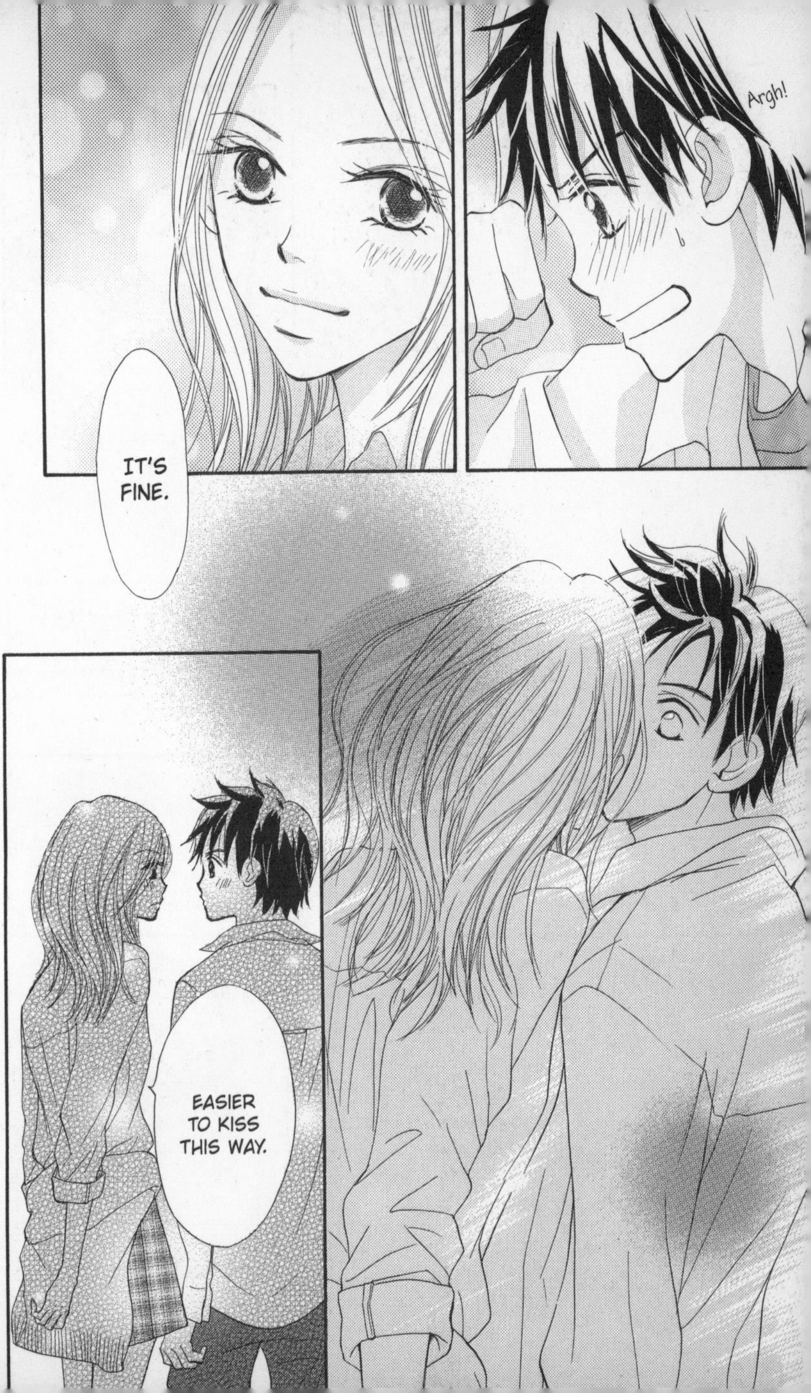
Argh!
IT'S FINE.
EASIER TO KISS THIS WAY.

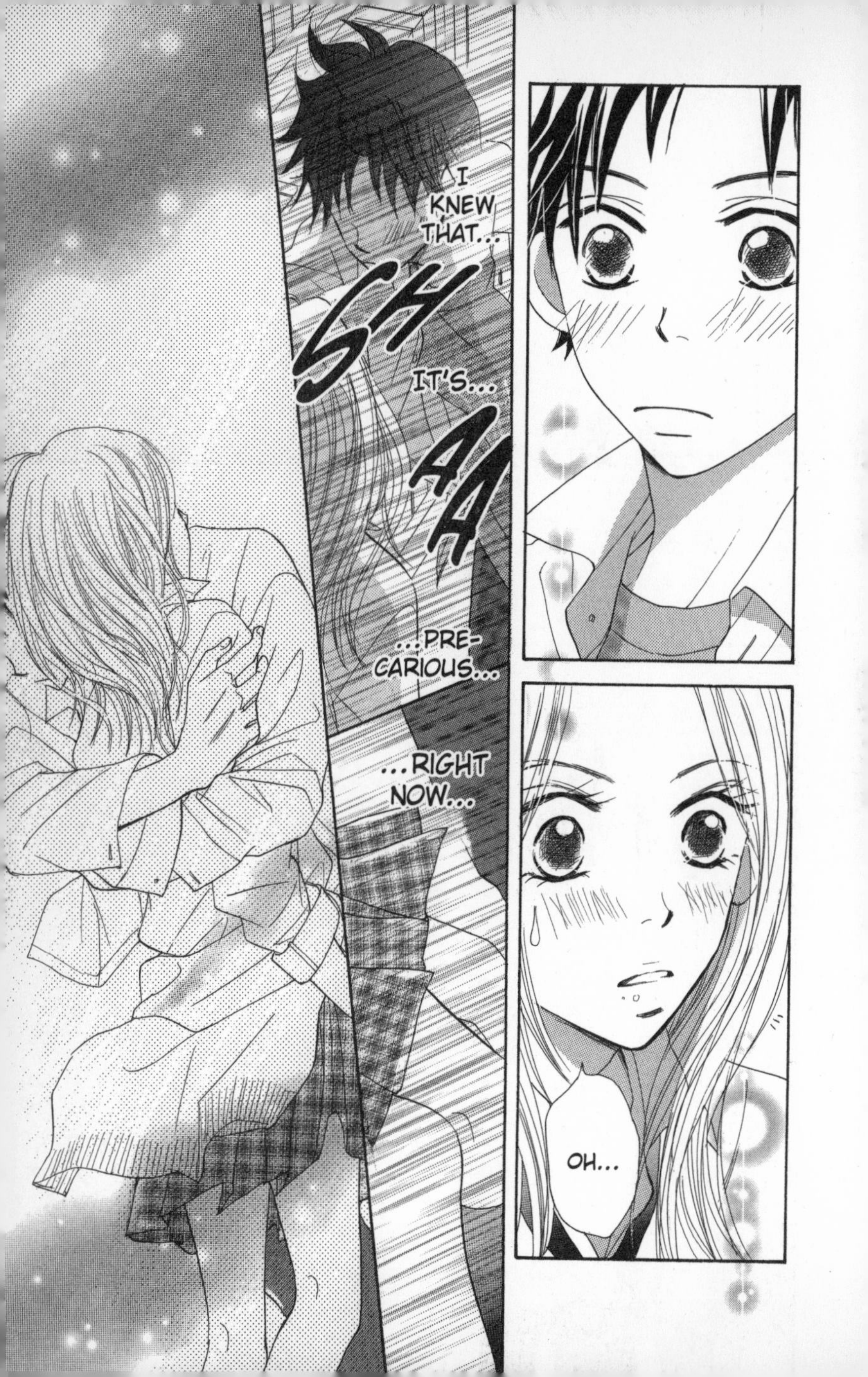
OH...
I KNEW THAT...
SHAA
IT'S...
...PRE-CARIOUS...
...RIGHT NOW...

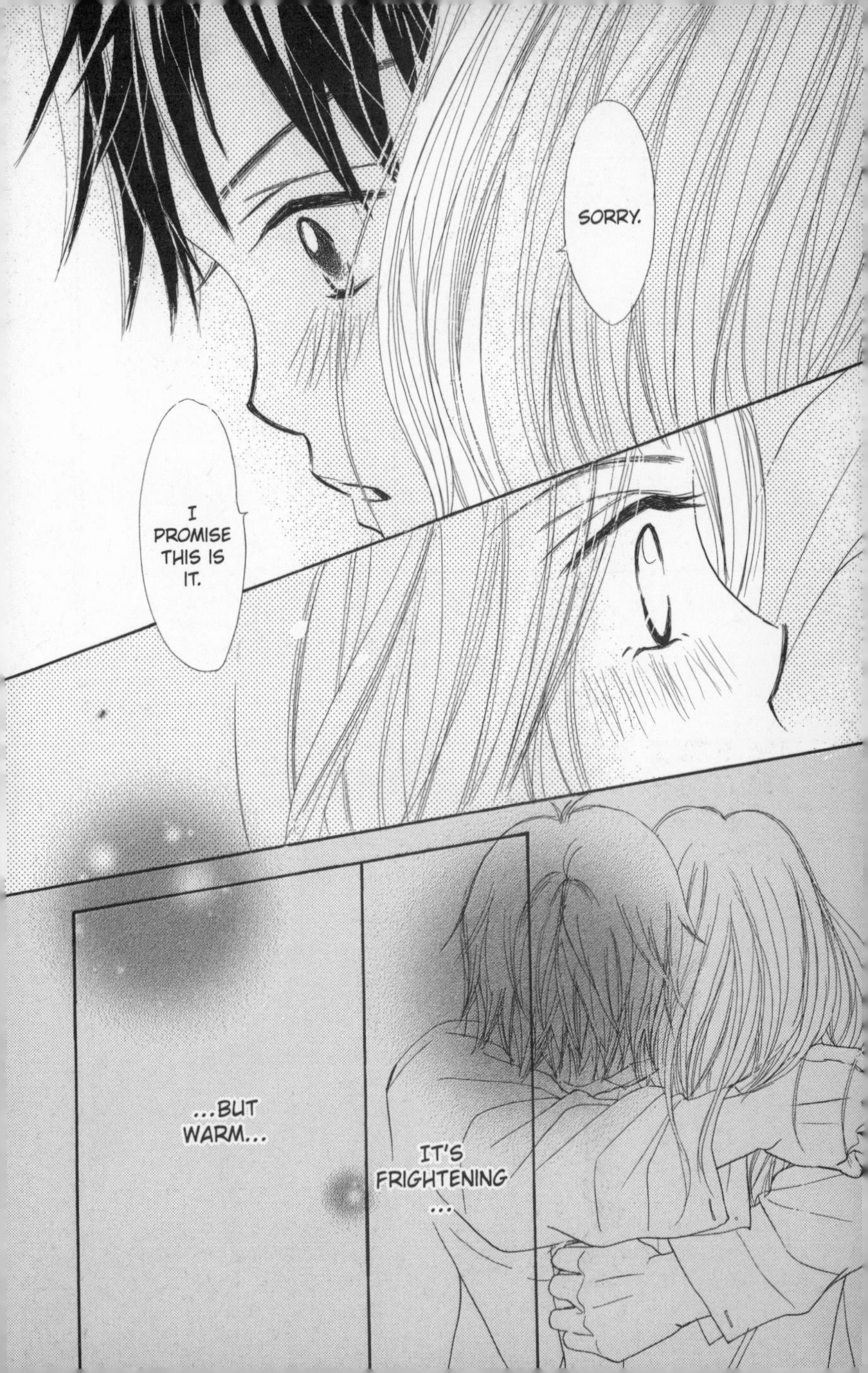
SORRY.
I PROMISE THIS IS IT.
IT'S FRIGHTENING ...
...BUT WARM...

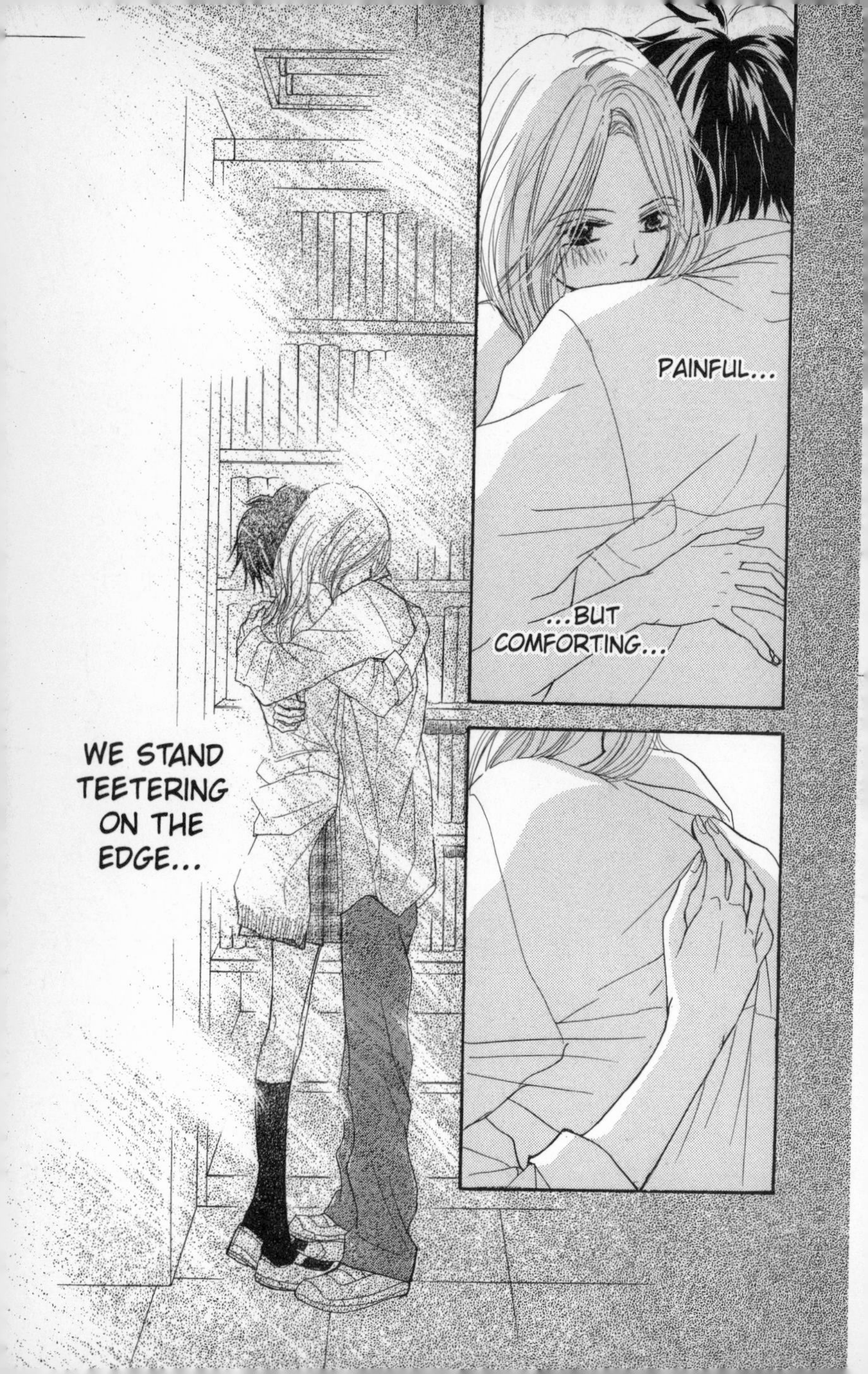
PAINFUL...
...BUT COMFORTING...
WE STAND TEETERING ON THE EDGE...

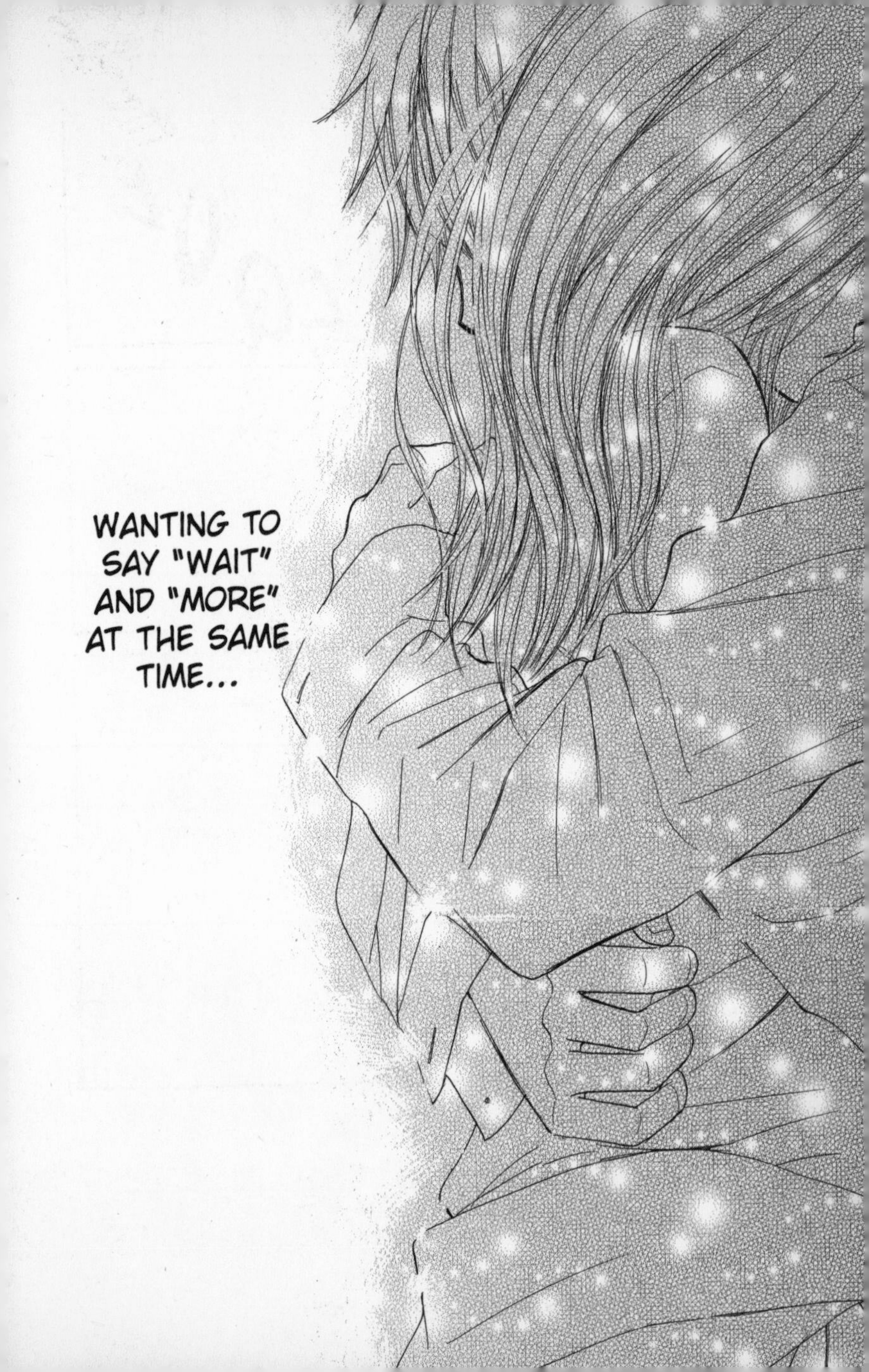
WANTING TO SAY "WAIT" AND "MORE" AT THE SAME TIME...

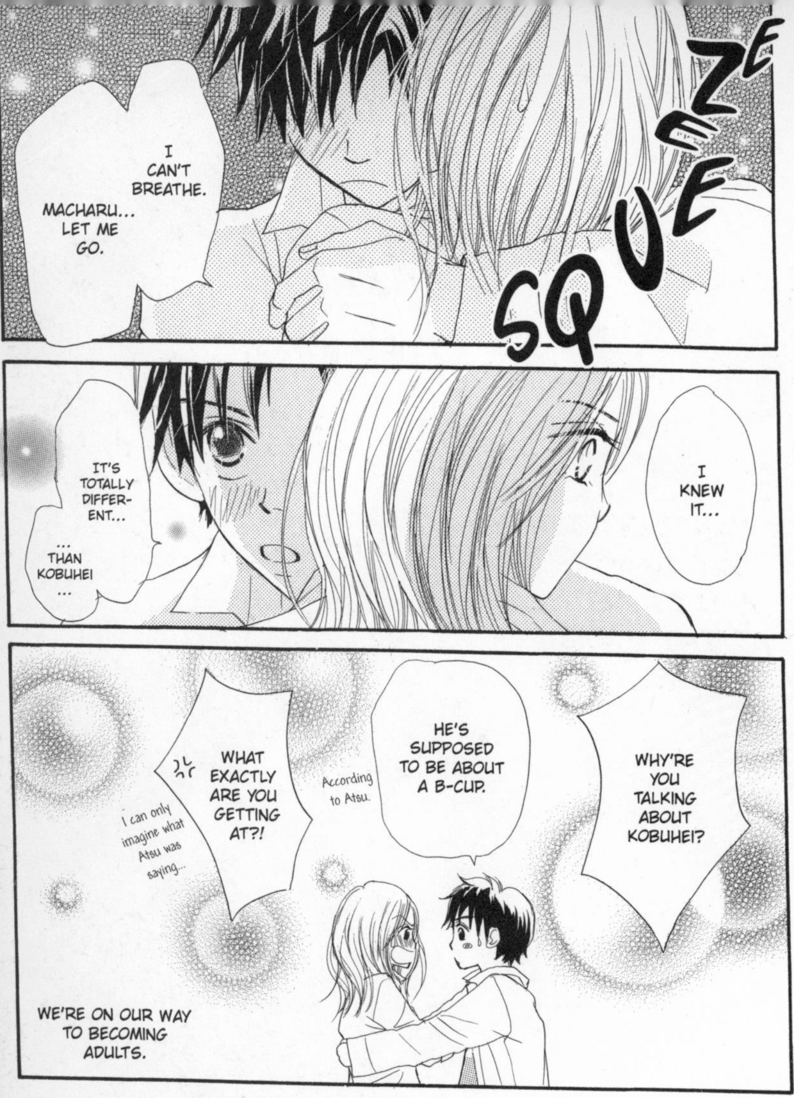
SQUEEZE
I CAN'T BREATHE.
MACHARU... LET ME GO.
I KNEW IT...
IT'S TOTALLY DIFFER-ENT...
...THAN KOBUHEI...
WHY'RE YOU TALKING ABOUT KOBUHEI?
HE'S SUPPOSED TO BE ABOUT A B-CUP.
According to Atsu.
WHAT EXACTLY ARE YOU GETTING AT?!
I can only imagine what Atsu was saying...
WE'RE ON OUR WAY TO BECOMING ADULTS.

HOW MUCH LONGER...?

MONKEY HIGH! ⑥ *THE END*

POSTSCRIPT

THANK YOU SO MUCH FOR YOUR SUPPORT! I'M SHOUKO AKIRA. VOLUME 6...! IS IT REALLY OKAY...? REALLY? ("NO! YOU ALWAYS MISS YOUR DEADLINES!" -EDITOR) I'D LIKE TO ADD COMMENTS ABOUT ALL THE DIFFERENT CHAPTERS.

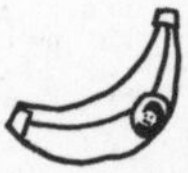

THE NUMBER OF BANANAS ON THE SPINE OF THE BOOK INCREASES BY VOLUME [IN THE ORIGINAL JAPANESE VERSION]. I THOUGHT IT WOULD BE A LITTLE TIGHT AFTER VOLUME 4, BUT WITH VOLUME 5, THERE'S A MONKEY STICKER! SO CUTE!! IT'S THE BLOOD AND TEARS OF THE DESIGNER!

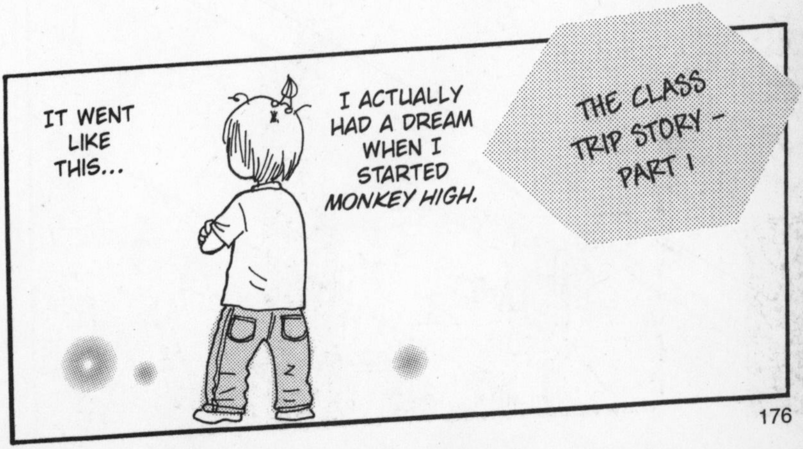
THE CLASS TRIP STORY - PART 1
I ACTUALLY HAD A DREAM WHEN I STARTED *MONKEY HIGH*.
IT WENT LIKE THIS...

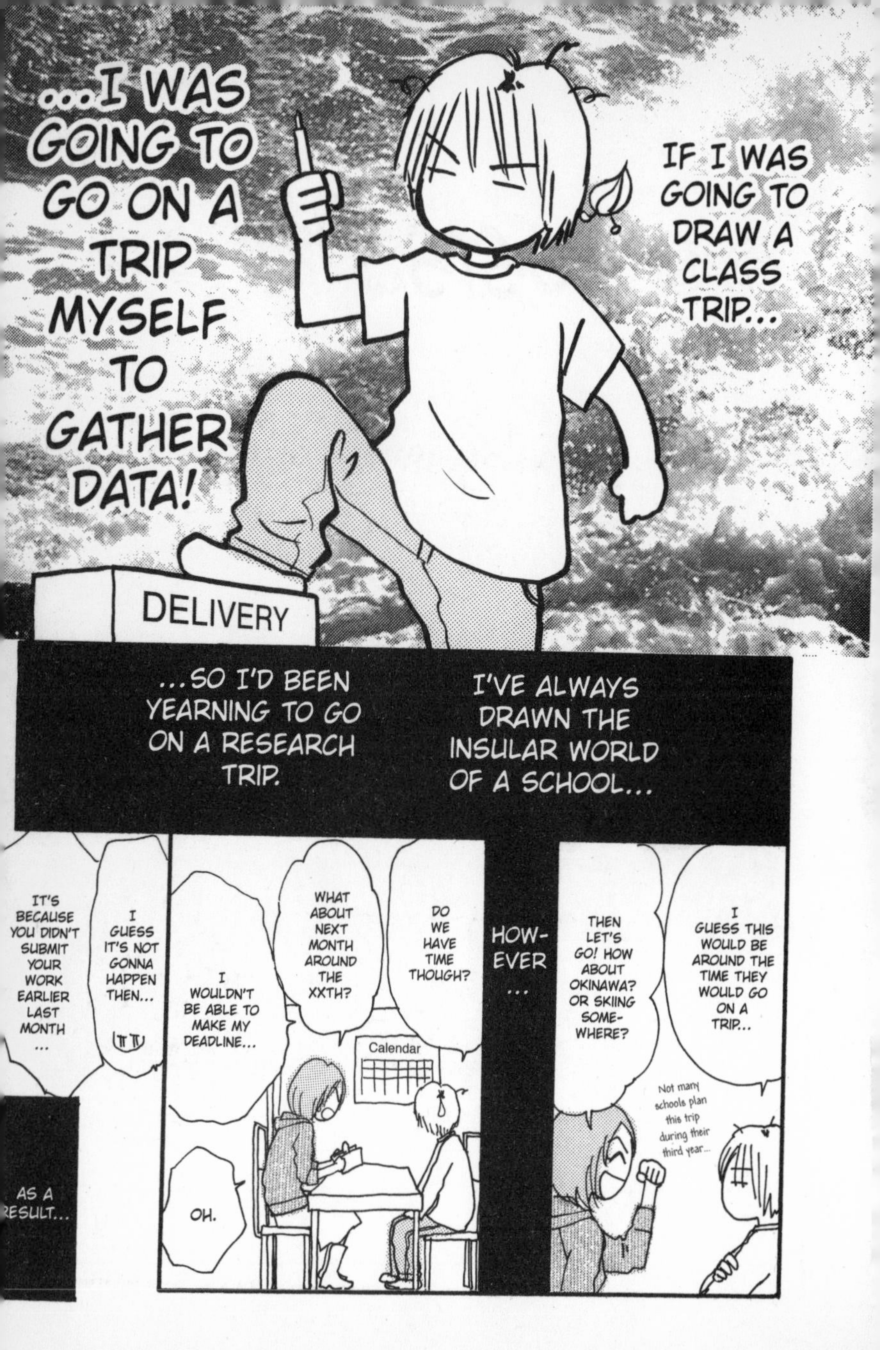
IF I WAS GOING TO DRAW A CLASS TRIP...
...I WAS GOING TO GO ON A TRIP MYSELF TO GATHER DATA!
DELIVERY
I'VE ALWAYS DRAWN THE INSULAR WORLD OF A SCHOOL...
...SO I'D BEEN YEARNING TO GO ON A RESEARCH TRIP.
I GUESS THIS WOULD BE AROUND THE TIME THEY WOULD GO ON A TRIP...
THEN LET'S GO! HOW ABOUT OKINAWA? OR SKIING SOME-WHERE?
Not many schools plan this trip during their third year...
HOW-EVER...
DO WE HAVE TIME THOUGH?
WHAT ABOUT NEXT MONTH AROUND THE XXTH?
Calendar
I WOULDN'T BE ABLE TO MAKE MY DEADLINE...
OH.
I GUESS IT'S NOT GONNA HAPPEN THEN...
IT'S BECAUSE YOU DIDN'T SUBMIT YOUR WORK EARLIER LAST MONTH...
AS A RESULT...

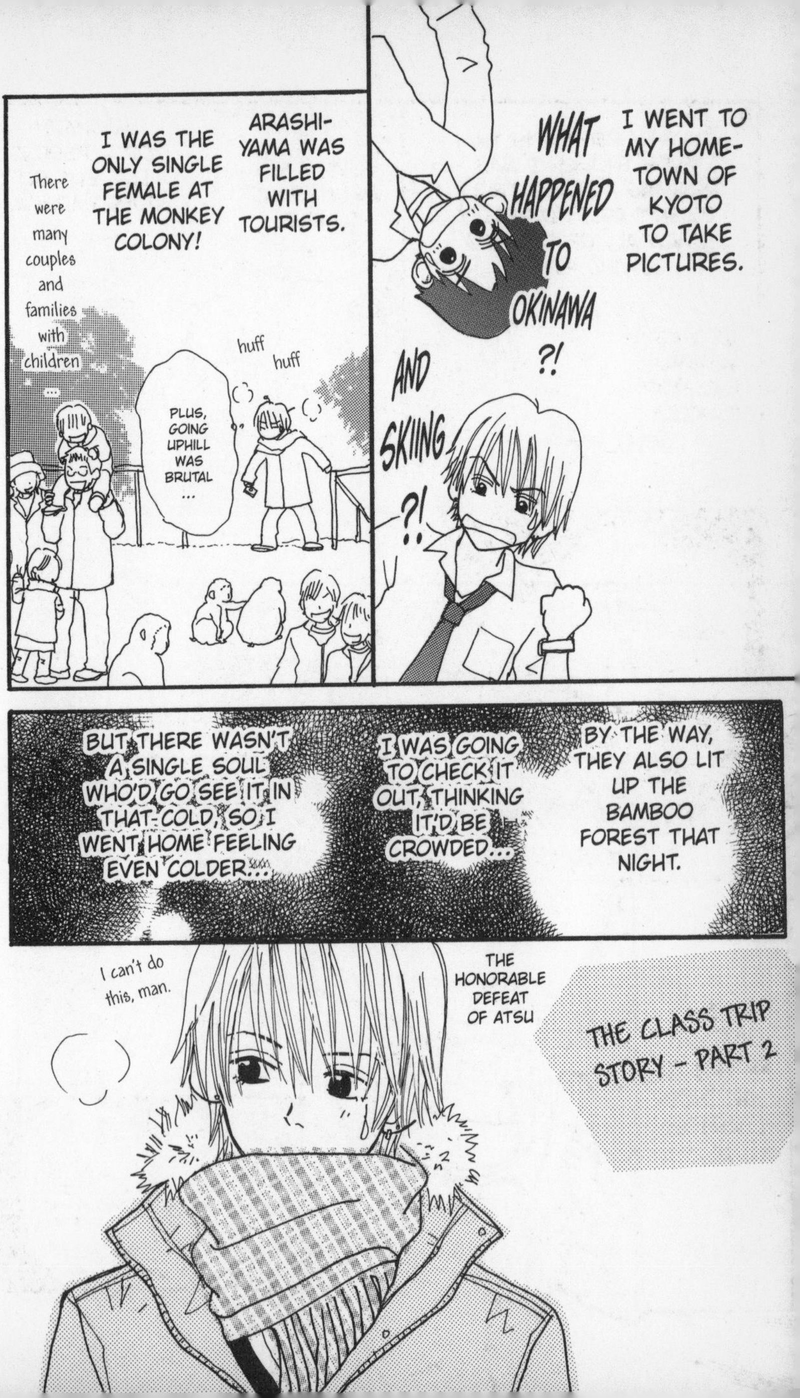
I WENT TO MY HOMETOWN OF KYOTO TO TAKE PICTURES.
WHAT HAPPENED TO OKINAWA ?!
AND SKIING ?!
ARASHIYAMA WAS FILLED WITH TOURISTS.
I WAS THE ONLY SINGLE FEMALE AT THE MONKEY COLONY!
There were many couples and families with children ...
huff huff
PLUS, GOING UPHILL WAS BRUTAL ...
BY THE WAY, THEY ALSO LIT UP THE BAMBOO FOREST THAT NIGHT.
I WAS GOING TO CHECK IT OUT, THINKING IT'D BE CROWDED...
BUT THERE WASN'T A SINGLE SOUL WHO'D GO SEE IT IN THAT COLD, SO I WENT HOME FEELING EVEN COLDER...
THE CLASS TRIP STORY - PART 2
THE HONORABLE DEFEAT OF ATSU
I can't do this, man.

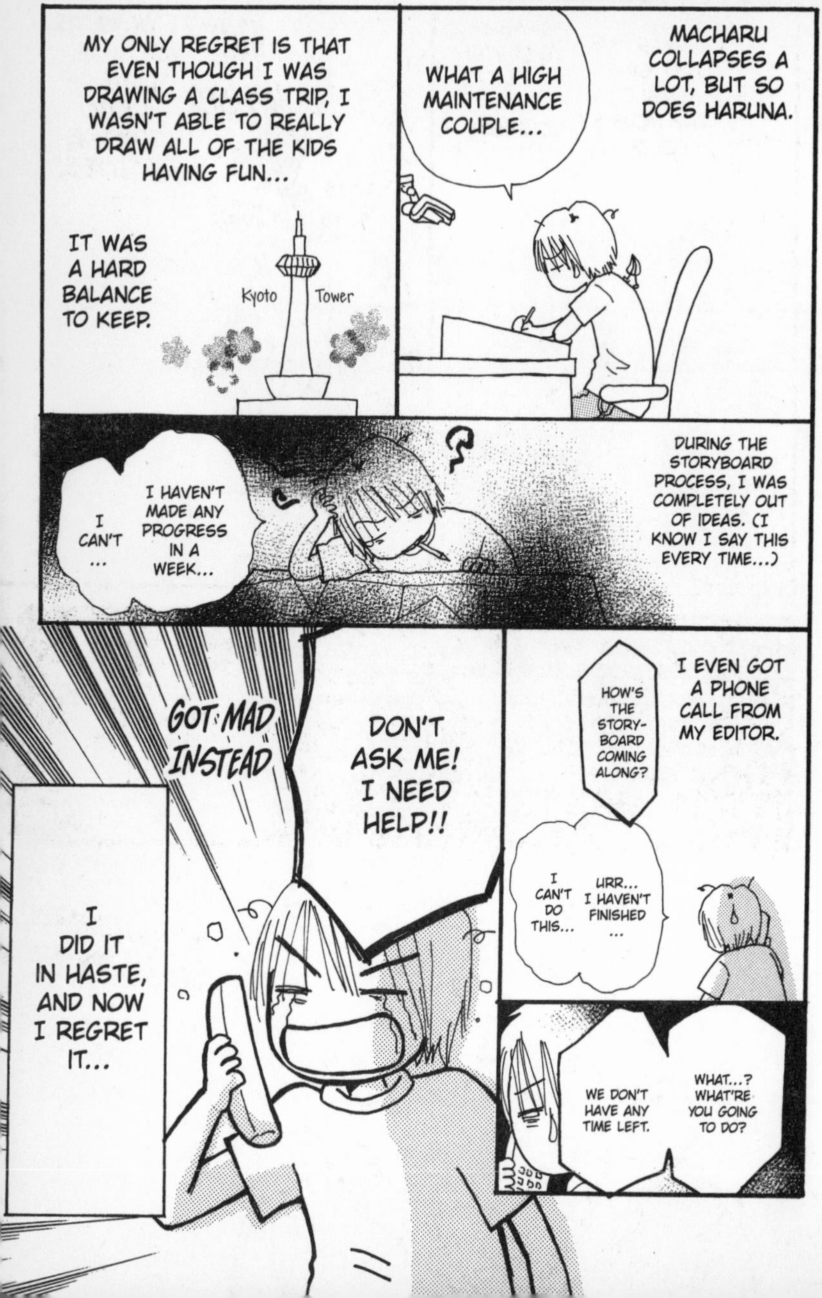
MACHARU COLLAPSES A LOT, BUT SO DOES HARUNA.
WHAT A HIGH MAINTENANCE COUPLE...
MY ONLY REGRET IS THAT EVEN THOUGH I WAS DRAWING A CLASS TRIP, I WASN'T ABLE TO REALLY DRAW ALL OF THE KIDS HAVING FUN...
IT WAS A HARD BALANCE TO KEEP.
Kyoto Tower
DURING THE STORYBOARD PROCESS, I WAS COMPLETELY OUT OF IDEAS. (I KNOW I SAY THIS EVERY TIME...)
I HAVEN'T MADE ANY PROGRESS IN A WEEK...
I CAN'T ...
I EVEN GOT A PHONE CALL FROM MY EDITOR.
HOW'S THE STORY-BOARD COMING ALONG?
URR... I HAVEN'T FINISHED ...
I CAN'T DO THIS...
WHAT...? WHAT'RE YOU GOING TO DO?
WE DON'T HAVE ANY TIME LEFT.
DON'T ASK ME! I NEED HELP!!
GOT MAD INSTEAD
I DID IT IN HASTE, AND NOW I REGRET IT...

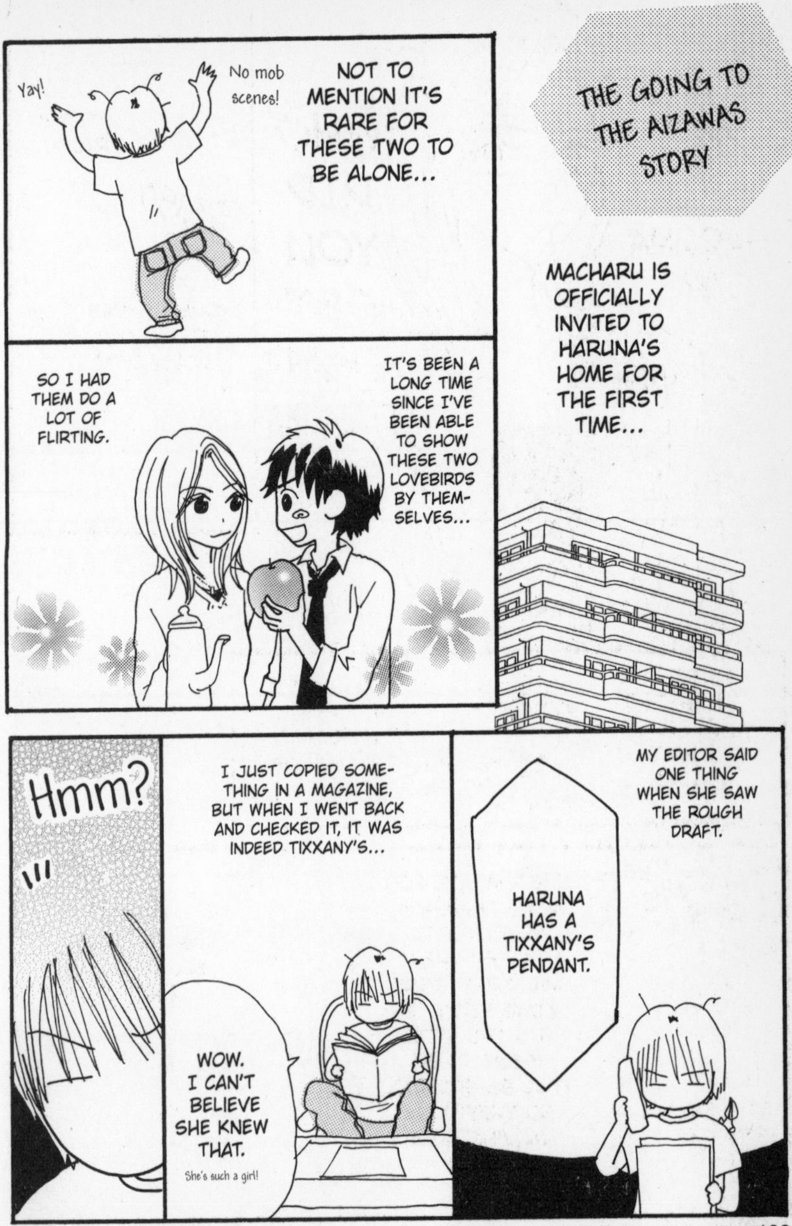
THE GOING TO THE AIZAWAS STORY
MACHARU IS OFFICIALLY INVITED TO HARUNA'S HOME FOR THE FIRST TIME...
NOT TO MENTION IT'S RARE FOR THESE TWO TO BE ALONE...
No mob scenes!
Yay!
IT'S BEEN A LONG TIME SINCE I'VE BEEN ABLE TO SHOW THESE TWO LOVEBIRDS BY THEM-SELVES...
SO I HAD THEM DO A LOT OF FLIRTING.
MY EDITOR SAID ONE THING WHEN SHE SAW THE ROUGH DRAFT.
HARUNA HAS A TIXXANY'S PENDANT.
I JUST COPIED SOME-THING IN A MAGAZINE, BUT WHEN I WENT BACK AND CHECKED IT, IT WAS INDEED TIXXANY'S...
WOW. I CAN'T BELIEVE SHE KNEW THAT.
She's such a girl!
Hmm?

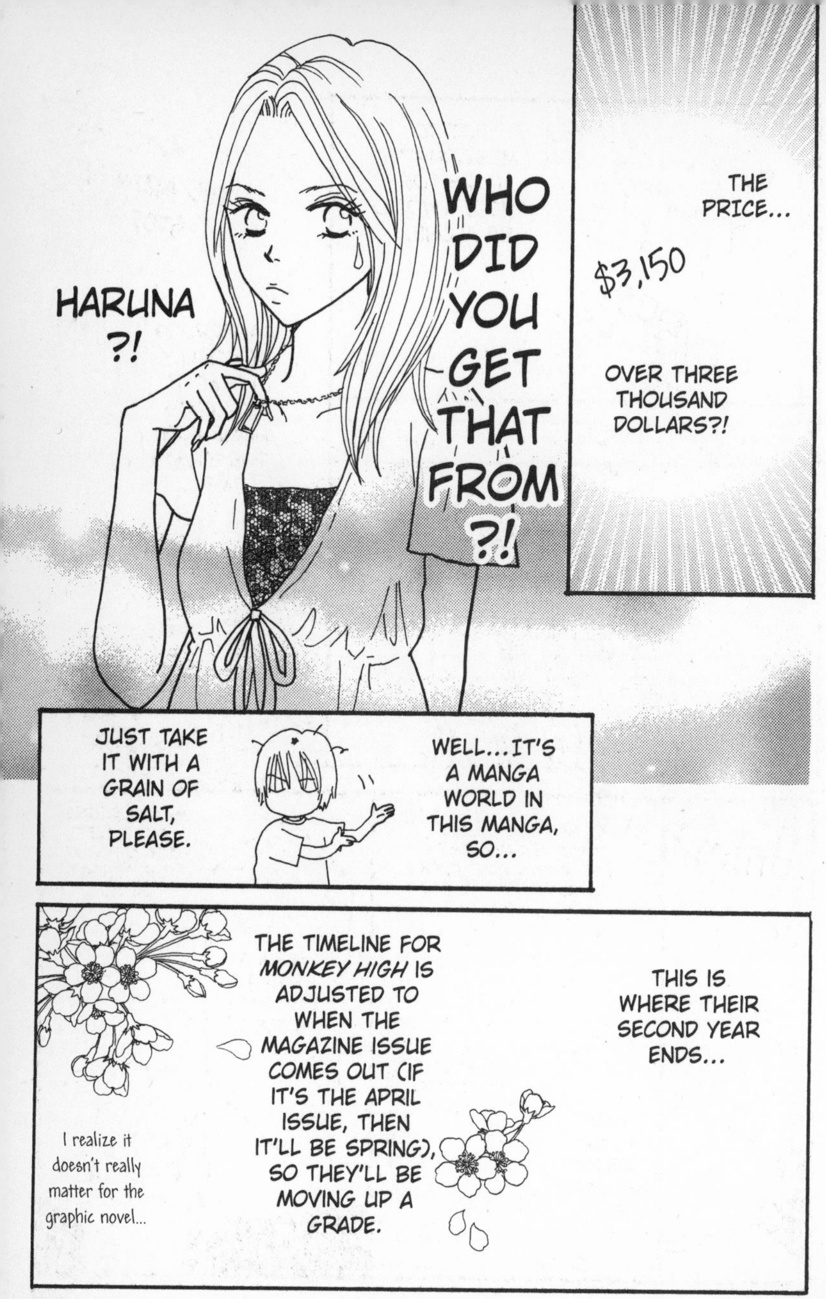
THE PRICE...
$3,150
OVER THREE THOUSAND DOLLARS?!
WHO DID YOU GET THAT FROM?!
HARUNA?!
WELL...IT'S A MANGA WORLD IN THIS MANGA, SO...
JUST TAKE IT WITH A GRAIN OF SALT, PLEASE.
THIS IS WHERE THEIR SECOND YEAR ENDS...
THE TIMELINE FOR *MONKEY HIGH* IS ADJUSTED TO WHEN THE MAGAZINE ISSUE COMES OUT (IF IT'S THE APRIL ISSUE, THEN IT'LL BE SPRING), SO THEY'LL BE MOVING UP A GRADE.
I realize it doesn't really matter for the graphic novel...

THE TOUCHING THE CHEST STORY

AND FINALLY AS THIRD-YEARS...

I WANTED TO DRAW A SCENE WHERE THE TOUCHING OF A CHEST OCCURRED SINCE IT'S NOT OFTEN DEPICTED IN SHOJO MANGA (PROBABLY FOR A REASON)...

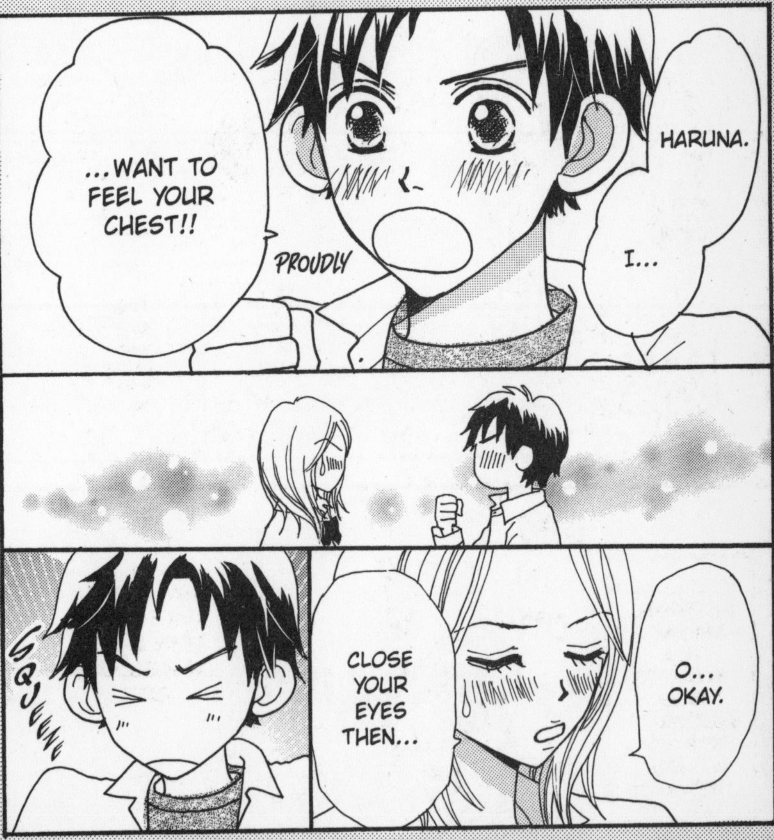
HARUNA.
I...
...WANT TO FEEL YOUR CHEST!!
PROUDLY
O... OKAY.
CLOSE YOUR EYES THEN...
SQUEEZE

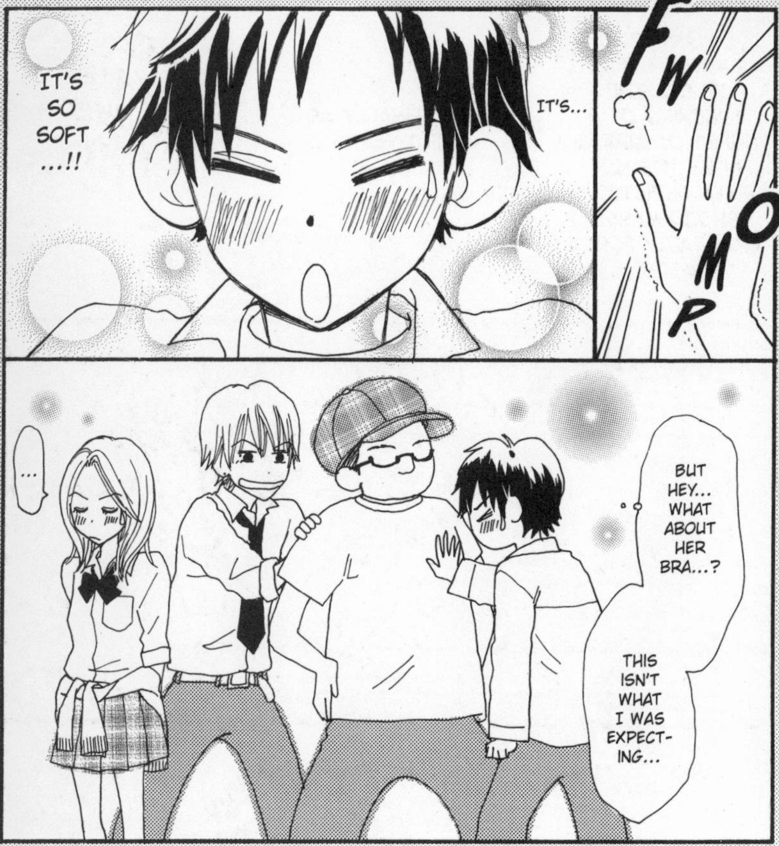
FWOMP
IT'S...
IT'S SO SOFT...!!
BUT HEY... WHAT ABOUT HER BRA...?
THIS ISN'T WHAT I WAS EXPECTING...
...

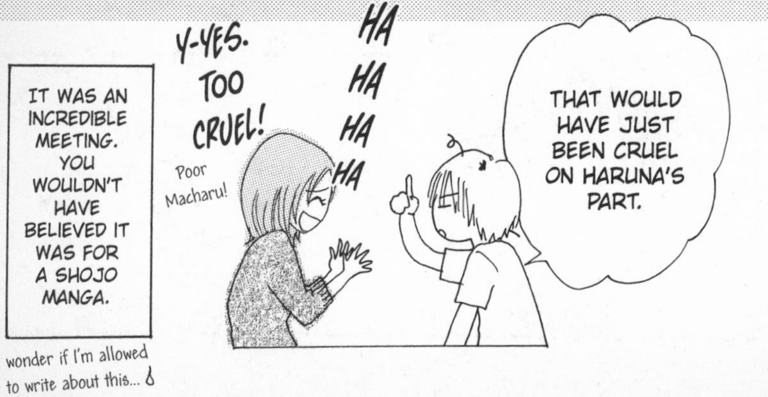
THAT WOULD HAVE JUST BEEN CRUEL ON HARUNA'S PART.
HA HA HA HA
Y-YES. TOO CRUEL!
Poor Macharu!
IT WAS AN INCREDIBLE MEETING. YOU WOULDN'T HAVE BELIEVED IT WAS FOR A SHOJO MANGA.
I wonder if I'm allowed to write about this...

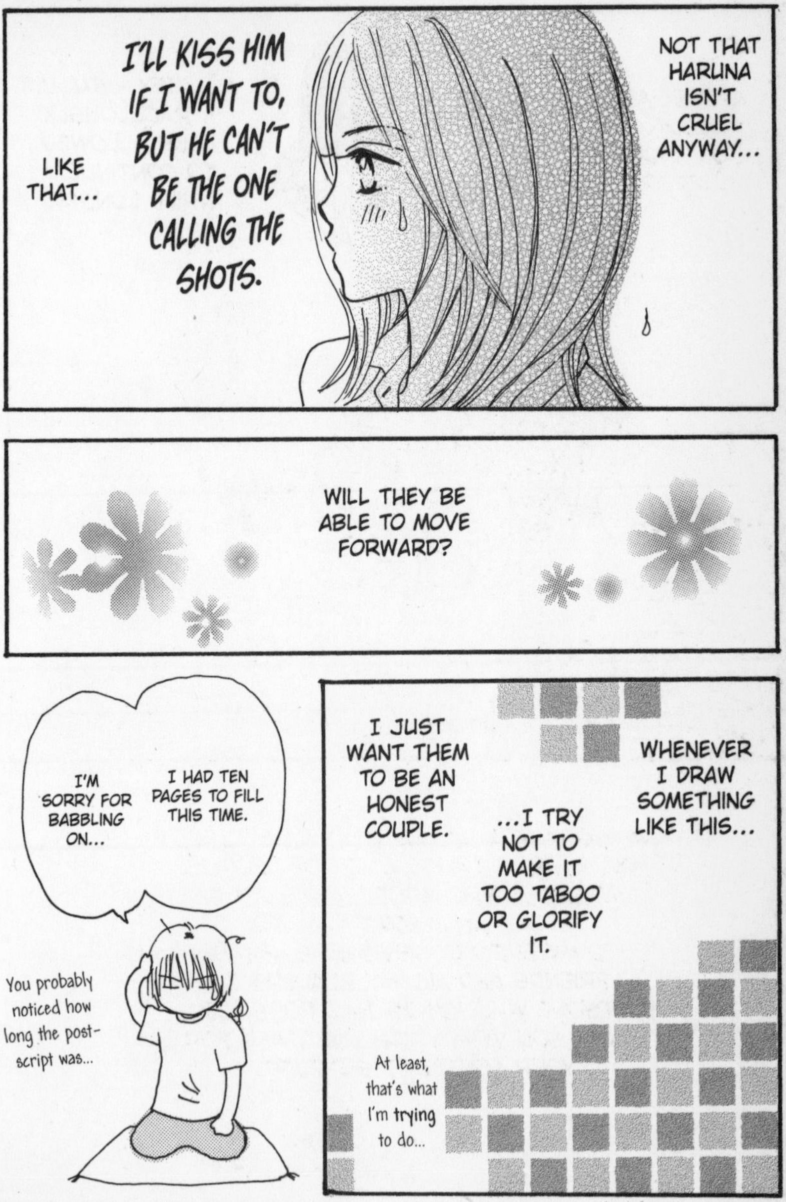
NOT THAT HARUNA ISN'T CRUEL ANYWAY...
I'LL KISS HIM IF I WANT TO, BUT HE CAN'T BE THE ONE CALLING THE SHOTS.
LIKE THAT...
WILL THEY BE ABLE TO MOVE FORWARD?
WHENEVER I DRAW SOMETHING LIKE THIS...
...I TRY NOT TO MAKE IT TOO TABOO OR GLORIFY IT.
I JUST WANT THEM TO BE AN HONEST COUPLE.
At least, that's what I'm trying to do...
I HAD TEN PAGES TO FILL THIS TIME.
I'M SORRY FOR BABBLING ON...
You probably noticed how long the post-script was...

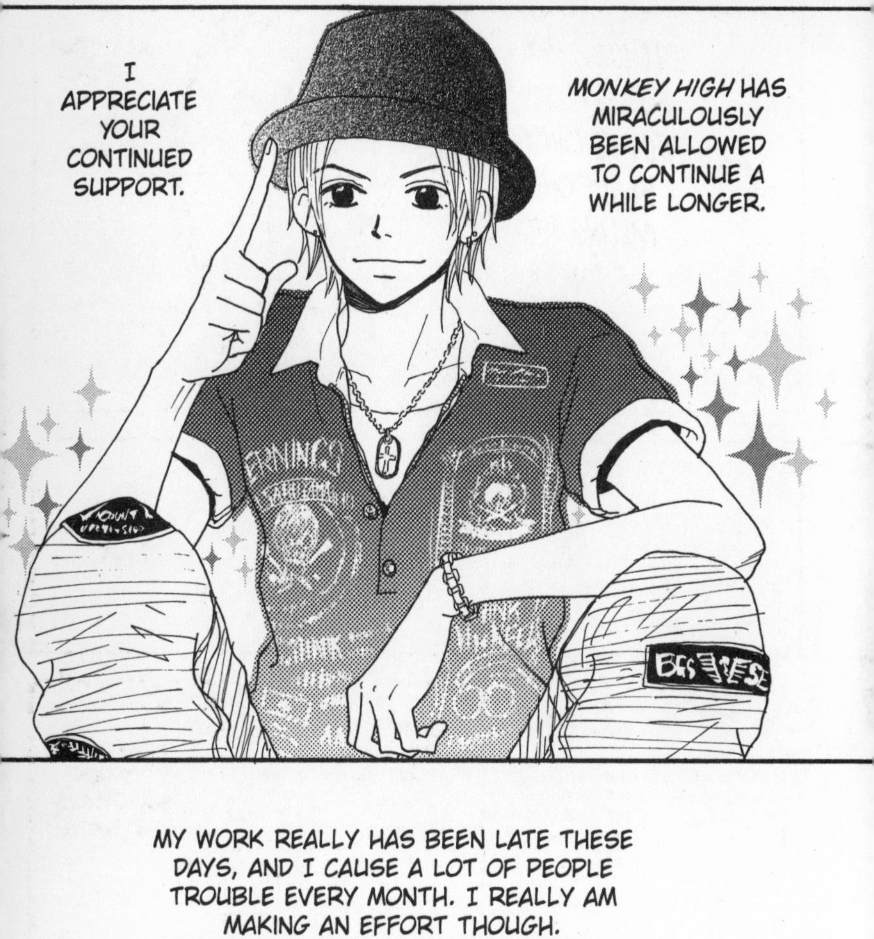
MONKEY HIGH HAS MIRACULOUSLY BEEN ALLOWED TO CONTINUE A WHILE LONGER.
I APPRECIATE YOUR CONTINUED SUPPORT.

MY WORK REALLY HAS BEEN LATE THESE DAYS, AND I CAUSE A LOT OF PEOPLE TROUBLE EVERY MONTH. I REALLY AM MAKING AN EFFORT THOUGH.
TO MY EDITORS, DESIGNERS, FAMILY, FRIENDS AND ALL MY READERS... EVERYONE WHO MAKES THIS POSSIBLE... THANK YOU VERY MUCH AND I ASK FOR YOUR CONTINUED SUPPORT.

June 2007
Shouko Akira

Slightly confused by all the monkeying around? Here are some notes to help you out!

Page 4: Masaru
Even though everyone refers to him by his nickname, Macharu's real name is "Masaru," which means "superior" in Japanese. Interestingly enough, *saru* by itself means "monkey."

Page 12, panel 5: Ryoma Sakamoto
Ryoma Sakamoto (1835-1867) is considered a notable contributor to the modernization of Japan. He was a leader who envisioned Japan without a shogunate and worked towards creating a modern naval force.

Page 12, panel 7: Kiyomizu-yaki
Kiyomizu-yaki refers to the type of ceramics made in the area around Kyoto's famous Kiyomizu Temple. These wares are often characterized by intricate and refined designs in penetrating blue, yellow and green colors. They are also famous for their durability.

Page 13, panel 2: Kyo
The T-shirt Macharu is holding has a wordplay on the middle character—the character itself is the *kyo* in Kyoto but it also sounds like the word for "today" in Japanese.

Page 16, panel 4: Bakumatsu
The Bakumatsu refers to the latest part of the Tokugawa era (around 1853-1867) that is also considered the age of the last samurai.

Page 87, panel 5: Otosan
Otosan means "father" in Japanese.

Page 114, panel 6: Nama Yatsuhashi
Yatsuhashi is a Japanese confectionary from Kyoto that is made from rice flour, cinnamon and sugar. *Nama* (raw) *yatsuhashi* has a soft texture and can be eaten wrapped around red bean paste.

I was barely hanging on by my fingernails
and somehow made it to volume 6...
Thank you so very, very much.

—Shouko Akira

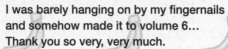

Volume 6...

I am savoring this moment...

Shouko Akira was born on September
10th and grew up in Kyoto. She currently
lives in Tokyo and loves soccer, cycling,
and Yoshimoto Shin Kigeki (a comedy
stage show based out of Osaka). Most of
her works revolve around school life and
love, including *Times Two*, a collection of
five romantic short stories.

MONKEY HIGH!
VOL. 6
The Shojo Beat Manga Edition

STORY AND ART BY
SHOUKO AKIRA

Translation & Adaptation/Mai Ihara
Touch-up Art & Lettering/John Hunt
Design/Hidemi Dunn
Editor/Amy Yu

Editor in Chief, Books/Alvin Lu
Editor in Chief, Magazines/Marc Weidenbaum
VP, Publishing Licensing/Rika Inouye
VP, Sales & Product Marketing/Gonzalo Ferreyra
VP, Creative/Linda Espinosa
Publisher/Hyoe Narita

SARUYAMA! 6 by Shouko AKIRA © 2007 Shouko AKIRA
All rights reserved.
Original Japanese edition published in 2007 by Shogakukan Inc., Tokyo.

The stories, characters and incidents mentioned in this publication
are entirely fictional.

Printed in Canada

Published by VIZ Media, LLC
P.O. Box 77010
San Francisco, CA 94107

Shojo Beat Manga Edition
10 9 8 7 6 5 4 3 2 1
First printing, June 2009

www.viz.com

store.viz.com

PARENTAL ADVISORY
MONKEY HIGH! is rated T for Teen
and is recommended for ages 13 and up.
This volume contains suggestive themes.
ratings.viz.com

love ★ com

By Aya Nakahara

Class clowns Risa and Ôtani join forces to find love!

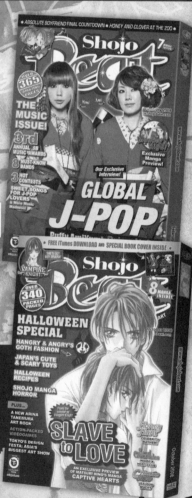